A Handbook to
THE ESSAYS OF
Michel de Montaigne

which includes
the Notes Upon the Text of the Translation by
GEORGE B. IVES
and a series of Comments Upon the Essays by
GRACE NORTON
to accompany Mr. Ives' translation

New York
THE HERITAGE PRESS

The special contents of this edition are copyright, 1946, by THE GEORGE MACY COMPANIES, INC. The translation by GEORGE B. IVES was first published, and was copyright, in 1925 by the HARVARD UNIVERSITY PRESS; from whom permission has been obtained for its reprinting here. The essay by ANDRE GIDE was translated by DOROTHY BUSSY and first published, and copyright, in 1939 by LONGMANS GREEN AND CO.; from whom permission has been obtained for its inclusion here.

Contents

THE NOTES AND COMMENTS WILL BE FOUND AS FOLLOWS:

For Book I, Chapter 1 . . . *beginning on page* 1531
For Book I, Chapter 2 1534
For Book I, Chapter 3 1538
For Book I, Chapter 4 1542
For Book I, Chapter 5 1544
For Book I, Chapter 6 1546
For Book I, Chapter 7 1548
For Book I, Chapter 8 1549
For Book I, Chapter 9 1551
For Book I, Chapter 10 1554
For Book I, Chapter 11 1556
For Book I, Chapter 12 1559
For Book I, Chapter 13 1560
For Book I, Chapter 14 1562
For Book I, Chapter 15 1575
For Book I, Chapter 16 1576
For Book I, Chapter 17 1577
For Book I, Chapter 18 1579
For Book I, Chapter 19 1581
For Book I, Chapter 20 1584
For Book I, Chapter 21 1597
For Book I, Chapter 22 1602
For Book I, Chapter 23 1603
For Book I, Chapter 24 1611
For Book I, Chapter 25 1616

Contents
[CONTINUED]

For Book I, Chapter 26 . . . *beginning on page* 1623
For Book I, Chapter 27 1637
For Book I, Chapter 28 1641
For Book I, Chapter 29 1648
For Book I, Chapter 30 1650
For Book I, Chapter 31 1652
For Book I, Chapter 32 1659
For Book I, Chapter 33 1662
For Book I, Chapter 34 1663
For Book I, Chapter 35 1665
For Book I, Chapter 36 1666
For Book I, Chapter 37 1668
For Book I, Chapter 38 1673
For Book I, Chapter 39 1675
For Book I, Chapter 40 1682
For Book I, Chapter 41 1686
For Book I, Chapter 42 1688
For Book I, Chapter 43 1694
For Book I, Chapter 44 1696
For Book I, Chapter 45 1698
For Book I, Chapter 46 1699
For Book I, Chapter 47 1702
For Book I, Chapter 48 1706
For Book I, Chapter 49 1713
For Book I, Chapter 50 1717
For Book I, Chapter 51 1720
For Book I, Chapter 52 1722
For Book I, Chapter 53 1723

Contents
[CONTINUED]

For Book I, Chapter 54 . . . *beginning on page* 1724
For Book I, Chapter 55 1726
For Book I, Chapter 56 1728
For Book I, Chapter 57 1733

For Book II, Chapter 1 . . . *beginning on page* 1737
For Book II, Chapter 2 1741
For Book II, Chapter 3 1746
For Book II, Chapter 4 1753
For Book II, Chapter 5 1754
For Book II, Chapter 6 1756
For Book II, Chapter 7 1761
For Book II, Chapter 8 1764
For Book II, Chapter 9 1769
For Book II, Chapter 10 1771
For Book II, Chapter 11 1775
For Book II, Chapter 12 1783
For Book II, Chapter 13 1872
For Book II, Chapter 14 1875
For Book II, Chapter 15 1876
For Book II, Chapter 16 1879
For Book II, Chapter 17 1886
For Book II, Chapter 18 1897
For Book II, Chapter 19 1899
For Book II, Chapter 20 1902
For Book II, Chapter 21 1904
For Book II, Chapter 22 1906
For Book II, Chapter 23 1907

Contents
[CONTINUED]

For Book II, Chapter 24 . . . *beginning on page* 1909
For Book II, Chapter 25 1910
For Book II, Chapter 26 1911
For Book II, Chapter 27 1913
For Book II, Chapter 28 1916
For Book II, Chapter 29 1918
For Book II, Chapter 30 1920
For Book II, Chapter 31 1921
For Book II, Chapter 32 1925
For Book II, Chapter 33 1927
For Book II, Chapter 34 1930
For Book II, Chapter 35 1934
For Book II, Chapter 36 1936
For Book II, Chapter 37 1941

For Book III, Chapter 1 . . . *beginning on page* 1952
For Book III, Chapter 2 1961
For Book III, Chapter 3 1964
For Book III, Chapter 4 1969
For Book III, Chapter 5 1974
For Book III, Chapter 6 1994
For Book III, Chapter 7 2001
For Book III, Chapter 8 2004
For Book III, Chapter 9 2013
For Book III, Chapter 10 2035
For Book III, Chapter 11 2045
For Book III, Chapter 12 2050
For Book III, Chapter 13 2060

A Handbook to
THE ESSAYS OF MONTAIGNE

BOOK ONE

CHAPTER I

By Divers Means a Like End is Attained

A. THE COMMENT BY MISS NORTON

THE earlier Essays of Montaigne, written before 1850, especially those of the first book,—are much less interesting than the later ones; they are greatly inferior in substance and in form. Many of them, indeed, do not deserve the name of Essays, a title subsequently invented by Montaigne: they are only what had been called *leçons* by his literary precursors—short compilations on one or another subject, with little or no addition of original thought, and demanding no sustained effort of author or reader.

That Montaigne placed this Essay at the opening of his volume does not indicate necessarily that it was the first he composed (some of those that follow are unquestionably earlier in date): its position may be due to a different cause. In its first form when published in 1580, this Essay was scarcely more than half as long as it became later; it concluded with the thought: "Truly man is a marvellously volatile, various, and wavering creature." And another expression of this idea—which was a dominant conception in his mind at the time of his first making himself known to the public—is found at the conclusion of the last Essay of the

1531

Notes and Comments

edition of 1580 (Book II, chapter 37): *C'est la plus générale forme que nature ait suivy que la variété.* This theme runs as a *Leit-motif* through the two books: and it is a not improbable hypothesis, suggested by M. Villey, that he intentionally opened and closed their pages with it.

It was perhaps ten years later that Montaigne returned to this Essay, preparing it for a new edition, and he inserted in the middle of it a personal sentence regarding his own tendency toward *la miséricorde et le pardon*, indicating by this personal touch confidence in his public, given him by the reception of the Essays on their first appearance.

And this, the first expression in the Essays of Montaigne's own nature, should not be passed over lightly. By this time—1588—he had spent a year in Italy, he had been for four years mayor of Bordeaux, he was in relation with the chief personages of the day, and it is probable that he had served in the royalist army. The effect of all this experience of life and men had caused him to recognize that, in contrast to the pervading ferocity of the times, he had *une merveilleuse lascheté vers la miséricorde et le pardon.* The word *lascheté* is significant. It did not have in Montaigne's mouth at all the modern sense of a lack of courage, but it did have the meaning of a lack of vigor, a certain *mollesse* of nature. He had read in Seneca's *De Clementia* that "all good men will manifest clemency and gentleness, but they will avoid pity [*misericordia*], for it is the weakness of a small soul giving way at the sight of other's ills." It is not in praise of himself that Montaigne speaks of this quality in himself; it is only one of the touches of that *Selbst-Portrat* which he painted in the Essays, and in painting it, depicted human nature.

A Like End is Attained

This apparent reminiscence of Seneca is only the first of hundreds. The Essays are more or less permeated throughout by his thoughts. In the earlier ones Montaigne repeatedly expresses his deep admiration for him personally and for his writings. Plutarch and Seneca, he says in the Essay "Of Books," are the books *qui me servent plus ordinairement*. Of all the works of Seneca, he best likes his Letters. Later, his admiration diminishes; he finds in him a certain artificiality, and comparing him (for a second time) to Plutarch, he says that the one touches more the reader's *esprit*, the other his *entendement*.

B. THE NOTES BY MR. IVES

1. The "Black Prince," son of Edward III. See Froissart.
2. Froissart, on the contrary, says that he showed mercy *only* to the three gentlemen.
3. Scanderbeg [Iskander Beg. *i. e.*, Prince Alexander] was an Albanian hero (1404-1466). Montaigne probably had in mind a passage in a work of Paulus Jovius, *Commentarii . . . e la vita di Scanderberg*, translated into French in 1544.
4. *La gentillesse.*
5. See Jean Bodin, *Methodus ad facilem historiarum cognitionem* (Proemium). It was the siege of Weinsberg, in 1140.
6. See Seneca, *De Clementia*, V.
7. *Mais non pas qu'on flechisse et compatisse avec eux.*
8. See Plutarch, *How far a man may praise himself.*
9. See Diodorus Siculus, XIV, 29.
10. See Plutarch, *Political Precepts,* where the citizen is called Stheno.

Notes and Comments

11. *Ibid.* The city was Præneste. The mistake was made by Amyot in the first edition of his translation (1572), where Montaigne found it. It was corrected in Amyot's edition of 1574. In the first edition the Essay ended here.
12. *Qui le chamailloient de toutes parts.*
13. See Quintus Curtius, IV, 6.
14. See Diodorus Siculus, XXVII, 4.

CHAPTER II

Of Sadness

A. THE COMMENT BY MISS NORTON

OF this Essay the first sentence and the last are the most interesting. The first: "I am one of those least subject to this emotion"; and the last: "I am little subject to such violent emotions. My sensitiveness is naturally not keen, and I harden and deaden it every day intentionally." It is to be observed that these sentences were not in the Essay as first published in 1580; they were added eight years later, like those of the same character we have noted in the first Essay. It was during the intervening years that Montaigne had discovered a purpose for his writing, an aim for his thoughts, in the description, the delineation of himself

Of Sadness

as an aid in the study of man. The sentences above quoted are among the first lines of his self-portraiture.

The Essay opens with narratives exhibiting the effects of successive sorrows on some souls; those that receive the first blow with rigid calmness and are overwhelmed by a later, lighter one. The old account of the painting of the sacrifice of Iphigenia and the turning Niobe to stone are introduced as symbolising that extremity of grief that cannot be represented. It is Dryden's thought (in the "Threnodia Augustalis"):—

>   Sure there's a lethargy in mighty woe;
>   Tears stand congealed and cannot flow,
> And the sad soul retires into her inmost room.
> Tears for a stroke foreseen afford relief.
>   But unprovided for a sudden blow,
>   Like Niobe we marble grow
>   And petrify with grief.

The tearless and fatal grief of a "seigneur allemand" is depicted (an addition in 1595); and then the essayist passes, through the violent emotions of love, to those caused by pleasure; unlooked-for delight may kill, and of this he gives a list of examples. An extreme emotion of shame, of mortification, may be deadly, as proved by Diodorus the Dialectician. And with this the Essay cut itself short in 1580. In 1588 another sentence was added, which, as I have said, echoed the first sentence of the Essay and connects itself with the expression in the "Apologie" (Book II, chapter 12) when, speaking of the evil of excessive sensibility, he says: *Il nous faut abestir pour nous assagir.*

Notes and Comments

B. THE NOTES BY MR. IVES

1. This line first appeared in 1588.

2. *Tristezza.* This word is open to various shades of meaning: sadness, sorrow, melancholy—even a gloomy, melancholy moroseness.

3. See especially St. Augustine, *De Civitate Dei*, XIV.

4. See Herodotus, III, 14.

5. *Un prince des nostres.* Charles de Guise, Cardinal of Lorraine. This expression is to be distinguished from *un de nos princes,* which is used for members of French families, the houses of France and of Bourbon; the former is used for the house of Lorraine, which was foreign by origin. The cardinal was at the Council of Trent in 1563, at the time of the assassination of his brother François de Guise, and of the death also, after the battle of Dreux, of a younger brother, the Grand Prior.

6. Timanthes, 4th century B.C. See Cicero, *Orator*, XXII; Pliny, *Natural History*, XXXV, 10; Valerius Maximus, VIII, 2, *ext.* 6; Quintilian, *Institutio Oratoria*, II, 13.

7. *Diriguisse malis.*—Ovid, *Metamorphoses*, VI, 304. Montaigne adapted the original form of the verb (*diriguitque*) to his context.

8. *Et via vix tandem voci laxata dolore est.*—Virgil, *Æneid*, XI, 151.

9. About 1556. See Paulus Jovius, *Historiæ sui Temporis*, XXXIX. In 1595, the phraseology of these last sentences was changed somewhat, without changing the sense.

10. *Chi può dir com'egli arde è in picciol fuoco.*—Petrarch, *Sonnet* 137.

11.   *Misero quod omnes Eripit sensus mihi. Nam simil te,*

Of Sadness

> *Lesbia, aspexi, nihil est super mi*
>   *Quod loquar amens.*
> *Lingua sed torpet, tenuis sub artus*
> *Flamma dimanat, sonitu suopte*
> *Tinniunt aures, gemina teguntur*
>   *Lumina nocte.*   —Catullus, LI, 5.

12. *Qui se laissent gouster et digerer.*

13. *Curæ leves loquuntur, ingentes stupent.*—Seneca, *Hippolytus*, Act II, sc. 3, v. 607.

14.   *Ut me conspexit venientem, et Troia circum*
> *Arma amens vidit, magnis exterrita monstris,*
> *Diriguit visu in medio; calor ossa reliquit;*
> *Labitur, et longo vix tandem tempore fatur.*
>   —Virgil, *Æneid*, III, 306.

15. These and similar examples of death caused by joy are found collected in many works in Latin of different periods. Montaigne did not take them from their original sources. The "Roman woman" and Dionysius and Diodorus (below) came from Pliny's *Natural History*, VII, 54; Sophocles and Talva from Valerius Maximus, IX, 12, *ext.* 5.

16. See Guicciardini, *Storia d'Italia*, XIV.

17. *Apprehension.* Montaigne uses this word frequently in the sense of "the action of feeling anything emotionally"—an obsolete sense of the similar English word.

18. *Je l'encrouste et espessis . . . par discours.*

CHAPTER III

Our Feelings Extend Themselves Beyond Our Perceptions

A. THE COMMENT BY MISS NORTON

THIS Essay, like the last one, begins with an *addition*, and includes many, some made in 1588, some in 1595. It is now nine pages long; at first, in 1580, it was only three—a mere *leçon*; it began with the passage concerning Bertrand du Guesclin, and ended with that about the Emperor Maximilian; just a string of anecdotes. It was probably written about 1572.

The reflections, the comments, the remarks that now accompany the stories—the note of the moralist—are what constitute the interest of these pages for us. They are somewhat incoherent, but turn for the most part on the lack of wisdom shown in dwelling in the future, in not remaining *chez nous*.

And we have in this connection the statement for the first time of Montaigne's great principle—that of Socrates: "Do what is thine to do, and know thyself"; *Fay ton faict et te cognoy*.

An interesting paragraph is that regarding the desirableness of examining into the actions of princes after their death. We may find here a hint of one of Montaigne's great characteristics, his reverence for laws, his obedience to legal authority, united with an independence of mind

Our Feelings Extend Themselves

which enables him always to judge of the man apart from the office.

B. THE NOTES BY MR. IVES

1. *Nos affections s'emportent au dela de nous.*
2. The first three pages were added in 1588 or 1595.
3. *Calamitosus est animus futuri anxius.*—Seneca, *Epistle* 98.6.
4. In the *Timæus*.
5. *Ut stultitia etsi adepta est quod concupivit nunquam setamen satis consecutam putat: sic sapientia semper eo contenta est quod adest, neque eam unquam sui pœnitet.* —Cicero, *Tusculan Disputations*, V, 18.

In the edition of 1595, the following translation is substituted for this Latin passage: *Comme la folie, quand on luy octroyera ce qu'elle desire, ne sera pas contente, aussi est la sagesse contente de ce qui est present, ne se desplait jamais de soy.*

6. See Cicero, *Tusc. Disp.*, III, 15.
7. See Diodorus Siculus, I, 6.
8. See Book XXXV, 48.
9. See Tacitus, *Annals*, XV, 67, 68.
10. The last phrase, *à luy et à tous meschans comme luy*, was added in 1595.
11. See Herodotus, VI, 58.
12. See the *Nicomachæan Ethics*, I, 10.
13.   *Quisquam*
    Vix radicitus et vita set tollit, et eiicit:
    Sed facit esse sui quiddam super inscius ipse,
    Nec removet satis a projecto corpore sese et
    Vindicat.—Lucretius, III, 877, 878, 882, 883.

1539

Notes and Comments

The numbering here followed is that adopted by Cyril Bailey in the Oxford texts. *Quisquam* is an addition of Montaigne's. The original has *Nec* instead of *Vix* in the second line, and, at the end, *et illum se fingit,* instead of *sese et vindicat.*

14. See Jean Bouchet, *Annales d'Aquitaine.*
15. See Guicciardini, *Storia d'Italia,* XII.
16. See Plutarch, *Life of Nicias.*
17. See Idem, *Life of Agesilaus.*
18. Changed to Zischa [Ziska] in 1595. Montaigne's source for this is uncertain. The fact is mentioned in various sixteenth-century compilations.
19. See Lopez de Gomara, *Histoire Générale des Indes,* III, 22.
20. Bayard was killed at the river Sesia in 1524. See *Mémoires* du Bellay, book II. These memoirs treat of the events in France from 1513 to the death of King Francis I. They are the work of two brothers, Martin, Seigneur de Langey, and Guillaume, who became Seigneur de Langey on his brother's death. They consist of ten books, of which the 5th, 6th, and 7th were written by Guillaume, the others by Martin.
21. Philip II, of Spain.
22. Maximilian.
23. In the editions prior to 1588, the chapter ended here.
24. See Xenophon, *Cyropædeia,* VIII, 7, 26.
25. See Livy, Epitome of book XLVIII.
26. See Diogenes Laertius, *Life of Lycon.*
27. Cf. Cicero, *Tusc. Disp.,* I, 45. The following clause of 1588 is omitted: *et sauf les choses requises au service de*

Our Feelings Extend Themselves

ma religion si c'est en lieu où il soit besoing de l'enjoindre.

28. *Totus hic locus est contemnendus in nobis, non negligendus in nostris.*

29. And, as was said like a saint by a saint: *Curatio funeris, conditio sepulturæ, pompa exequiarum, magis sunt vivarum solatia quam subsidia mortuorum.*—St. Augustine, *De Civitate Dei*, I, 12.

30. See Plato, *Phædo;* Cicero, *Tusc. Disp.*, I, 43.
31. *Galand.*
32. The judges.
33. See Diodorus Siculus, XIII, 31, 32.
34. *De mesme pain souppe.* See Idem, XV, 9.
35. *Perdit le fruit tout net et contant.*
36.   *Quæris quo jaceas, post obitum, loco?*
        Quo non nata jacent.
   —Seneca, *Troades*, Act II, ll. 30, 31 (400, 401).
37.   *Neque sepulchrum, quo recipiat, habeat portum corporis,*
    Ubi, remissa humana vita, corpus requiscat a malis.
   —Ennius, quoted in Cicero, *Tusc. Disp.*, I, 44.

CHAPTER IV

How the Soul Vents Its Emotions On False Objects When True Ones Are Lacking

A. THE COMMENT BY MISS NORTON

THE title indicates the theme of this short Essay; it opens by declaring that "the mind when disturbed and excited" must have "*some* object to seize and work upon"; and thus we quarrel with even inanimate things—not only with inanimate things, but with the gods, with God himself. Man, and also the brute beasts, when inwardly moved, direct themselves to definite objects; and if circumstances do not furnish the emotions with a true object for their exercise, they create for themselves false objects; witness lap-dogs and the like; witness the blows and kicks given by children, and grown-up children, to inanimate things; witness inane curses. For another class of actions, due to inconscious bewilderment, consider the tearing of the hair, the beating of the breast, the knocking one's head against a wall, the defiance of the gods and of Fortune; all the *déréglements* of our human intelligence.

1542

How the Soul Vents its Emotions

B. THE NOTES BY MR. IVES

1. *Ventus ut amittit vires, nisi robore densæ*
   Occurrant silvæ spatio diffusus inani.
   —Lucan, III, 362.
2. In the *Life of Pericles*.
3. *Pannonis haud aliter post ictum sævior ursa,*
   Cum jaculum parva Lybis amentavit habena,
   Se rotat in vulnus, telumque irata receptum
   Impetit, et secum fugientem circuit hastam.
   —Lucan, VI, 220.
4. *Flere omnes repente offensare capita.*—Livy, XXV, 37. The two brothers were Publius and Cneius Scipio.
5. See Cicero, *Tusc. Disp.*, III, 26.
6. See Herodotus, VII, 35; Plutarch, *Of the Cure of Anger*.
7. See Herodotus, I, 189.
8. The text reads *pour le plaisir*, but this is thought to be an unquestionable misprint. See Seneca, *De Ira*, III, 22.
9. See Suetonius, *Life of Augustus*, 16.
10. See *Ibid.*, 23.
11. In the editions of 1580-1588, the text reads: *à Dieu mesmes à belles injures;* the last phrase was omitted in 1595.

1543

CHAPTER V

Whether the Commandant of a Besieged Stronghold Should Go Forth to Parley

A. THE COMMENT BY MISS NORTON

THIS is one of the Essays that show Montaigne's interest in military affairs. They are found only in the first Book, though traces of the essayist's familiarity with the life of a soldier are to be found throughout. Their subject-matter is now without interest for us. Our sieges and parleyings are of a different character from those of the sixteenth century. But Montaigne's treatment of these subjects is of importance to the student of his character, from its unconscious self-revelation.

Another point of interest may be found in the sentence in which Montaigne asserts, or at least suggests, that the civilization "among those nations whom we so unhesitatingly call Barbarians" may be in some respects equal to our own. The thought is like a forerunner of the later Essay "Of Cannibals."

B. THE NOTES BY MR. IVES

1. *Entregets d'accord.* See Livy, XLII, 43.
2. The following passage, down to the line from the

Should the Commandant go Forth to Parley

Æneid, "Dolus an," etc., was substituted in the edition of 1595 for the following reading of 1580-1588: *Si est-ce que le Senat Romain, à qui le seul advantage de la vertu sembloit moyen juste pour acquerir la victoire, trouva cette pratique laide et deshonneste, n'ayant encores ouy sonner à ses oreilles cette belle sentence:—*

3. See Plutarch, *Life of Pyrrhus*.

4. See Idem, *Life of Camillus*.

5. See Livy, XLII, 43, for the whole story. The addition of the edition of 1595 is almost a literal translation.

6. *Dolus an virtus quis in hoste requirat?*—Virgil, *Æneid*, II, 390.

7. Montaigne did not take this remark from Polybius, but from the *Politiques* of Justus Lipsius, V, 17.

8. *Eam vir sanctus et sapiens sciet veram esse victoriam, quæ salva fide et integra dignitate, parabitur.*—Florus, I, 12, 6. This quotation, also, Montaigne took, not from the original, but from the same page of Lipsius.

9.   *Vosne velit an me regnare hera, quidve ferat fors,*
    Virtute experiamur.
    —Ennius, in Cicero, *De Officiis*, I, 12.

10. *Si à pleine bouche.*

11. Goulard, *Histoire du Portugal*, XIV, 16.

12. See Giovanni Villani, *Cronica*, VI, 75.

13. See Plutarch, *Life of Lysander*.

14. See *Mémoires* du Bellay, I, 22.

15. Guicciardini, IV; du Bellay, I, 29. Guicciardini was governor of Reggio.

16. See Plutarch, *Life of Eumenes*.

17. See Froissart, I, 209.

CHAPTER VI

The Hour of Parley is a Dangerous Time

A. THE COMMENT BY MISS NORTON

AGAIN we have consideration of the principles of warfare; the first paragraph more interesting than before because concerned with conditions that occurred in 1569, the siege of the little village of Mussidan in Montaigne's immediate neighbourhood. Montaigne, it has been observed, disclaims with covert irony the accusation of treason brought against the besieging royalists. In another century, he admits, there might have been some colour in the accusation, but in the present one, "Our ways are entirely unlike former rules of conduct, and we should not expect to place confidence in one another until the last pledge of engagement has been given."

Later paragraphs narrate other sixteenth-century incidents. The classical illustrations were added in 1595.

There are two little personal touches, both expressive of moral feeling. "I am surprised," he says, "at the extension Xenophon gives these privileges [of war] . . . and I do not accede to the measure of his dispensation in all things and everywhere" (1595).

The Hour of Parley is a Dangerous Time

B. THE NOTES BY MR. IVES

1. Mussidan was besieged in April, 1569. See de Thou.
2. See Livy, XXXVII, 32.
3. See Plutarch, *Apothegms of the Lacedæmonians*.
4. In the first instance, Montaigne wrote in the Latin text of this passage: *Casilinum inter colloquia, cunctationemque petentium fidem, per occasionem captum est* (Livy, XXIV, 19), for which he later substituted the translation.
5. *Neminem id agere ut ex alterius prædetur inscitia.* —Cicero, *De Off.*, III, 17.
6. In the *Cyropædeia*.
7. See Guicciardini, V, 2.
8. Montaigne is here in error. The incident he narrates occurred at the siege of Dinan (in the neighbourhood of Liège) in 1554. He very likely knew of it by oral report. See de Thou, and G. Paradin, *Continuation de l'histoire de notre temps*.
9. *Ce pas de clerc.*
10. See Guicciardini, XIV, 5; also, du Bellay, II, 43.
11. See du Bellay, IX, 328.
12.   *Fu il vincer sempre mai laudabil cosa,*
      Vincasi o per fortuna o per ingegno,—
          —Ariosto, *Orlando Furioso*, Canto XV, 1.
13. See Cicero, *De Off.*, III, 10.
14. *Malo me fortunæ pœniteat quam victoriæ pudeat.*
15.   *Atque idem fugientem haud est dignatus Orodem*
    Sternere nec jacta cæcum dare cuspide vulnus;
    Obvius adversoque occurrit, seque viro vir
    Contulit, haud furto melior, sed fortibus armis.
            —Virgil, *Æneid*, X, 732.

CHAPTER VII

That Our Actions Should Be Judged by Our Intentions

A. THE COMMENT BY MISS NORTON

THE central passage of this Essay, that beginning "We can not be held responsible beyond our strength and our resources," expresses the thought that it is not the actual result of our actions but what we desire should be the result—our intentions—that is to be judged by the laws of duty. It is a comment on the title.

Stories precede and follow it; the subject of the first is the effect of our death, or other involuntary circumstances, on our promises and pledges. This tragedy was a recent event (1568) when Montaigne was writing, and it made a great sensation. But the special point on which Montaigne dwells—the entreaty of Count Egmont—is mentioned in no account of the event. M. Villey says: "Je crois que Montaigne tient ce fait de la tradition orale. . . . Montaigne est ici, probablement, la première source à laquelle nous puissions nous référer."

The second story notes the insufficiency of the justice we may do, and the injustice we may do after our death.

Montaigne, passing judgement on these examples, says: "It would seem" that death could not free Henry VII from his pledge; and that death was not necessary to release Count Egmont from his obligation.

1548

Of Idleness

These pages simply mirror the moral reflections that were passing through Montaigne's mind in the early days of his authorship, before his individual method and meaning had become defined to himself.

B. THE NOTES BY MR. IVES

1. In 1506. See du Bellay, I, 7.
2. In 1568.
3. In 1580: *ausquels il fit trancher la teste.*
4. Henry VII.
5. Count Egmont.
6. Book II, 121.

CHAPTER VIII

Of Idleness

A. THE COMMENT BY MISS NORTON

IN an Essay written some seven years later ("Of the affection of fathers for their children," Book II, chapter 8), Montaigne thus refers to his state of mind at this time: "It was a melancholy mood, and consequently one much opposed to my natural disposition, brought about by weariness of the solitude in which a few years ago I buried myself, which first put into my head this idle thought of writing."

It is not physical but mental idleness that Montaigne

1549

Notes and Comments

has in mind, and he declares that, if the mind is not occupied with a definite subject, which guides it and restrains it, it wanders hither and thither in the vague field of dreams. It is of his own experience he is thinking. He tells us here that he had lately withdrawn from public affairs, and had sought solitude, thinking thus to benefit his mind by allowing it to follow its own course. But no, he found that now, aimlessly wandering, it created such chimerical and fantastic imagination, disorderly and meaningless, that he had begun to write them down, so that he might in time shame his own intelligence.

I cannot believe that these "chimères et monstres fantasques" which he thought well to "mettre en rolle" are to be found in any of the Essays. His contemplation of them would seem to have led him to their exact opposite, the simple statement of facts and comment upon them, which marks the character of his first "manner." The Essays show no trace of *ineptie* and *étrangeté*.

B. THE NOTES BY MR. IVES

1. See Plutarch, *Marriage Precepts*.
2. *Sicut aquæ tremulum labris ubi lumen ahenis*
   Sole repercussum, aut radiantis imagine Lunæ
   Omnia percolitat late loca, jamque sub auras
   Erigitur, summique ferit laquearia tecti.
   —Virgil, *Æneid*, VIII, 22.
3. *Velut ægri somnia, vanæ Finguntur species.* —Horace, *Ars Poetica*, 7.
4. *Quisquis ubique habitat, Maxime, nusquam habitat.* —Martial, VII, 73.
5. *Variam semper dant otia mentem.*—Lucan, IV, 704.

1550

CHAPTER IX

Of Liars

A. THE COMMENT BY MISS NORTON

THAT Montaigne should enter on the subject of liars by a discourse on his own memory is humorously characteristic, and it is not so strange an opening as it may seem. It has been known from ancient days that a good memory is necessary if one would successfully tell lies, and Montaigne feels that it somewhat consoles him for lack of memory, to be thus hindered by Nature from lying. "In truth, lying is an accursed vice." He declares his own memory to be singularly bad, so extraordinarily bad that he says, jestingly, it might really be a cause for renown. This statement has been much commented on, and has been accused of being a falsehood and an affectation. There is no ground for such accusation; the Essays give no proof of either an accurate memory or a long one. Montaigne's mind was too full of *thoughts* to make and retain *records*.

In this connection he notes a curious fact, that those of the country about him "do not perceive any difference between memory and understanding," which his friend Charron in some sort, later confirmed, saying, "The common people, whose judgement is never sound, more greatly admire [*fait plus de feste de*] memory than imagination or understanding."

Notes and Comments

Montaigne continues by remarking regretfully that the same words that describe a lack of memory imply ingratitude; and that it is said of him himself,—"qui ne scait rien si bien faire qu'estre amy,"—"he has forgotten his promise ... he has forgotten to do or say this or that ... for me. Certainly," he declares, "I can easily forget, but to be indifferent about the service my friend has asked of me, that I am not."

He consoles himself for this deficiency by two results of it: the one, that he cannot tell long stories—so often too long! and the other, that he quickly forgets offences, and that places and books seen and read for a second time "always charm me with the freshness of novelty."

This paragraph so stood in 1588; in 1595 his prime consolation was that this *misère* preserved him from ambition, and strengthened in him more intellectual faculties.

He then starts off on considerations of the relations between memory and lying, and the dangers that ensue if the memory *n'est bien assurée*. In the earliest form of the Essay he went on immediately with the two stories the first of which is evidently the occasion of it. In 1588 he inserted the paragraph beginning: "Whereof I have often seen amusing proof," and ending, "if there be the reputation there cannot be the effect"; and in 1595 the paragraph beginning "In truth," and ending with "silence."

These two added pages, interesting in themselves, are somewhat incoherent and confusing where they stand and do not well preface the stories.

In the passage regarding the education of children (chapter 26 of this Book) we have the first expression—there are many later ones—of Montaigne's thoughtful study of ed-

Of Liars

ucation; a study of its principles which caused his precepts to rank among those that no change of beliefs or fashions can impair.

B. THE NOTES BY MR. IVES

1. This sentence appeared in the first edition but was afterward dropped.
2. See Plato, *Critias,* near the beginning.
3. That is, lack of memory.
4. Lack of memory.
5. Referring back to "I thus somewhat console myself: in the first place" (page 42).
6. See Cicero, *Oratio pro Ligurio,* XII: *Oblivisci nihil soles, nisi injurias.*
7. See Herodotus, V. 105.
8. See Quintilian, *Institutio Oratoria,* IV, 2; Nigidius, in Aulus Gellius, XI, 11, and in Nonius, V, 80.
9. *Entre dire mensonge et mentir.*
10. Cf. Book II, chap. 18 ("Of Lying"): *C'est un vilain vice que le mentir.*
11. See St. Augustine, *De Civ. Dei,* XIX, 7.
12. *Ut externus alieno non sit hominis vice.*—Pliny, *Natural History,* VII, 1.
13. *D'avoir mis au rouet.*
14. *Taverna.*
15. See du Bellay, IV (an. 1533).
16. Probably taken by Montaigne from the *Apologie pour Hérodote* (XV, 24) of H. Estienne, who translated it from Erasmus, *De Lingua.*

CHAPTER X

Of Readiness or Unreadiness of Speech

A. THE COMMENT BY MISS NORTON

AS we turn the pages of this volume of the Essays, more and more we slip into the mood of *conversation*. Montaigne is *talking* to us, and soon we are so interested that we find ourselves answering him, discussing with him, and perhaps not listening to him, because we are thinking of what he *has* said or what he *may* say.

The peculiar interest of these few pages is that Montaigne here treats not only in general of the subject in hand, but incidentally of his own nature in relation to it. The Essay opens with the remark that some men are always ready for eloquent speech while others need time and preparation. As it is chiefly preachers and lawyers who have need of eloquence, it seems to Montaigne that the slow-witted would make the best preachers, and the quick-witted the best lawyers; and he alleges reasons for this belief, and tells as comment on it a story of a famous lawyer of his day. In France, at least, there are more able lawyers than preachers, he thinks. But he who can say nothing without preparation, and he who speaks none the better for having plenty of time *sont en pareil degré*. Severus Cassius was said to speak best when suddenly called upon. Here our attention is caught by

Of Speech

the words (printed in 1580): "I know by experience that inborn disposition which cannot sustain eager and laborious premeditation."

He goes on to speak of works that "smell of the oil and the lamp," and remarks that eagerness to do well hinders the outpouring of the soul, like water when pressing against too small an outlet. This is the effect of all strong passions; the soul must be "solicited," not "shaken"; but it must be moved; "excitement is its life and is favourable to it." He says gaily of himself that his talk is worth more than his writings, "if there can be a choice where there is nothing of value"; and the talk ends with a delightful laugh over his confession of those *subtilités* that he often loses so well, that he can never discover their meaning himself.

B. THE NOTES BY MR. IVES

1. *Onc ne furent à tous toutes graces données.*—La Boëtie.
2. *Le boute-hors si aisé.*
3. *Carrière.*
4. *See du Bellay, IV.*
5. *See Seneca (the Rhetorician), Controversiæ, III, Pref.*
6. In the editions previous to 1588 this sentence read thus: *Je cognois bien privement et par ordinaire experience, ceste condition de nature qui ne peut soustenir une vehemente premeditation, tant pour le defaut de la memoire et difficulté du chois des choses et de leur disposition, que pour le trouble qu'une attention vehemente luy apporte d'ailleurs.*

1555

CHAPTER XI

Of Prognostications

A. THE COMMENT BY MISS NORTON

IN writing of "prognostications" Montaigne foreruns Bacon in the belief that (in Bacon's words), "They ought all to be despised, and ought to serve but for winter talk by the fireside."

The story of the Marquis de Salluce was the occasion of this Essay, and was originally almost the whole of it; the page that precedes it only gives the reasons why it seemed to Montaigne remarkable; and the verses of Horace brought the Essay to a close in 1580.

In 1588 the next sentence (dropped in 1595) was: "I should much prefer to manage my affairs by the cast of dice than by such dreams"; and it was followed by the paragraph beginning: "I see some who annotate their almanacs." After the sentence, "There would be more certainty . . ." came the remark (afterward somewhat changed): "I have seen sometimes to their hurt . . ." Then came immediately: "The Demon of Socrates," and the Essay ended as now.

In 1595 the Latin quotations of the first page were, all but one, added; also two immediately following the Horace quotation, and the paragraph about the Tuscans and that about Plato. A line or two after, another Latin citation.

Of Prognostications

Again a line or two, and the story of Diagoras and the saying of Cicero were inserted. Before "The Demon of Socrates" were pushed in the books of Joachim and Leon and the remarks that follow.

This sketch gives an idea of the sometimes unfortunate and often confusing changes the Essays underwent from the many additions at various times. They render them not simple growths, but complicated agglomerations.

B. THE NOTES BY MR. IVES

1. *Cur isto modo jam oracula Delphis non enduntur non modo nostra ætate sed jamdiu, ut modo nihil possit esse contemptius?*—Cicero, *De Divin.*, II, 57.
2. In the *Timæus*.
3. *Trepignement*.
4. *Aves quasdam rerum augurandarum causa natas esse putamus.*—Cicero, *De Nat. Deor.*, II, 64.
5. *Multa cernunt aruspices, multa augures provident, multa oraculis declarantur, multa vaticinationibus, multa somniis, multa portentis.*—*Ibid.*, II, 65.
6.   *cur hanc tibi, rector Olympi,*
   Sollicitis visum mortalibus addere curam,
   Noscant venturas ut dira per omina clades?
   Sit subitum quodcunque paras, sit cæca futuri
   Mens hominum fati; liceat sperare timenti.
                          —Lucan, II, 4-6, 14, 15.
7. *Ne utile quidem est scire quid futurum sit; miserum est enim nihil proficientem angi.*—Cicero, *De Nat. Deor.*
8. That is, divination.
9. See du Bellay, VI; de Thou, I, 37.
10. In Italy.

Notes and Comments

11. That is, to rebel and change his allegiance.
12.   *Prudens futuri temporis exitum*
Calignosa nocte premit Deus
  Ridetque, si mortalis ultra
   Fas trepidat

. . . .
     Ille potens sui
Lætusque deget, cui licet in diem
  Dixisse, vixi, cras vel atra
   Nube polum pater occupato
Vel sole puro.
   Horace, *Odes*, III, 29.29—32, 41-45.

13. *Lætus in præsens animus quod ultra est;*
Oderit curare.   —*Ibid.*, II, 16.25.

The Essay ended here in the early editions.

14. *Ista sic reciprocantur, ut et, si divinatio sit, dii sint; et, si dii sint, sit divinatio.*—Cicero, *De Divin.*, I, 6.
15. *Nam istis qui linguam avium intelligunt,*
Plusque ex alieno jecore sapiunt quam ex suo,
Magis audiendum quam auscultandum censeo.
     —See *Ibid.*, I, 57.
16. See *Ibid.*, II, 23.
17. See the *Timæus*, and the *Republic*, book V.
18. See the *Republic*, book V. Plato does not say "banished," but "secretly dispersed among the other citizens."
19. *Quis est enim, qui, totum diem jaculans, non aliquando collineet.*—Cicero, *De Divin.*, II, 59.
20. *Ce seroit plus de certitude, s'il y avoit regle et verité a mentir tousjours.*
21. Those of the almanac students.
22. See Cicero, *De Nat. Deor.*, I, 37.

23. *De Divin.*, I, 3.
24. A.D. 1130-1202.
25. Leo VI, the Philosopher, A.D. 865-911. See Chalcondylas (tr. Vigenère), I, 8.
26. On the intentional obscurity of the seers, see Cicero, *De Divin.*, II, 54, 56.
27. *Opinion prompte, vehemente et fortuite.*

CHAPTER XII

Of Steadiness

A. THE COMMENT BY MISS NORTON

THIS Essay was built up from the two examples of escape from danger which made the whole of it in 1580.

The second and third paragraphs, the one beginning "Many very warlike nations," and the other "Regarding the Scythians," were inserted in 1595, and break the continuity of thought.

The last sentence was added in 1588, and is one of the indications of Montaigne's experience as a soldier.

B. THE NOTES BY MR. IVES

1. *Et le jeu de la constance se joue.*

Notes and Comments

2. See *Laches*.
3. *De pied ferme.*
4. See Herodotus, IV, 126, 127.
5. In the invasion of 1536. See du Bellay, VII.
6. *Sus le theatre aux arenes.*
7. Catherine de Medicis, widow of Henri II, and mother of François II, Charles IX, and Henri III.
8. *Bien luy servit de faire le cane.*
9. This passage (to the end of the chapter), added after 1588, is a close imitation of Aulus Gellius, XIX, 1. But Montaigne probably took it from the summary given by St. Augustine in *De Civ. Dei*, IX, 4, where the verse of Virgil also is found.
10. *Mens immota manet; lacrimæ volvuntur inanes.*
—Virgil, *Æneid*, IV, 449.

CHAPTER XIII

The Ceremony at Interviews of Kings

A. THE COMMENT BY MISS NORTON

ALL subjects belong to conversation, and so all matters may be touched upon in these Essays. Montaigne recognises this, and also that the topic he now takes up

The Ceremony at Interviews of Kings

is not a very interesting one, when he says: "There is no subject so trivial as not to deserve a place in this medley"—this collection of fragments. It is of royal ceremonies and of courtesies among "the great" that he talks. He had just been reading Guicciardini, and the account of the meeting of the Pope and emperor at Boulogne, in 1532, had entertained him and so he transported it to his own pages.

In 1562 there was published *Anales et croniques de France depuis la destruction de Troyes jusques au temps des roy Louis onzieme,* with additions bringing it down to the year of publication. The first part was composed by "feu maistre Nicolle Gilles," who had been "secrettaire iudiciaire du Roy, et controlleur de son tresor." Montaigne owned a copy of this volume and made in it some hundred and seventy annotations. It became in our day the property of the well-known Montaigne scholar, M. Dezeimeris, who has published an elaborate study of it.

Among many other indications that Montaigne may have had it occasionally in mind when writing, M. Dezeimeris suggests that a passage in the additions, "De l'entree de l'empereur et son fils, Roy des Romains [Charles] en la ville de Paris," might have been the occasion of this Essay.

The little personal touch, "For my part . . . I do away with all ceremony," was inserted in 1588, and was changed in 1595 to "so far as I can."

In a later Essay ("Of Vanity," Book III, chapter 9) Montaigne says: "There is more of heartbreak than of consolation in taking leave of one's friends [when setting out on a journey]; I willingly forget this duty of our manners"; a detail of the feeling expressed earlier here.

1561

Notes and Comments

B. THE NOTES BY MR. IVES

1. *Rapsodie.*
2. *Si on l'en traine jusques en sa taniere.*
3. Clement VII. The same interview was referred to in chap. 10, *supra,* page 48. See du Bellay, IV.
4. Charles V. It was in 1532. See Guicciardini, XIX, 6.
5. *Le prennent de ce biais.*
6. *La science de l'entregent.*

CHAPTER XIV

That the Savour of Goods and Ills Depends in Large Part on the Idea that We have of Them

A. THE COMMENT BY MISS NORTON

THIS title reminds one of Hamlet's saying, "There is nothing either good or bad but thinking makes it so." The opening sentence enlarges and defines the meaning of the title, and then Montaigne goes on to question whether this be true: let us see if this can be maintained.

He thinks that one proof that it is true is the difference of the ideas of different men about death: by one it is re-

The Savour of Goods and Ills

garded as the most horrible of things, by another as the sovereign good of nature. As one way of meeting death he instances the many jokes that have been uttered by persons on their way to execution; as another, the women who bury or burn themselves with the dead bodies of their husbands, or the self-destruction of men and women in time of war or political trouble. (Here he tells a striking fact that he had learned from his father.) Then follows an inserted passage about the Jews in Portugal—from whom Montaigne's mother was descended, which fact perhaps made their history the more interesting to him.

He then tells the story of Pyrrho pointing out in a storm at sea, for the emulation of his companions, the composure of a pig; and Montaigne questions whether we do not ill employ the intelligence that has been given us for our greatest good, in struggling against the universal order of things. *L'universel ordre des choses*—we have here, as has been remarked by M. F. Strowski, *Montaigne* (1906), p. 31, one of the *Leit-motives* of Montaigne's thought.

The Essayist now contemplates the other ills of human life. "Very good," you will answer; "your precept is well enough for death: but what will you say of poverty? and what of pain?" He answers that with regard to pain, "Here it is not all imagination.... I grant that it is the worst mischance of our being," and that poverty is to be dreaded—but dreaded only—because it throws us into the arms of pain, by hunger and cold, thirst and heat. He says that to himself the idea of pain *is* terrible, "there is no man on earth who shuns it as much as I."

A striking example occurs in just these pages of the self-contradictions not infrequent in the Essays, and which are

Notes and Comments

due to the different passages being written at different periods of Montaigne's life and then joined together as if they were consecutive in thought as well as in position. He says, "I find *by experience* that it is chiefly the unendurableness [*l'impatience*] of the thought of death that makes pain unendurable to us." In the next paragraph we read: "I have not had, thanks be to God, *much familiarity* with it [pain]." The first sentence was written after the second one. His sufferings from the stone (what he calls "the colic") did not begin till 1573, and the greater part of the Essay we are considering was written somewhere about 1572. The sentence regarding his "experience" of pain did not appear till 1595, three years after his death, and during the last twenty years of his life he suffered greatly and frequently.

It is extremely interesting to remember in this connection that the daily records made by his secretary when travelling with him give proof that Montaigne's endurance of pain was singularly heroic.

If we cannot annihilate pain, we can diminish it by patience. So he thought in 1580; so he proved in later years. Besides, if there were not pain to be defied, how should we give evidence of courage, strength, and resolution? Again, pain can not be at once violent and long.

(This strange assertion is a striking testimony to the increased power that medicine and surgery have acquired to preserve life even in conditions of great suffering. And Montaigne seems quite to forget the result of great natural strength of constitution. His contemporary Brantôme describes himself as stretched on his bed for four years in torture, in consequence of being crushed by his horse falling upon him.)

The Savour of Goods and Ills

In a passage added in his last years he reaches the assurance that the soul cannot bring into harmony with herself "the perceptions of the body and all other external things"; and that it behooves us to "arouse her all-powerful springs."

He combats in an obscure sentence an opinion thus expressed by Plato in the "Phaedo" (Jowett's translation):

"The soul of the true philosopher abstains from pleasures and desires and pains and fears, as far as she is able; . . . because each pleasure and pain is a sort of nail which nails and rivets the soul to the body, and engrosses her and makes her believe that to be true which the body affirms to be true; and from agreeing with the body and having the same delights she is obliged to have the same habits and ways." Montaigne says, No: in yielding to pain and pleasure we rather disunite the body and the soul—and (as I understand him) remove ourselves from the government of the body by the soul, which makes our greatest comfort. But this view finds a pseudo-contradiction in an opinion expressed just before, to the effect, seemingly, that the soul would do well to let the body entirely alone.

Then in his favorite fashion, he cites examples: the endurance of the pains of child-birth; the constancy of Lacedæmonian children; the fortitude of Mucius Scævola; the contempt of pain that women show in the pursuit of beauty; the wounds given as pledges of good faith—in which connection he tells of an incident he had witnessed, about which we may wonder whether it had any personal interest for him; and the self-inflicted tortures of pious and fanatic souls—which he himself had seen often. Then comes an inserted passage of instances of composure at death of friends and children, where occurs one of the personal ex-

Notes and Comments

pressions which have been foolishly misjudged. He says that he has borne the loss of two or three of his children, who died when babies, not without regret, but without *fascherie;* that is, without grief, distress (the meaning of the word in his day).

And he adds that while by the greater number and the most healthy-minded among men it is considered that to have many children is a great fortune, "I and some others consider the lack of them good fortune." We may well believe that this feeling originated in part from the disastrous condition of public affairs in that age—one of the most tragic in history.

Montaigne could meet them himself with equanimity, but he recognized the manifold sufferings of every kind which they caused to countless individuals. Childless parents were to be congratulated.

All this shows, as Cicero said, "the source of suffering is not in the nature of things but in our opinion of them."

If our opinion may make us disregard what is commonly counted as evil, so, on the other hand, it may enhance the value of good. And (after a rather incoherent and difficult page added many years later) he proceeds to show this by his own example in relation to the use of his property, through diffuse and wanderings pages, concluding: "Affluence then and indigence depend on each man's opinion."

His last word is that among all the reasons for despising death and enduring pain there must be some which man can accept. If not, "What can be done for him who has no courage to support either death or life?"

It may be observed that Montaigne borrowed much in this Essay from Seneca, especially from Epistle 78.

1566

The Savour of Goods and Ills

B. THE NOTES BY MR. IVES

1. In the edition of 1595, this chapter became Chapter 40, and the numbers of all the intervening chapters were changed accordingly. Not until Chapter 41 is the numbering the same in all editions.

2. Epictetus, *Enchiridion*, 10. Montaigne probably took it from Stobæus, *Sermon* 117. This proverb—

Ταράσσει τοὺς ἀνθρώπους οὐ τὰ πράγματα,
ἀλλὰ τὰ περὶ τῶν πραγμάτων δόγματα

—was inscribed in Greek on one of the beams of Montaigne's library.

3. *De nous bander pour le party qui nous est le plus ennuyeux.*

4. *Elles n'entrent en nous que par composition.*

5. Montaigne repeats the same thought in almost the same words in the Essay, "A Custom of the Isle of Cea," Book II, chap. 3: *Et ce n'est pas la recepte à une seule maladie: la mort est la recepte à tous maux.*

6.   *Mors utinam pavidos vita subducere nolles,*
      Sed virtus te sola daret.
—Lucan, IV, 580.

7. See Cicero, *Tusc. Disp.*, V, 40.

8. This whole passage follows closely Seneca's thought in *Epistle* 70.

9. All these instances are taken from the *Apologie d'Hérodote* of H. Estienne (XV, 20).

10. In 1588: *que se departir de ses opinions, quelles qu'elles fussent.*

11. See Jean Bouchet, *Annales d'Aquitaine* (1477).

·1567

Notes and Comments

In the *Édition Municipale* the passage relating to the practice of suttee in the kingdom of Narsinga is inserted at this point; but in the edition of 1595 it is more appropriately placed a little further on. See page 63.

12. *Vogue la gallée!*

13. See Bonaventure Des Periers, *Les Nouvelles Recreations*.

14. This name was often given by the Portuguese and others to Vijayanagar. The Hindu Empire of Vijayanagar included for 200 years, from the middle of the fourteenth to the middle of the sixteenth century, the whole of Southern India below the 15th degree of latitude.

15. See Goulard's translation of Bishop Osorio's *Histoire du roi Emmanuel de Portugal* (1581).

16. See Plutarch, *Life of Brutus*.

17. See Diodorus Siculus, V, 29.

18. John II reigned from 1481 to 1495. This whole narrative is summarised from Osorio's *Emmanuel of Portugal*, of which Montaigne sometimes, as here, made use of the Latin text, and sometimes of Goulard's translation.

19. Reigned from 1495 to 1521.

20. See Du Haillant, *Histoire de France* (1576). This sentence, which first appeared in 1595, is not found in the *Édition Municipale*.

21. *Quoties non modo ductores nostri,* says Cicero, *sed universi etiam exercitus, ad non dubiam mortem concurrerunt!*—Cicero, *Tusc. Disp.*, I, 37.

22. *Enracinee en son cueur par divers visages de discours.*

23. See Diogenes Laertius, *Life of Pyrrho*.

24. *Si nous en devenons plus lasches.* This phrase, added in 1595, does not appear in the *Édition Municipale*.

The Savour of Goods and Ills

25. In 1588: *pour sa commodité et avantage?* In a letter written to M. de Mesmes (1570) Montaigne said: *Tous ce qui est sous le ciel employe les moyens et les outils que nature luy a mis en main . . . pour l'agencement et commodité de son estre.*

26. See Cicero, *Tusc. Disp.*, II, 6.

27. See *Ibid.*, 25.

28. *Qui nisi sunt veri, ratio quoque falsa sit omnis.*—Lucretius, IV, 485.

29. *Aut fuit, aut veniet, nihil est præsentis in illa.*—Etienne La Boëtie, *Satire* addressed to Montaigne.

30. *Morsque minus pœnæ quam mora mortis habet.*—Ovid, *Heroïdes*, X, 82 (Epistle of Ariadne to Theseus).

31. *Malam mortem non facit, nisi quod sequitur mortem.*—St. Augustine, *De Civ. Dei*, I, 11.

32. *Avida est periculi virtus.*—Seneca, *De Providentia*.

33. *Non enim hilaritate, nec lascivia, nec risu aut joco, comite levitatis, sed sæpe etiam tristes firmitate et constantia sunt beati.*—Cicero, *De Fin.*, II, 20.

34. *Lætius est, quoties magno, sibi constat honestum.*—Lucan, IX, 404.

35. *Si gravis [dolor], brevis; si longus, levis.*—Cicero, *De Fin.*, II, 29. Translated by Montaigne before quoting. Cf. Seneca, *Epistles* 34 and 78.

36. See Seneca, *Epistle* 78.

37. *Memineris maximos morte finiri; parvos multa habere intervalla requietis; mediocrium nos esse dominos: ut si tolerabiles sint feramus, sin minus, e vita, quum ea non placet, tamquam e theatro exeamus.*—Cicero, *De Fin.*, I.

38. In the early editions, including 1588, there followed here the clause, *c'est d'avoir en trop de commerce avec le*

Notes and Comments

corps—a thought borrowed from Seneca, *Epistle* 78: *Illud autem est quod imperitos in vexatione corporis male habet; non assueverent animo esse intensi; multum illis cum corpore fuit.* On the Bordeaux copy of 1588 *(Edition Municipale),* Montaigne first substituted for this clause: *Et de nous armer d'elle contre la mollesse du corps;* this he afterwards struck out, and added the long passage that follows in the text, in which, however, he made many changes.

39. That is, the soul.
40. *Tous autres accidens.*
41. *Qui le tiennent sous boucle.*
42. *Plato craint nostre engagement aspre a la dolur et a la volupte, d'autant qu'il oblige et atache par trop l'ame au corps. Moi plustost, au rebours, d'autant qu'il l'en desprent et descloue.* See Plato, *Phædo.*
43. See Seneca, *Epistle* 78.
44. See Cicero, *Tusc. Disp.,* II, 23.
45. *Tantum doluerunt,* says St. Augustine, *quantum doloribus se inseruerunt.—De Civ. Dei,* I, 10.
46. See *Genesis,* III, 16: In sorrow thou shalt bring forth children.
47. See Plutarch, *Of Love,* XXXIV.
48. In 1580-1588: *(car le larrecin y estoit action de vertu, mais par tel si qu'il estoit vilain qu'entre nous d'y estre surpris).*
49. See Plutarch, *Lycurgus.* Montaigne refers again to this and the following story, and comments on them, in Book II, chap. 32.
50. The editions of 1580-1588 add: *pour ne troubler le mystère.* See Valerius Maximus, III, 3, *ext.* 1.
51. See *Tusc. Disp.,* V, 27.

The Savour of Goods and Ills

52. *Nunquam naturam mos vinceret, est enim ea semper invicta; sed nos umbris, deliciis, otio, languore, desidia animum infecimus; opinionibus maloque more delinitum mollivimus.*—Ibid.

53. See Livy, II, 12.

54. See Seneca, *Epistle* 78, for these two anecdotes.

55. See Aulus Gellius, XII, 5.

56. *Quis mediocris gladiator ingemuit. Quis vultum mutavit unquam? Quis non modo stetit, verum etiam decubuit turpiter? Quis cum decubuisset ferrum recipere jussus, collum contraxit?*—Cicero, *Tusc. Disp.*, II, 17.

57. 1580: *et l'en surnommoit on Madame l'Escorchée.*

58. *Vellere queis cura est albos a stirpe capillos,*
    Et faciem dempta pelle referre novam.
    —Tibullus, I, 8.45.

59. *Pour faire un corps bien espaignolé.* This word is used only by Montaigne, and by him only here. It is a French form of a Gascon word signifying *habitude, façon d'être des Espagnols.*

60. Henri III. See de Thou (an. 1574).

61. In 1595, this passage was so changed as to read: *Quand je viens de ces fameux Estats de Blois, j'avois veu peu auparavant une fille en Picardie.*

62. See Guillaume Postel, *Des Histoires Orientales.*

63. A small Turkish silver coin.

64. *Porter la croix.*

65. The "witness" whom Montaigne refers to, he believed to be Joinville; but unfortunately the edition of his *Chronicles* which Montaigne read was extremely inaccurate, and this statement about King Louis is not found in modern editions.

Notes and Comments

66. Eleanor. She married, first, Louis XI; then, Henry II of England.

67. See Jean Bouchet, *Annales d'Aquitaine*.

68. This was Fulke III, who died in 1040. Montaigne found this account in a French translation of the *De Rebus Gestis Francorum*, of Paulus Æmilius of Verona, published in 1539.

69. Montaigne describes in the *Journal* of his travels a similar scene that he witnessed (some time after this passage was written) in Rome, on Good Friday, 1581.

70. See Cicero, *Tusc. Disp.*, III, 28.

71. This "some one" was Gaston de Foix, comte de Gurson and de Fleix, marquis de Trans. One of his sons was the husband of the Diane de Foix to whom the essay, "De l'Institution des Enfans" (Book I, chap. 26) was dedicated. Montaigne wrote in his *Ephemerides: Julius 29, 1587, le côte de Gurson, le côte de Fleix, & le chevalier, trois freres mes bôs S^{rs} & amis, furent tués à Môcrabeau en Agenois en un côbat fort aspre pour la service du roi de Navarre.*

72. In 1595 this passage was made to read: *qu'il ne la prinst à faveur et gratification singuliere du Ciel. Je n'ensuis ces humeurs monstreuses.*

73. *Ex quo intelligitur non in natura, sed in opinione esse ægritudinem.*—Cicero, *Tusc. Disp.*, III, 28.

74. See Plutarch, *Apothegms of Kings*, etc.

75. *Ferox gens nullam vitam rati sine armis esse.*—Livy, XXXIV, 17. This sentence, beginning "Cato, when," was manifestly inserted in the wrong place.

76. St. Carlo Borromeo, Archbishop of Milan, 1538-1584.

The Savour of Goods and Ills

77. The philosopher Democritus. See Aulus Gellius, X.
78. *La plus commune et la plus saine part des hommes.*
79. See Diogenes Laertius, *Life of Thales.*
80. *Sur quoi je m'advise que nous sommes grands mesnagiers de nostre mise. Selon qu'elle poise, elle sert de ce mesme qu'elle pois. Nostre opinion ne la laisse jamais courir a faus fret.*
81. Aristippus. Montaigne refers to this again in Book II, chap. 11. Among other sources, this statement is found in Diogenes Laertius *(Life of Aristippus)* and in Horace, *Satires*, II, 3. 100.
82. See Seneca, *Epistle* 17.
83. *En maniere que j'en rendoy une loyauté mesnagere et aucunement piperesse.*
84. See Plutarch, *Life of Cæsar.*
85. *Tot per impotentia freta?*—Catullus, IV, 19.
86. That is, associations of religion or of instruction.
87. *Au delà de.*
88. *Fortuna vitrea est; tunc, cum splendet frangitur.*—This sentence is from Publius Syrus; but Montaigne found it in the *Politiques* of Justus Lipsius, V, 18.
89. *Faber est suæ quisque fortunæ.*—Sallust, *De Republica Ordinanda*, I, 1.
90. *In divitiis inopes, quod genus egestatis gravissimum est.*—Seneca, *Epistle* 74.
91. Seneca, *De Tranquillitate Animi*, VIII, 3.
92. See the *Laws*, I, not far from the beginning, where Plato says not exactly this, but something like it.
93. Montaigne is in error here: it was Dionysius the elder. See Plutarch, *Apothegms of Kings*, etc.
94. That is, in the "second condition." See page 80.

1573

Notes and Comments

95. *Non esse cupidum pecunia est, non esse emacem vectigal est.*—Cicero, *Paradoxa Stoicorum,* VI, 3.
96. *Divitiarum fructus est in copia, copiam declarat satietas.*—Cicero, *Paradoxa,* VI, 2.
97. See Xenophon, *Cyropædeia,* VII, 3.35-50.
98. That is, the "elderly prelate."
99. Fortune.
100. See Seneca, *Epistle* 98.
101. *Accessions:* probably a misprint for *accessoires.*
102. See Plutarch, *Of Vice and Virtue.*
103. This passage is taken from Seneca, *Epistle* 71.
104. *Opinio est quædam effeminata ac levis, nec in dolore magis quam eadem in voluptate: qua quum liquescimus fluimusque mollitia, apis aculeum sine clamore ferre non possumus. Totum in eo est ut tibi imperes.*—Cicero, *Tusc. Disp.,* II, 22.
105. See Seneca, *Epistle* 12: *Malum est in necessitate vivere; sed in necessitate vivere necessitatis nulla est.*
106. On the Bordeaux copy of 1588, Montaigne first wrote the source of this sentence: *Nemo nisi sua culpa diu dolet;* then erased it, and substituted this translation.

CHAPTER XV

Unreasonable Persistence in the Defence of a Stronghold is Punished

A. THE COMMENT BY MISS NORTON

THE subject of this Essay has so little to do with our own day that the first sentence is the only one of general interest. This sentence is an admirable expression of Montaigne's esteem for *moderation,* his constant desire to maintain the *mean.* He recognises, as Shakespeare does, that

> Virtue itself turns vice, being misapplied.
> *(Romeo and Juliet)*

Elsewhere, in the "Apology" (Book II, chapter 12), he says, speaking of the limits and boundary lines of all knowledge, "An extreme degree has a wrong quality as with virtue."

And again, in the Essay "Of Moderation" (Book I, chapter 30), "We can so hold virtue as to render it sinful."

B. THE NOTES BY MR. IVES

1. *On est puny pour s'opiniastrer à une place sans raison.* —[*Place* = *place forte.*]
2. See du Bellay, II. Montmorency was not made

constable till fifteen years later, but had been made a marshal three years before.

3. The word "capitaine," as used by Montaigne, denotes simply a commander of troops. The brothers du Bellay (both of whom wrote memoirs) were at one time or another at the head of troops. See du Bellay, VIII.

4. *Ibid.*, IX.

5. See Goulard, *Histoire du Portugal*, XIV, 15.

CHAPTER XVI

Of the Punishment of Cowardice

A. THE COMMENT BY MISS NORTON

ANOTHER exhibition of Montaigne's familiarity in thought with military matters. And it was not in thought merely that he was familiar with them. How much of a soldier he himself had been is a matter of discussion, but it is quite certain that he had lived in camps and borne the fatigue of marches.

The first sentence gives the text of the Essay. But the most important passage is that where Montaigne refers to the "view of those who condemn capital punishment for heretics and unbelievers." It was hardly safe to do more than to hint at such an opinion—to drop it as Montaigne does here into the middle of a page; but we shall see later how earnestly he himself held it.

1576

A Proceeding of Some Ambassadors

B. THE NOTES BY MR. IVES

1. See du Bellay, X. He surrendered Boulogne to Henry VIII in 1545.
2. See Diodorus Siculus, XII, 4.
3. *Suffundere malis hominis sanguinem quam effundere.*—Tertullian, *Apologeticum*. The original has *maluit*.
4. See Ammianus Marcellinus, XXIV, 4. This fact concerns the Emperor Julian the Apostate, when fighting with the *Persians* in A.D. 363, just before his death.
5. *Ibid.*, XXV, 1.
6. See Livy, XXV, 7, 22; XXVI, 1.
7. See du Bellay, II.
8. *Ibid.*, VII. The Comte de Nansau led an army into Picardy in 1537, and the citizens of Guise showed both cowardice and pusillanimity.

CHAPTER XVII

A Proceeding of Some Ambassadors

A. THE COMMENT BY MISS NORTON

I SOMETIMES wonder whether Montaigne wrote his title at the head of his sheet of paper, and then, pausing a moment and thinking of first one and then another thing in connection with it, caught suddenly a thought that he

Notes and Comments

wished to put in words and began the Essay. Or did he sit with pen near at hand and jot down from time to time an interesting passage in the book he was reading, or the memory or fancy or reflection that came to his mind; and when a few pages were thus brokenly written, did he then choose his title from one of the many subjects touched upon?

At all events we hear nothing of *ambassadors* till halfway through the Essay, and then to very little purpose; but the first sentence of the first paragraph, and the second paragraph are of much interest,—much importance, one may say,—as furnishing some of those details with regard to Montaigne's own mind and manners, which aid us to form our conception of him. The Essay is truly of the proceedings of Montaigne, rather than of ambassadors.

The special ambassadorial proceeding that it treats of is the dissimulation and even concealment of the truth which ambassadors sometimes practise toward their masters.

B. THE NOTES BY MR. IVES

1. Cf. the old proverb: *Table vaut escole notable*—Table-talk is an excellent schoolmaster.
2. *Basti al nocchiero ragionar de' venti,*
   Al bifolco dei tori, et le sue piaghe
   Conti'l guerrier, conti'l pastor gli armenti.
   —An Italian translation of Propertius, II, 1.43, which Montaigne found in Stefano Guazzo's *Civil Conversation*.
3. See Plutarch, *Apothegms of the Lacedæmonians*.
4. See *De Bello Gallico*, IV, 17.
5. See Diodorus Siculus, XV, 6. Montaigne speaks of this in the essay "Of Presumption," Book II, chap. 17.

Of Fear

6. *Optat ephippia bos piger optat arare caballus.*—Horace, *Epistles*, I, 14.43.
7. *Les menees, intelligences, et pratiques.*
8. Guillaume du Bellay.
9. See du Bellay, V.
10. Of France.
11. See Aulus Gellius, I, 13.24.
12. See *Ibid.*: *Quod esset ditissimus, quod nobilissimus, quod eloquentissimus, quod jurisconsultissimus, quod pontifex maximus.*
13. *Deus mas de navire.*

CHAPTER XVIII

Of Fear

A. THE COMMENT BY MISS NORTON

MONTAIGNE may say, if he pleases, that he is not *un bon naturaliste* (natural philosopher), but every page of his writing shows how intimately he knew human nature; and this little disquisition on Fear is full of truths derived, as usual, from his observation of others and of himself. If he did not know (as he says) what were the springs of fear, he well knew what were the effects of the currents of both private fear and public fear. He had "seen" (probably when with the army) many people beside themselves with fear, and he had read of delirious flights into the very

Notes and Comments

mouth of danger, and of trance-like stupidities of inaction, and of seeming courage, all caused by this strange passion.

And his conclusion from all this is,—and herein he truly shows himself *bon naturaliste,*—"The thing I am most afraid of is fear."

A somewhat irrelevant sentence: "Those who are in extreme dread . . . of being exiled . . ." brings vividly before us the *fortunes* of those days, the causes for fear, for "constant anguish," of which *we* know nothing.

B. THE NOTES BY MR. IVES

1. *Obstupui, steteruntque comæ, et vox faucibus hæsit.*—Virgil, *Æneid,* II, 774.
2. *Bon naturaliste.*
3. The "croix blanche" of France, and the "croix rouge" of Spain.
4. In 1527. See du Bellay, III.
5. See du Bellay, VIII, for this and the next episode.
6. See Tacitus, *Annals,* I, 63.
7. *Adeo pavor etiam auxilia formidat.*—Quintus Curtius, III, 2.
8. See the *Annals* of Zonaras. This chronicler died in 1130. His work was published at Basle in 1557, but Montaigne used a French translation published in 1560.
9. *Juste.* Montaigne uses the word several times, as here, in the Latin sense. It was the battle of Trebia, in 218 B.C., which Livy describes in Book XXI, 56. Montaigne refers to it again in the Essay, "Of the Custom of wearing Clothes," Book I, chap. 36.
10. See Cicero, *Tusc. Disp.,* III, 27.
11. *Tum pavor sapientiam omnem mihi ex animo ex-*

Our Fortune after Death

pectorat.—Ennius, *apud* Cicero, *Tusc. Disp.*, IV, 8. This passage, beginning with "Could there be a keener" (11 lines above), and ending with this line of Ennius, does not appear on the Bordeaux copy of 1588, but there is a mark indicating an interlineation, and a piece of wafer used to affix an additional sheet. The passage as it stands first appeared in 1595.

12. See Diodorus Siculus, XV, 7.15-17.
13. See Plutarch, *Of Isis and Osiris*.

CHAPTER XIX

That Our Fortune Must not be Judged of Until After Death

A. THE COMMENT BY MISS NORTON

THIS Essay is entirely described by its title. Its interest is at once increased and diminished by the fact that many of the opinions Montaigne here set forth he disavowed in later years.

It was written (except the last two paragraphs) in 1572, when he was not quite forty years old, and when he had not passed beyond the ideas about death that were familiar to his generation. In after years he was far from considering the day of death as "the master day"; and the wish expressed in the last sentence, it is matter for rejoicing that he was

1581

Notes and Comments

able to accomplish—"one of my chief endeavours regarding my own end is that it may carry itself well, that is to say, quietly and insensibly." The last words in the original are *quietement et sourdement,* and the passage is undoubtedly one that Pascal stigmatizes when he says: "Il ne pense qu'à mourir lachement et mollement par tout son livre." The word *sourdement* is to be noted. Montaigne substituted it (in the posthumous edition) for *seurement,* and it is open to question whether he did not thereby modify the conception. Cotgrave defines *sourdement* as "privately . . . in huggermugger, without any din or noise."

From what Montaigne says elsewhere of his preference for dying away from home, and of the common confusion and distresses of a death-bed (see Book III, chapter 12, a few pages from the beginning, and Book I, chapter 20, last sentence), it is possible to believe that he was thinking of external quietness as well as of that of the soul.

It may be that in the last paragraph, he refers to La Boëtie's death; but the phrase "a glorious end,"—*une fin pompeuse,*—unless the word may be understood as descriptive simply of moral *stateliness,* sounds oddly in regard to his friend's peaceful and domestic passing from life; as also does the statement about this death leading to "the power and the fame" to which the personage had aspired. La Boëtie's fame was in some part of Montaigne's creating. It would seem as if Montaigne were speaking of some great public character. But of whom? Henri, duc de Guise, has been suggested; but that is absurd. A brutal assassination is not *une fin pompeuse;* and neither honour nor honours followed the duke after death. The allusion to the execution of Mary, Queen of Scots was added in 1595.

1582

Our Fortune After Death

B. THE NOTES BY MR. IVES

1.   *Scilicet ultima semper
Expectanda dies homini est, dicique beatus
Ante obitum nemo supremaque funera debet.*
—Ovid, *Metamorphoses*, III, 135.

2. Passages in square brackets omitted in 1595.

3. See Herodotus, I, 86. Montaigne had already referred to this saying of Solon in chapter 3 of this Book.

4. See Plutarch, *Apothegms of the Lacedæmonians*.

5. An allusion to Philip, son of Perseus. See Plutarch, *Life of Paulus Æmilius*.

6. An allusion to the familiar story of Dionysius the tyrant, driven from his realm by Timoleon.

7. See Cicero, *Tusc. Disp.*, I, 35.

8. See Guicciardini, IV.

9. Mary, Queen of Scots, widow of François II. She was executed in 1587, but this passage did not appear in the Essays until after Montaigne's death.

10. This last sentence is not in the *Édition Municipale*, but was added in 1595.

11.   *Usque adeo res humanas vis abdita quædam
Obterit, et pulchros fasces sævasque secures
Proculcare, ac ludibrio sibi habere videtur.*
—Lucretius, V, 1233.

12. See Seneca, *Epistle* 98: *Incrementa lente exeunt, festinatur in damnum.*

13. *Nimirum hac die una plus vixi mihi quam vivendum fuit.*—Macrobius, *Saturnalia*, II, 7.

14. *D'un esprit bien né.*

15. *Parler françois.*

1583

Notes and Comments

16. *Nam veræ voces tum demum pectore ab imo Ejiciuntur, et eripitur persona, manet res.*
—Lucretius, III, 57.

17. See Seneca, *Epistle* 26, 4: *Ille laturus sententiam de omnibus annis meis dies veneret.*

18. The Essay ended here in editions before 1588.

19. See Seneca, *Epistle* 24.

20. See Plutarch, *Apothegms of Kings*, etc.

21. Epaminondas.

22. *Dans la fleur de son croist.*

23. *Sourdement:* substituted in 1595 for *seurement*.

CHAPTER XX

That to Think as a Philosopher is to Learn to Die

A. THE COMMENT BY MISS NORTON

THIS Essay opens with a consideration of the meaning of the sentence of Cicero which forms its title; and continues with the assertion that to lose the fear of death is part of that pleasure, or *volupté* (as Montaigne chooses to call it from a wilful desire to shock those to whom this word "is so abhorrent"), which is "the final object of our

To Think as a Philosopher

aim"; and from this he passes into a noble passage regarding the *pleasure of virtue*, condemning those "who instruct us that her quest is hard and laborious." The last sentence could hardly be finer. (The whole paragraph belongs to 1595.)

Continuing, he says: "The end of our career is death; it is the unavoidable thing in full sight." The original text has a deeper significance than can easily be conveyed in English; the phrase is: Death "est le but de nostre carriere . . . c'est l'object de nostre visee"; this can be paraphrased: "the winning post of our race . . . the object of our aim."

In one of the latest and noblest of the Essays ("Of Physiognomy," Book III, Chapter 12) he precisely contradicts this remark; he had risen from a theological to a humane conception of death. He recognises that "If we have known how to live, it is unreasonable to teach us how to die . . . if we have known how to live steadily and quietly, we know how to die in like manner. . . . It is my opinion that it [death] is indeed the close but not the aim of life [*c'est bien le bout, non pourtant le but de la vie*]; it is its end, its extremity, not, however, its object; life should be its own aim and purpose [*elle doibt estre elle mesme à soi sa visée, son desseing*]; its true study is to order and guide it, and patiently to support it [*se souffrir*]. Among the number of several other offices which the general and principal chapter of knowing how to live includes, is this article of knowing how to die, and it is among the lightest, if our fears did not give weight to it." Here we have the mature Montaigne, serene, simple, natural. In this present Essay he was dominated by Seneca; he had not yet shaken off the conventional emotions of his day; he was still *youthful* in mind, though,

1585

Notes and Comments

as he tells us, he was at this time 39 years old.

Regarding the considerations he here turns to as to the common length of life, it is worth observing, as showing the different standard for it in his day and ours,—and not less in his day and earlier (Bible) days,—that he speaks of this age of 39 as beyond the usual term of life. This has a strange sound to our ears. The next point he touches upon is a curious one—the question whether or not the majority of famous men have died before they were 35; and this becomes more interesting when connected with a kindred question that he raises in a later Essay: whether or not the greater number of noble actions on record have been performed before the age of 30 years. He thinks so: "Yes, often in the life of the same man"; that is, even when the same men have lived on to later years.

The greater part of this Essay would seem to have been written somewhere about the date he gives in the course of it—the 15th March, 1572. But in the last part, which is not very closely connected with the rest, he made additions before its publication in 1580. Some discrepancies result; for instance on one page he says: "I have enjoyed to the present time very vigorous health, very seldom interrupted"; on another he says: "When I was well I had much more dread of sicknesses than since I have them." He was attacked by the malady of the stone in 1573; by 1580 he had suffered from it.

From the paragraph beginning "These examples," the chief interest is in observing the action of the essayist's thought, the state of mind at that time.

There is only a sentence here and there that is worth remembrance, except the address of Nature to Man (imitated

To Think as a Philosopher

from Lucretius) asserting Death to be a part of the constitution of the universe, and largely composed of passages from Seneca. Regarding the rest, we feel with Lord Bacon: "Much of the doctrines of the philosophers seem to me to be more fearful and cautionary than the nature of things requires: thus they increase the fear of death in offering to cure it; for when they would have a man's whole life be but a discipline or preparation to die, they must needs make men think that it is a terrible enemy, against whom there is no end of preparing." (*Advancement of Learning*, II, 21.5.)

This criticism is of precisely opposite tone to that made by Pascal *(Pensées)*, who, speaking directly of Montaigne, says: "His somewhat free and light feelings about some passages of life can be excused, but his wholly pagan feelings about death cannot be excused; for one must relinquish all piety, if one does not desire to die, at least, in a Christian manner; now, throughout his book he has in mind only to die weakly and gently."

No, not *lachement et mollement*, but *quietement et sourdement;* or, in still better phrase, *constamment et tranquillement*.

B. THE NOTES BY MR. IVES

1. See *Tusc. Disp.*, I, 30.
2. See *Ibid.*, 31.
3. See Cicero, *De Fin.*, II, 27.
4. See *Ecclesiastes*, III, 12.
5. *Transcurramus solertissimas nugas.*—Seneca, Epistle 117.
6. *Mais quelque personnage que l'home entrepreigne, il joue tousjours le sien parmy.*

Notes and Comments

7. *Volupté*=earthly delight.
8. *Plaisir.*
9. That is, "they who proceed to instruct us."
10. *Car c'est une bonne portion de l'effaict, et consubstantielle.*
11. In 1580-1588, *Voylà pourquoy toutes les sectes des philosophes . . . à cet article de nous instruire à la mespriser.*
12. See Pliny, *Natural History*, VII, 51.
13.   *Omnes eodem cogimur; omnium*
       Versatur urna, serius ocius
         Sors exitura et nos in æternum
           Exsilium impositura cymbæ.
                —Horace, *Odes*, II, 3.25.
14. See Seneca, *Epistle* 74.
15. *Quæ quasi saxum Tantalo semper impendet.*—Cicero, *De Fin.*, I, 18.
16.   *non Siculæ dapes*
    Dulcem elaborabunt saporem,
      Non avium cytharæque cantus
        Somnum reducent.—Horace, *Odes*, III, 1.18.
17.   *Audit iter, numeratque dies, spacioque viarum*
    Metitur vitam, torquetur peste futura.
           —Claudian, *In Rufinum*, II, 137.
18. *Qui capite ipse suo instituit vestigia retro.*
              —Lucretius, IV, 472.
19. That is, the testament.
20. See Plutarch, *Life of Cicero*.
21. *Feu*, deceased, or, as we say, "late." The derivation of the word is uncertain, whether from the Latin *functus* (deceased), or, through the Italian, from the Latin *fuit* (he was). According to Hatzfeld and Darmesteter, from the

To Think as a Philosopher

vulgar Latin *fatutus:* who has fulfilled his destiny *(fatum)*.

22. In 1565 Charles IX of France decreed that the year should begin on January 1, instead of at Easter; but the decree was not carried into effect until two years later.

23. The editions of 1580-1588 add: *y pensent aussi peu les uns que les autres.*

24. Montaigne reasserts this belief in the Essay "Of Age," Book I, chap. 57.

25. In 1580 and 1582 we have, *et ce fameux Mahumet aussi.*

26. *Quid quisque vitet, nunquam homini satis Cautum est in horas.*—Horace, *Odes,* II, 13.13.

27. This was Bertrand de Got, Archbishop of Bordeaux, Pope from 1305 to 1314, under the name of Clement V. Montaigne jestingly calls him "my neighbour" because he was of Bordeaux. The Duc de Bretaigne was Jean II, died 1305. Montaigne took this from *Les diverses leçons* of Pierre de Messie, translated from the Spanish in 1552.

28. Henri II, in 1559.

29. Philippe, son of Louis le Gros: his horse was frightened by a hog. See Jean Bouchet, *Annales d'Aquitaine.*

30. *A l'airre* (1580-1588); *à l'airte (Éd. Mun.).* This phrase was borrowed from the Italian *all'erte* (on the height), and was used in the sense that Montaigne gives it, by Baïf and others.

31. This legend came originally from Valerius Maximus, IX, 12, *ext.* 2; but Montaigne apparently took it from the *Officina* of Ravisius Textor.

32. Anacreon. See Valerius Maximus, IX, 12, *ext.* 8.

33. These last three instances are taken from Pliny, *Natural History,* VII, 33 and 53.

Notes and Comments

34. John XXII. The names of these five, and the manner of their deaths, are taken from Ravisius Textor, *Officina*.

35. Bebius and Caius Julius, as well as Cornelius Gallus (above), are found in a longer list given by Pliny, *Natural History*, VII, 53.

36. This last clause well illustrates the difference between French and English usage in the matters of gender. In such impersonal expressions as "it seems," where the neuter pronoun is always used in English, the French use the masculine pronoun: *"il* me semble." Again, all nouns in French being either masculine or feminine, the pronoun always follows in gender the noun for which it stands; whereas in English we personify certain nouns as masculine or feminine according to no fixed rule. *Mort* (death) being feminine, the feminine pronoun *elle* is always used; while if we personify Death, we always speak of it as "he."

37. That is, that it does not matter. Compare Montaigne's change of note in later Essay, Book III, chap. 12.

38. *Le meilleur jeu que je me puis donner, je le prens.*

39. *Prætulerim . . . delirus inersque videri,*
Dum mea delectent mala me, vel denique fallant,
Quam sapere et ringi.—Horace, *Epistles*, II, 2.126.

40. *En dessoude;* from *de* and *soude*, a variant of *soudain*.

41. *Nempe et fugacem persequitur virum,*
Nec parcit imbellis juventæ
Poplitibus timidoque tergo.
—Horace, *Odes*, III, 2.14.

42. *Ille licet ferro cautus se condat ære,*
Mors tamen inclusum protrahet inde caput.
—Propertius, III, 18.25.

To Think as a Philosopher

43. Cf. Seneca, *Epistle* 4.
44. See Plutarch, *Banquet of the Seven Sages;* Herodotus, II, 78.
45.   *Omnem crede diem tibi diluxisse supremum;*
    Grata supervenient, quæ non sperabitur hora.
                       —Horace, *Epistles*, I, 4.13.
46. This and the four sentences following are taken from Seneca, *Epistle* 26.
47. See Idem, *Epistle* 78.
48. Perseus. See Plutarch, *Life of Paulus Æmilius.*
49. Songecreux.
50. *Jucundum cum ætas florida ver ageret.*
                        —Catullus, LXVIII, 16.
51. *Et qu'autant m'en pendoit à l'oreille.*
52. *Jam fuerit, nec post unquam revocare licebit.*
                        —Lucretius, III, 915.
53. *Tout ce qui peut estre faict une autre jour, le peut estre aujourd'hui.*
54. Cf. Seneca, *Epistle* 49.
55. *Nemo altero fragilior est: nemo in crastinum sui certior.*—Idem, *Epistle* 91.
56.   *Quid brevi fortes jaculamur ævo*
    Multa?   —Horace, *Odes*, II, 16.17.
57. The last words, from "if it be not," are found only in the *Édition Municipale.*
58. The edition of 1595 adds: *Les plus mortes morts sont les plus saines.* (The deadest deaths are the most healthful.) This is not found in the *Édition Municipale.*
59.   *Miser, o miser, aiunt, omnia ademit*
    Una dies infesta mihi tot præmia vitæ.
                        —Lucretius, III, 898.

Notes and Comments

60.   *Manent opera interrupta minæque*
       Murorum ingentes. —Virgil, *Æneid*, IV, 88.
The original has *pendent* instead of *manent*.

61. The *Édition Municipale* has *pour n'en voir la fin;* all other texts, *pour en voir la fin.*

62. The passage in brackets is omitted in the *Édition Municipale* and in 1595.

63.   *Cum moriar, medium solvar et inter opus.*
                    —Ovid, *Amores*, II, 10.36.

64.   *Illud in his rebus non addunt, nec tibi earum*
      Jam desiderium rerum super insidet una.
                    —Lucretius, III, 900.

65. See Plutarch, *Life of Lycurgus.*

66.   *Quin etiam exhilarare viris convivia cæde*
      Mos olim, et miscere epulis spectacula dira
      Certantum ferro, sæpe et super ipsa cadentum
      Pocula, respersis non parco sanguine mensis;
                    —Silius Italicus, XI, 51.
Montaigne took it from J. Lipsius, *Saturnalium sermonum libri duo*, I, 6.

67. See Herodotus, II, 78. Cf. p. 114 *supra.*

68. See such lists in Pliny, *Natural History*, VII; Valerius Maximus, IX, 12; also Rabelais, IV, 18.

69. A philosophical writer—a pupil of Aristotle. See Cicero, *De Off.*, II, 5.

70. This is an idea that constantly recurs in Seneca's letters.

71. The editions of 1580-1588 add: *Je reconnoy par experience que.*

72. Cf. the Essays, "Of Experience" (Book II, chap. 6), and "Of the Resemblance of Children to their Fathers"

1592

To Think as a Philosopher

(Book II, chap. 37), near the beginning.
73. In *De Bello Gallico*, VII, 84.
74. That is, illness.
75.   *Heu! senibus vitæ portio quanta manet.*
    —Maximianus (or Pseudo-Gallus), *Elegies*, I, 16.
76. Seneca *(Epistle* 77) tells this, not of a soldier, but of an old prisoner.
77. That is, Nature's.
78.   *Non vultus instantis tyranni*
      Mente quatit solida; neque Auster
    Dux inquieti turbidus Adriæ,
    Nec fulminantis magna Iovis manus.
    —Horace, *Odes*, III, 3.3.
79. *Faire la figue.*
80. Cf. Seneca, *Epistle* 26, at the end.
81.   *in manicis et*
Compedibus sævo te sub custode tenebo.
Ipse Deus, simul atque volam, me solvet. Opinor,
Hoc sentit: Moriar; mors ultima linea rerum est.
    —Horace, *Epistles*, I, 16.76.
A figurative allusion to chariot races is intended. The *alba linea* marked the goal.
82. *Le discours de la raison.*
83. See St. Augustine, *De Civ. Dei*, I, 11.54.
84. See Diogenes Laertius, *Life of Socrates*. In the passage of Laertius from which Montaigne took this, there is previously a mention of the thirty tyrants, by which he was misled. The thirty tyrants had fallen four years before the death of Socrates. It was the Athenians, as Laertius says, who decreed his death.
85. See Seneca, *Epistle* 77.

Notes and Comments

86. *Ainsi nous despouillames nous de nostre ancien voile en y entrant.*

87. See Cicero, *Tusc. Disp.*, I, 39.

88. This refers back to the sentence a few lines above: "Is there not more harm in dreading them all than in enduring one of them?" The following pages, almost to the end of the chapter, are reminiscent of the famous passage in the third book of Lucretius (near the end). It may be observed that in 1580 Montaigne's text in this Essay was built up on borrowings from Lucretius, illustrated and filled out by translations of Seneca. The additions of 1588 are chiefly from Lucretius. Those of the *Édition Municipale* are almost all from Seneca. Very often the sentences in French following the quotations from Lucretius are paraphrases of connecting lines not quoted.

89.   *inter se mortales mutua vivunt*
  Et quasi cursores vitaï lampada tradunt.
        —Lucretius, II, 76, 79.

90. The text here is of peculiar grammatical construction: *Changerayje pas pour vous cette belle contexture des choses.*

91. That is, in shunning it.

92.   *Prima, quæ vitam dedit, hora, carpsit.*
    —Seneca, *Hercules Furens*, Act. III, 874.

93.   *Nascentes morimur, finisque ab origine pendet.*
    —Manilius, *Astronomica*, IV, 16.

94. The phrase *Et ne mouriez jamais trop tost* stood here in 1580, but was dropped in 1588.

95. See Lucretius, III, 935.

96.   *Cur non ut plenus vitæ conviva recedis?*
        —Idem, 938.

To Think as a Philosopher

97.   *Cur amplius addere quæris*
Rursum quod pereat male, et ingratum occidat omne?
—Lucretius, III, 941.

98. See Seneca, *Epistle* 99.

99.   *Non alium videre patres; aliumve nepotes*
            Aspicient.
—Manilius, I, 522. Montaigne took this quotation from Vivès's Commentary on St. Augustine; *De Civ. Dei*, XI, 4.

100.   *Versamur ibidem, atque insumus usque.*
—Lucretius, III, 1080.

101.   *Atque in se sua per vestigia volvitur annus.*
—Virgil, *Georgics*, II, 402.

102.   *Nam tibi præterea quod machiner, inveniamque*
Quod placeat, nihil est; eadem sunt omnia semper.
—Lucretius, III, 944.

103. See Seneca, *Epistle* 30.

104. Cf. Lucretius, III, 1087-1089, 1092-1094.

105.   *Licet, quod vis, vivendo vincere secla,*
            Mors æterna tamen nihilominus illa manebit.
—Idem, III, 1090.

106.   *In vera nescis nullum fore morte alium te,*
            Qui possit vivus tibi te lugere peremptum,
            Stansque jacentem;
—Idem, III, 885.

107.   *Nec sibi enim quisquam tum se vitamque*
                        requirit.
Nec desiderium nostri nos afficit ullum.
—Idem, III, 919, 922.

108.   *multo mortem minus ad nos esse putandum,*
Si minus esse potest quam quod nihil esse videmus.
—Idem, III, 926.

Notes and Comments

109. Cf. Cicero, *Tusc. Disp.*, I, 38.
110. See Seneca, *Epistle* 69.
111.   *Respice enim quam nil ad nos ante acta vetustas*
       Temporis æterni fuerit. —Lucretius, III, 972.
112. See Seneca, *Epistle* 77.
113. See Idem, *Epistle* 49.
114. See Idem, *Consolatio ad Marciam*, 20; *Epistle* 93.
115. See Idem, *Epistle* 61.
116. See Idem, *Epistle* 77.
117.   *Omnia te vita perfuncta sequentur.*
                                 —Lucretius, III, 968.
118. See Seneca, *Epistle* 77.
119.   *Nam nox nulla diem, neque noctem aurora*
                                 secuta est,
    Quæ non audierit mistos vagitibus ægris
    Ploratus, mortis comites et funeris atri.
                                 —Lucretius, II, 578.
120. See Seneca, *Epistle* 107.
121. See Idem, *Epistle* 91.
122. See Idem, *Epistle* 93.
123. See Lucian, *Dialogues of the Dead*, XXVI.
124. See Diogenes Laertius, *Life of Thales*.
125. See Seneca, *Epistle* 117.
126. See Idem, *Epistle* 120.
127. See Seneca, *Epistle* 24.
128. See *Ibid.*

CHAPTER XXI

Of the Power of Imagination

A. THE COMMENT BY MISS NORTON

AGAIN the first page is interesting from our interest in Montaigne personally. It was added in 1595. The next following ones may be skipped as simply illustrating the power of credulity in the matter of physical marvels, which Montaigne possessed in common with his contemporaries—which was a part of the ignorance of the age. But when he says, "Some attribute the scars of King Dogabert and of Saint Francis to the power of imagination," we find here one of those thoughts of an entirely modern character which are frequent with him. The next sentence, "It is said that by it bodies are sometimes lifted from their places," might have served as a motto a generation ago for the Theosophists. But he is in the truth when he says ("Of Custom," p. 145 *infra*), "Miracles exist from our ignorance of Nature, not in Nature herself."

In this Essay, as sometimes elsewhere, Montaigne carries his habitual frankness of speech to an extreme. He recounts some questionable physiological phenomena caused by the force of the imagination, and does not hesitate to call things by their names.

It is to be remembered that refinement of language was

Notes and Comments

not insisted upon in his day, and that, in the minds of his contemporaries, his freedom would excite no surprise or displeasure.

There is a passage of intelligent observation about animals, which are subject, like ourselves, to the power of imagination; but his discourse on beasts goes on to include some marvellous tales, resembling those we shall have to deal with later in the "Apology"; and about these he divests himself of responsibility by closing with a "So they say. For the anecdotes that I borrow, I refer them to the consciences of those from whom I receive them." He regards his conclusions as founded on reason—as having, as it were, a sort of *a priori* truth; and if these examples happen to be false, and do not therefore strengthen his arguments, then let some one else find others that do; there must be plenty of them, he thinks: "If I do not rightly comment on them, let another comment for me."

The last paragraph of the Essay adds Plutarch's authority to this theory of the slightness of connection between a text and its illustrations. All the last page was added in 1595.

To return, for a moment, to an earlier page (136): where he now says: "Some one saw lately at my home a cat watching a bird," he said in 1580, not "some one," but "My father saw one day"—a pleasant little picture of the elder Montaigne walking in his garden with open eyes. And he says that all this Essay—"this vagary"—has arisen from a tale told him "by an apothecary in the household of my late father."

Very original and interesting considerations of the historical truth in his own writings conclude the Essay.

1598

Of the Power of Imagination

B. THE NOTES BY MR. IVES

1. *Fortis imaginatio generat casum.*—Source unknown.
2. *Chacun en est heurté, mais aucuns en sont renversez.* In 1580-1588, the sentence read: *Chacun en est feru, mais aucuns en sont transformez.*
3. That is, the imagination.
4. Later, in chapter 12 of Book II, Montaigne exclaims: *Combien en a rendu malades la seule force de l'imagination!*
5. These two words were added in 1595, which fact would seem to indicate that one, or both, of the editors of 1595 had heard the story from Montaigne's lips and knew who the "rich old man" was.
6. That is, the old man.
7. See Seneca (Rhetor), *Controversia,* IX.
8. *S'eschauffe si avant en son harnois.*
9. *Ut quasi transactis sæpe omnibus rebus profundant Fluminis ingentes fluctus, vestemque cruentent.*
   —Lucretius, IV, 1035.
10. There are tales and references, more or less full, in Valerius Maximus, Pliny, and Ovid, of or to *some* Cyppus who suddenly found himself behorned; but none of these mentions the *combat des taureaux,* or speaks of it as an effect of imagination. Montaigne seems to have taken the story from the *Diverses Leçons* of Pierre Messie (1552).
11. This story is told by Herodotus (I,85); but Montaigne did not read Herodotus till a later date than that at which this Essay was written, and consequently did not derive it from him.
12. See Lucian, *On the Goddess of Syria;* Plutarch, *Life of Demetrius.*

Notes and Comments

13. See his *Natural History*, VII, 4.

14. *Vota puer solvit, quæ fœmena voverat Iphis.*
—Ovid, *Metamorphoses*, IX, 794. The first word, in the original, is *Dona*.

15. Montaigne in his *Journal de Voyage*.

16. See *De Civ. Dei*, XIV, 24.

17. *A qui il ne falloit que faire ouir.*

18. *Ces plaisantes liaisons des mariages.*

19. Jacques Pelletier of Mans (1517-1582), whom Sainte-Beuve speaks of as *mathematicien, physicien, médecin, grammairien, et avec tout cela versificateur habile.*

20. *Luy porter le resveillon.*

21. *Se demesler.*

22. *Gentil compaignon par tout ailleurs.*

23. See Herodotus, II, 181. Montaigne gives a twist of his own to this story, to make it an illustration of the force of imagination. It was Laodice, not Amasis, who made *vœux et promesses à Venus*.

24. That is, the women.

25. It was Theano, his wife. See Diogenes Laertius, *Life of Pythagoras*.

26. See Augustine, *De Civ. Dei*, XIV, 24, and the commentary of Vivès thereon.

27. *Qu'il tient son maistre a peter d'une haleine.*

28. See Suetonius, *Life of Claudius*. The last sentence does not appear in the *Édition Municipale*.

29. This passage is as incoherent in the original as in translation. Montaigne, it would seem, had in mind Socrates's conversation with Diotima, reported in the *Symposium*. His words recall Diotima's saying: *Viri sane mulierisque congressu fœtus partusque proverit. Est autem opus*

Of the Power of Imagination

hoc divinum, et in animali ipso mortali immortale hoc est conceptio scilicet et generatio. This is the Latin translation of Ficino, which Montaigne habitually used.

30. Guillaume de Maris. See Messie, *Diverses Leçons.*

31. See Lucretius, III, 493, and *passim.* Cf. Book II, chap. 12, *infra: car un cheval accustumé aux trompettes, aux harquebusades, et aux combats, que nous voyons tremousser et fremir en dormant, estendu sur sa litiere, comme s'il estoit en la meslée, il est certain qu'il conçoit en son ame un son de tambourin sans bruict, une armée sans armes et sans corps.*

32.   *Dum spectant oculi læsos, læduntur et ipsi,*
    Multaque corporibus transitone nocent.
              —Ovid, *Remedium Amoris,* 615.

33. See Pliny, *Natural History,* VII, 2.

34. *De la seule veue.* See Pliny, *Natural History.*

35. See Pierre Messie, *Diverses Leçons,* II, 7.

36. *Nescio quis teneros oculus mihi fascinat agnos.*—Virgil, *Eclogues,* III, 103.

37. This refers to an anecdote told by St. Jerome, and repeated in all the sixteenth-century dissertations on the force of the imagination, almost always accompanied by the two facts that follow it in Montaigne, the "girl from near Pisa" and "Jacob's sheep."

38. See *Genesis,* XXX, 38 ff.

39. See Ambroise Paré, *Des Monstres.*

40. In 1580: *Mon père vit un jour.*

41. The Essay ended here in editions prior to 1588.

42. *Si je ne comme bien, qu'un autre comme pour moy.* In the first part of this addition the *Édition Municipale* shows the various forms in which Montaigne tentatively

Notes and Comments

expressed his thought before making a final decision. At this point he added, then deleted: *Ce n'est pas mal parler que mal comer.*
    43. *Un tour de l'humaine capacité.*
    44. *Similitudes.*

CHAPTER XXII

One Man's Profit is Another's Loss

A. THE COMMENT BY MISS NORTON

THE extravagant statements here made by Montaigne show that he had not accepted that "general truth" of the Stoics that "whatever is profitable to any man is profitable also to other men" (as Marcus Aurelius phrases it) —a doctrine that in its largest sense is accepted by us today. And the sayings of this dreary page would seem to come more naturally from the cold heart of a La Rochefoucauld, or the unreasonable brain of a Rousseau, than from the genial, friendly, liberal soul of Montaigne. They do in fact come from the philosophic Seneca. This unimportant little chapter is only a reproduction of a passage in the *De Beneficiis*. It may be noted that the sentence about "the ministers of religion" is Montaigne's own.

If we accept as true the statement of the last sentence that the birth of any thing causes the death of that from which it springs, it may be observed that it is precisely as

Of Custom

true a way of stating the fact—and it sounds more cheerful!—to say that death creates life.

The quotation from Lucretius at the close is fantastically irrelevant, especially when traced to its original connection—a passage (about the colour of bodies of matter) too abstruse and abstract to give any account of here. Munro translates these lines: "For whenever a thing changes and quits its proper limits, at once this change of state is the death of that which was before."

B. THE NOTES BY MR. IVES

1. See Seneca, *De Beneficiis*, VI, 38.
2. See Stobæus, *Sermon* 100.

CHAPTER XXIII

Of Custom, and the Inadvisability of Changing an Established Law

A. THE COMMENT BY MISS NORTON

THE examples by which, in opening this Essay, Montaigne attempts to show the power of habit are neither very interesting nor very credible. We must remember that he disclaims responsibility for the facts that he relates, and we find here an odd pell-mell of the true and the false.

Notes and Comments

We are entertained by little personalities about his "perfumed doublet" and the tower in which he lived and the bell that he heard every day. And, later, the excellent remarks on the education of children are a prelude to those that follow in a subsequent Essay, and include a delightful testimony to the effect of education on Montaigne himself. The last sentence deserves to be written in letters of gold: "In every thing and everywhere my eyes are enough to keep me straight; there are no others which watch me so closely, or which I more respect."

This is a part of a long passage inserted in 1595, which breaks in upon illustrations, not exactly of the force of habit, but of the power of training; and the essayist then passes on to example of the odd customs of diverse nations —slipping here from one signification of the word *coûtume* —custom, habit—to another.

We may, with little loss, skip here several pages, and we then find ourselves at one of the most interesting passages we have yet come to in the Essays: "The laws of the conscience." But this passage, like many others, is made difficult and confused by being written at different periods, and the parts never properly fused together: it is three overlapping "formations." The first sentence is of 1595, the next of 1588, the next three of 1580. And the next (whole) page of 1595. It is therefore almost impossible, without long, and one may say *imaginative,* study of such passages, to follow closely Montaigne's train of thought; but even a hasty, if not a careless, reading may discover something of the largeness, the freedom, the *vitality* of his thought, and its force of subtle observation.

From these graver matters Montaigne passes to the con-

Of Custom

sideration of the fantasticalness of custom in dress; but he soon swings back into matters of state, considering the question whether it is of use to change laws that have been established by long custom. The passage is of interest, not only in itself (as a discussion of political principles), but historically, as Montaigne's view of his own time and its conditions of government.

The last pages of the Essay contain Montaigne's recognition that in cases of extreme necessity the old laws should give way to new regulations; and he quotes Plutarch's praise of Philopœmen.

M. Villey remarks that the many compilers of the sixteenth century took evident pleasure, as Montaigne did, in collecting examples of strange customs; and other contemporary writers, who do not give examples, insist on the force of custom. (See La Boëtie in *Le Contr'un*.) Many, like Montaigne, hold to the necessity of keeping exactly to the usages of one's native land. In the Italian authors this is especially a law of social intercourse. In others, particularly in the political writers, it is a rule of intellectual prudence and of political conversation. These two points of view are both found in this Essay.

M. Villey's résumé of the Essay presents its main outlines in a manner greatly to assist the reader:

"This Essay may be divided into two parts: (1) setting forth the power of custom and the strangeness of its effects; (2) declaring the necessity, in spite of the inanity of our usages, of following them and of avoiding all novelty. On one side, as on the other, Montaigne expresses ideas familiar to his contemporaries, and in 1580 he does so by means of examples that are frequently met with in the writings of

Notes and Comments

the time. He only adds to these some facts borrowed from Plutarch's Lives, which was then his habitual reading. He is here seen to be penetrated by the feeling of relativity, and beginning to formulate his political and religious conservatism. In 1588 both parts have been considerably developed, the first by a great number of illustrations borrowed from Lopez de Gomara, the second extended by very personal developments that would seem to be inspired by the civil troubles. In 1595 both parts receive again numerous and very important additions, which prove how great Montaigne's interest continued to be in the questions he had here treated of. Herodotus, and works on the expeditions of the Portuguese to the Indies, furnished him with new customs; but especially Montaigne adds some very rich developments, many of which are directly derived from his personal experiences, while others come from abundant reading of ancient authors, as Pliny, Livy, etc., but principally from Cicero, whose conservatism singularly charmed Montaigne."

B. THE NOTES BY MR. IVES

1. *La Coûtume* here stands for both personal habits and national customs.

2. It can be found in Stobæus, *Sermon* 29; in Quintilian, I, 9; and in the *Adages* of Erasmus, I, 11, 51.

3. *Usus efficacissimus rerum omnium magister.*—Pliny, *Natural History*, XXVI, 2; taken by Montaigne from the *Politiques* of J. Lipsius.

4. Book VII, at the beginning.

5. Mithridates, King of Pontus. See Aulus Gellius, XVII, 16.

Of Custom

6. *D'araignées* (spiders' webs); but the context shows that it must have been spiders. See below, *les apastoient* ("and fed them"). See Messie, *Diverses Leçons*, I, 26.

7. This and the following particulars are found in Lopez de Gomara, *Histoire Générale des Indes*. A French translation by Martin Fumée was published in 1569.

8. *Consuetudinis magna vis est. Pernoctant venatores in nive; in montibus uri se patiuntur. Pugiles cœstibus contusi ne ingemiscunt quidem.*—Cicero, *Tusc. Disp.*, II, 17.

9. See Idem, *Somnium Scipionis*, VI, 19.

10. *Coupures et muances.*

11. *Collet de fleurs.*

12. *Effraye.*

13. See Diogenes Laertius, *Life of Plato*. Laertius says that he reproved a man who was gambling with dice.

14. *Plus pure et plus forte qu'elle est plus gresle.* Changed in 1595 to: *plus pure et plus naifve, qu'elle est plus gresle et plus neuve.*

15. *Pour m'estre duit.*

16. A small copper coin worth one sixth of a sou.

17. This person is noted in many journals of this time.

18. This clause is omitted in the edition of 1595.

19. *J'en vy un autre, estant enfant.* A similar case is mentioned by Ambroise Paré, in *Des Monstres*.

20. That is, those of custom.

21. *Non pudet physicum, id est speculatorem venatoremque naturæ, ab animis consuetudine imbutis quærere testimonium veritatis.*—Cicero, *De Nat. Deor.*, I, 30.

22. This example, and all of those following which were added in 1588 *(b)*, down to line 5 on page 151 *infra*, are taken, sometimes with slight variations, from the *His-*

Notes and Comments

toire Générale des Indes by Lopez de Gomara.

23. *Se coucher sur les propres.*

24. Gomara does not mention being eaten by birds; but see Plutarch, *That vice alone is enough to make a man miserable.*

25. See Herodotus, IV, 172. At this point Montaigne wrote on the Bordeaux copy of 1588: *Ou le peuple adore certeins Dieus*[,] *Mars*[,] *Bacchus*[,] *Diane*[;] *Le Roy un dieu particulier pour soi*[,] *Mercure,* which he afterwards struck out, and inserted in chapter 42 of this Book: see page 348.

26. See Goulard, *Histoire du Portugal.*

27. See Lopez de Castaneda, *Histoire de la decouverte et de la conquête des Indes par les Portugais* (book XIV), from which Goulard derived most of his material.

28. See Herodotus, IV, 168.

29. See Herodotus, II, 35.

30. See Idem, IV, 191.

31. See Idem, IV, 180.

32. The edition of 1595 adds here: *sans distinction de parenté.* We return now for a moment to the text of 1580.

33. See Herodotus, IV, 172.

34. See Idem, IV, 176.

35. An allusion to the republic of the Amazons.

36. Especially the Thracians. See Valerius Maximus, II, 6, *ext.* 12. The text of 1580-1588 is here slightly shortened, but without change of meaning.

37. See Xenophon, *Cyropædeia,* I, 2.

38. See Plutarch, *Of the virtuous deeds of women.*

39. See Herodotus, III, 38.

40. See Aristotle, *Nicomachæan Ethics,* VII, 5.

Of Custom

41. *Ne s'en en peut desprendre sans remors, ny s'y appliquer sans applaudissement.*

42. See Valerius Maximus, VII, 2, *ext.* 18.

43. *Ce qui est hors des gonds de coutume, on le croit hors des gonds de raison.*

44. This last sentence is not found in the *Édition Municipale*, but was added in 1595.

45. See Herodotus, III, 38.

46. *Nil adeo magnum, nec tam mirabile quicquam*
Principio, quod non minuant mirarier omnes
Paulatim.
—Lucretius, II, 1028.

47. In 1580-1588: *si chetif et si foible.*

48. These two words added in 1595.

49. Of their condemnation.

50. See Plato, *Laws* (Jowett, Amer. Ed., V, 217-221).

51. See Diogenes Laertius, *Life of Chrysippus.*

52. See Isocrates, *Oratio ad Nicoclem*, VI, 18.

53. *Les loix Latines et Imperiales.* See Paulus Jovius.

54. That is, the lawyers and the nobility.

55. The king.

56. *Ceux-là la robbe longue, ceux-cy la courte en partage.*

57. See Plato, *Crito;* Diogenes Laertius, *Life of Socrates.*

58. Νόμοις ἕπεσθαι τοῖσιν ἐγχωροις καλόν.
—M. Villey thinks that Montaigne found this in a collection of Greek sentences compiled by Crispin (1569).

59. *En voicy d'un autre cuvée.*

60. Zaleucus, the legislator of the *Locrians*. See Diodorus Siculus, XII, 4; Plato, *Phædo.*

61. Lycurgus. See Plutarch, *Life of Lycurgus.*

Notes and Comments

62. See Idem, *Apothegms of the Lacedæmonians.*
63. See Valerius Maximus, II, 6, *ext.* 7.
64. In 1588: *depuis vingt-cinq ou trente ans.*
65. *C'est à elle à s'en prendre au nez.*
66. *Heu! patior telis vulnera facta meis.*
—Ovid, *Heroïdes,* II, 48 (Epistle of Phyllis to Demophoön).
67. See Thucydides, III, 52. Montaigne probably took it from Plutarch, *How to distinguish a flatterer from a friend.*
68. *Honesta oratio est.*—Terence, *Andria,* I, 1.114.
69. *Adeo nihil motum ex antiquo probabile est.*
—Livy, XXXIV, 54.
70. *Ad deos id magis quam ad se pertinere; ipsos visuros ne sacra sua polluantur.*—Livy, X, 6.
71. See Herodotus, VIII, 36.
72. *Quis est enim quem non moveat clarissimis monumentis testata consignataque antiquitas.*—Cicero, *De Divin.*
73. See Isocrates, *Oratio ad Nicoclem.*
74. *Et que nous ne devons pas suivre, mais contempler avec estonnement; actes de son personnage, non pas du nostre.*
75. *Quum de religione agitur, T. Coruncanium, P. Scipionem, P. Scævolam, pontifices maximos, non Zenonem aut Cleanthem aut Chrysippum sequor.*—Cicero, *De Nat. Deor.,* III, 2. *This addition of the Édition Municipale,* beginning in the last line but one of p. 161, appears in only a few copies of 1595; in some copies it was inserted by Mademoiselle de Gournay by a *carton.* It first appeared properly in the edition of 1602.
76. *Soubs quelle enseigne se jette elle à quartier?*

Different Results of Counsel

77. *Contre ceux qui ont la clef des champs.*

78. *Aditum nocendi perfido præstat fides.*—Seneca, *Œdipus*, III, 686.

79. This was not Octavius, afterward Augustus, but Octavius who was consul with Cinna, and of whom Plutarch speaks at some length in the *Life of Marius*.

80. Agesilaus. See Idem, *Life of Agesilaus*.

81. Alexander the Great. See Idem, *Life of Alexander*.

82. See Idem, *Life of Lysander*.

83. To stay the breaking out of the Peloponnesian War. The ambassador was Polyarces. See Idem, *Life of Pericles*.

84. See Idem, *Parallel between Flaminius and Philopœmen*.

CHAPTER XXIV

Different Results of the Same Counsel

A. THE COMMENT BY MISS NORTON

IT is pleasant to think of Montaigne and Jacques Amyot (1503-1593), "evêque d'Auxerre," talking together; pleasant, not because Amyot was "grand aumosnier de France," but because he was the famous translator of Plutarch, the writer of whom Montaigne says in a later Essay ("Business To-morrow"), "I give . . . the palm to Jacques

1611

Notes and Comments

Amyot over all our French authors, not only for simplicity and purity of language wherein he surpasses all others," and for this and for that; "but especially I am grateful to him for having culled out and chosen a book so worthy and so opportune, to make a present of it to his country. We ignoramuses had been lost if this book had not lifted us out of the mire." We see that in the whole course of the Essays Montaigne felt himself indebted to Amyot.

So Jacques Amyot was talking to him (one would like to know when and where) about "one of our princes." This particular prince of Amyot's story was François, duc de Guise, surnamed *le Balafré*, who was assassinated in 1563, and whose death we have already heard of in the second Essay. Here we learn how, the year before, he escaped assassination (by a Protestant) by "sermonising" his would-be murderer. This story is followed by a long translation from Seneca of the similar story of Augustus, which Corneille has celebrated in his *Cinna*. These two stories are intended to "point the moral," that the *rightest* path is the *safest:* "The safest way ... is, in my opinion, to throw oneself on the side in which there is the most uprightness" and justice. A characteristic conclusion for Montaigne to reach.

But in reaching this conclusion, Montaigne has taken a most wandering course, and has discussed the share that fortune has in the success of medicine, of poetry and painting, and of military enterprises; so large a share that he believes (as his title says): in "different results of the same counsel." The passage about medicine is amusing; it is the first of his repeated Molière-like outbursts against the medical profession.

The title does not fit closely to the rest of the Essay, the

Different Results of Counsel

greater part of which was added in 1588, and which is occupied with the uselessness of attempting to prevent conspiracies by punishments, and with the torment a ruler must suffer who is suspicious of those about him.

The passage connected with these thoughts, beginning, "Those who teach princes watchful distrust," probably refers to Henri III and Henri IV. The noble lines, "Courage... displays itself... as nobly in a doublet as in armour," seem a forerunner of those of Lowell *(Commemoration Ode):*

> Life may be given in many ways,
> And loyalty to truth be sealed
> As bravely in the closet as the field.

Montaigne himself also says in the preceding paragraph, "Valour is not shown in war alone." On a later page there is a striking account of a scene Montaigne witnessed "when a child" (in 1548, when he was 15 years old). The "great city" was Bordeaux; and the poor gentleman who was killed was named Moneins.

The passage on the next page connects itself with the fact that in May, 1585 (during Montaigne's mayoralty), there was a great review of all the "citizens' companies" of Bordeaux; an occasion of possible excitement and danger.

B. THE NOTES BY MR. IVES

1. François, duc de Guise (Le Balafré).
2. *Les tenants et aboutissants* = *tout ce à quoi quelqu'un se tient et se rapporte.*
3. See Seneca, *De Clementia,* I, 9.
4. *Par le faveur d'un simple libertin.*

Notes and Comments

5. François de Guise was assassinated at the siege of Orleans, in 1563, by Poltrot de Meré.

6. *Celles que l'autheur y a mises et apperçeües.*

7. See Plutarch, *How a man may praise himself*, and *Life of Sylla*. This clause was added in the second edition.

8. *Il survient des allegresses fortuites et des fureurs estrangeres.*

9. This clause—"and when . . . straight one"—was added in the second edition (1582).

10. The duc de Guise.

11. See Seneca, *Epistle* 4.8.

12. See Plutarch, *Apothegms of Kings, Life of Dion*.

13. See Idem, *Life of Alexander;* Quintus Curtius, III, 6.9. Montaigne probably took it from Witart's translation of Arrian's history of Alexander.

14. In 1588: *La vaillance n'est pas seulement à la guerre* (Valour is not shewn in war alone).

15. This addition on the margin of the Bordeaux copy is in the handwriting of Mlle. de Gournay; but certain words were stricken out in Montaigne's manner.

16. See Livy, XXVIII, 17.

17. *Habita fides ipsam plerumque fidem obligat.*—Livy, XXII, 22. It is impossible to reproduce exactly the play upon words permitted in Latin by the two-fold meaning of *fides: trust (confidence),* and *good faith.*

18. *A une vie ambitieuse et fameuse il faut, au rebours, prester peu, et porter la bride courte aux soubçons.*

19. Louis XI.

20.   *Stetit aggere fulti*
    Cespitis, intrepidus vultu; meruitque timeri
    Nil metuens.   —Lucan, V, 316.

Different Results of Counsel

21. *Douceur.*
22. *Il recevra bien plutost.*
23. *En pourpoinct.*
24. *Il la devoit avaller toute, et n'abandonner ce personnage.*
25. *Il luy advint . . . de saigner du nez.*
26. Montaigne refers to the review held at Bordeaux in 1585, during his mayoralty.
27. *Gaillardes.*
28. Here ends the 1588 addition, starting on page 170.
29. See Suetonius, *Life of Cæsar*, LXXV.
30. *Apprentissage.* See Plutarch, *Apothegms of Kings.*
31. *De quoy ils ne sentent le vent.*
32. See Villani, *Universal History*, part II, 1, 12.
33. *Passer une fois le pas.*
34. Montaigne seems to have combined two stories related by Appian.
35. *D'appeller les mains ennemies, c'est un conseil un peu gaillard.*

CHAPTER XXV

Of Pedantry

A. THE COMMENT BY MISS NORTON

THIS is one of the simplest in construction of the Essays; it is really about "pedantry." First, Montaigne considers the character of pedants, and the esteem, or rather disesteem, in which they are held, and its causes; and the differences between the pedants of his day and the philosophers of old days. He thinks that men of learning have become contemptible because of the mistaken character of their education, and that neither masters nor scholars are more *able* because of *learning*. "We labour only to fill the memory," he says, "and we leave the understanding and the conscience empty." And then, with a droll little return on himself, he says that this is just what he does in this book; "it is a wonder how nicely this folly finds an example in me." This is a most unmerited little humorous piece of self-blame! His criticism here of works that have no *nourishment* in them is peculiarly inapplicable to his own writings. The sentence,—a very characteristic one,—"a parrot could speak as wisely," shows how little Montaigne could fall into any parrotry of thought or expression.

The next page is the story of a wealthy Roman who fancied himself a man of learning because he had in his pay learned men who talked for him. Such a man resembles "those whose learning resides in their costly libraries."

Of Pedantry

Montaigne continues in the same vein, insisting that all learning is useless to us that we do not make our own, that we do not *digest*.

The "teachers" of his day, like the sophists in Plato's time, were in Montaigne's eyes "of all men those who promise to be most useful to mankind, and alone of all men they not only do not improve what is entrusted to them . . . but they injure it."

On another page he tells an amusing story of one of these senseless beings whom he had seen at his own house; which leads on to a passage of beautiful, noble praise of his friend Adrianus Turnebus.

Later Montaigne gives an interesting sketch of his views of a proper Civil Service Examination—the passage beginning: "There are some of our Parliaments . . ."

Returning to his former train of thought, Montaigne speaks of learning as "a dangerous weapon" for those who do not know how to use it—and therefore women had better not be trusted with it.

A passage about "this purpose of enriching ourselves" sounds as if it had been written yesterday.

"The reason that I was seeking just now," I think refers to the beginning of the Essay and to his quest for the causes of the low esteem in which men of learning were held.

Then he gets among the ancients, and dwells on the point that the Persians "taught virtue to their children as other nations do letters," in which the Lacedæmonians resembled them; and he speaks of the difference between the education given to the children of Sparta and those of Athens, and in this connection brings Socrates forward.

The last paragraph of the Essay is on the thesis that learn-

Notes and Comments

ing lessens warlike impulses, and it is interesting from the examples taken from Montaigne's own times.

In view of the inferences that may be drawn from the additions made to this Essay in 1595, M. Villey remarks:

"It is worth observing that in 1595 the point of view of Montaigne in this Essay seems somewhat different from what it was in the text of 1580. In 1580 Montaigne was especially inspired by Seneca and by Plutarch, who both criticise only pretended knowledge; and in like manner Montaigne's aim was to combat, as the title indicates, the pedantry of his age; and he expresses strongly his admiration for the men of true learning, for the great philosophers of antiquity. In 1595 he weakens these praises, undoubtedly with reserve, it not being his purpose to correct himself, but, none the less, in a significant manner, he borrows from Plato numerous sarcasms against the philosophers, who seem to him to lack completely practical sense; especially in the additions which close the chapter, he strongly affirms the idea that knowledge is profitable only to a small number of estimable minds, and when spread abroad among the masses, it is injurious to the moral character and to the military spirit."

B. THE NOTES BY MR. IVES

1. The word is used in its original sense of teacher.
2. *Magister.*
3. *Perdois-je mon latin.*
4. See Plutarch, *Life of Cicero.*
5. *Magis magnos clericos non sunt magis magnos sapientes.*—Proverb, found also in Rabelais, *Gargantua*, I, 39.
6. Probably Marguerite, afterwards Queen of Navarre.

Of Pedantry

7. *Courbe et croupi.*

8. *Par la liberté Comique.*

9. This much of the addition of 1595 is translated from the *Theætetus* of Plato, XXIV.

10. *Odi homines ignava opera, philosophia sententiæ.*—Pacuvius, in Aulus Gellius, XIII, 8.

11. See Plutarch, *Life of Marcellus.* This is a condensation of Plutarch's description of the works executed by Archimedes; the thoughts which Montaigne ascribes to Archimedes himself, Plutarch ascribes to Plato.

12. The philosophers.

13. See Diogenes Laertius, *Life of Crates.*

14. See Idem, *Life of Heraclitus.*

15. See Idem, *Life of Empedocles.*

16. See Cicero, *De Divin.*, I, 49; Diogenes Laertius, *Life of Thales.*

17. See Aristotle, *Politics*, I, 7.

18. *A mes gens;* that is, the philosophers.

19. That is, the very great reason why the *clericos* are not *magis magnos sapientes.* See page 177.

20. *Du jugement et de la vertu, peu de nouvelles.*

21. See Seneca, *Epistle* 88.

22. See Seneca, *Epistle* 89, near the end.

23. See Plutarch, *How to know whether one improves in the practice of virtue.*

24. *Mettre au vent.*

25. *Non pour les garder, car je n'ay point de gardoires.*

26. See Plutarch, *How to know whether one improves in the practice of virtue.*

27. *Apud alios loqui didicerunt, non ipsi secum.*—Cicero, *Tusc. Disp.*, V, 36.

Notes and Comments

28. *Non est loquendum, sed gubernandum.*—Seneca, *Epistle* 108.

29. This is Montaigne's own translation: M. Villey suggests that the meaning is: "To blow is easy enough, but we have to move the fingers to play on the bag-pipe."—It is difficult to see the connection between this whole interpolated passage and the subject under discussion.

30. See Seneca, *Epistle* 33.7.

31. Calvisius Sabinis. See Seneca, *Epistle* 27.5.

32. *Selon son gibier.*

33. That is, as those also remind me.

34. *Lexicon.* This word had not been used before Montaigne except by Ronsard; it is in no French dictionary.

35. See Plutarch, *On Hearing*.

36. See Cicero, *Academic Questions*, II, 1. In 1580-1588, this passage read: *si grand capitaine et si advisé, sans l'essay et sans experience.*

37. Μισῶ σοφιστὴν, ὅστις οὐχ αὑτῷ σόφος.
—Euripides, in Stobæus, *Sermon* 3. (See also Cicero, *Epistulæ Familiares*, XIII, 15.) In 1580-1588, Montaigne supplied a French translation: *Je haï, dict-il, le Sage qui n'est pas sage pour soy-mesmes.*

38. *Ex quo Ennius: Nequicquam sapere sapientem, qui ipse sibi prodesse non quiret.*—Cicero, *De Off.*, III, 15.

39.   *Si cupidus, si*
  Vanus et Euganea quamtumvis vilior agna.
                        —Juvenal, *Satires*, VIII, 14.

40. *Non enim paranda nobis solum, sed fruenda sapientia est.*—Cicero, *De Fin.*, I, 1; but Montaigne probably borrowed it from Justus Lipsius, *Politics*, I, 10.

41. For "Dionysius" read "Diogenes the Cynic." See

Of Pedantry

Diogenes Laertius, *Life of Diogenes*.
42. *Un meilleur branle*.
43. See Plato, *Meno*, XXVIII.
44. See Idem, *Protagoras*, XVI.
45. *Sçavanteaux. Lettreferits*=letter-stricken.
46. *Une belle robe*.
47. *Vos, O patritius sanguis, quos vivere par est*
Occipiti cæco, posticæ occurrite sannæ.
—Persius, *Satires*, I, 61.
48. *(b) Queis arte benigna*
Et meliore luto finxit præcordia Titan.
—Juvenal, *Satires*, XIV, 34.
49. In 1580-1588: *Et qu'elle nous amende, ou elle est vaine et inutile*.
50. Ὡς οὐδέν ἡ μάθησις ἦν μὴ νοῦς παρῇ,
—Stobæus, *Sermon* 3.
51. *Non vitæ sed scholæ discimus*.—Seneca, *Epistle* 106. Montaigne took the sentence from the *Politics* of Justus Lipsius.
52. See Seneca, *Epistles* 71 (near the end) and 110.
53. See Idem., *Epistle* 36.3.
54. *Ut fuerit melius non didicisse*.—Cicero, *Tusc. Disp*., II, 4.
55. See G. Corrozet: *Les divers propos memorables des nobles et illustres hommes de la chrestienté*.
56. *Des lettres;* that is "literary learning," so to speak.
57. *Nous est aujourd'hui proposée*. The earlier editions read *en butte* for *proposée*.
58. *Postquam docti prodierunt, boni desunt*.—Seneca, *Epistle* 95.
59. That is, the reason for the low esteem in which men

1621

Notes and Comments

of learning were held. See the beginning of the Essay.

60. *Tel a la veue clere, qui ne l'a pas droite.*
61. Near end of book III, and beginning of book IV.
62. *Asotos ex Aristippi, acerbos ex Zenonis schola exire.* —Cicero, *De Nat. Deor.,* III, 31.
63. See *Cyropædeia,* I.
64. See the *First Alcibiades.*
65. See Plutarch, *Apothegms of the Lacedæmonians,* and *Life of Lycurgus.*
66. Near the beginning.
67. That is, the Persians'.
68. See *Cyropædeia,* I, 3. It was the mother of Astyages who asked Cyrus the question.
69. *Mon regent.*
70. *De droit fil.*
71. *Au propre des effets.*
72. *Afin que ce ne fut une science en leur ame.*
73. See Plutarch, *Apothegms of the Lacedæmonians.*
74. See *Ibid.*
75. See *Ibid.,* and *Life of Agesilaus.*
76. See Plato, *Hippias Major.*
77. *Les fermit et aguerrit.*
78. Cf. Book II, chap. 12: *La vieille Rome me semble avoir bien porté de plus grande valeur, et pour la paix et pour la guerre, que cette Rome sçavante qui se ruyna soy-mesme.*

CHAPTER XXVI

Of the Education of Children

A. THE COMMENT BY MISS NORTON

THIS Essay, I think, is one of the first in which Montaigne really tried the force of his own wing, when he first left the nest where he had been "brooded" by Plutarch and Seneca and the other ancient authors, and where the historians of his own day were his companions. Now, no longer merely hopping from twig to twig, he struck out into the open air and under the wide sky with bolder flight.

Several indications in its pages make it certain that it was written in 1579 or 1580, that is, seven or eight years later than most of the preceding Essays. And this circumstance gives a peculiar touch and emphasis to his summing up, in the first pages, of his own capacities and abilities. It is not too fanciful, I think, to trace here some indication of a perhaps scarcely conscious break between his earlier intellectual life of incoherent but fertilising reading, and his later life of incoherent but fruitful thinking, of which these Essays are the record.

"History," he says, "is my chief pursuit in the way of books." His reader continually appreciates how great an influence Montaigne's knowledge of historic thought and facts had upon the formation of his own ideas. And in the

Notes and Comments

education of a child Montaigne believed that history should hold a capital place. The object of education for him was to learn how to live reasonably, an art that can be learned only by personal study of life; and in M. Villey's words: "History is life treasured up in books. It is an indefinite prolongation of our experience." (*Livres d'Histoire Moderne, utilisés par Montaigne*, p. 19.)

The next sentence the perceptive reader has been waiting for through all the preceding pages, and through all the following ones he hears it echo: "Poetry, which I love with a special inclination."

How well, how nobly, how vigorously he loved the poets, we shall learn from later pages. Sainte-Beuve says: "No French writer, including the rightly called poets, has had as high an idea of poetry as he."

Like the greater thinker of ancient days, Plato, whose vein of poetic thought lay still deeper—so did the thinker and poet, Montaigne, write of Education. Not because Plato did, but because to such minds the breeding of the race seems the essential thing. The making of legislators was in their eyes of more importance than lawmaking.

Montaigne fully appreciates the arduousness of the work. "The greatest and most important difficulty," he says, "of human knowledge seems to lie where it concerns itself with the bringing up and education of children."

Montaigne had no thought of writing for posterity as he penned these quiet and simple pages. He felt only that, having lately been thinking and writing about *pedantisme*, it would interest and please him now to write a friendly letter to a pretty lady whom he had known as a young girl (being her father's familiar friend), whose marriage (in

Of the Education of Children

1579) he had lately helped to arrange, and who was soon going to present her husband, he hoped, with a son.

How shall this boy be educated? As carelessly and ignorantly and ineffectually as many young nobles of the day? As strangely as Montaigne himself? No, Montaigne thinks, let it be reasonably and intelligently. And so thinking, he lays down the main lines of an education that to-day could for the most part be bettered only by being carried further; an education for boys—girls were not in his mind.

A few passages may be recognised as applying more to the education that men should give themselves than to that suitable for a youth. When Montaigne says: "Let him make him sift every thing," M. Félix Hémon justly remarks *(Cours de Littérature—Montaigne)*: "To examine every thing, to sift every thing, to accept nothing simply on authority and on credit, suggests in advance the Cartesian system, admirable for men but difficult of application in the education of boys, and almost impossible in that of children, of whom there would be danger of making precocious reasoners and precocious sceptics."

These lines have been followed by the thinkers who have succeeded Montaigne, and the path they made by hacking and hewing is the road—the highway of education—along which we now lead our children—our sons—as a matter of course. It must never be forgotten in reading Montaigne's views on this topic, that they were original in large measure. Rabelais was to some degree his precursor, Erasmus also, and other less well-known men; but Montaigne was the forerunner of Locke and of Rousseau, the two writers who have most influenced the principles of education, the one in England, the other in France.

Notes and Comments

B. THE NOTES BY MR. IVES

1. Charlotte-Diane de Foix was the daughter of Frédéric de Foix, comte de Candale, and of Françoise de la Rochefoucauld. In 1579, she married her cousin, Louis de Foix, comte de Gurson, who, with his two brothers, was killed at the battle of Moncrabeau, in 1587.

2. *Qui n'a gousté des sciences que la crouste premiere en son enfance.*

3. Arithmetic, geometry, music, astronomy.

4. In 1580-1588: *estude de Platon, ou d'Aristote.*

5. The editions of 1580-1588 add: *ce n'est pas mon occupation.*

6. See Seneca, *Epistle* 108.10.

7. See Plutarch, *Table-Talk.*

8. *Disant que voire.*

9. This sentence substituted for *car autrement j'engendrois des monstres: comme font les ecrivains indiscrets,* etc., of the earlier editions.

10. See Diogenes Laertius, *Life of Chrysippus.*

11. See Idem, *Life of Epicurus.*

12. That is, one of the passages borrowed from other authors by "the indiscreet writers of our time."

13. *Peintures* in earlier editions.

14. *Incompatible.*

15. *Si je leur pouvoy tenir palot, je serois honneste homme, car je ne les entreprens que par où ils sont les plus roides.*

16. *Conduire son dessein sous les inventions anciennes rappiecées par cy par la.*

17. *Je ne dis les autres, sinon pour d'autant plus me dire.*

Of the Education of Children

18. The reference is to *Lelii Capilupi cento ex Virgilio de vita monacorum* (Venice, 1543).
19. *Politica, sive civilis doctrinæ* (Leyden, 1589).
20. Recurring to the point at which the interpolation of the *Édition Municipale* begins, on page 198.
21. *Inepties.*
22. See Book II, chap. 17.
23. Chap. 25, "Of Pedantry."
24. *Genereux* (Latin *generosus*).
25. He had signed the contract as proxy for the bridegroom's parents.
26. See Plato, *Theages.*
27. See Plutarch, *Why divine justice sometimes postpones the punishment of evil deeds.*
28. See *Ibid.*
29. See the *Republic,* books III, IV, and VII.
30. See Seneca, *Epistle* 74.
31. That is, our teachers.
32. *Il commençast à la mettre sur la montre.*
33. See Cicero, *De Fin.*, II, 1.2.
34. *Obest plerumque iis qui discere volunt auctoritas eorum qui docent.*—Idem, *De Nat. Deor.*, I, 5.
35. That is, his pupil's.
36. The pupil.
37. In the early editions, *mais de son jugement.*
38. The tutor's.
39. The original addition of 1588 began with these sentences, which were stricken out in 1595: *On ne cherche reputation que de science. Quand ils disent: "C'est un homme sçavant," il leur semble tout dire.*
40. *Nunquam tutelæ suæ fiunt.*—Seneca, *Epistle* 33.

1627

Notes and Comments

41. *Un honneste homme.*

42. *Dogme.* This word was introduced into the French language by Montaigne.

43. *Inanité* also was first used by Montaigne.

44. *Accessoire = malencontre.* Cf. Molière, *École des Femmes*, IV, 6:

> *Et tout ce qu'elle a pu, dans un tel accessoire,*
> *C'est de me renfermer dans une grande armoire.*

"*Ce dernier sens,*" says Littré, "*tombé en désuétude, est ancien.*"

45. *Tout passer par l'estamine.*

46. This last clause, inserted on the Bordeaux copy, then stricken out, then restored, was omitted in the edition of 1595.

47. *Che non men che saper dubbiar m'aggrada.*—Dante, *Inferno*, XI, 93. Taken by Montaigne from Guazzo's *Civil Conversation*. This verse first appeared in the second edition of the Essays (1582).

48. See Seneca, *Epistle* 33.

49. *Non sumus sub rege; sibi quisque se vindicet.—Ibid.*

50. See Seneca, *Epistle* 84.

51. See Idem, *Epistle* 12.

52. See Idem, *Epistle* 84; Plutarch, *On Hearing.*

53. See Seneca, *Epistle* 84.

54. See Plutarch, *Which animals are the more crafty.*

55. *On nous les placque en le memoire toutes empennées.*

56. See Seneca, *Epistle* 33.

57. Cf. Plutarch, *How we should read the poets.*

58. That is, for education.

Of the Education of Children

59. It had already become a customary thing for the nobility to travel to broaden their knowledge.

60. *Boire chaut, boire froit.*

61.   *Vitamque sub dio et trepidis agat*
    In rebus.   —Horace, *Odes*, III, 2.5.

62. That is, supported by the body.

63. *Ahane=éprouve une grande fatigue en faisant quelque chose.*

64. *Labor callum obducit dolori.*
    —Cicero, *Tusc. Disp.*, II, 15.

65. He now recurs to the discussion of the evils of children being tied to their parents.

66. That is, over the pupil.

67. That is, the pupil.

68. *Licet sapere sine pompa, sine invidia.*—Seneca, *Epistle* 103.

69. *Si quid Socrates et Aristippus contra morem consuetudinem fecerint . . . idem sibi ne arbitretur licere; magnis enim illi et divinis bonis hanc licentiam assequebantur.*—Cicero, *De Off.*, I, 41.

70. Cf. Book III, chap. 8: *Je festoye et caresse la verité en quelque main je le trouve, et m'y rends alaigrement, et luy tends mes armes vaincus de loing que je la vois approcher.*

71. *En chaise.*

72. *Neque, ut omnia quæ præscripta et imperata sint defendat, necessitate ulla cogitur.*—Cicero, *Academica*, II.

73. That is, the courtiers.

74. That is, in relation to the character of their master.

75. Cf. Book III, chap. 8: *Tous les jours la sotte contenance d'un autre m'advertit et m'advise.*

Notes and Comments

76. *Quæ tellus sit lenta gelu, quæ putris ab æstu;*
Ventus in Italiam quis bene vela ferat.
—Propertius, IV, 3.39.

77. *C'est un vain estude, qui veut;* in the editions prior to 1588, there was no punctuation after *veut*, followed by this clause, *et qui ne se propose autre fin que le plaisir.*

78. See the *Hippias Major*, at the beginning.

79. That is "the lengthy reflections."

80. *Mettre en place marchande.*

81. Plutarch, *Of False Shame*. He quotes this as a joke.

82. See Idem, *Apothegms of the Lacedæmonians.*

83. See Plutarch, *Of Banishment;* Cicero, *Tusc. Disp.*

84. *Ne laissent pas de galler le bon temps.*

85. That is, the Savoyard.

86. Cf. Henri Estienne, *Apologie pour Hérodote (discours préliminaire).*

87. See Cicero, *Tusc. Disp.*, V, 3.

88.   *quid fas optare, quid asper*
Utile nummus habet; patriæ charisque
    propinquis
Quantum elargiri deceat; quem te Deus esse
Jussit, et humana qua parte locatus es in re;
Quid sumus, aut quidnam victuri gignimur.
—Persius, *Satires*, III, 69-72, 67.

89. *Et quo quemque modo fugiatque feratque laborem.*
—Virgil, *Æneid*, III, 459.

90. *Entre les ars liberaux, commençons par l'art qui nous faict libres.* I have tried, at some sacrifice, to reproduce the play upon the words *libereaux* and *libres*. This whole passage is a paraphrase of part of Seneca, *Epistle* 88.

91. *En celles mesmes qui le sont.*

Of the Education of Children

92. See Diogenes Laertius, *Life of Socrates;* Plato, *Euthydemus.*

93.   *Sapere aude,*
Incipe; vivendi recte qui prorogat horam,
Rusticus expectat dum defluat amnis; at ille
Labitur, et labetur in omne volubilis ævum.
          —Horace, *Epistles*, I, 2.40.

94. *Quid moveant Pisces, animosaque signa Leonis,*
    Lotus et Hesperia quid Capricornus aqua.
          —Propertius, IV, 1.89.

95.   Τί πλειάδεσσι κἀμοι
    Τί δ' ἀστράσι βοώτεω;
          —Anacreon, XVII, 10.

96. See Diogenes Laertius, *Life of Anaximenes.*
97. The earlier editions, including 1588, have *musique.*
98. Theodorus Gaza (1398-1478), a Greek scholar.
99. The earlier editions, including 1588, add: *rien qui vous chatouille.*
100. *Ergotismes.*
101. That is, to philosophy.
102. See Plutarch, *Of oracles that have ceased to speak.*
103.   *Deprendas animi tormenta latentis in ægro*
    Corpore, deprendas et gaudia: sumit utrumque
    Inde habitum facies.—Juvenal, *Satires,* IX, 18.
104. See Seneca, *Epistle* 59.16.
105. See Idem, *De Ira,* III, 13.
106. *Lui faire toucher au doigt.*
107. Heroines of the *Orlando Furioso.*
108. *Luy faut.*
109. Referring to the image of virtue on a lonely rock, page 216.

Notes and Comments

110. The clause in brackets omitted in 1595.
111. *Qu'il faut colloquer les enfans.* See Plato, *Republic;* Jowett, (American edition), vol. iii, p. 104.
112. *Udum et molle lutum est; nunc, nunc properandus, et acri*
Fingendus sine fine rota.
—Persius, *Satires,* III, 23.
113. See Seneca, *Epistle* 49.5.
114. *Ces ergotistes.*
115. *Ce sont abus;* literally, this is *(i. e.,* our methods are) misspending.
116. Alexander. See Plutarch, *Of the fortune of Alexander.*
117. *Arts et sciences.*
118. *Petite hinc, juvenesque, senesque,*
Finem animo certum, miserisque viatica canis.
—Persius, *Satires,* V, 64.
119. See Diogenes Laertius, *Life of Epicurus.*
120. In the earlier editions, *dans un college.*
121. Cf. Book I, chap. 39, "Of Solitude," page 328. *Les livres sont plaisans; mais si de leur frequentation nous en perdons en fin la gayeté et la santé, nos meilleures pieces, quittons les: je suis de ceux qui pensent que leur fruict ne pouvoit contrepeser cette perte.*
122. See Diogenes Laertius, *Life of Carneades.*
123. See Plutarch, *Table-Talk.*
124. See *Ibid.*
125. *Æque pauperibus prodest, locupletibus æque;*
Et, neglecta, æque pueris senibusque nocebit.
—Horace, *Epistles,* I, 1.25.
126. *Il chomera moins.*

Of the Education of Children

127. *Il n'en faut pas faire à deux.*
128. See Plutarch, *Of the preservation of health.*
129. See Plato, *Laws,* book VII.
130. See Quintilian, *De Inst. Orat.,* I, 3.
131. Diogenes Laertius, *Life of Speusippus.*
132. See Plato, *Laws,* book VII, *passim.*
133. See Diogenes Laertius, *Life of Pyrrho.*
134. See Plutarch, *Of Envy and Hatred.*
135. See Idem, *Life of Alexander.*
136. *Multum interest utrum peccare aliquis nolit aut nesciat.*—Seneca, *Epistle* 90.
137. See Plutarch, *Life of Alcibiades.*
138. *Omnis Aristippum, decuit color, et status, et res.*
—Horace, *Epistles,* I, 17.23.
139.   *Quem duplici panno patientia velat*
Mirabor, vitæ via si conversa decebit,
Personamque feret non inconcinnus utramque.
—*Ibid.,* 17.25, 26, 29.

By taking words in a forced sense, and by omitting two lines, Montaigne thus adapts to his context a passage which Horace intended to be taken in just the opposite sense.

140. See Plato, *The Rivals.*
141. *Hanc amplissimam omnium artium bene vivendi disciplinam vita magis quam litteris persequuti sunt.*—Cicero, *Tusc. Disp.,* IV, 3.
142. See *Ibid.,* V, 3. At this point, Montaigne first wrote, then erased, the following on the Bordeaux copy of 1588: *Suivant le dogme de Antisthene maintenant que la vertu n'avoit besoin ny des disciplines ny des paroles ny des effaicts, qu'elle suffisoit à soi Hegesias.*
143. See Diogenes Laertius, *Life of Diogenes.*

Notes and Comments

144. That is, something written by Diogenes.
145. See Diogenes Laertius, *Life of Diogenes*.
146. *Qui disciplinam suam, non ostentationem scientiæ, sed legem vitæ putet; quique obtemperet ipse sibi, et decretis pareat.*—Cicero, *Tusc. Disp.*, II, 4.
147. *Nos discours.*
148. See Plutarch, *Apothegms of the Lacedæmonians.*
149. *Regens.*
150. *Verbaque prævisam rem non invita sequentur.*
 —Horace, *Ars Poetica*, 311.
151. *Cum res animum occupavere, verba ambiunt.* —Seneca, *Controversiæ*, III, (*Prœmium*).
152. *Ipsæ res verba rapiunt.*—Cicero, *De Fin.*, III, 5.
153. See Tacitus, *Dialogues de Oratoribus*, XIX. The name is *Aper*. Montaigne misconstrues the text.
154. See Plutarch, *Apothegms of the Lacedæmonians.*
155. See Idem, *Political Precepts.*
156. See Idem, *Life of Cato.* It was not Cicero's eloquence, but his jokes, at which Cato is said to have laughed.
157. *Pour cela, non force.*
158. *Emunctæ naris, durus componere versus.*
 —Horace, *Satires*, I, 4.8.
159. *Coustures.*
160. *Tempora certa modosque, et quod prius ordine verbum est,
Posterius facias, præponens ultima primis,
Invenias etiam disjecti membra poetæ.*
 —Horace, *Satires*, I, 4.58, 59, 62.
By omitting two lines, Montaigne reverses the thought.
161. See Plutarch, *Of the renown of the Athenians.*
162. *Les choses et la matière.*

Of the Education of Children

163. *Plus sonat quam valet.*—Seneca, *Epistle* 40.5.

164. Our pupil.

165. See Idem, *Epistle* 49.6.—The following sentence was written by Montaigne on the Bordeaux copy of 1588, then erased: *Voies ce qu'il en semble a Platon en l'Euthydème: et par tout la guerre jurée de Socrates a l'encontre des Sophismes.*

166. *Pourquoi le deslierai je, puis que, tout lie, il m'empesche?* See Diogenes Laertius, *Life of Aristippus.*

167. See Diogenes Laertius, *Life of Chrysippus.*

168. *Contorta et aculeata sophismata.*—Cicero, *Academica*, II, 24.

169. *Qui se destournent de leur voye un quart de lieue.*

170. *Aut qui non verba rebus aptant, sed res extrinsecus arcessunt, quibus verba conveniant.*—Quintilian, *De Inst. Orat.*, VIII, 3.

171. *Sunt qui alicujus verbi decore placentis vocentur, ad id quod non proposuerant scribere.*—Seneca, *Epistle* 59.5.

172. *Pour la coudre sur moi.*

173. *Peigné.*

174. *Hæc demum sapiet dictio, quæ feriet.*
—*Epitaph* of Lucan.

175. The following passage of the editions of 1580 and 1582 was omitted in all later editions: *Qu'on luy repoche hardiment ce qu'on reprochoit à Seneque, que son langage estoit de chaux vive, mais que le sable en estoit a dire.*

176. *Quæ veritati operam dat oratio, incomposita sit et simplex.*—Seneca, *Epistle* 40.4.

177. *Quis accurate loquitur, nisi qui vult putide loqui?*
—Idem, *Epistle* 75.

Notes and Comments

178. *N'y entendoit rien.*
179. See Diogenes Laertius, *Life of Epicurus.*
180. See Plato, *Laws,* book I.
181. In the earlier editions: *Ceux-cy sont les miens.*
182. See Stobæus, *Sermon* XXXVI.
183. *De cet inconvenient qui estoit en usage.*
184. *En nourrice, et avant le premier desnouement de ma langue.*
185. *Jargonner.*
186. *On le donne aux autres en François;* that is, to be turned into Latin.
187. He died at 26.
188. In 1580 the last clause read: *et avoit un joueur d'espinette pour cet effect.*
189. *La debonnaireté et facilité de complexion.*
190. *De la faineantise, non pas de la malice.*
191. The clause in brackets is in the edition of 1595, but not in the *Édition Municipale.*
192. *Enlumineur.*
193. *Alter ab undecimo tum me vix ceperat annus.*
—Virgil, *Eclogues,* VIII, 39.
194. *Aristoni tragico actori rem aperit: huic et genus et fortuna honesta erant; nec ars, quia nihil tale apud Græcos pudori est, ea deformabat.*—Livy, XXIV, 24.

CHAPTER XXVII

It is Unwisdom to Leave to Our Knowledge the Decision of What is True and What is False

A. THE COMMENT BY MISS NORTON

THIS is one of the Essays which are important as expressing Montaigne's power of criticism. It must be compared and contrasted with a later one, "Of Cripples" (Book III, chapter 11), if we would know Montaigne's mind. Here he is feeling his way, there he has found it; here he is as a bird beating against the walls of the room into which he has accidentally entered; later he has flown out of the window and is at ease in the space and freedom that are his natural elements. The subject of his discourse in both these Essays is *miracles;* and it was of these two that Pascal was thinking when he wrote: "How I condemn those who question about miracles! Montaigne speaks in a right manner of them in two places. In one [the later Essay] we see how prudent he is; none the less in the other he is a believer, and throws scorn on the incredulous."

This is quite true; and yet I think it would be a mistake to draw the inference from these or any other of Montaigne's writings that he believed less in his later days than in his earlier. He was never, often as he is so called, a sceptic;

Notes and Comments

he only was more clearly aware of his own ignorance, of the necessary limitations of human knowledge, than most men —and by just that was wiser than most men. "Montaigne—the Sceptic" Emerson writes of; but he defines "scepticism" as "the attitude assumed by the thinker in relation to the particulars which society adores, but which he sees to be reverend only in their tendency and spirit. *The ground occupied by the sceptic is the vestibule of the temple.*"

Montaigne's thought clarified with years; he saw more and more distinctly the essential principles of life, and more and more definitely and *unquestioningly believed* in them. How far at any time he believed in the dogmas of the church he never left, I think he himself hardly knew, and very little cared. It was principles of *action*, not dogmas of faith, that seemed to him of importance. For these he cared almost *passionately*, strange as the word may sound to some ears when applied to his conditions of feeling. And here, to my apprehension, lies one of the great differences between him and a man of recent days, who has sometimes been compared to him—Renan. Renan's philosophical detachment from the usual objects of ambition was not due to an absence of ambition, but to peculiar ambitions; whereas Montaigne's sole ambition was to appear in his own eyes "un honnête homme." This may be called a common ambition, but few men have felt it with Montaigne's ardour and intensity, and for very few has it been their sole ambition, as with him. How many men could use his proud words: "In every thing and everywhere my eyes are enough to keep me straight; there are no others which watch me so closely or which I more respect." This may really be considered the *motto* of his life.

What is True and What is False

I have wandered far from his views of miracles—apparently, not really, far; for every thing that Montaigne says is so illuminated by what he was, that his opinions are of double force when one has become familiar with his personality and hears his very voice as he utters them.

Here, for instance, where Montaigne says, "We must judge things with more reverence for this infinite power of nature," Bacon answers (having also in his thought Montaigne's expression about *des enchantements, des sorcelleries*), "Neither am I of opinion in this history of marvels, that superstitious narratives of sorceries, witchcrafts, charms, dreams, divinations, and the like, where there is an assurance and clear evidence of the fact, should be altogether excluded. For it is not yet known in what cases, and how far, effects attributed to superstition participate of natural causes."

B. THE NOTES BY MR. IVES

1. *C'est folie de rapporter le vrai et le faux à nostre suffisance.*
2. *Ut necesse est lancem in libra ponderibus impositis deprimi, sic animum perspicuis cedere.*—Cicero, *Academica*, II, 12.
3. *Quelque suffisance outre la commune.*
4. *Où je ne peusse pas mordre.*
5.   *Somnia, terrores magicos, miracula, sagas,*
      Nocturnos lemures portentaque Thessala.
                —Horace, *Epistles*, II, 2.208.
6.   *Jam nemo, fessus satiate videndi,*
      Suspicere in cœli dignatur lucida templa.
                —Lucretius, II, 1038.

Notes and Comments

7.   *Si nunc primum mortalibus adsint*
Ex improviso, ceu sint objecta repente,
Nil magis his rebus poterat mirabile dici,
Aut minus ante quod auderent fore credere gentes?   —*Ibid.*, 1033.

8. *Scilicet et fluvius, qui non est maximus, ei est*
Qui non ante aliquem majorem vidit, et ingens
Arbor homoque videtur; et omnia de genere omni
Maxima quæ vidit quisque, hæc ingentia fingit.
—Lucretius, VI, 674.

9. *Consuetudine oculorum assuescunt animi, neque admirantur, neque requirunt rationes earum rerum quas semper vident.*—Cicero, *De Nat. Deor.*, II, 38.

10. In earlier editions, *puissance de Dieu.*

11. This epigram is ascribed to various sages—by Diogenes Laertius to Solon; but it is oftenest given to Chilo. See Diogenes Laertius, *Life of Thales;* Aristotle, *Rhetoric*, II, 12; Pliny, *Natural History*, VII, 32.

12. Book III, chap. 17; it was in 1385.

13. See Nicolle Gilles, *Annales et Chroniques de France*, etc.

14. See Plutarch, *Life of Paulus Æmilius.*

15. The text has *dirons nous pas.*

16. See Bouchet, *Annales d'Aquitaine.*

17. *Passe = soit, ne faites pas attention, laissez passer.*

18. *D'un train.*

19. See St. Augustine, *De Civ. Dei*, XXII, 8. The three following examples are taken from the same work.

20. *Qui ut rationem nullam afferrent, ipsa auctoritate me frangerent.*—Cicero, *Tusc. Disp.*, I, 21.

CHAPTER XXVIII

Of Friendship

A. THE COMMENT BY MISS NORTON

THIS Essay is based on the friendship between Montaigne and La Boëtie, and there could not be a more fitting motto for it than a stanza of Ben Jonson's fine ode to the two friends, Sir Lucius Cary (afterward Lord Falkland) and Sir Henry Morison.

Jonson speaks of the

> simple love of greatness and of good,
> That knits brave minds and manners more
> than blood,—

adding:—

> This made you first to know the why
> You liked; then, after, to apply
> That liking: and approach so, one the t'other,
> That either grew a portion of the other.

Before reading this Essay there should be read the letter Montaigne wrote to his father at the time of La Boëtie's death in 1563—fourteen years before this Essay was written. The causes of Montaigne's ardent and admiring affection for him are there, not set forth, but revealed; and after reading the letter, and thus passing day after day with Montaigne by the bed of his dying friend, we find ourselves

Notes and Comments

reading between the lines of the Essay a full record of the personal emotion which years could not dull. A touching indication of the permanent strength of this emotion is given in the Journal kept by Montaigne when travelling in 1580. He was ill, and he says: "This morning, writing to M. Ossat [the cardinal and famous statesman], I fell into such sad thoughts of M. de la Boëtie, and was so long a time engrossed by them that it did me much harm." In connection with the letter to his father should also be read Montaigne's four letters to L'Hôpital, M. de Foix, and two other gentlemen, about the writings and character of La Boëtie. These are to be found in several of the French editions of the Essays.

That Montaigne's estimate of La Boëtie was not due merely to his profound friendship is proved by the judgements of other contemporaries. De Thou mentions "three great men" whom France lost in 1563, and counts La Boëtie as one of them, though he was but thirty-three years years old. It is also a proof of the strength of his character and abilities, that his writings may still be read with interest. He is the noblest representative of those men of his time who derived strength from the teachings of antiquity. His love of mankind, his faith in human nature, his lofty and ardent passion for public welfare, and the high simplicity and sincerity of his course of life, made him, in Montaigne's phrase, *un grand homme de bien*. In his writings may be discovered a vehement and somewhat utopian nature, but also excellent good sense, with peculiar sweetness and delicacy of feeling. Montaigne speaks of "la tendre amour qu'il portoit à sa miserable patrie," and there is expression of it in a Latin poem addressed to Montaigne and another friend,

Of Friendship

and probably written about 1560. Americans may take a special interest in these verses, because, confiding to his friends his wish to fly from "these cruel days," to "bid a long and last farewell to my native land," his thoughts turn to "those unknown tracts of earth extending to the West" where are found *vacuas sedes et inania regna*. "Here must we go, thither must we bend our oars and turn our sails." Imagine Montaigne and La Boëtie coming here a hundred years before the Pilgrim Fathers!

How warmly La Boëtie returned Montaigne's affection is testified in his will, where, leaving him his books, he speaks of "M. de Montaigne ... mon intime frère et immutable amy."

This Essay is not merely narrative. In the first pages Montaigne treats of friendship in general, and argues that the highest friendship has no other "cause and end and fruit" but itself.

He then considers the friendship of children to their fathers, which he thinks is rather to be called respect; and that of brothers, which must be somewhat uncertain. And to compare the affection we bear women to friendship—ah, that cannot be! it is quite too inferior a passion!

As we read Montaigne's account of his "first meeting" with La Boëtie, there is something that recalls Hamlet's words to Horatio:

> Since my dear soul was mistress of her choice,
> And could of men distinguish, her election
> Hath seal'd thee for herself;

and throughout the Essay we are reminded, naturally, of what other men have said in love and praise of their dead

Notes and Comments

friends. Montaigne speaks of "the four years when it was given me to enjoy the sweet companionship and society of this personage." Tennyson says (*In Memoriam*):

> The path by which we twain did go,
>   Which led by tracts that pleas'd as well,
>   Through four sweet years arose and fell
> From flower to flower, from snow to snow.

Montaigne writes, untranslatably: "Depuis le jour que je le perdis, je ne foys que trainer languissant." Dryden (*Threnodia Augustalis*):

> No wife, no brother, such a grief could know,
>   Nor any name but friend.

If, in connection with this Essay, one reads the fine essay by Bacon on the same subject, one may perceive that that was written by a *moralist*, this by a *poet*.

B. THE NOTES BY MR. IVES

1.   *Desinit in piscem mulier formosa superne.*
                             —Horace, *Ars Poetica*, 4.
2. In the earlier editions this clause occurred here: *n'ayant pas attaint le dix huitiesme an de son aage.*
3. 1562. La Boëtie's "notes" have recently (1917) been published by M. Bonnefon in the *Revue de l'Histoire Littéraire de la France*.
4. In 1571, *La Mesnagerie de Xenophon*, etc.
5. *Nos hommes.*
6. *Société.*
7. See Aristotle, *Ethics*, VIII, 1.4.
8. That is, of companionship.
9. That is, with friendship.

1644

Of Friendship

10. See chap. 23, page 149.
11. A literal translation of a wholly incomprehensible sentence. In the earlier editions this sentence followed: *l'amitié n'en vient jamais là.*
12. See Diogenes Laertius, *Life of Aristippus.*
13. See Plutarch, *Of Brotherly Love.*
14.   *et ipse*
    Notus in fratres animi paterni.
                              —Horace, *Odes,* II, 2.6.
15.   *neque enim est dea nescia nostri*
    Quæ dulcem curis miscet amaritiem.
                              —Catullus, LXVIII, 17.
16.   *Come segue la lepre il cacciatore*
    Al freddo, al caldo, alla montagna, al lito;
    Ne piu l'estima poi che presa vede,
    Et sol dietro a chi fugge affretta il piede.
                        —Ariosto, *Orlando Furioso,* X, 7.
17. La Boëtie.
18. *Quis est enim iste amor amicitiæ? Cur neque deformem adolescentem quisquam amat, neque formosum senem?*—Cicero, *Tusc. Disp.,* IV. 33.
19. See Plato, *Symposium* (discourse of Pausanias).
20. That is, from the Academy.
21. That is, to the frenzy.
22. That is, the Academy.
23. See Plato, *Symposium* (discourse of Pausanias).
24. See Plato, *Symposium.*
25. *Amorem conatum esse amicitiæ faciendæ ex pulchritudinis specie.*—Cicero, *Tusc. Disp.,* IV, 34.
26. Of friendship.
27. *Omnino amicitiæ, corroboratis jam confirmatisque*

Notes and Comments

ingeniis et ætatibus, judicandæ sunt.—Idem, *De Amicitia.*

28. *Qu'elles effacent et ne retrouvent plus la couture qui les a jointes.*

29. By Montaigne himself, in 1571.

30. La Boëtie was born in 1530, Montaigne in 1533.

31. That is, that belonged solely to either of us.

32. That is, Tiberius's.

33. See Cicero, *De Amicitia*, XI; Plutarch, *Parallel between Tiberius and Gaius;* Valerius Maximus, IV, 7.1.

34. At this point in the early editions (1580 to 1588) occurs the sentence, *de laquelle il se pouvoit respondre comme de la sienne.*

35. *Il tenoit la volonté de Gracchus en sa manche, et par puissance et par connoissance.*

36. *Cet harnois.*

37. *Nos ames ont charrié si uniement ensemble.*

38. See Aulus Gellius, I, 3.

39. See Diogenes Laertius, *Life of Aristotle.*

40. See *Ibid.*

41. *Qui faict le liberal.* In the early editions the reading was, *Qui faict l'honneste et le courtois.*

42. That is, the friend.

43. *Qu'il le redemandoit à ses amis, non qu'il le demandoit.* See Diogenes Laertius, *Life of Diogenes.*

44. *Heritiers.*

45. See Lucian, *Toxaris*, XXII.

46. *La chose la plus une et unie.*

47. See Xenophon, *Cyropædeia*, VIII, 3.

48. *Tous les ressorts.*

49.   *Mihi sic usus est; tibi, ut opus est facto, face.*
      —Terence, *Heautontimorumenos*, I, 1.28.

Of Friendship

50. *A la familiarité de la table j'associe le plesant, non le prudant; au lict la beauté avant la bonté; en la societé du discours, la suffisance, voire sans la preud'homie.*

51. See Plutarch, *Life of Agesilaus.*

52. *Laches.*

53. *Nil ego contulerim jucundo sanus amico.*
 —Horace, *Satires,* I, 5.44.

54. See Plutarch, *On Brotherly Love.*

55. *Ayant prins en payement.*

56. *De ce personnage.*

57.   *quem semper acerbum,*
Semper honoratum (sic, Dii, voluistis), habebo.
 —Virgil, *Æneid,* V, 49.

58. *Nec fas esse ulla me voluptate hic frui*
Decrevi, tantisper dum ille abest meus particeps.
 —Terence, *Heautontimorumenos,* I, 1.97.
Montaigne adapted the text to suit his purpose.

59. *Illam meæ si partem animæ tulit*
Maturior vis, quid moror altera,
    Nec charus æque, nec superstes
   Integer? Ille dies utramque
Duxit ruinam. —Horace, *Odes,* II, 17.5.

60. *Quis desiderio sit pudor aut modus*
Tam chari capitis. —Horace, *Odes,* I, 24.1.

61.   *O misero frater adempte mihi!*
Omnia tecum una perierunt gaudia nostra,
   Quæ tuus in vita dulcis alebat amor.
Tu mea, tu moriens fregisti commoda, frater;
   Tecum una tota est nostra sepulta anima,
   Cujus ego interitu tota de mente fugavi
Hæc studia atque omnes delicias animi.

Notes and Comments

Alloquar? audiero nunquam tua verba
      loquentem?
Nunquam ego te, vita frater amabilior,
Aspiciam posthac? At certe semper amabo.
                    —Catullus, LXVIII, 20; LXV, 9.

62. *Dixhuict* in 1580-1588. Montaigne originally intended to add La Boëtie's tract, *La Servitude Volontaire*, at the end of this chapter.

63. In the earlier editions, including 1588, the following sentence appeared: *Ce sont 29. sonnets que le sieur de Poiferré homme d'affaires et d'entendement, qui le connoissoit long temps avant moy, a retrouvé par fortune chez luy, parmy quelques autres papiers, et me les vient d'envoyer; dequoy je luy suis tres-obligé, et souhaiterois que d'autres qui detiennent plusiers lopins de ses escris, par-cy, par-là, en fissent de mesmes.*

CHAPTER XXIX

Nine-and-twenty Sonnets of

Etienne de la Boëtie

A. THE COMMENT BY MISS NORTON

WE have here only a paragraph of introduction of his friend's verses, addressed by Montaigne to Madame de Grammont. This dedication, which appeared in 1580,

Nine-and-Twenty Sonnets

was probably written as early as 1576.

Madame de Grammont was known as *la belle Corisande d'Andouins*. She was by birth Diane, vicomtesse de Louvigny; she married in 1567 Philibert, comte de Grammont et de Guiche. He was killed at the siege of La Fère in 1580. Montaigne noted in his *Ephemerides* "6 aout, l'an 1580 mourut au siege de la fere, môsr de gramôt qui m'étoit fort amy; qui avoit été frapé d'un coup de piece 4 jours auparaunt, moi etat au d'siege." In the Essay "Of Diversion" (Book III, chapter 4), he says: "I went with several other of his friends to conduct to Soissons the body of monsieur de Gramont from the siege of la Fere, where he was killed."

B. THE NOTES BY MR. IVES

1. Referring to the volume of *Vers François* of La Boëtie, published by Montaigne in 1572.

2. That is, the verses in the volume referred to in the preceding note.

3. The 29 sonnets were printed in all editions down to and including 1588. In place of the above sentence written by Montaigne on the Bordeaux copy of 1588, on which he struck out the sonnets, we find in 1595 the following: *Ces vingt-neuf sonnetz d'Estienne de la Boëtie, qui estoient mis en ce lieu, ont esté despuis imprimez avec ses œuvres.* The edition of the sonnets which led Montaigne to omit them here has never been discovered.

CHAPTER XXX

Of Moderation

A. THE COMMENT BY MISS NORTON

THE motto for this chapter might be taken from Molière's *Misanthrope*:

> La parfaite raison fuit toute extremité
> Et veut que l'on soit sage avec sobrieté.

"Moderation" was the law of Montaigne's life, but he treats of it without any special eloquence or force, and with only limited illustrations. He repeats here in other words the observation he has made in the fifteenth Essay, that all virtues, if too extravagantly practised, may become vices.

The quotation from St. Paul he here makes use of was one of the many inscriptions in his library. In 1775 the question was proposed by the French Academy, as the subject for a prize of eloquence: "En quoi consiste l'esprit philosophique conformément à ces paroles: *Non plus sapere quam oportet sapere?*" This question has not yet been answered. Is it asked as often as it might be?

We find here one of the few *cheerless* passages of the Essays, that which begins: "Is not man a pitiful creature?" a cheerlessness occasioned by facts existing far more in Montaigne's day than, happily, in our own. From this "impression" we pass on rather disconnectedly to the matter of human sacrifice.

Of Moderation

B. THE NOTES BY MR. IVES

1. *Insani sapiens nomen ferat, æquus iniqui,*
Ultra quam satis est virtutem si petat ipsam.
—Horace, *Epistles*, I, 6.15.

2. See *Epistle to the Romans*, XII, 3: *Dico enim . . . omnibus qui sunt inter vos, non plus sapere quam oportet sapere, sed sapere ad sobrietatem.*—For I say . . . to every man that is among you, not to think of himself more highly than he ought to think, but to think soberly.

3. *Tel grand.* Probably King Henri III.

4. That is, the first stone for walling up the door of the Temple, in which he had taken refuge. See Diodorus Siculus, XI, 45; Cornelius Nepos, *Pausanias*, V.

5. See Diodorus Siculus, XII, 19; Valerius Maximus, II, 7.6. Livy (IV, 29, and VIII, 7) denies this.

6. See the *Gorgias*.

7. See the *Secunda Secundæ*, question 154, art. 9.

8. *La parantelle.*

9. *Les sciences.*

10. Epaminondas. See Plutarch, *Political Precepts*.

11. See Cicero, *De Off.*, I, 40.

12. See Spartianus, *Ælius Verus*.

13. Eusebius and Nicephorus.

14. *Fortunæ miseras auximus arte vias.*
—Propertius, III, 7.32.

15. *Faict bien sottement l'ingenieuse.*

16. *Comme elle faict favorablement et industrieusement d'employer ses artifices a nous peigner et farder les maux.*

17. See Tacitus, *Annals*, VI, 3.

1651

Notes and Comments

18. The chapter ended here in the editions before 1588.
19. Amurath II. See Chalcondylas, *History of the Fall of the Grecian Empire*, VII, 4.
20. That is, to defray the cost of their sacrifice. See Gomara, *Histoire Générale des Indes*, II, 7.
21. Cortez.
22. See Gomara, *Don Fernando Cortes*.

CHAPTER XXXI

Of Cannibals

A. THE COMMENT BY MISS NORTON

IT has been remarked (by M. Gilbert Chinard) that this chapter is one of those in which most definitely appears a desire on Montaigne's part to give a lesson to his contemporaries, to urge them to free themselves from their prejudices, to listen to the voice of our *grande et puissante mère Nature*.

And it may be added that it is notable that these pages are composed with a closer connection of ideas than is usual with Montaigne. The connecting thread of thought, often so slight with him, is here perceptible throughout.

This Essay, like that on Education, is curiously precur-

Of Cannibals

sory of the beliefs of Rousseau. It is the praise, not of a state of *savagery*, but of a state alien to our conditions of civilisation—a state which Montaigne is inclined to consider—as Rousseau does—a state of *nature*. Montaigne does not call it so; and indeed he is less interested, evidently, about this point than in the fact that "every one calls *barbarie* whatever is not his own custom."

Montaigne's thoughts had been turned in this direction by the comparatively recent discovery of America, more especially by the really recent interest of the French in South America—which they called *la France antartique*.

A few dates may be helpful in enabling us to enter into the views held by Montaigne and his contemporaries.

It should be remembered that Columbus died (in 1506) in the firm belief that his discoveries were parts of Asia; and it was not till 1513 that the Pacific Ocean was made known (by Balboa), a discovery that Montaigne seems not to have appreciated. The conquest of Mexico, by Cortez, was in 1519-1521, and that of Peru, by Pizarro, in 1531-1532. We shall see later (in the Essay "Of Coaches") how much Montaigne had occupied himself with the conditions of the civilisations thus known—which were called barbarisms.

M. Gilbert Chinard in an interesting chapter on Montaigne as "un defenseur des Indiens," in his *L'Exotisme Americain* (1911), remarks on the essential difference of tone between this Essay on Cannibals and that on Coaches, written many years later. M. Chinard expresses a somewhat strange surprise that Montaigne, in this earlier Essay, says nothing of the atrocities of the Spaniards toward the French, and he offers, as a possible explanation, a belief that Montaigne was opposed by his principles to all colonial en-

Notes and Comments

terprises, and was convinced that his fellow countrymen had no right over Brazil, and that those who had gone thither as fortune-seekers had had only the luck they deserved.

Later, the moral problem created by the conquest of America interested him; and, while, in this first Essay, we perceive only the results of his curiosity, his love of investigation, his liking for picturesque details, in the later one we feel that his conscience has been touched; he considers the matter from a wider point of view, and he puts himself clearly on the side of the original possessors of the country against their barbarous conquerors, as a defender of the Right and of Humanity.

The peoples with whom Montaigne chiefly concerned himself in this Essay were those of Brazil, which was discovered in 1550—first by the Spaniards, and a few months later by the Portuguese, who obtained the mastery. In 1555-1560 the amiral de Coligny made an attempt to found a Protestant settlement in America. Chevalier Nicolaus Durard de Villegaignon in 1555 led two ships to Brazil, and founded a colony on an island in the Bay of Rio de Janeiro. Geneva sent fourteen missionaries thither, but Villegaignon suddenly joined the Catholic Church, and his defection ruined the colony. Many of the settlers returned to France in 1557,—when Montaigne was twenty-four years old,— and probably later the particular wanderer came back, from whom Montaigne says he gained much of the information he here dwells on. It is to be feared that the remarks Montaigne makes on the value of his testimony, and that of the "seamen and merchants" he brought to Montaigne, have not the firmest foundation; but the interest of the Essay lies not in the facts Montaigne believed, but in the inferences

Of Cannibals

he draws from them. As M. Levaux has said: "It must be acknowledged that Montaigne has singularly amplified what a man whom he describes as a 'simple, plain fellow' could have related to him. It is an interpreted narrative; what Montaigne reproved others for doing, he here himself does."

What more natural! And how Montaigne would have liked to hold up to the light this bit of human nature in himself, if he had chanced to perceive it! Again we feel that he writes as a *poet*, not as an historian, and not quite as a philosopher. And this Essay has a link with poetry that gives it the greatest possible extraneous interest that it could possess. Shakespeare read it, and with such warmth of interest and appreciation that he quoted it. Nothing could be more delightful to the lover of Montaigne than that in "The Tempest,"—one of the most beautiful of the plays, one most closely connected with Shakespeare personally, and written in the noblest maturity of his mind,—nothing could be more delightful, I say, than to find imbedded in it a long quotation from Montaigne (Act II, scene 1). Shakespeare took it quite certainly from the translation of Florio.

(It is to be observed that Shakespeare read the word "idle" as referring to *men;* in Montaigne "oisives" refers to *occupations.* It may be mentioned, by the way, that Florio's volume is the only book which we certainly know to have belonged to Shakespeare. The British Museum has a copy with his autograph on the fly-leaf. That was published in 1603, and "The Tempest" was written in 1610.)

M. Villey remarks: "Much was written in the sixteenth century about the cannibals. It is interesting to examine carefully the assertions of Montaigne in relation to those of

Notes and Comments

his contemporaries. Besides the great cosmographs of Thevet, of Belleforest, and of Munster (we know that this last was in Montaigne's library), and the great histories of the Indies, like that of Lopez de Gomara, it is particularly instructive to read the narratives of the companions of Villegaignon: that of André Thevet, 'Les Singularetez de la France antartique' (1563); and the relation of Jean de Léry, 'Histoire d'un voyage fait en la terre de Brésil, autrement dit Amérique' (1578)."

B. THE NOTES BY MR. IVES

1. See Plutarch, *Life of Pyrrhus*.
2. See Plutarch, *Life of Flamminius*, III. But Plutarch says it of Flaminius himself, not of his army.
3. See Livy, XXXI, 34.
4. *Par la* voye *de la raison, non par la* voix commun.
5. In 1580-1588: *Comme on dict, et le dit-on de ceux, ausquels l'appetit et la faim font plus desirer de viande, qu'ils n'en peuvent empocher; je crains aussi* (omitted in the *Édition Municipale*).
6. *Le golfe de la mer Majour;* that is, the Black Sea.
7. See the *Timæus*, XXII, XXIV, XXV. Cf. Benzoni's *Storia del Monde Nuovo*.
8.   *Hæc loca, vi quondam et vasta convulsa ruina,*
    Dissiluisse ferunt, cum protinus utraque tellus
    Una foret. —Virgil, *Æneid*, III, 414.
9.   *sterilisque diu palus aptaque remis*
    Vicinas urbes alit, et grave sentit aratrum.
    —Horace, *Ars Poetica*, 65.
10. That is, rivers.
11. This is taken practically word for word from Chau-

Of Cannibals

veton's translation of Benzoni's history, just cited, and is said to be a translation of the treatise περὶ Θαυμάσιων Ἀκουσμάτων, sometimes ascribed to Aristotle; see page 66 of the Teubner Edition of Aristotle's *De Plantis*, etc.

12. That is, the "lords."
13. Than the Atlantis fable. See page 272.
14. See page 271.
15. *Mire.*
16. *Sauvages.*
17. *Par tout où sa pureté reluit.*
18.   *Et veniunt ederæ sponte sua melius,*
 Surgit et in solis formosior arbutus antris,
   Et volucres nulla dulcius arte canunt.
       —Propertius, I, 2.10.
19. *L'utilité de son usage.*
20. See Plato, *Laws*, book X.
21. *Soudeure humaine.*
22. *Viri a diis recentes...* —Seneca, *Epistle* 90.
23. *Hos natura modos primum dedit.*
    —Virgil, *Georgics*, II, 20.
24. *En une contrée de païs tres-plaisante et bien temperée.*
25. *Artifice.*
26. *Sert de flang.*
27. A Byzantine lexicographer.
28. *Presche en commun toute la grangée.*
29. See Herodotus, IV, 69.
30. *Et qu'il soit ainsi.*
31. See Diogenes Laertius, *Life of Chrysippus*, and *Life of Zeno*; Sextus Empiricus, *Hypotyposes*, III, 24.
32. *Se De Bello Gallico*, VII, 77, 78.

Notes and Comments

33.   *Vascones, fama est, alimentis talibus usi
        Produxere animas.*   —Juvenal, XV, 93.
34. *La seule jalousie de la vertu.*
35. *Cette pleine possession de biens par indivis.*
36.   *Victoria nulla est
        Quam quæ confessos animo quoque subjugat
        hostes.*
            —Claudian, *De Sexto Consulatu Honorii*, 248.
37. See the *History* of Chalcondylas, V, 9.
38. *Si succederit de genu pugnat.*—Seneca, *De Providentia*, II. The modern text has *occiderit*.
39. Cf. Idem, *De Constantia*, VI. Text of 1580-1588: *il est vaincu par effect, et non pas par raison; c'est son malheur qu'on peut accuser, non sa lascheté.*
40. See Diodorus Siculus, XV, 16.
41. *Le vray vaincre a pour son rolle l'estour, non pas le salut.*
42. *Forme.*
43. See St. Augustine, *De Civ. Dei*, XVI, 15 and 38. Some confusion is created by the fact that Leah and Rachel were "the wives of Jacob."
44. See Suetonius, *Augustus*, LXXI.
45. *Leur fit espaule.* See Plutarch, *Of the virtuous deeds of women.*
46. *Cordon.*
47. *Comme je presuppose qu'elle soit desia avancée.*
48. In 1562.
49. Montaigne himself.
50. The editions of 1580-1588 add: *et bien souls.*

CHAPTER XXXII

That It is with Sobriety that We Should Undertake to Judge of the Divine Decrees

A. THE COMMENT BY MISS NORTON

THIS short Essay, which was written in 1572, is one of the contemplations of human affairs in relation to religious theories which Montaigne fell into oftener in his earlier than in his later writings; and which he more or less summed up in the "Apologie." The chief point he makes here is that no support or authority is given to religious beliefs by any course of present events; and in proof of this he alleges the recent battles of the civil war. The arrangement of his sentences does not represent the dates of these battles quite accurately. The battle of Jarnac was fought the 13th of March, 1569, by the duc d'Anjou (afterward Henri III) on the part of the king (Charles IX) and the Catholics, against the prince de Condé and the amiral de Coligny, the Protestant chiefs. The excellent Castelnau—one of the most skilful and celebrated diplomatists of the sixteenth century, and equally distinguished for his character of wisdom and moderation—took part in the battle, and in his "Mémoires" has given an account of it. One of the first things that he says is: "The duke, seeing that this day he should be prepared to

Notes and Comments

meet the enemy, having followed his good and praiseworthy habit of beginning his morning by placing himself under the protection of God, desired to receive the precious body of our Lord, as did the princes and some of the officers of our army." Equally fervent prayers we may be sure were not lacking on the Huguenot side: Montaigne was not far from believing that

> The prayers of Christian, Turk and Jew
> Have one sound up there in the blue;

certainly he did not believe that either Catholic or Protestant prayers had much influence that day at Jarnac.

The affair of La Rochelabeille came off three months later in June, 1569; it was only a great skirmish between the troops of the amiral de Coligny and the duc d'Anjou—when the duke did not choose to risk giving battle, partly because of a heavy rain. The Protestants had no great reason to pride themselves on it; and there is something pathetic in their putting it forward, as Montaigne says they did, as a proof of divine favour.

The battle of Moncontour took place the 3d of October (1569). For a time the fortunes of the day were variable, though Coligny was fighting with only 18,000 men exhausted by long efforts, while the duc d'Anjou was strong with 25,000 fresh troops. The young Henri de Navarre (Henri IV), sixteen years old, witnessed the battle from a neighbouring height where he was placed with a body of troops, and he was restrained only by Coligny's commands from joining in the fray. Coligny's immense courage availed only to dignify the victory of the duke. Coligny was wounded and obliged to retreat.

To Judge of the Divine Decrees

Montaigne's conclusion, from all these events, is that good fortune and ill fortune befall alike the saint and the sinner. "He maketh his sun to rise on the evil and on the good, and sendeth rain on the just and on the unjust."

B. THE NOTES BY MR. IVES

1. *Et puis, n'estant point subjectes à nos discours ordinaires, elles nous ostent le moyen de les combattre.*
2. In the *Critias*.
3. *Et id genus omne.*—Horace, *Satires*, I, 2.2.
4. *De suivre leur esteuf:* "foolishly to rely on, strayne himself for, or follow after, incertainties."—Cotgrave.
5. *Injuste.*
6. See Gomara, *Histoire Générale des Indes*, III, 22.
7. That is, divine approval.
8. *S'ils n'ont un peuple du tout à leur mercy.*
9. That is, those who had the advantage at La Rochelabielle, namely, the Protestants.
10. At Lepanto (1571).
11. See Jean Bouchet, *Annales d'Aquitaine*.
12. See Lampridius, *Heliogabalus*, XVII.
13. *D'en faire sottement nostre profit.*
14. The meaning here is not at all clear. The text is: *une belle preuve sur ses adverseres;* a variant reading of the *Edition Municipale* has *à ses adverseres.* See *De Civ. Dei*, I, 8.
15. See Plutarch, *Of Curiosity*.
16. *Quis hominum potest scire consilium dei? aut quis poterit cogitare quid velit dominus?*—Book of Wisdom, IX.

CHAPTER XXXIII

Of Avoiding Pleasures at the Cost of Life

A. THE COMMENT BY MISS NORTON

THIS title does not mean that Montaigne thought it well to do so, but that he was considering the opinions of the ancients. He had always known that they thought it was time to die when there was more pain than pleasure in living; but he had only lately learned that Seneca and Epicurus also counselled their friends to die rather than live a worthless life. And Montaigne then remarks that the same feeling may be found among *nos gents* (that is, among moderns with religious beliefs), save that, with "Christian moderation," they do not seek death at their own hands.

B. THE NOTES BY MR. IVES

1. Ἤ ζῆν ἀλύπως, ἤ θανεῖν εὐδαιμόνως.
   Καλὸν τὸ θνήσκειν οἷς ὕβριν τὸ ζῆν φέρει.
   Κρεῖσσον τὸ μη ζῆν ἐστὶν ἤ ζῆν ἀθλίως.
2. See Seneca, *Epistle* 22.3.
3. See Idem, *Epistle* 23.5.
4. *Elle luy mourut.*
5. *Singulière.* See Jean Bouchet, *Annales d'Aquitaine.*
6. *Ce fut une morte embrassée avec singulier contentement commun.*

CHAPTER XXXIV

That Fortune is Often Met with in the Train of Reason

A. THE COMMENT BY MISS NORTON

THIS Essay is only a collection of historic stories, and of more or less authentic and more or less incredible facts; and its inherent dullness is only occasionally relieved by a jest from Montaigne, as when he quotes: "Fortune is better advised than we"; which were the last words of the Essay in 1580. M. Villey remarks: "These anecdotes and others of the same kind are multiplied in such compilations as those of Messie and Bouoystuau. Montaigne was slow to loose himself from their habits. However, his Essays of this kind are few in number."

B. THE NOTES BY MR. IVES

1. Cæsar Borgia.
2. See Guicciardini, VI.
3. *Conjugis ante coacta novi dimittere collum,*
   Quam veniens una atque altera rursus hyems
   Noctibus in longis avidum saturasset amorem.
   —Catullus, LXVIII, 81.
4. See the *Mémoires* of Martin du Bellay, II.
5. *Semble il pas que ce soit un sort artiste?*—"On peut remarquer que Montaigne n'emploie pas ce mot [*artiste*]

Notes and Comments

adjectivement avant son voyage en Italie, et c'est lui seulement qui l'emploie dans ce sens: qui montre de l'art, de l'intention, selon les regles de l'école et de l'art."

6. See Jacques de Lavardin, *Histoire de G. Castriot*.
7. Fortune.
8. See Bouchet, *Annales d'Aquitaine*.
9. Son of Hugh Capet.
10. *Recheut toutes-fois tout empanné.*
11. See *Mémoires* du Bellay, II.
12. See Pliny, *Natural History*, VII, 51 (50).
13. See Idem, XXXV, 10.
14. Wife of Edward II. See Froissart, I, 10.
15. Ταυτόματον ἡμῶν καλλίω βουλεύεται.
    —Menander.

Montaigne found this in the collection published in 1569 by Jean Crispin. He translates the line after quoting it.

16. *Comme ils se guignoient l'un l'autre.*
17. See Plutarch, *Life of Timoleon*.
18. *Cette fortune surpasse en reglement les regles de l'humaine prudence.*
19. Fortune.
20. *De retirer encore des playes leurs bras sanglants et armés.*
21. *Nœud.*
22. See Appian, IV, 21.

CHAPTER XXXV

Of a Defect in Our Administration of Cities

A. THE COMMENT BY MISS NORTON

EACH of the three paragraphs of this little Essay has its separate interest: the first because of the reference to Montaigne's father (whom he always speaks of with the highest and warmest regard).

The interest of the next paragraph lies in the character and position of the two men to whom it refers; and in Montaigne's expressions concerning them, his wish to be of material service to their like has a characteristic simplicity and sincerity and earnestness of delightful quality.

The third and last paragraph has little to do with what precedes, but connects itself with Montaigne's thought of his father. The Essay closes with a vigorous avowal of Montaigne's belief in the advantages of keeping a diary.

B. THE NOTES BY MR. IVES

1. In 1580-1588 occurs this phrase: *Es commandemens qui luy estoyent tombez en main.*
2. An Italian archæologist and poet, 1479-1552.
3. 1515-1563.
4. *Quels trains y ont passe; combien [de temps?] arreste.*

CHAPTER XXXVI

Of the Custom of Wearing Clothes

A. THE COMMENT BY MISS NORTON

MONTAIGNE thinks that, as all other beings are perfectly furnished with what is needful for the maintenance of their existence, it is not to be believed that man alone is created in an "indigent" condition; and therefore we had (perhaps) better go naked and see what comes of it; or, at least, this might be well if custom had not made impossible what is not so by nature. He tells a story of a question asked of "one of our beggars" which Locke ("Of Education," § 5) puts into the mouth of an Athenian who addressed it to a Scythian philosopher. The story may be told as often as you please without inducing us to go *en chemise* today.

Montaigne passes on, as he says, "d'une autre piece," to the consideration of the material effects of cold, and to the difficulties and calamities caused by it in warfare; and then twists back again, oddly enough, to the clothes and the utensils of the King of Mexico, which last paragraph was added in 1588.

B. THE NOTES BY MR. IVES

1. *Ecclesiastes*, IX, 3. *Omnium quæ sub sole sunt fortuna et lex par est.* This sentence was inscribed on the beams of Montaigne's library.

Of the Custom of Wearing Clothes

2. *Exactement fourny ailleurs de filet et éguille pour maintenir son estre.*

3.   *Proptereaque fere res omnes aut corio sunt,*
    Aut seta, aut conchis, aut callo, aut cortice
    tectæ.   —Lucretius, IV, 935.

4. The following clause, found in 1580, but not in 1588 or in the *Édition Municipale*, was restored in 1595: *et sous bien plus rude ciel que le nostre.*

5. See Guillaume Postel *Histoire des Turcs*.

6. See Cicero, *De Senectute*, X.

7. See Herodotus, III, 12.

8. See Plutarch, *Apothegms of the Lacedæmonians*.

9. See Suetonius, *Life of Cæsar*.

10.   *tum vertice nudo*
    Excipere insanos imbres, cœlique ruinam.
    —Silius Italicus, I, 250.

11. See Gasparo Balbi, *Travels in the East Indies*.

12. *Merveilleusement.* See Plato, *Laws*, book XII.

13. Stephen Bathori.

14. *Apres le nostre.* Henri de Valois, duc d'Anjou, King of Poland, 1573-1574; afterwards Henri III of France.

15. See Pliny, *Natural History*, XXVIII, 6.

16. *D'une autre piece.*

17. See *Mémoires* of du Bellay, X.

18.   *Nudaque consistunt formam servantia testæ*
    Vina, nec hausta meri, sed data frusta bibunt.
    —Ovid, *Tristia*, III, 10.23.

In the first edition the Essay ended here.

19. See Strabo, VII. In M. Villey's opinion, this source is very uncertain, and the passage does not indicate that Montaigne had read Strabo's geography.

Notes and Comments

20. See Livy, XXI, 54.
21. See Xenophon, *Anabasis*, IV, 4.5.
22. See Diodorus Siculus, XVII, 18. The edition of 1595 adds: *et nous en pouvons aussi voir.*
23. See Lopez de Gomara, *Histoire Générale des Indes.*

CHAPTER XXXVII

Of the Younger Cato

A. THE COMMENT BY MISS NORTON

WHAT Montaigne says of himself and what he says of the men of his time in the first two pages of this Essay give one a very strong impression both of the moral isolation in which he felt himself to be living, and of the sincerity with which he disclaimed for himself any great moral elevation. But no man could have a warmer appreciation of the heights of virtue than Montaigne, and he only does himself justice in declaring that, so great is his delight in noble and generous actions, with "great names" he would gladly boost them to raise them higher—"*je la prendrois volontiers à leur prester quelque tour d'espaules pour les haulser.*"

This Essay is nominally about Cato the Younger, Cato "junior." He was "the junior" of his great-grandfather Cato the Censor; and he is known as Cato of Utica, merely because Utica was the scene of his death.

Of the Younger Cato

He was only forty-nine when he died—when he killed himself in despair at the triumphant successes of Cæsar. All his life he was the enemy—the immitigable enemy, the vigorous opponent—of tyranny; justice, rigid justice, unmoved by favour, untouched by compassion, was the object of his devotion. This stern severity of character was accepted as high virtue, and excited extraordinary reverence. His firmness of purpose could not be weakened by flattery or daunted by violence, and his disinterestedness was unquestioned. He was a great public servant and kept untiring watch and ward over public affairs. But he lacked the practical ability, the sound judgement, the large views that would have been needed to be a wise leader in those tumultuous days; and he vainly strove to form, between the Party of Cæsar and the party of Pompey, a party of the Commonwealth. And when the civil war broke out, the most important part he played was that of a patriotic philanthropist. A year or two later, he was entrusted by the Senate with troops, whom he managed not very competently, and carried to Africa, where he formed a junction with other Roman generals and became second in command. The whole army was the next year utterly routed by Cæsar; and Cato immediately sought refuge in death from the despotism he abhorred.

From that moment he has been the object of interminable panegyric. Cicero magnificently leads the endless procession of his praisers with a separate eulogy that has been lost, and with beautiful expressions in his "De Officiis"; and following Cicero, come the great historians, Plutarch and Tacitus and Sallust, and then the poet Juvenal and the philosopher Seneca, and among these great men the five poets whom it is the purpose of the Essay to bring together for

Notes and Comments

comparison and criticism: Martial, Manilius, Lucan, Horace, and Virgil. In this connection we have one of Montaigne's admirable sayings about poetry, which is capable of being generalised to relate to all Art: "To a certain slight extent it can be judged of by maxims and by skill, but the excellent, the ineffable, the divine, is above rules and the power of judgement."

He says of himself: "From my earliest childhood, poetry has had the power to pierce and transport me"; and he tells us how he liked first Ovid and then Lucan and now Virgil: as a man might say in these days, that as a boy he admired Moore, and then Byron, and at last Milton.

As we read these pages, it is interesting to remember that Dante makes Cato the warden of Purgatory. The thought was perhaps suggested to him by the very line of Virgil that Montaigne quotes. As Cato stands on the shores of Purgatory, his countenance is illumined with the light of the four stars which are the four Virtues—Justice, Prudence, Fortitude, and Temperance; and it is foretold of him that he will be clothed in glory at the last day. Dante takes him as the symbol of Liberty, for, as Virgil says to him: "non ti fu per lei amara in Utica la morte" (for the sake of Liberty not bitter to thee was death in Utica).

The purpose of Purgatory is the gaining of freedom from sin through purification, the winning of spiritual Liberty; and, therefore, the lover of Liberty is a fit guardian of the realm.

Erasmus thought that Cicero could hardly be denied admittance to Heaven. Dante places Cato on the way to it, far removed from the Limbo of the heathen and the dreadful wood of the suicides. He writes of him in the "Convito"

Of the Younger Cato

with the greatest reverence. The passage ends thus: "With his name it is fitting to close that which was to be said here of the signs of nobleness, because this nobleness displays all these signs in him at all times of his life."

Montaigne's words seem almost a modern echo of the same thought when he says that Cato "was truly a pattern that Nature chose, to show to how great a height human virtue and steadfastness could attain."

B. THE NOTES BY MR. IVES

1. In 1580-1588: *Je croy aysement d'autruy beaucoup de choses, où mes forces ne peuvent attaindre.*
2. *Je m'insinue fort bien en leur place.*
3. *Sunt qui nihil laudent, nisi quod se imitari posse confidunt.* —Cicero, *Tusc. Disp.*, II, 1.
4. *virtutem verba putant, ut Lucum ligna.* —Horace, *Epistles*, I, 6.31. In the original text this is a question—"putes?" The quotation was added in 1582.
5. *Quam vereri deberent, etiamsi percipere non possent.* —Cicero, *Tusc. Disp.*, V, 2. The text is changed slightly; Cicero is speaking of philosophy, Montaigne of virtue.
6. *Purement vertueuse* in 1580-1588.
7. *Chez l'ouvrier.*
8. See Herodotus, IX, 70. This is said to have occurred at the battle of Platæa, not Potidæa.
9. *A qui les veut estendre, quelle diversité d'images ne souffre nostre interne volonté.*
10. *Leur prester quelque tour d'espaule à les hausser.* See Book II, chap. 17: *Je tesmoigne volontiers de mes amis*

1671

Notes and Comments

par ce que j'y trouve de louable, et d'un pied de valeur j'en fais volontiers un pied et demy.

11. Referring to "the greater number of the intelligent men of my time," at the beginning of the paragraph.

12. Plutarch. See *Of the malignity of Herodotus*.

13. The edition of 1580 adds: *et de ceux qui font l'honneur la fin de toutes actions vertueuses.*

14. See Plato, *Io*.

15. See Book I, chap. 26 ("Of the Education of Children"), near the beginning, for another reference by Montaigne to his passion for poetry.

16. *Sit Cato, dum vivit, sane vel Cæsare major.*
—Martial, *Epigrams*, VI, 32.
Montaigne gives his own significance to this line, which in the original is not of a wholly flattering character.

17. *Et invictum, devicta morte, Catonem.*
—Manilius, *Astronomica*, IV, 87.

18. *Victrix causa diis placuit, sed victa Catoni.*
—Lucan, *Pharsalia*, I, 128.

19. *Et cuncta terrarum subacta,*
Præter atrocem animum Catonis.
—Horace, *Odes*, II, 1.23.

20. *Les noms.* Cotgrave, *sub verbo* "nom": "a fame, bruit, report; whence, *Il en a le nom.*"

21. *His dantem jura Catonem.*
—Virgil, *Æneid*, VIII, 670.

CHAPTER XXXVIII

How We Weep and Laugh at One and the Same Thing

A. THE COMMENT BY MISS NORTON

MONTAIGNE here touches, not very deeply, not very interestingly, on the manysidedness of human emotions. Macbeth asks:

> Who can be wise, amaz'd, temperate and furious,
> Loyal and neutral, in a moment? No man,

he says; but, perhaps, as truly it might be answered, "Every man—in his own heart." At any rate, we may certainly mourn and rejoice over the same event, and Montaigne, after his wont, brings forward many anecdotes to prove this.

The motif of the Essay would seem to have been suggested by three passages in Plutarch: that about Antigonus in the Life of Pyrrhus, about Cæsar in the Life of Pompey, and about Timoleon in his Life.

Some touches of personal portraiture are found here: his emotions on leaving home, and when he scolds his valet, and when he scolds himself. In a later Essay ("On Anger") he gives a further account of his angers, and says: "Sometimes, too, it happens that I pretend to be angry, for the management of my household, without any real emotion."

Notes and Comments

B. THE NOTES BY MR. IVES

1. See Plutarch, *Life of Pyrrhus.*
2. Charles the Bold, killed in 1477, at Nancy.
3. In 1364; see Froissart.
4. *Et cosi aven che l'animo ciascuna*
   Sua passion sotto el contrario manto
   Ricopre, con la vista hor' chiara hor' bruna.
   —Petrarch, *Sonnet* 81.
5. See Plutarch, *Life of Cæsar,* and *Life of Pompey.*
6. *tutumque putavit*
   Jam bonus esse socer; lachrimas non sponte cadentes
   Effudit, gemitusque expressit pectore læto.
   —Lucan, IX, 1037.
7. *Ne soient que masque et fard.*
8. *Hæredis fletus sub persona risus est.*
   —Publius Syrus, in Aulus Gellius, XVII, 14.
9. *Estne novis nuptis odio Venus, anne parentum*
   Frustrantur falsis gaudia lachrimulis,
   Ubertim thalami quas intra limina fundunt?
   Non, ita me divi, vera gemunt, juverint.
   —Catullus, LXVI, 15.
10. *Bran du fat.*
11. See Tacitus, *Annals,* XIV, 4.
12. *Largus enim liquidi fons luminis, ætherius sol*
    Inrigat assidue cœlum candore recenti,
    Suppeditatque novo confestim lumine lumen.
    —Lucretius, V, 281.
13. See Herodotus, VII, 45, *et seq.;* Valerius Maximus, IX, 13, *ext.* 1.

14. That is, the imagination's.
15.   *Nil adeo fieri celeri ratione videtur*
      Quam sibi mens fieri proponit et inchoat ipsa.
      Ocius ergo animus quam res se perciet ulla,
      Ante oculos quarum in promptu natura videtur.
                              —Lucretius, III, 182.
16. See Plutarch, *Life of Timoleon;* Diodorus Siculus, XVI, 65.

CHAPTER XXXIX

Of Solitude

A. THE COMMENT BY MISS NORTON

THE longer Essays are almost without exception the most interesting; and this is one to be read and re-read. Not that there is any profound or original thought in it, and it is very often diffuse; but the thought is never trivial, and the phrase is never commonplace. It is the expression—as intimate as it is simple—of the mind of one of our fellow men, whom it would be a pleasure to resemble.

He begins by questioning what it is that makes us desire solitude, and remarks that if it be "to live more at leisure and at ease," we do not always choose the right path. "We

Notes and Comments

carry our fetters with us. . . . Our sickness is of the soul. . . . Let us win from ourselves the power to live alone in good earnest and thus to live at our ease." This thought he enlarges upon in the passage on the next page (321) beginning: We "must have wives, children," and closing with the noble phrase that the soul "can be its own company: it has the means of attack and of defence, of giving and of receiving." It has been said of this Essay,—

> Il m'enseigne à n'avoir affection pour rien;
> De toutes amitiés il détache mon ame.

But, in truth, that is not its spirit. It is not addressed to men in active life; it speaks to, and of, those to whom solitude is becoming, for whom it is reasonable "to take leave of society betimes"; and it is not the counsel of selfishness, but of generosity, when he declares: "The greatest thing in the world is to know how to belong to oneself."

Nowhere can be found nobler moral precepts than here. The passage beginning about "the beggar at my door" shows the dramatic philosophising which was one of Montaigne's most characteristic qualities. He was constantly essaying to put his mind into the mind of another, to *chausser son biais*, and evidently felt it to be a strengthening exercise.

The last two pages are a sort of *cento*, paraphrasing, more or less, passages from two or three of Seneca's letters, and phrases from Epicurus. Throughout the whole Essay are embedded thoughts to be found in Seneca's writings which, passing through Montaigne's mind, take his imprint, so that the analogous passages in Seneca can not be precisely referred to; but a reader familiar with the two writers recognises the strong resemblance.

1676

Of Solitude

B. THE NOTES BY MR. IVES

1. See Lucan, II, 383. Lucan is speaking of Cato of Utica.
2. *Qu'ils se battent la conscience.* "Analogue," Says M. Villey, "à 'se frappe la poitrine.' "
3. See Diogenes Laertius, *Life of Bias.*
4. *Ecclesiastes* (not *Ecclesiasticus*), VII, 28.
5. *Rari quippe boni: numero vix sunt totiden, quot Thebarum portæ, vel divitis ostia Nili.*
   —Juvenal, XIII, 26.

   Probably from Buchanan's *De Jure Regni Scotorum.*
6. *Toutes les deux sont dangereux; et de leur ressembler par ce qu'ils sont beaucoup, et d'en haïr beaucoup, par ce qu'ils sont dissemblables.* See Seneca, *Epistle* 7.8.
7. See Diogenes Laertius, *Life of Bias.*
8. Taken from Goulard's French translation of Bishop Osorio's *History of Portugal* (Latin).
9. See Seneca, *Epistle* 28.6, 7.
10. See Diodorus Siculus, XII, 4. M. Villey thinks it probable that Montaigne found this fact elsewhere than in Diodorus: *Les Sources et l'Évolution des Essais,*.I, 115.
11. See Diogenes Laertius, *Life of Antisthenes.*
12. *ratio et prudentia curas,*
    Non locus effusi late maris arbiter, aufert.
    —Horace, *Epistles,* I, 2.25.
13. *et*
    Post equitem sedet atra cura.
    —Idem, *Odes,* III, 1.40.
14. *Hæret lateri letalis arundo.*
    —Virgil, *Æneid,* IV, 73.

Notes and Comments

15. See Seneca, *Epistle* 104.7.
16.   *Quid terras alio calentes*
     Sole mutamus? patria quis exul
        Se quoque fugit?
                      —Horace, *Odes*, II, 16.18.
17. See Seneca, *Epistle* 28.3.
18. *Vous ensachez le mal.*
19. *En les branlant et secouant;* this curious statement was added in the edition of 1582.
20.   *Rupi jam vincula dicas:*
   Nam luctata canis nodum arripit; attamen illi,
   Cum fugit, a collo trahitur pars longa catenæ.
                     —Persius; *Satires*, V, 158.
21.   *Nisi purgatum est pectus, quæ prœlia nobis*
   Atque pericula tunc ingratis insinuandum?
   Quantæ conscindunt hominem cuppedinis acres
   Sollicitum curæ, quantique perinde timores?
   Quidve superbia, spurcitia, ac petulantia?
     quantas
   Efficiunt clades? quid luxus desidiæque?
                     —Lucretius, V, 43.
22. *In culpa est animus qui se non effugit unquam.*
                     —Horace, *Epistles*, I, 14.13.
Translated by Montaigne before quoting.
23. *Ainsin il la faut ramener et retirer en soi.* See Seneca, *De Tranquillitate Animi*, XIV, and *Epistle* 7.8.
24. See Idem, *Epistle* 9.18, and *De Constantia Sapientis*, V; Diogenes Laertius, *Life of Stilpo*.
25. See Idem, *Life of Antisthenes*.
26. See St. Augustine, *De Civ. Dei*, I, 10.
27. *Une arriere-boutique toute nostre, toute franche.*

Of Solitude

28. *In solis sis tibi turba locis.*—Tibullus, IV, 13.12.
29. See Diogenes Laertius, *Life of Antisthenes.*
30. *Tout pituiteux, chassieux et crasseux.*
31. *Nulles nouvelles.*
32. *Vah! quemquamne hominem in animum instituere, aut*
  Parare, quod sit charius quam ipse est sibi?
  —Terence, *Adelphi*, I, 1.13.
33. See Diogenes Laertius, *Life of Thales.*
34. *A nostre aise.*
35. *Prinses.*
36. See Seneca, *Epistle* 74.
37. *Rarum est enim ut satis se quisque vereatur.*—Quintilian, X, 7.24.
38. The source of this is unknown. A passage in Stobæus was cited first by Coste, later by Le Clerc; but M. Villey, in his Notes to the *Édition Municipale*, points out the unsatisfactoriness of this reference.
39. That is, in the faculty of grasping a new idea.
40. The allusion is to Democritus.
41. The allusion is to Crates.
42.   *Tuta et parvula laudo,*
  Cum res deficiunt, satis inter vilia fortis:
  Verum, ubi quid melius contingit et unctius, idem
  Hos sapere, et solos aio bene vivere, quorum
  Conspicitur nitidis fundata pecunia villis.
  —Horace, *Epistles*, I, 15.42.
43. See Seneca, *Epistle* 28.6.
44. See Diogenes Laertius, *Life of Arcesilaus.* The philosopher was generous with his "utensils" in that he used to

Notes and Comments

lend them to his friends; and when they were poor, he did not reclaim them. Cf. Seneca, *Epistle* 5.6.

45. *Je voy jusques à quels limites va la necessité naturelle.*
46. *J'essaye de chausser mon ame à son biaiz.*
47. This seems to connect with the passage on page 325, ending "glorious and worthy of imitation."
48.   *Conentur sibi res, non se submittere rebus.*
—Horace, *Epistles*, I, 1.19.
The original reads: *Et mihi res, non me rebus, subjungere conor.*
49. *La mesnagerie.*
50. See Sallust, *Catiline*, IV.
51. See Xenophon, *Œconomicus*, I, 20; Cicero, *De Senectute*, XVII.
52.   *Democriti pecus edit agellos*
    Cultaque, dum peregre est animus, sine
        corpore velox.—Horace, *Epistles*, I, 12.12.
53. *En cette pleine et grasse retrait.*
54. Pliny, *Epistles*, I, 3. The name of his correspondent was *Caninius* Rufus.
55. See Cicero, *Orator*, XLIII.
56.   *Usque adeo ne*
Scire tuum nihil est, nisi te scire hoc sciat alter?
—Persius, *Satires*, I, 23.
57. That is, the advice of Pliny to C. Rufus, to devote himself to the study of letters.
58. *Nous retombons toujours de fièvre en chaud mal*
59. *Le mesnagier.*
60. See Seneca, *Epistle* 51.13. Properly *Philetas*.
61.   *Unusquisque sua noverit ire via.*
—Propertius, II, 25.38.

1680

Of Solitude

62. *Au mesnage.*
63. *Consolent et conseillent.*
64. *Tacitum sylvas inter reptare salubres,*
 Curantem quidquid dignum sapiente bonoque
 est. —Horace, *Epistles*, I. 4.4.
65. *A tous nos dents et nos griffes.*
66. The edition of 1580 adds: *et les alonger de toute nostre puissance.*

67. *Quamcunque Deus tibi fortunaverit horam,*
 Grata sume manu, nec dulcia differ in annum.
 Carpamus dulcia; nostrum est
 Quod vivis: cinis et manes et fabula fies.
 —Persius, *Satires*, V, 151.

68. That is, the ambitious, in solitude.
69. *Tun, vetule, auriculis alienis colligis escas?*
 —*Ibid.*, I, 22.
70. Epicurus and Seneca.
71. See Seneca, *Epistle* 19.2.
72. See Idem, *Epistle* 22.9.
73. See Idem, *Epistle* 19.4.
74. *Science et suffisance.*
75. See Seneca, *Epistle* 7.9.
76. See Idem, *Epistle* 7.11.
77. See *Ibid.*
78. See Idem, *Epistle* 7.10.
79. See Idem, *Epistle* 68.
80. See *Ibid.*
81. See Idem, *Epistle* 25.5.
82. *Observentur species honestæ animo.*—Cicero, *Tusc. Disp.*, II, 22.
83. Pliny and Cicero.

CHAPTER XL

Reflection Concerning Cicero

A. THE COMMENT BY MISS NORTON

THE first sentence refers to the preceding Essay, in which he has compared the philosophy, the principles, of Cicero and Pliny (the Younger) with those of Seneca and Epicurus; and there is hardly more about Cicero in this present Essay than in the other. The first pages are taken up (more or less consecutively) with the thesis that it is not well for an eminent man to excel in matters which are not suitable to his position, and, as a corollary, that the perfection of writing well adds little to a man's greatness. That is, that the most beautiful style is of value only for what it expresses. What would modern writers say to this?

That this was Montaigne's sincere opinion is certain, but it is not lacking in dignity; and the remarks about the stories way he does not here note, by a singularly exquisite perception of the beauty of artistically used language. He says elsewhere (Book III, chapter 5): "When I behold those noble modes of expression, so vivid, so profound, I do not say this is speaking rightly, I say it is thinking rightly."

And it was because the thought seemed to him far more valuable than the expression, that he disliked (as he says in this Essay) to hear the language of his own Essays praised.

Reflection Concerning Cicero

(This is, of course, a passage inserted after the first edition.) The pleasant boast that follows, that no writer has filled his pages with solider or more abundant matter, is so true that it is not lacking in dignity; and the remarks about the stories and the quotations that he makes use of indicate how important it is for his reader to read *between the lines*. The reward is great for "those who may fall in with my way of thinking."

The last three pages of this Essay are one of the very interesting passages of self-*description*; and there is here one of the touching references to his dead friend La Boëtie, when he speaks of his lack of such companionship as he once had had, of intercourse which would lead him on, uphold him, and lift him up: *Le commerce qui m'attirast, me soustinst et souslevast.*

B. THE NOTES BY MR. IVES

1. That is, Pliny and Cicero on the one side, Seneca and Epicurus on the other.

2. See Cicero to Lucceius, *Epistulæ ad Familiares*, V, 12; Pliny to Tacitus, *Letters*, VII, 33.10.

3. *Pieça faict perdre ces histoires.*

4. Cf. Book II, chap. 18, at the beginning: *César et Xenophon ont eu dequoy fonder et fermir leur narration en la grandeur de leurs gestes comme en une baze massive et solide.*

5. See Prologue to *Adelphi* and *Heautontimoroumenos*.

6. See Plutarch, *Life of Pericles*.

7. *J'ay veu de mon temps, en plus fortes termes, des personnages qui tiroient d'escrire et leurs titres et leur vocation, desadvouer leur apprentissage, corrompre leur plume et affecter l'ignorance de qualité si vulgaire et que nostre peuple*

Notes and Comments

tient ne se rencontrer guere en mains sçavantes: se recommandans par meilleures qualitez.

8. See Plutarch, *Life of Demosthenes.*
9.   *Imperet bellante prior, jacentem*
          Lenis in hostem.
                —Horace, *Carmen Sæculare*, 51.
10.   *Orabunt causas alii, cœlique meatus*
    Describent radio, et fulgentia sidera dicent;
    Hic regere imperio populos sciat.
                —Virgil, *Æneid*, VI, 849.

In the original this is part of the address of Anchises to Æneas, and the last line reads:—
    Tu regere imperio populos, Romane, memento.

11. See Plutarch, *Life of Pericles.*
12. See Idem, *Apothegms of Kings*, etc., and *How to tell a flatterer from a friend.*
13. See Idem, *Apothegms of Kings*, etc.
14. See Idem, *Life of Pericles* (Preamble).
15. *Ce n'est pas tant eslever les mots, comme c'est deprimer le sens, d'autant plus piquamment que plus obliquement.*
16. *Non est ornamentum virile concinnitas.*—Seneca, *Epistle* 95.2.
17. *La vertu.*
18. Seneca and Epicurus. See Seneca, *Epistle* 21.3.
19. That is, the wise men.
20. That is, the writers.
21. See Book II, chap. 10, for a juster appreciation of Cicero's letters and his eloquence.
22. See Seneca, *Epistle* 52.14.
23. *Se donne corps elle mesme.*

Reflection Concerning Cicero

24. *Pour nous faire toucher au doigt son naturel.*
25. See Plutarch, *Apothegms of Kings*, etc.
26. Referring to La Boëtie.
27. *Car de negotier au vent.*
28. *Un stile comique et privé.*
29. *Presentations.*
30. *Faire sentire une plus expresse volonté et plus respectueuse (= respective).*
31. *J'honore le plus ceus que j'honore le moins:* that is, I do the least honour to those for whom I feel the most honour. This sentence of the *Édition Municipale* supplants this (omitted) of 1588: *ceux que j'ayme me mettent en peine, s'il faut que je le leur die.*
32. Translator of the *Æneid* (1507-1566).
33. *En brodure.*
34. On the title-page of the edition of 1580, the author's name is followed by the words: "Chevalier de l'Ordre du Roy, & Gentil-homme ordinaire de sa Chambre"; and in 1582 he added the further *titre*, "Maire & Gouverneur de Bourdeaus." But these were all omitted in 1588.

CHAPTER XLI

Of Not Giving Away One's Glory

A. THE COMMENT BY MISS NORTON

THE title of this Essay is not very lucid, and Florio was misled into translating it "That a man *should* not communicate his glory." What Montaigne had in mind was that a man *does* not often give freely to another the glory, the honour, which is due to himself. It may be said that there are not many men who have much "glory" to give away; and that more rarely still could they find any one to give it to. As Montaigne says: "All other things fall within the field of communication; we give our property and our lives to meet the needs of our friends; but to part with what does one honour and to bestow on another one's glory—that is seldom seen."

But that this has sometimes chanced to be done, Montaigne's stories give more or less proof. There are seven of them in two or three pages.

Number one is of a military officer throwing away his own reputation to cover the disgrace of his soldiers.

Number two, of an imperial councillor opposing his master's judgement, though it was his own also, in order that all the success of the event might be attributed to the emperor.

Number three, of the mother of a dead son declaring that

Of Not Giving Away One's Glory

his city possessed many citizens greater and more valiant than he.

Number four, of King Edward at the battle of Crécy, refusing to go to the assistance of the Black Prince.

Number five, of Lælius unselfishly promoting the greatness of Scipio.

Number six, of a king who said that things went well, not so much because he knew how to rule as because the people knew how to obey.

Number seven, of a bishop who chose to fight in battle, but not to obtain any fruit and glory from his fierce and bloody exertions, and therefore handed over all his prisoners to his friends.

One can trace the connection in Montaigne's mind of each one of these stories with his subject; but it may be observed that number six (of the popular king) is the only one that really fits.

B. THE NOTES BY MR. IVES

1. *La fama, ch'invaghisce a un dolce suono*
   Gli superbi mortali, e par si bella,
   E un echo, un sogno, anzi d'un sogno un ombra
   Ch'ad ogni vento si dilegua e sgombra.
   —Tasso, *Jerusalem Delivered*, XIV, 63.

2. *Quia etiam bene proficientes animos tentare non cessat.*—St. Augustine, *De Civ. Dei*, V, 14.

3. *Si intestine que vous avez peu que tenir à l'encontre.*

4. See Cicero, *Oratio pro Archia Poeta*, X.

5. See Plutarch, *Life of Marius*.

6. That is, the Emperor.

7. See *Mémoires* du Bellay, VI; Brantôme, *Vies des*

Notes and Comments

Hommes Illustres Etrangers; de Thou, *Histoire de France.*

8. See Plutarch, *Apothegms of the Lacedæmonians.*

9. See Froissart, I. In 1580 the Essay ended here.

10. *Semper enim quod postremum adjectum est, id rem totam videtur traxisse.*—Livy, XXVII, 45.

11. See Plutarch, *Political Precepts.*

12. *La chose publique demeuroit sur ses pieds.*

13. See Plutarch, *Ibid.*; and *Apothegms of the Lacedæmonians.*

14. See Jean du Tillet, *Receuil des Rois de France,* etc. (M. Villey, *Livres d'Histoire Moderne utilisés par Montaigne,* pp. 145-148.)

15. See Jean du Tillet, *Receuil des Rois de France.*

CHAPTER XLII

Of the Inequality between Us

A. THE COMMENT BY MISS NORTON

THE opening of this essay—the first few pages—is characteristically vigorous and characteristically derived from Seneca; then, characteristically again, it wanders off to the King of Thrace and Alexander the Great, between whose names occurs a noble passage on royalty.

Of the Inequality between Us

The rest of the Essay is chiefly occupied with considerations of the disadvantages of royalty. Princely advantages are, as it were, imaginary. King Henry's great speech ("Henry V," Act IV, scene 1) is a magnificent commentary on it. And Montaigne's later Essay "De l'incommodité de la grandeur" (Book III, chapter 7) continues the theme.

B. THE NOTES BY MR. IVES

1. See Plutarch, *That beasts make use of reason.*
2. *Il parle de la suffisance de l'ame et qualités internes.*
3.   *Hem vir viro quid præstat!*
                              —Terence, *Phormio*, III, 3.7.
4. *Et qu'il y a autant de degrez d'esprits qu'il y a d'ici au ciel de brasses, et autant innumerables.*
5. See Seneca, *Epistle* 16.
6.   *Volucrem*
Sic laudamus equum, facili cui plurima palma
Fervet, et exultat rauco victoria circo.
                      —Juvenal, *Satires*, VIII, 57.
7. See Seneca, *Epistle* 41.7.
8. *Un chat en poche.*
9. See Seneca, *Epistle* 80.
10.   *Regibus hic mos est: ubi equos mercantur,*
        opertos
Inspiciunt, ne, si facies, ut sæpe, decora
Molli fulta pede est, emptorem inducat hiantem,
Quod pulchræ clunes, breve quod caput, ardua
     cervix.   —Horace, *Satires*, I, 2.86.
11. See Seneca, *Epistle* 80.
12. See Idem, *Epistle* 92.
13. See Idem, *Epistle* 76.

Notes and Comments

14. See *Ibid.*
15. *La fortune n'y a elle que voir?*
16. See Seneca, *Epistle* 76.
17. *Sapiens, sibique imperiosus,*
    Quem neque pauperies, neque mors, neque
        vincula terrent,
    Responsare cupidinibus, contemnere honores
    Fortis; et in seipso totus, teres atque rotundus,
    Externi ne quid valeat per læve morari,
    In quem manca ruit semper fortuna?
        —Horace, *Satires*, II, 7.83.
18. *Sapiens, pol! ipse fingit fortunam sibi.*
        —Plautus, *Trinummus*, II, 2.84.
19. *Nonne videmus*
    Nil aliud sibi naturam latrare, nisi utqui
    Corpore sejunctus dolor absit, mentre fruatur,
    Jucundo sensu cura semota metuque?
        —Lucretius, II, 16.
20. In the early editions, including 1588, this catalogue of qualities reads: *ignorante, stupide et endormie, basse, servile, pleine de fiebvre et de frayeur, instable.*
21. *D'une plaisante maniere, et bien rencherie.*
22. See Herodotus, V, 7.
23. See Seneca, *Epistles* 76 and 80.
24. *Scilicet et grandes viridi cum luce smaragdi*
    Auro includuntur, teriturque thalassina vestis
    Assidue, et Veneris sudorem exercita potat.
        —Lucretius, IV, 1126.
25. *Ille beatus introrsum est. Istius bracteata felicitas est.*—Seneca, *Epistles* 119 and 115.
26. *Non enim gazæ neque consularis*

Of the Inequality between Us

Summovet lictor miseros tumultus
Mentis et curas laqueata circum
Tecta volantes.
—Horace, *Odes*, II, 16.9.

27. *Re veraque metus hominum, curæque sequaces,*
Nec metuunt sonitus armorum nec fera tela;
Audacterque inter reges rerumque potentes
Versantur, neque fulgorem reverentur ab auro.
—Lucretius, II, 48.

28. *Bonnettades.*

29. Cf. Seneca, *Epistle 17*.

30. *Nec calidæ citius decedunt corpore febres,*
Textilibus si in picturis ostroque rubenti
Jacteris, quam si in plebeia veste cubandum est.
—Lucretius, II, 34.

31. See Plutarch, *Apothegms of Kings*, etc., and *Life of Alexander*.

32. See Idem, *Apothegms of Kings*, etc., where the poet is called Hermodotus.

33. *C'est un homme pour tous potages.*

34. *Puellæ*
Hunc rapiant; quicquid calcaverit hic rosa fiat.
—Persius, *Satires*, II, 38.

35. *Hæc perinde sunt, ut illius animus qui ea possidet,*
Qui uti scit, ei bona; illi qui non utitur recte, mala.
—Terence, *Heautontimoroumenos*, I, 3.21.

36. *Non domus et fundus, non æris acervus et auri*
Ægroto domini deduxit corpore febres,
Non animo curas; valeat possessor oportet,

Notes and Comments

Qui comportatis rebus bene cogitat uti.
Qui cupit aut metuit, juvat illum sic domus aut res,
Ut lippum pictæ tabulæ, fomenta podagram.
—Horace, *Epistles*, I, 2.47.

37. See Plato, *Laws*, book II. This passage of the *Laws* is translated thus by Dr. Jowett: "I plainly declare that evils as they are termed are goods to the unjust, and only evils to the just; and that goods are truly good to the good, but evil to the evil."

38. *Passion de l'ame.*

39. *Totus et argento conflatus, totus et auro.*
—Tibullus, I, 2.70.
Montaigne substitutes *conflatus* for *contextus* of the original.

40. *Si ventri bene, si lateri est pedibusque tuis, nil*
Divitiæ poterunt regales addere majus.
—Horace, *Epistles*, I, 12.5.

41. See Plutarch, *Whether aged men should meddle in public affairs.*

42. *Ut satius multo jam sit parere quietum,*
Quam regere imperio res velle.
—Lucretius, V, 1129.

43. See Amyot's *Epistre au Roy* at the head of his translation of Plutarch's *Morals*.

44. See Xenophon, *Hiero*.

45. *Pinguis amor nimiumque potens in tædia nobis*
Vertitur, et stomacho dulcis ut esca nocet.
—Ovid, *Amores*, II, 19.25.

46. See Xenophon, *Hiero*.

47. *Plerumque gratæ principibus vices,*

Of the Inequality between Us

Mundæque parvo sub lare pauperum
Cænæ, sine aulæis et ostro,
Sollicitam explicuere frontem.
—Horace, *Odes*, III, 29.13.

48. See G. Postel, *Histoire des Turcs*.
49. See Chalcondylas, *Histoire de la Décadence de l'Empire Grec*, etc.
50. Princes.
51. *In civitate* (Ficino's Latin translation).
52. *Outre ce que les taches s'agrandissent selon l'eminence et clarté du lieu où elles sont assises.*
53. See Plutarch, *Political Precepts*.
54. See Xenophon, *Hiero*.
55. That is, our own princes.
56. The maréchal de Brissac, in 1534.
57. The maréchal de Montluc, in 1550.
58. *Roytelets*. As Cæsar says nothing like this of the Gauls, Coste, followed by later commentators, suggested that Montaigne, by a lapse of memory, refers here to what Cæsar says of the *Germans*, in *De Bello Gallico*, VI, 23.
59. *Paucos servitus, plures servitutem tenent.*—Seneca, *Epistle* 22.11.
60. *Maximum hoc regni bonum est,*
Quod facta domini cogitur populus sui
Quam ferre tam laudare.
—Seneca, *Thyestes*, II, 1.30.
61. See Ammianus Marcellinus, XXII, 10. It was the lawyers, not the courtiers, who praised him.
62. See Aurelius Victor, *Augustan History*. But M. Villey thinks it likely that Montaigne took this illustration from Crinitus, *Commentariorum de honesta disciplina*.

Notes and Comments

63. *Le rebut.* See Plutarch, *Banquet of the Seven Wise Men.*
64. See Plutarch, *Life of Pyrrhus.*
65. *Nimirum quia non bene norat quæ esset habendi Finis, et omnino quoad crescat vera voluptas.*
—Lucretius, V, 1432.
Lucretius is not speaking of Pyrrhus.
66. *Je m'en vais clorre ce pas:* a military expression.
67. *Mores cuique sui fingunt fortunam.*—Cornelius Nepos, *Life of Atticus,* II. Erasmus comments at length on this sentence in his *Adages,* II, 4.30.

CHAPTER XLIII

Of Sumptuary Laws

A. THE COMMENT BY MISS NORTON

MONTAIGNE judges the sumptuary laws of his day to be unwise; not that he would not have different degrees of rank distinguished,—"which in truth I consider to be most essential in a state,"—but that there are better ways "to regulate the foolish and idle expenses of the table and of apparel." He seems to think that the spring of reformation is in the "inclination" of the king; and he gives a

Of Sumptuary Laws

curious list of the follies that would immediately disappear if the court would frown on them.

The sentence beginning: "In all things, save only those that are evil, change is to be dreaded," is a literal translation from Plato *(Laws)* and the next is immediately derived from him. Compare Lord Bacon ("Of Innovations"): "New things piece not so well; but though they help by their utility, yet they trouble by their inconformity; besides, they are like strangers, more admired and less favoured."

M. Villey remarks: "To understand the opportuneness of this Essay, we must remember that in the sixteenth century, under the influence of Italy, luxury developed with extreme rapidity, fashions were transformed with exceptional promptitude, and incessantly kings intervened by laws and edicts to prevent the deplorable consequences of these excesses. It was thought of great importance to distinguish ranks by costumes and not to permit the common people to dress like the great. Fortunes were often lost in this fearful racing toward luxury, where each one strove to go beyond his neighbour. Public finances equally suffered; for, certainly at the beginning of the century, and in great part through the whole of it, silks and objects of personal adornment came from Italy, and thus every year important sums were drained out of the country. At last it was evident that this question interested the morality of the nation."

The first sumptuary law was enacted in 1518; followed by others in 1532, 1543, 1549, 1561, 1573, 1577, 1583.

B. THE NOTES BY MR. IVES

1. *La tresse d'or.*
2. *Vilité.*

1695

Notes and Comments

3. *Homme de ville* = *bourgeois;* in 1580, *homme de néant;* in 1588, *homme de peu.*
4. See Diodorus Siculus, XII, 20. The Essay ended here in 1580.
5. *Quidquid principes faciunt, præcipere videntur.*—Quintilian, *Declamations,* III.
6. *Garderobbe.*
7. That is, princes.
8. *Tercelets et quartelets de roys.*
9. *Vitieuses.*
10. See Plato, *Laws,* book VII.

CHAPTER XLIV

Of Sleep

A. THE COMMENT BY MISS NORTON

MONTAIGNE had been struck by the accounts in Plutarch's Lives of the profound sleep of some great men at the moment of their most important affairs; and evidently wondering at these stories, he simply brought them together here, with little comment.

Montaigne apparently had not happened to read Dr. Johnson's note on Miranda's sleep (in "The Tempest").

Of Sleep

He says: "I believe experience will prove that any violent agitation of the mind easily subsides in slumber." Nor had he had the pleasure of reading Voltaire, or he would certainly have added to his other stories what Voltaire tells concerning "le grand Condé." The duc d'Enghein (as he then was), following the example of Alexander, slept never more peacefully than on the night before the battle of Rocroy.

It has been noted that the modern hero was even more remarkable than the ancient, since Alexander—a trained warrior—was to meet an already twice-conquered enemy, while Condé, who had just been put at the head of the army, was going to his first battle with a formidable foe.

B. THE NOTES BY MR. IVES

1. See Seneca, *Epistle* 20.3.
2. See Plutarch, *Life of Alexander*.
3. See Idem, *Life of Otho*.
4. See Idem, *Life of Cato of Utica*.
5. *Escrimeurs à outrance = escrimeurs qui sont engagés à donner la vie pour leurs maîtres.*
6. See Plutarch, *Life of Cato of Utica*.
7. In the early editions, 1580-1588, this sentence was made to apply to Alexander and Otho, as well as to Cato: *de la grandeur de courage de ces trois hommes.*
8. See Suetonius, *Life of Augustus*.
9. See Plutarch, *Life of Sylla*.
10. See Plutarch, *Life of Paulus Æmilius*.
11. See Pliny, *Natural History*, VII, 51.
12. Herodotus (IV, 25) says that he does not believe what Montaigne states as a fact alleged by him.
13. See Diogenes Laertius, *Life of Epimenides*.

CHAPTER XLV

Of the Battle of Dreux

A. THE COMMENT BY MISS NORTON

THIS was the first battle of the civil wars. It was fought December 19, 1562, in the reign of Charles IX. The Reformers for a time believed themselves to have won the day: but the duc de Guise renewed the combat by bringing up troops from the rear, and after a bloody struggle the Protestant army was driven from the field. The prince de Condé was made prisoner and 8000 men lost their lives.

Montaigne here defends the duc de Guise against the accusation of having seen the constable de Montmorency and his troops in danger, and not having gone to their assistance. In his defence he cites ancient examples which he thinks *germein* to the case of monsieur de Guise.

B. THE NOTES BY MR. IVES

1. De Montmorency.
2. *Attendant l'avantage de la voir en queue.*
3. See Plutarch, *Life of Philopœmen.*
4. See Idem, *Life of Agesilaus.* It was the battle of Coroneia, 394 B.C.

CHAPTER XLVI

Of Names

A. THE COMMENT BY MISS NORTON

AS Montaigne himself says, it is *une galimafrée* that he sets before us here; but his art makes a mere salad as nutritious as it is palatable.

His first "article" is that some names are in ill-repute, and that others, in royal houses, seem in especial favour; and in this connection he gives an illustration of the extraordinary number of *Guillaumes*, among gentlemen, at the end of the twelfth century. Then he remarks that it is well, not only to have "bon nom," that is, "crédit et réputation," but also "un nom beau"—a name that can easily be pronounced and remembered. "Socrates thinks it a matter worthy a father's attention to give well-sounding names to his children." Next he tells a story about the naming of a chapel at Poitiers; and to this he adds (in 1595) a not very relevant story about the effect of music on the passions. Then comes an interesting passage of ironical comment on the follies in the matter of names of the "Reformed Church" in his own day, follies the like of which, in England, Scott has made familiar to us. Then he praises Jacques Amyot for not having *translated* the Latin names.

He goes on to speak with much good sense of the *vilain usage* of calling each one by the name of his estate and lord-

Notes and Comments

ship; but he gives no indication of being aware that his own forbears had placed his own family in just the situation he deplores. *La maison noble de Montaigne* was bought in 1477 by Ramon Eyquem, the great-grandfather of Michel Montaigne; and the title *de Montaigne* was first assumed by Michel's father; while Michel himself was the first to drop the name of Eyquem. (It has been a troublesome business to disentangle the family of Montaigne from the previous family who owned the chateau.) The considerations to which he is here led "draw me perforce," he says, "into another field"; and he bursts into an eloquent outcry at our folly in thinking that we can attach to ourselves the bubble reputation, which we go seeking even in the cannon's mouth. Eloquent it is, and poetical, but illogical enough, since it can make not the slightest difference to us whether we pass to posterity by one or another name, so long as we are rightly known by our own deeds.

But his thought, illogical or not, goes at last to the deepest of questions, and he asks (in 1595) what perception have the dead of the fame that lives after them, of the glory that keeps their memory green. "Dieu le sçait." For him, it was not true that

> major famæ sites est, quam Virtutis;—

but fame has, none the less, proclaimed his name.

B. THE NOTES BY MR. IVES

1. See Jean Bouchet, *Annales d'Aquitaine*.
2. *Par un froid rencontre.*
3. See Bouchet, *ubi supra*.
4. Brawn.

Of Names

5. Salt cod.
6. Porpoise.
7. See Ælius Spartianus (*Augustan History*, V), whose words are repeated almost literally by Crinitus, *De Honesta Disciplina*, whence Montaigne derived the example.
8. See Villey, *Les livres d'histoire moderne utilisés par Montaigne*. Montaigne apparently took this from Bouchet.
9. Presumably, his translation of Plutarch.
10. *Appanage.*
11. *Où autant de partages, autant de surnoms.*
12. His friend.
13. The last clause, beginning "and endows," is not found in the *Édition Municipale*, but was added in 1595.
14. *Pour tous potages.*
15. See Lucian, Δική Φονέντων (*The Judgement of the Vowels*).
16.   *Non levia aut ludicra petuntur*
      Præmia. —Virgil, *Æneid*, XII, 764.
17. *Faits.*
18. See Suetonius, *Life of Otho*.
19.   *Id cinerem et manes credis curare sepultos?*
                      —Virgil, *Æneid*, IV, 34.
20.   *Consiliis nostris laus est attonsa Laconum.*
—Cicero, *Tusc. Disp.*, V, 17; translated from the Greek. This is the first of four elegiac verses engraved on the base of the statue of Epaminondas at Thebes. See Pausanias, IX.
21.   *A sole exoriente supra Mætis paludes*
      Nemo est qui factis me æquiparare queat?
                      —Cicero, *Tusc. Disp.*, V, 17.
22. Cf. Book II, chap. 16, *infra: Il y a une famille à Paris et à Montpelier qui se surnomme Montaigne; une autre,*

Notes and Comments

en Bretaine et en Saintonge, de la Montaigne. Le remuement d'une seule syllable meslera nos fusées, de façon que j'auray part à leur gloire, et eux, à l'adventure, à ma honte.

23.   *ad hæc se*
Romanus, Graiusque, et Barbarus Induperator
Erexit, causas discriminis atque laboris
Inde habuit, tanto major famæ sitis est quam
Virtutis.   —Juvenal, X, 137.

CHAPTER XLVII

Of the Uncertainty of

Our Judgement

A. THE COMMENT BY MISS NORTON

THE promise of general interest which this title holds out is disappointed, for the uncertainty of judgement of which the Essay treats is that which is concerned with matters of war; and the chief interest of these pages now lies in the proofs they contain of how much of a soldier Montaigne was, and to how great a degree military affairs attracted his attention.

The various points of uncertainty of judgement he touches on here are:—

Of the uncertainty of our Judgement

1. Whether a conquered enemy should be pursued to extremity.
2. Whether soldiers should be richly armed.
3. Whether soldiers should be suffered to brave and insult the enemy.
4. Whether generals ought to disguise themselves before a battle.
5. Whether it is best to fall upon an enemy, or to wait for an attack.
6. Whether it is best for a prince to await his enemy in his own territory, or to go to attack him upon his territory.

All these questions are illustrated by instances from ancient and modern history, giving weight to decisions now on this side, now on that, regarding the same point.

B. THE NOTES BY MR. IVES

1.   Ἐπέων δὲ πολὺς νόμος ἔνθα καὶ ἔνθα.
—Homer, *Iliad*, XX, 249.
Montaigne translates the line after quoting it. It is one of the inscriptions on the walls of his library.

2.   *Vinse Hannibal, et non seppe usar' poi*
    Ben la vittoriosa sua ventura.
—Petrarch, *Sonnet* 82.

3. That is, to agree with Petrarch.
4. October 3, 1569.
5. August 10, 1557.
6.   *Dum fortuna calet, dum conficit omnia terror.*
—Lucan, VII, 734.

7. *Et lui chaussa bien autrement les esperons quand ce fut à son tour.* At Pharsalia. See Plutarch, *Life of Cæsar*, and *Life of Pompey*.

1703

Notes and Comments

8. Cf. Jean Bodin, *Les six livres de la République*, V, 5; Rabelais, I, 43; G. du Bellay, *Instructions sur le faict de la guerre*, II, 2.

9. April 11, 1512.

10. Or Cerisoles. A victory won by the French under François de Bourbon, comte d'Enghien, over the Spaniards under the marchese del Guasto, April 14, 1544.

11. *Gravissimi sunt morsus irritatæ necessitatis.*—Justus Lipsius, *Politics*, V, 18; after Porcius Latro.

12.   *Vincitur haud gratis jugulo qui provocat hostem.*
            —Lucan, IV, 275.

13. See Diodorus Siculus, XII, 25.

14. See Jean Bouchet, *Annales d'Aquitaine*.

15. See Plutarch, in the *Life* of each of these three.

16. See Suetonius, *Life of Cæsar*.

17. See Xenophon, *Cyropædeia*, IV, 3.

18. That is, if he be richly armed.

19. See Livy, IX, 40.

20. The Romans.

21. See Aulus Gellius, *Noctes Atticæ*, V, 5.

22. See Plutarch, *Apothegms of the Lacedæmonians*.

23. *Il leur remit par ce moyen le cœur au ventre.*

24. See Plutarch, *Life of Otho*.

25. That is, the device of disguising oneself.

26. *Mais aussi il en cuida encourir l'autre inconvenient.* See Plutarch, *Life of Pyrrhus*, where the name is to be found as Megacles.

27. See Idem, *Life of Alexander*.

28. See Idem, *Lives of Agis and Cleomenes*.

29. *Pied coy.*

30. See Plutarch, *Life of Pompey*. Plutarch puts the

Of the uncertainty of our Judgement

criticism in Cæsar's mouth. The "very words" are, of course, those of Amyot's translation of Plutarch.

31. *Voila ce qu'il dict pour ce rolle.*

32. *Qui est esbranlé.*

33. Cyrus and Artaxerxes, in 401 B.C. See Xenophon, *Anabasis*, I, 8.17, 19. Xenophon does not mention Clearchus.

34. *Tout bellement.*

35. *Pour leurs personnes, et pour leurs armes à trait.*

36. See Plutarch, *Conjugal Precepts*. Plutarch says, according to Amyot: *Si les ennemis leur venoient courir sus avec grands cris, qu'ils les receussent sans mot dire: et au contraire, s'ils venoient les assaillir en silence, qu'eulx courussent avec grands cris à l'encontre.* Either Montaigne's memory betrayed him, therefore, or he had some other authority in mind.

37. *Maison.*

38. *Que celuy qui met la nappe tombe toujours des despens.*

39. *Dans nos entrailles.*

40. *De donner loy au combat;* that is, to choose the moment for the battle to begin.

41. "See *Mémoirs* du Bellay, VI, 184, and especially G. Du Bellay, *Instructions sur le faict de la guerre*, II, 3, where the arguments on both sides are given at great length, and where the question is generalised as by Montaigne. See also a discussion of the same question in Bodin's *République*, V, 5, and especially Machiavelli's *Discourse on the First Decade of Livy*, where numerous arguments and examples from ancient times are set forth on both sides, many of which arguments and examples are found in Montaigne.

Notes and Comments

But du Bellay, unlike Montaigne, who reaches no conclusion, decides distinctly in favour of the offensive, while Machiavelli advises those who are well armed to await the enemy on their own soil, and those who are ill equipped to carry the war into their neighbour's territory."—Note of M. Villey in *Édition Municipale*.

    42. See Plutarch, *Life of Scipio;* Livy, XXIX, 24-35. It was in the Second Punic War.

    43. See Plutarch, *Life of Hannibal;* Livy, XXX, 19-35.

    44.   *Et male consultis pretium est; prudentia fallax;*
Nec fortuna probat causas sequiturque merentes;
Sed vaga per cunctos nullo discrimine fertur.
Scilicet est aliud quod nos cogatque regatque
Majus, et in proprias ducat mortalia leges.
                                    —Manilius, IV, 95.

    45. See Plato, *Timæus*.

CHAPTER XLVIII

Of Steeds

A. THE COMMENT BY MISS NORTON

THIS is again an Essay more or less about warfare; but it has a more personal note of interest than the last: for Montaigne was himself never so content as when on horseback—"It is the place in which I find myself best off, wheth-

Of Steeds

er well or sick." And naturally he cared for all kinds of horses, even *destriers*, of which name the Essay opens by offering an explanation. Then it speaks of the horses (and their names) that were anciently so trained that the rider could change from one to another while in motion. And then Montaigne refers to what appears to have been the training of horses in his own day," to succor their masters," and gives two illustrations of the same sort of training, one from ancient and one from modern history. Thence he passes to the training of the horses of the Mamelukes.

Next, he speaks of the excellence of the horsemanship of Cæsar and of Pompey; and of the horses of Cæsar and Alexander, a passage which in 1588 followed (more naturally) the "Roman nobles." Then of his own love of riding and its healthfulness. Then of the Parthian habit of being constantly on horseback. Then of cavalry being dismounted by their officers to prevent their running (or rather riding) away; and of the Romans always taking possession of the horses as well as the arms of the peoples they conquered; adding a curious fact, that at that day no Christian or Jew in Turkey was allowed to own a horse.

These last matters were inserted in 1595; originally the line of thought ran on naturally from the fact of the Roman captains dismounting their soldiers to the fact of the French, during the English wars, finding it to their advantage to fight on foot. Thence he passes to the consideration of the best kind of arms, and has no good word to say for firearms: of pistols, "I hope we shall some day give up the use." He prefers the ancient *phalarica*, which he describes with other inventions, whereby the Italians of old supplied the want of powder and shot.

Notes and Comments

All this learning, and more, belongs to 1595. In 1588 he was thinking rather of Maistre Pierre Pol—why and wherefore does not very clearly appear; apparently only because he had been reading Monstrelet, and was going to quote him on the subject (to which he here recurs) of the training of horses. He quotes Cæsar, too, and cites the Massilians, who rode without saddle or bridle, which Montaigne says that he had, with wonder, seen done. Then he quotes the letters of Guevara, with a fine slash of criticism at them; and then *The Courtier*, which we may believe he had liked better. All these quotations are about riding on mules, which, he adds, the Abyssinians think dignified—the Abyssinians whose prince is "le Prettejan," or, as we know him in English, Prester John. Then we are told about the horses of the Assyrians and the horses of Cyrus, and how the Scythians and the Turks, the Muscovites and the Tartars, drank their horses' blood, and the Cretans their urine.

There follows a paragraph on the subject, always interesting to Montaigne (and to us), about "these newly discovered people of the Indies" and how they believed the horses of the Spaniards, as well as their masters, to be superior beings. Then he passes over to the East Indies and elephant- and camel- and ox-riding, and quotes "some one in our time." (How many books he read!) And then—oh, why!—Quintus Fabius Maximus Rutilianus comes plunging in, fighting against the Samnites!

Then comes "le duc de Muscovie" paying reverence to the Tartars: and the Emperor Bajazet escaping from Tamburlane, and Crœsus meeting serpents; and we have a perfectly "displaced" sentence about "un cheval entier" and the Lacedæmonians clipping the horses they led in triumph,

Of Steeds

followed by another sentence about Alexander.

By this time we have lost all thread of continuous interest, and we accept with what gratitude we can a page of mere entertainment about monsieur de Carnavalet, and a man at Constantinople, and the Prince of Sulmone at Naples, and feats of circus-riding.

B. THE NOTES BY MR. IVES

1. *Des Destries*, usually assumed to be a misprint for *Destriers*.
2. Cf. Book I, chap. 26, p. 227.
3. See Suetonius, *Life of Tiberius*.
4. *A destre*.
5. *Quibus, desultorum in modum, binos trahentibus equos, inter acerrimam sæpe pugnam, in recentem equum ex fesso armatis transsultare mos erat; tanta velocitas ipsis, tamque docile equorum genus.*—Livy, XXIII, 29.5.
6. *Coustillier*.
7. *Accueilli*.
8. That is, Onesilus. See Herodotus, V, 111, 112.
9. Charles VIII of France.
10. The king. See Paulus Jovius, *History of his Time;* Comines, VIII, 6.
11. See Paulus Jovius, *ubi supra*. In this passage about the Mamelukes the translation follows the text of 1595, the Bordeaux copy of 1588 being imperfect, owing to the fact that part of the sentence was cut off in rebinding.
12. See Plutarch, *Life of Pompey*.
13. See Idem, *Life of Cæsar*. Montaigne may have taken this from Beroald's Commentary on Suetonius's *Life of Cæsar*.

Notes and Comments

14. See Aulus Gellius, V, 2.
15. See Suetonius, *Life of Cæsar*, and Beroald's Commentary.
16. In the *Laws*.
17. See Pliny, *Natural History*, XXVIII, 14. This, too, Montaigne probably took from Beroald's Commentary.
18. In 1580-1588: *loy de Cyrus*.
19. See Xenophon, *Cyropædeia*, IV, 3.22. Probably taken from Beroald's Commentary.
20. *Se promener.*
21. See Justinus, XLI, 2. Probably taken from Beroald's Commentary.
22. See Suetonius, *Life of Cæsar*.
23. *Quo haud dubie superat Romanus.*—Livy, IX, 22.
24. The Romans.
25. *Arma proferri, jumenta produci, obsides dari jubet.* —Cæsar, *De Bello Gallico*, VII, 11.2, and *passim*.
26. *Le Grand Seigneur.*
27. See Xenophon, *Cyropædeia*, IV, 3.15-21.
28. That is, those fought on foot.
29. *Cedebant pariter, pariterque ruebant Victores victique, neque his fuga nota neque illis.* —Virgil, *Æneid*, X, 756.
30. *Primus clamor atque impetus rem decernit.*—Livy, XXV, 41.6.
31. *Et quo ferre velint permittere vulnera ventis: Ensis habet vires, et gens quæcunque virorum est, Bella gerit gladiis.* —Lucan, VIII, 384.
32. The pistol. "The essay which Montaigne announces here, and which he actually wrote, has not come down to

Of Steeds

us: it was stolen from him by a secretary. Cf. Book II, chaps. 9 and 37 (near the beginning)."—M. Villey.

33. That is, the Romans.

34. *Magnum stridens contorta phalarica venit,*
Fulminis acta modo. —Virgil, Æneid, IX, 705.

35. *Saxis globosis funda mare apertum incessentes, coronas modici circuli, magno ex intervallo loci, assueti trajicere: non capita modo hostium vulnerabant, sed quem locum destinassent.*—Livy, XXXVIII, 29.4 and 7.

36. *Ad ictus mœnium cum terribili sonitu editos, pavor et trepidatio cepit.*—Livy, XXXVIII, 5.

37. *Non tam patentibus plagis moventur, ubi latior quam altior plaga est, etiam gloriosus se pugnare putant; idem, cum aculeus sagittæ aut glandis abditæ introrsus tenui vulnere in speciem urit, tum, in rabiem et pudorem tam parvæ perimentis pestis versi, prosternunt corpora humi.*—Ibid., 21.

38. See Xenophon, *Anabasis*, IV, 2.28.

39. See Diodorus Siculus, XIV, 12.

40. See Enguerrand Monstrelet, *Chroniques*, I, 46.

41. *Ibid.*, I, 56. The editions of 1580-1588 add at this point: *Je ne sçay quel maniement ce pouvoit estre, si ce n'est celuy de nos passades.*

42. *Selles et bardelles.*

43. See Cæsar, *De Bello Gallico*, IV, 1.

44. *Et gens quæ nudo residens Massilia dorso,*
Ora levi flectit frænorum nescia, virga.
—Lucan, IV, 682.

45. *Et Numidæ infræni cingunt.*
—Virgil, Æneid, IV, 41.

Notes and Comments

46. *Equi sine frenis, deformis ipse cursus, rigida cervice et extento capite currentium.*—Livy, XXXV, 11.

47. Alphonso XI of Leon and Castile. See Antoine de Guevara, *Epîtres Dorées*.

48. The Essay ended here in 1580.

49. By Baldasarre Castiglione; book II, chap. 3.

50. "Paulus Jovius, in the *History of his Time* (XVIII), has something to say of the mules of the Abyssinians, but I have found no source for Montaigne's exact statement."—M. Villey.

51. See Xenophon, *Cyropædeia*, III, 3.26, 27.

52. *Mettoit les chevaux de son escot.*

53. See *Ibid.*, VIII, 1.38.

54.   *Venit et epoto Sarmata pastus equo.*
       —Martial, *Liber Spectaculorum*, III, 4.

55. See Valerius Maximus, VII, 6, *ext.* 1.

56. See Paulus Jovius, *Ordo ac Disciplina Turcicæ Militiæ.*

57. See Lopez de Gomara, *History of Fernando Cortez.*

58. *Aux Indes de decà.*

59. See Arrian, *Anabasis of Alexander the Great.*

60. Rullianus.

61. See Livy, VIII, 30.

62. *Id cum majore vi equorum facietis, si effrenatos in hostes equos immittitis; quod sæpe romanos equites cum laude fecisse sua, memoriæ proditum est. Detractisque frenis, bis ultro citroque cum magna strage hostium, infractis omnibus hastis, transcurrerunt.*—Idem, XL., 40.5-7. The first two sentences are from an address of Flaccus to his troops. The last describes their obedience.

63. *Cette reverence.*

64. See H. de Fulstin, *Histoire des Rois de Pologne.*
65. See H. de Fulstin, *ubi supra.*
66. See Chalcondylas, *History of the Decline of the Greek Empire*, III, 12.
67. See Herodotus, I, 78.
68. *Nous appellons un cheval entier.*
69. See Plutarch, *Life of Nicias.*
70. See Quintus Curtius, VII, 7.32.
71. *A mener un cheval à raison.*
72. See G. Lebelski, *Description of the games and magnificent spectacles at Constantinople on the occasion of the circumcision of the son of Amurath.* In Latin; French translation published in 1583.
73. A Spanish sixpence.

CHAPTER XLIX

Of Ancient Customs

A. THE COMMENT BY MISS NORTON

"I PROPOSE to put together here some ancient customs which I remember, some like our own and others different, to the end that, having in our minds this continual variation of human things, we may have a more enlightened and stable judgement concerning them."

Notes and Comments

Thus Montaigne describes the subject and object of this Essay. In execution the subject does not prove particularly interesting, nor the object very vigorously or effectively enforced. As with most of these pseudo-historical studies of Montaigne's, the facts are too disconnected, too little strung on thought; they gain no value by being brought together.

There is much animated good sense in his remarks: as when, in his opening paragraph, he ridicules his countrymen for the changeableness of their fancies in the fashions of dress. The customs he speaks of are, first, the habit of the Romans, which still existed in his day in France, of fighting with the sword while wrapped in a short cloak; and the also still existent old-time French custom of stopping passers-by; the ancient custom of bathing, in connection with which he speaks of the then prevailing fashion among French women of having the hair of the forehead plucked out. He speaks of the ancient custom of eating in a recumbent position, of the custom of kissing one's own hands as a sign of respect, and of the habit of the Venetians of kissing one another on meeting. Elsewhere (Book III, chapter 5) Montaigne says that "the form of salutation which is peculiar to our nation changes by its facility the quality of the charm of kisses"—which, taken with this passage, would seem to imply that in France at that time the kiss of salutation passed between men and women but not between men. He is interested in the custom of the ancients of cooling their wine with snow, and of having their meats served on chafing-dishes; and about "portable kitchens," such as he had himself seen.

He discourses of the fish-pools of the ancients; and as-

Of Ancient Customs

serts that modern men are not capable of rivalling those of old in luxury and magnificence any more than in their virtues—"souls, in proportion as they are less strong, have less means to do either very well or very ill." Then he remarks on the most honourable place at table among the Romans being the middle; and of their paying no attention to whether they named themselves before or after those to whom they spoke or wrote. Then he goes back to their baths, and says that men and women were there together. Then he gives a jump and lands among the ancient Gauls, whose mode of wearing their hair was of the "fashion that has been revived by the effeminate and foolish usage of this age," that is, long in front and short behind. Back to the Romans again, and how they paid their watermen on embarking, "which we do after we have reached the landing." Then the manner in which they lay in the bed, and the manner in which they drank; and how their lackeys looked; and how the ladies of Argos and Rome wore white for mourning, "as ours were wont to do, and as they should continue to do, if my advice were followed."

B. THE NOTES BY MR. IVES

1. Cf. chap. 31, page 271: *Je ne scay, dit-il* [Pyrrhus], *quels barbares sont ceux-cy (car les Grecs appelloyent toutes les nations estrangeres barbares), mais la disposition de cette armée que je voy n'est aucunement barbare.*
2. *Sinistras sagis involvunt, gladiosque distringunt.*—Cæsar, *De Bello Civili*, I, 75.
3. See Cæsar, *De Bello Gallico*, IV, 5.2.
4. See Seneca, *Epistle* 86.
5. See *Ibid*.

Notes and Comments

6. *Quod pectus, quod crura tibi, quod brachia vellis.* —Martial, II, 62.1.

7. *Psilotro nitet, aut arcida latet oblita creta.* —Idem, VI, 93.9.

8. See Seneca, *Epistle* 108.23.

9. *Inde thoro pater Æneas sic orsus ab alto.* —Virgil, *Æneid*, II, 2.

10. See Plutarch, *Life of Cato of Utica*.

11. *Gratatusque darem cum dulcibus oscula verbis.* —Ovid, *De Ponto*, IV, 9.13.

12. *At tibi nil faciam, sed lota mentula lana.* —Martial, II, 58.11.

13. *Pusi sæpe lacum propter si ac dolia curta Somno devincti credunt se extollere vestem.* —Lucretius, IV, 1026.

14. See Seneca, *Epistle* 78.23.

15. *Has vobis epulas habete lauti; Nos offendimur ambulante cœna.* —Martial, VII, 48.4.

16. *Le haut bout d'entre eux, c'estoit le milieu.*

17. See Plutarch, *Life of Flaminius*. Amyot's words are: *De maniere que es chansons que les Poëtes en feirent, et que le meme peuple chantoit par les villes à la louange de ce faict d'armes, on mettoit tousjours les Ætoliens devant les Romains.*

18. *Inguina succinctus nigra tibi servus aluta Stat, quoties calidis nuda foveris aquis.* —Martial, VII, 35.2.

19. See Sidonius Apollinaris, V, 239.

20. *Dum as exigitur, dum mula ligatur, Tota abit hora.* —Horace, *Satires*, I, 5.13.

Of Democritus and Heraclitus

21. The alcove-side of King Nicomedes.—Suetonius, *Life of Cæsar*.
22. That is to say, they put water in it.
23.   *Quis puer ocius*
Restinguet ardentis falerni
Pocula prætereunte lympha?
—Horace, *Odes*, II, 11.18.
24. *Et ces champisses contenances de nos laquais.*
25.   *O Jane, a tergo quem nulla ciconia pinsit,*
Nec manus auriculas, imitata est mobilis albas,
Nec linguæ quantum sitiet canis Apula tantum!
—Persius, *Satires*, I, 58.
26. See Plutarch, *Roman Questions*, XXVI.

CHAPTER L

Of Democritus and Heraclitus

A. THE COMMENT BY MISS NORTON

THE Essay opens with a recognition of the universal usefulness of the judgement, and Montaigne says that in the essays—the tests—he here makes of it (he does not allude to his writings in the modern sense of essays) he avails himself of every opportunity; and he goes on to describe the assistance it gives him; and, still further, his

Notes and Comments

manner of composing, and the advantages of it to a man of not more assured and powerful mind than himself.

But his avoidance of going to the bottom of things does not (he implies) conceal from the reader the manner of man he is; "every motion reveals us"; and in fact, perhaps, the soul is best seen "when she is jogging quietly along."

In its higher planes of existence it is more carried on the winds of passions, and is more engrossed by each separate thing to which it gives itself. This train of thought leads to a passage—"Things by themselves . . ." etc.—where the extreme use of figures (not at all common with Montaigne) makes the understanding somewhat difficult.

(When I say this style is not frequent with Montaigne, I mean the extreme and confusing use of figurative language. Never was there a writer who made such incessant and illuminating use of figurative expressions of a kind that interpret themselves with the utmost plainness. It is what gives his style its constant beauty of *colour*.)

Returning from this thought, that it is our opinion of a thing and not the thing itself which affects us (one of the dominant doctrines of the Stoic philosophy), Montaigne recurs to the thought that every chord of our mind may be touched and sounded by commonplace conditions, bringing forward in illustration the game of chess—"that foolish and puerile game," as he thinks it: "I dislike it and shun it because it is not play enough." And he again insists that "every occupation of a man betrays and reveals him equally with any other."

Originally Democritus and Heraclitus came on the stage before now: this long philosophy was inserted in 1595; but it is of little consequence when they appear, as

Of Democritus and Heraclitus

they have but small parts to play. They are introduced only as figure-heads of two different ways of judging of this poor human creature who cannot disguise himself and whose state may be considered either as ridiculous or sorrowful.

B. THE NOTES BY MR. IVES

1. That is, of the action of the judgement.
2. The judgement.
3. *A effleurer.*
4. The edition of 1595 adds: *et me trompois en mon impuissance.*
5. This whole passage is so perplexing that it is given at length, that readers may interpret it for themselves. *La santé, la conscience, l'autorité, la science, la richesse, la beauté, et leurs contraires se despouillent à l'entrée, et recoivent de l'ame nouvelle vesture, et de la teinture qu'il luy plait: brune, verte, claire, obscure, aigre, douce, profonde, superficielle, et qu'il plait à chacune d'elles; car elles n'ont pas verifié en commun leurs stile, regles, et formes; chacune est reine en son estat.*
6. Than in playing chess. *Je ne me vois et retaste plus universellement en nulle autre posture.*
7. *Alter Ridebat, quoties a limine moverat unum Protuleratque pedem; flebat contrarius alter.*
   —Juvenal, *Satires*, X, 28.
8. See Plutarch, *Life of Alexander;* Cicero, *Tusc. Disp.*
9. See Plutarch, *Life of Brutus.*
10. See Diogenes Laertius, *Life of Aristippus.*
11. See *Ibid.*

CHAPTER LI

Of the Vanity of Words

A. THE COMMENT BY MISS NORTON

It is easy to understand that Montaigne would have no respect for "the art of rhetoric"; for the tongue that could "make the worse appear the better reason"; for the eloquence "that makes it its business to deceive . . . our judgement and to debase and corrupt the essence of things." He says that Socrates and Plato defined it as the "art of deceiving and flattering." But he might have remembered that Diogenes Laertius (whom he quotes so often) said that Socrates himself (forerunning Milton's Satan) was ridiculed by Aristophanes "as making the worse appear the better reason." Montaigne thinks that eloquence flourishes less in a monarchical government than under other forms of administration, for one well-educated man (as a prince may be supposed to be) is less under the influence of its poison than the ignorant commonalty. There was never any orator of renown known to come from Macedonia or Persia.

All this philosophy about "la vanité des paroles" was suggested to Montaigne, he says, by a talk he had just been having with an Italian he had taken into his service, the former maître d'hôtel of a cardinal, whose elaborate dis-

Of the Vanity of Words

course about his office and "the science of the gullet" seemed highly ridiculous to Montaigne. And not less so seemed to him the big words of architects (or mere house-builders), pilasters, architraves, Corinthian and Doric style, and the like, when they were only busy about a kitchen door. And all the strange names used by grammarians—metonomy and metaphor—are rather absurd when they concern the chatter of a chambermaid.

But of far more importance than these trivial *piperies* is the custom of calling State officers by titles too big for their duties and powers; and worse still the unworthy bestowal of such a surname as "Divine" on such a man as Aretino—"which in my opinion will be matter of reproach some day to our age."

        B. THE NOTES BY MR. IVES

1. See Plutarch, *Apothegms of the Lacedæmonians*.
2. See Plutarch, *Life of Pericles*.
3. The rhetoricians.
4. See Quintilian, II, 15.
5. See *Ibid.*, II, 16; Plato, *Gorgias, passim*.
6. See G. Postel, *Histoire des Turcs*.
7. See Quintilian, II, 16.
8. *Où tous ont tout peu* [*pu*].
9. See Livy, X, 22.
10. That with which the Essay opens.
11.   *Nec minimo sane discrimine refert Quo gestu lepores, et quo gallina secetur.*
          —Juvenal, *Satires*, V, 123.
12.   *Hoc salsum est, hoc adustum est, hoc lautum est parum,*

Notes and Comments

Illud recte; iterum sic memento; sedulo
Moneo quæ possum pro mea sapientia.
Postremo, tanquam in speculum, in patinas,
  Demea,
Inspicere jubeo, et moneo quid facto usus sit.
  —Terence, *Adelphi*, III, 3.71.

13. See Plutarch, *Life of Paulus Æmilius*.
14. In *Amadis de Gaule*.
15. *Pellegrin* = *pelerin*.

CHAPTER LII

Of the Parsimony of the Ancients

A. THE COMMENT BY MISS NORTON

THIS is merely a record of the parsimony—or carefulness about expenses—of Regulus and of Cato, of Scipio, Homer, Zeno, and Tiberius Gracchus.

B. THE NOTES BY MR. IVES

1. *Valet de labourage.*
2. See Valerius Maximus, IV, 4.6.
3. See Plutarch, *Life of Cato the Censor*.
4. See Valerius Maximus, IV, 3.13.
5. See Seneca, *Consolatio ad Albinam*, XII.
6. See Plutarch, *Life of Tiberius Gracchus*.

CHAPTER LIII

On a Saying of Caesar's

A. THE COMMENT BY MISS NORTON

THIS *mot de César*, from the "De Bello Civili," is the last sentence of the Essay, and was translated by Montaigne himself (in the early editions): "It happens by a common natural weakness that we both trust more, and fear more, things that we have not seen and that are hidden and unknown." The thoughts with which Montaigne leads up to this do not concern themselves so much with the subject of the saying, as with the point that man's imperfection is demonstrated by the inconstancy of his desires. Even the philosophers have never been able to discover the sovereign good of man.

B. THE NOTES BY MR. IVES

1. *Dum abest quod avemus, id exsuperare videtur*
   Cætera; post aliud, cum contigit illud, avemus
   Et sitis æqua tenet. —Lucretius, III, 1082.
2. *Nam, cum vidit hic, ad usum quæ flagitat usus.*
   Omnia jam ferme mortalibus esse parata,
   Divitiis homines et honore et laude potentis
   Affluere atque bona natorum excellere fama,
   Nec minus esse domi cuiquam tamen anxia
   corda,
   Atque animum infestis cogi servire querelis:

Notes and Comments

*Intellexit ibi vitium vas efficere ipsum,
Omniaque illius vitio corrumpier intus,
Quæ collata foris et commoda quæque venirent.*
—Lucretius, VI, 9, 10, 12-14, 16-19.
This text differs slightly from the modern text, as does also that of Lambin (Paris, 1563), the edition Montaigne used.

3. *Communi fit vitio naturæ et invisis, latitanibus atque incognitis rebus magis confidamus, vehementiusque exterreamur.*—Cæsar, *De Bello Civili*, II, 4. In all the editions from 1580 to 1588, the essay closed with the following translation of the passage quoted: *Il se fait, par un vice ordinaire de nature, que nous ayons et plus de fiance et plus de crainte des choses que nous n'avons pas veu, et qui sont cachées et inconnues.*

CHAPTER LIV

Of Trivial Minutiae

A. THE COMMENT BY MISS NORTON

AFTER all the dry little morsels—*leçons* (in the old sense of the word) rather than "essays"—we have been munching, we come to a bit with more flavour, a more juicy slice. The pleasantness of this Essay is in the personal touch,—in seeing Montaigne playing games with his family,—in that, and in one other passage that I shall speak of directly. I am inclined to believe that the title of the Es-

Of Trivial Minutiae

say and its first page were merely intended to give,—in a certain inverted, reverted fashion,—by the contempt thrown on trifles, a certain dignity or decorum to the trivial amusement "we" had just been indulging in *chez moy*. The game was, who could think of the greatest number of things, called by the same name, that were unlike each other and at the two extremes.

He passes on, evidently, from what they could have said in a game, to what the game had made him think of, and he goes deeper and deeper in thoughts that became later a "Pensée" of Pascal. But what is of most interest is the passage where, after praising the "simple peasants" as few men of his age would have thought of doing, but as he does over and over again, he goes on to praise "the poetry of the people." It was the first time that the phrase had been heard; and his appreciation of this form of poetry is a delightful expression of the freedom and delicacy of his own poetic perceptions.

B. THE NOTES BY MR. IVES

1. See Plutarch, *Table Gossip:* "Xenocrates says that the number of *syllables* made by the letters combined and mingled together amounts to one hundred million, two hundred thousand."
2. See Quintilian, II, 20.
3. See Plutarch, *The Opinions of Philosophers*.
4. *Ardeur de courage.*
5. "Montaigne certainly alludes to Garcia V, called 'Le Trembleur,' the twelfth King of Navarre, son of Sancho Garcia. He reigned near the close of the tenth century."—M. Villey.

Notes and Comments

6. *Elle s'en transiroit tout à plat.*
7. See Aristotle, *De Auscultationibus Mirabilibus.* Montaigne interprets the text inaccurately.
8. *La bestise et la sagesse se rencontrent en mesme point de sentiment et de resolution à la souffrance des accidens humains.*
9. The wise.
10. *Doctorale.*
11. *Parfaicte selon l'art.*
12. *Esprits communs et vulgaires, ny guiere aux singuliers et excellens.* In 1580 the last clause reads *esprits grossiers et ignorans, ny guiere aux delicats et savans.* And this sentence is added: *Ils trouveroint place entre ces deux extremités.*

CHAPTER LV

Of Odours

A. THE COMMENT BY MISS NORTON

THE title does not seem to promise much of interest, but interest is awakened by one of the first sentences; for it has the personal expression that is the charm of the Essays. "The most exquisite odour for a woman is to have no odour," Montaigne remarked in 1580, when all the poets around him were singing in rapturous phrases the

Of Odours

odorous breath of woman. Listen to Ronsard describing "les beautés qu'il voudrait en s'amie."

> La dens d'ivoire, odorante l'haleine
> A qui s'egalerait à peine
>   Les doux parfums de la Sabée
>   Ou toute l'odeur dérobée
> Que l'Arabie heureusement amène.

This was the fashion of the day. Montaigne, with the ancients, was of another mind. The remark that follows has the same flavour of old-time opinions; and it is worth observing that Montaigne suppressed it in his later editions; but there are yet some hearts that welcome it.

This Essay in the first edition consisted only of this one paragraph. It ended with "Posthume, non bene olet, qui bene semper olet" (Martial); in the next important edition (1588) Montaigne added another page or two, of which one paragraph is interesting from its theory of the use of incense, and another from its account of the luxurious possibilities and practices of the day.

B. THE NOTES BY MR. IVES

1. See Plutarch, *Life of Alexander.*
2.   *Mulier tum bene olet, ubi nihil olet.*
                       —Plautus, *Mostellaria*, I, 3.117.
3. The last clause was omitted in 1595.
4.   *Rides nos, Coracine, nil olentes;*
    Malo quam bene olere, nil olere.
                        —Martial, VI, 55.4.
5.   *Posthume, non bene olet, qui bene semper olet.*
                        —Martial, II, 12.4.

Notes and Comments

6. *A estre entretenu.*
7.   *Namque sagacius unus odoror,*
Polypus, an gravis hirsutis cubet hircus in alis,
Quam canis acer ubi lateat sus.
—Horace, *Epodes*, XII, 4.
8. See Herodotus, IV, 75.
9. See Diogenes Laertius, *Life of Socrates.*
10. *Avoir eu ma part de l'art.*
11. See Paulus Jovius. *History of his Time.* The king was Muley Hassan.

CHAPTER LVI

Of Prayers

A. THE COMMENT BY MISS NORTON

THIS Essay originally (in 1580) began with the sentence, "I know not whether I am mistaken." In 1582 the first lines were added, with the exception of the sentence concerning "l'Eglise catholique, apostolique et romaine," which was added in 1595. M. Villey observes: "This declaration, which appeared for the first time in the edition of 1582, was unquestionably induced by the warning given Montaigne by the *maestro del sacre palazzo*, of which Montaigne speaks in his *Journal de Voyage.*" He there says (18th March, 1580): "To-day in the evening, my Es-

Of Prayers

says were returned to me corrected in accordance with the judgement of the Docteurs Moines. The Maestro del sacre palazzo had been able to judge of them only by the report of some French Frater, he [*i. e.*, the Maestro] not at all understanding our language; he was entirely satisfied by the explanations I gave of each article that had been censured."

This is one of the Essays that Montaigne most added to, particularly in the editions during his own life. Long passages were added everywhere; an especially long one, from "Nor surely is it right to see the holy book . . . tossed about," to "would force me, perhaps, to be silent" (pages 27-31); which again was increased by a long addition in 1595. In 1580 the Essay was about a third only of its present length: in 1588 nearly two thirds.

It is an Essay not remarkable in thought or expression, but of great personal interest as showing (to my mind) the entire simplicity and sincerity of Montaigne's feeling about matters of religion. He writes as a respectful and obedient son of the Church, on a matter which lies not outside, but, one may say, *beneath*, the prescriptions of the Church,— a matter intimately concerning every human soul,—the meaning and use of Prayer. He first expresses the strength of his sentiment about the Lord's Prayer, and then his conviction that we should not invoke God's aid "without considering whether the occasion be reasonable or unreasonable." Our prayer must arise from a pure heart; "otherwise we ourselves present to him the rods wherewith to chastise us." To pray *par usage*, to pray without praying, to give "to the vices their hour, to God his hour"—what an unnatural conscience that can thus find peace! And what must we think of the prayers of those who persist in vicious habits?

Notes and Comments

Are they so bold as to ask forgiveness . . . without repentance?"

His thought turns to the discussions he had had perhaps with his Protestant brother. Montaigne's brother undoubtedly thought that in him Montaigne) there was evident "some brightness of mind," and perhaps accused him of hypocrisy. The last sentence of this paragraph is very interesting as an expression of his nature. Then, still somewhat thinking of the Protestants, perhaps, he speaks of the reasonableness of the Church's prohibition of the indiscriminate use of the Psalms (it is to be remembered that they had been set to gay music at Court); and enlarging on this subject, he declares that to the reading of the Bible, "we should always add this exordium of our divine service, *Sursum corda.*" And he expresses his sense of the dangers arising from too many translations. "Are we sure," he asks, "that in the Basque country and in Brittany there are enough judges to confirm the translation made into their language? The universal Church has no decision to make more difficult or more important."

The passage that follows, "One of our Greek historians" to the quotation from Epicurus, was added in 1595 and is uninteresting, since it is only a rather misplaced and obscure setting forth (by means of historical examples) of the point he is *about* to make—that religion should not be talked about, and *discussed*, and made *common*. This he maintains more openly and clearly on the next page; and in connection with this he expresses his sympathy with the Protestant feeling about the name of God.

He then passes back (curiously enough, by the way of Xenophon) to the worse than absurdity of praying to God

Of Prayers

when our hearts are full of sinful thoughts; and gives a little scoff at women in general, apropos of Queen Margaret of Navarre (whom he quite misrepresents).

The Essay closes with a paragraph eloquent from its earnestness, and which (excepting the reference to Plato and the quotation from Horace) belonged to the first draft.

B. THE NOTES BY MR. IVES

1. These first sentences, exclusive of that added in 1595, first appeared in the second edition in 1582. In the 1580 edition the Essay began with the next sentence.
2. See Plato, *Laws*, book X.
3. *Si, nocturnus adulter,*
   Tempora Santonico velas adoperta cucullo.
   —Juvenal, *Satire*, VIII, 144.
4. *Il se rameine, mais soudain il rechoit.*
5. *Comment pastissoit il ce discours en son courage?*
6. *Indigestible agonie.*
7. *Disparité:* a word of Montaigne's coinage.
8. *Conscience.*
9. That is, the people.
10. That is, the different sects.
11. The Greek historian was Nicetas, but Montaigne took this and the following examples from Justus Lipsius's *Adversum Dialogistam*, etc.
12. Sisinnius.
13. Andronicus.
14. Montaigne misread his Lipsius here. The scene took place in a tent *near* Lopadius. Lopadius was a lake, not a man.
15. *Profanes.* See Plato, *Laws*, book I. Plato does not

Notes and Comments

distinctly name women.

16. See Bishop Osorio, *History of King Emmanuel of Portugal*.

17. See Plutarch, *Of Love*.

18. *Raisons*.

19. That is, the "he . . . who should say, on the contrary," etc. See above.

20. *Verbis indisciplinatis*—St. Augustine, *De Civ. Dei*, X, 29.

21. *Et à moi avec, à l'avanture, de m'en taire.*

22. *A nostre commerce et société.*

23. *Quæ, nisi seductis, nequeas committere divis.*
—Persius, *Satires*, II, 4.

24. *Hoc ipsum quo tu Jovis aurem impellere tentas, Dic agedum, Staio: "Proh Juppiter! O bone," clamet, "Juppiter!" At sese non clamet Juppiter ipse?*
—Persius, *Satires*, II, 21.

25. See the *Heptameron*, Journée III, Nouvelle 25.

26. *Une religieuse reconciliation.*

27. *Tacito mala vota susurro Concipimus.* —Lucan, V, 104.

28. *Haud cuivis promptum est murmurque humilesque susurros Tollere de templis, et aperto vivere voto.*
—Persius, *Satires*, II, 6.

29. *Clare cum dixit: Apollo! Labra movet, metuens audiri: pulchra Laverna, Da mihi fallere, da justum sanctumque videri; Noctem peccatis et fraudibus objice nubem.*
—Horace, *Epistles*, I, 16.59.

Of Age

The goddess Laverna was the protector of thieves and of all kinds of frauds.

30. See Plato, *Second Alcibiades.*
31. *Mais qu'elles suivent la prudence.*
32. *Contexture.*
33. See Plato, *Laws,* book IV.
34.   *Immunis aram si tetigit manus,*
      Non somptuosa blandior hostia
        Mollivit aversos Penates,
     Farre pio et saliente mica.
                —Horace, *Odes,* III, 23.17.

CHAPTER LVII

Of Age

A. THE COMMENT BY MISS NORTON

UNLIKE the last, this Essay is scarcely changed from its first draft (one unimportant sentence was added in 1588 and another in 1595); and it has the pleasant, simple, conversational character that belongs to the "middle period" of the Essays. It need not detain us long. The chief thing to be noted in it is the impression Montaigne had of the usual length of human life: he thought that the common opinion gave many more years to it than facts justify. One might think that his impression was created by the

Notes and Comments

conditions of violence in those days, so abounding in wars and pestilences, were not the causes of the deaths he happens to specify—falls and shipwrecks and pleurisies, as well as *la peste*—exactly those which lie outside the dangers of battlefields. Perhaps he is right in believing that "to die of old age is a rare, peculiar, and extraordinary death"; but he surely exaggerates not a little in saying that "it is an exemption which nature bestows by special favour upon a single person in the course of two or three centuries."

The next sentence, regarding "the age we have reached," is somewhat obscure. Cotton and his follower Hazlitt throw a brave bridge across by arranging it "that when once *forty years*, we should consider it as an age to which very few arrive." I take Montaigne's meaning to be that any age (of discretion) we have reached, we should consider as an age to which very few arrive. This interpretation is confirmed by the first sentence of the next paragraph.

There is much good sense in what he says here of the mistake made in not giving to young men the management of affairs. He thought men should be put to work early and kept at work late, "for the public good." And there is much interest in what he says about the force of the soul in youth. He certainly goes too far in saying that the man who at twenty had not given proof of his powers will never do so; and one may question his belief that the greater number of noble deeds have been done by men under thirty: "deeds" perhaps, *actions* in the strict meaning of the word, yes; but *works*; it would be strange doctrine to say of the great men of the last generation, Lincoln and Gladstone and Darwin and Tennyson and Bismarck and Moltke and Ranke and Dollinger and Newman, that they were "great men after

Of Age

the age of thirty years in comparison with all others, but not in comparison with themselves."

M. Villey has shown that the greater number of the Essays of the first Book were written in or about 1572. And he remarks: "At this period it is only by exception that he makes use of his own judgement. He seems to call his compositions *fantasies* [Book II, chapter 8], not *essais*, and the word *fantasies* there signified simply ideas, impressions on the brain; it did not at all imply the shade of originality, of the exceptional, which it has for us to-day. Perhaps towards the later of these years Montaigne had his title [Essais] in mind; still this is doubtful; at least, at this time, he began to refer more to his judgement. But it is only much later that he will fully avow the legitimate employment of it, that on every subject he will make use of a veritable sounding of his judgement and his experience."

When Montaigne wrote the dissertation which opens this Essay, it was already very clearly his purpose to test his judgement; but it suffices to compare this chapter (of which the date is uncertain) with the chapters of 1579, to perceive immediately how much Montaigne's conception changed in the interval. He now does not only test his judgement, he tests his life.

B. THE NOTES BY MR. IVES

1. See Plutarch, *Life of Cato of Utica*. Plutarch's account indicates that Cato was indignant with his friends, not because he thought himself of a fit age to die, but because he thought himself of a fit age to decide whether or not he should die.

2. *Cours*.

Notes and Comments

3. *Et la moins en usage.*
4. See Suetonius, *Life of Augustus.*
5. See Aulus Gellius, X, 28.
6. *Vocation.*
7. Augustus.
8. That is, thirty years.
9. Cf. the closing sentences of Book III, chap 2.
10. *Ubi jam validis quassatum est viribus ævi*
    Corpus, et obtusis ceciderunt viribus artus,
    Claudicat ingenium, delirat linguaque mensque.
    —Lucretius, III, 451.

BOOK TWO

CHAPTER I

Of the Inconstancy of Our Actions

A. THE COMMENT BY MISS NORTON

SOME of Montaigne's Essays seem as if he had *talked* them rather than written them, as if they had been reported by a better than Boswell; we seem to hear the delicate intonations of his voice, which convey his meaning almost as much as his words do, and to see the smile that throws light on the sentence. This Essay is not one of those, but rather merely opens the door of his mind to us when he is in a mood of quiet meditation, not inclined to say much. There is something almost more like Bacon than like Montaigne himself in its sobriety of tone, in the absence of personal reference (except for one interesting passage), and in its admirable *generalisations;* but Bacon never wrote with the *simplicity* of thought and quick vividness of phrase that here, as elsewhere, is the special force of Montaigne.

He keeps comparatively close to his subject throughout. In the opening pages he characteristically illustrates the inconstancy, if not of our actions, at least of our words, by the examples of Marius and Boniface VIII and Nero and Augustus. Such is the natural instability of our conditions of mind that it is foolish to try to form of any man an impres-

Notes and Comments

sion logically coherent, not self-contradictory—a foolish mistake to represent any man with an *air universel* by which all his actions are to be interpreted.

He quotes Seneca's definition of the chief end of wisdom, that it is "to will and not will constantly the same things," and justly remarks that this is not *nostre façon ordinaire;* rather, that our words are so chameleon-like that on each one of our actions should be passed a separate judgement, since it is the force of circumstances more often than not that makes us do good or evil, well or ill.

Even the valour of Alexander was not without its *taches.* All nobleness that is not ingrained in us forsakes us at moments. "Virtue chooses not to be followed but for herself, and if we sometimes borrow her mask for other use, she soon tears it from our face."

B. THE NOTES BY MR. IVES

1. *De mesme boutique.*
2. See Plutarch, *Life of Marius.*
3. See Jean Bouchet, *Annales d'Aquitaine.*
4. See Seneca, *De Clementia,* II, 1.
5.   *Malum consilium est quod mutari non potest.*
        —Publius Syrus, in Aulus Gellius, XVII, 14.4.
6. *Qu'il s'est faict lascher entier et indecis aux plus hardis juges.*
7. See Seneca, *Epistle* 20.5.
8. See the *Funeral oration on the soldiers who died at Chæronea.*
9.   *Quod petiit spernit; repetit quod nuper omisit;*
      Æstuat, et vitæ disconvenit ordine toto.
        —Horace, *Epistles,* I, 1.98.

Of the Inconstancy of Our Actions

10. See Seneca, *Epistle* 20.6.
11. *Ducimur ut nervis alienis mobile lignum.*
—Horace, *Satires*, II, 7.82.
12. See Seneca, *Epistle* 23.8.
13. *Nonne videmus*
Quid sibi quisque velit nescire, et quærere semper
Commutare locum, quasi onus deponere possit?
—Lucretius, III, 1057.
14. *Tales sunt hominum mentes, quali pater ipse*
Juppiter auctifero lustravit lumine terras.
—Verses translated by Cicero (*Fragmenta Poematum*, lib. X) from the Odyssey (XVIII, 135), and taken by Montaigne from St. Augustine, *De Civ. Dei*, V, 28.
15. See Seneca, *Epistle* 52.1. Here Montaigne translates his author literally: *Fluctuamus inter varia consilia. Nihil libere volumus, nihil absolute, nihil semper.*
16. See Diogenes Laertius, *Life of Empedocles*.
17. *Discours;* that is to say, *la peinture de ces caractères.*
18. Cf. Seneca, *Epistle* 31.8.
19. See Plutarch, *Life of Pelopidas*.
20. *Verbis quæ timido quoque possent addere mentem.* —Horace, *Epistle, II*, 2.36.
21. *Quantumvis rusticus: Ibit,*
Ibit eo, quo vis, qui zonam perdidit, inquit.
—*Ibid.*, 39.
22. Mahomet.
23. See Chalcondylas, VIII, 13.
24. *Luy avoit mis le cœur au ventre; ce n'est un cœur ainsi formé par discours: ces circonstances le luy ont fermy.*
25. The Manichæans.

Notes and Comments

26. *Je me remue et trouble moy mesme par l'instabilité de ma posture.*
27. *Laborieux.*
28. *Ingénieux.*
29. See Seneca, *Epistle* 120.
30. *Nihil enim potest esse æquabile, quod non a certa ratione proficiscatur.*—Cicero, *Tusc. Disp.*, II, 27.
31. Arrian refers often to this weakness of Alexander.
32. See Plutarch, *Life of Alexander.*
33. *Voluptatem contemnunt, in dolore sunt molliores, gloriam negligunt, franguntur infamia.*—Cicero, *De Off.*, I, 21. This quotation is not in the edition of 1595.
34. *Qu'elle n'emporte la piece.*
35. *Cui vivendi via considerata atque provisa est.*—Cicero, *Paradoxa*, V, 1.
36. See Seneca, *Epistle* 20.2.
37. See *Epistle* 71.
38. See *Epistle* 93.
39. See *Epistle* 71.
40. *Nul vent fait pour celuy qui n'a point de port destiné.* "No helpe serves him that runnes uncertain courses (or knows not where to end them)."—Cotgrave.
41. See Cicero *(De Senectute)*, who says that Sophocles recited the play to the judges; see also Plutarch, *Whether an aged man*, etc.
42. See Herodotus, V, 29.
43. *Magnam rem puta unum hominem agere.*—Seneca, *Epistle* 120.
44. *Hac duce, custodes furtim transgressa jacentes,*
    Ad juvenem tenebris sola puella venit.
    —Tibullus, II, 1.75.

1740

CHAPTER II

Of Drunkenness

A. THE COMMENT BY MISS NORTON

As, in the last Essay, man is "of a shapeless and various contexture," so is the world only "variety and dissimilarity." It might seem from this opening sentence as if this Essay were a continuation of the last; but this is not exactly so true. Montaigne's point here is the difference between *vices*, their respective rank and measure.

"Drunkenness," he says, "seems to me a gross and brutish vice." But antiquity has not greatly decried this. Then he enters into some details regarding himself and his father. Then, "Let us go back to our bottles," he says; and he dwells on the advantages of drinking, especially for old men, passing into an admirable passage, which again seems to connect itself with the previous Essay: "To what vanity does the good opinion we have of ourselves carry us!" and leaving here all thought of "drunkenness," the Essay concludes with a long paragraph—a *cento* of quotations—to illustrate the theme that the "boastings" of those who defy the ills of life are a form of divine madness, and that "wisdom is a steady control of our souls."

No one of Montaigne's Essays is perhaps so remote from modern thought as this in its point of view of the subject it treats. Montaigne thought of drunkenness as a personal, not a national, vice; as being more or less degrading to in-

1741

Notes and Comments

dividuals, not as injuring classes and seriously affecting the life of a people. He wrote when it was wine, not alcohol, that was drunk. He wrote of all drinking-songs in the spirit of Omar Khayyam, with the liberal feeling of the ancient sages, in the tone of Pitt and his fellows, in the belief of St. Paul that "wine maketh glad the heart of man." His own nature was averse to drinking; he thought it *un vice grossier et brutal*, but one that harmed the public less than other vices. In the monstrous growth it has attained in the last hundred years, we now recognise it as one of our most terrible public enemies; and Montaigne's half-ironical words, that for pleasure's sake "we should never refuse an opportunity to drink," sound strangely enough.

More than half of this Essay was added in 1595—and it may be observed that of the three quotations in it from Plato, one is derived through Seneca, and the other two (direct) belong to the later-written portions.

The subject of this Essay was treated of more than once by Seneca, and repeatedly by Pierre Messie, Montaigne's contemporary, in his *Leçons*, from similar points of view.

B. THE NOTES BY MR. IVES

1. See Plutarch, *The Contradictions of the Stoics.*
2. *Quos ultra citraque nequit consistere rectum.*
   —Horace, *Satires*, I, 1.107.
3. *Nec vincet ratio hoc, tantundem ut peccet idemque*
   Qui teneros caules alieni fregerit horti,
   Et qui nocturnus divum sacra legerit.
   —Horace, *Satires*, I, 3.115.
4. *Et esleve le sien.*

Of Drunkenness

5. See Plato, *Charmides*.
6. *A qui le meilleur est tousjours en vice.*
7. *Genereux.*
8.   *Cum vini vis penetravit,*
Consequitur gravitas membrorum præpediuntur
Crura vacillanti, tardescit lingua, madet mens,
Nant oculi; clamor, singultus, jurgia gliscunt.
                  —Lucretius, III, 476, 478-80.
9. See Seneca, *Epistle* 83.
10.   *Tu sapientium*
Curas et arcanum jocoso
Consilium retegis Lyæo.
                  —Horace, *Odes*, III, 21.14.
11. *Tira le ver du nez.*
12. See Josephus, *De Vita Sua*, §44.
13. See Seneca, *Epistle* 83.
14.   *Externo inflatum venas de more Lyæo.*
                  —Virgil, *Bucolics*, VI, 15.
15. See Seneca, *Epistle* 83.
16.   *Nec facilis victoria de madidis, et*
Blæsis, atque mero titubantibus.
                  —Juvenal, *Satire* XV, 47.
17.   *Hoc quoque virtutum quondam certamine*
        magnum
Socratem palmam promeruisse ferunt.
                  —Pseudo-Gallus, *Elegy*, I, 47.
18. See Seneca, *De Tranquillitate Vitæ*, XV. He is speaking of Cato of Utica, not Cato the Censor.
19.   *Narratur et prisci Catonis*
Sæpe mero caluisse virtus.
                  —Horace, *Odes*, III, 21.11.

Notes and Comments

20. See Plutarch, *Life of Artaxerxes;* also *Table-Talk.*
21. In the edition of 1588 there follows here this sentence: *Platon luy attribue ce mesme effect au service de l'esprit,* which first appeared in that edition.
22. See G. Bouchet, *Les Serées*, I, 1; Herodotus, I, 133.
23. *Qui choquent quasi tous de plus droit fil la société publique.*
24. *Mais il la prenoit mal.*
25. *Lotz.* "Lot = (about) our pottle."—Cotgrave.
26. Lechery.
27. *Damerets.*
28. That is, not in Latin.
29. By Bishop Antonio de Guevara.
30. *Du primsaut.*
31. These sentences, not found in the Bordeaux copy of 1588, were added in 1595: *Et par ce qu'en la viellesse, nous apportons le palais encrassé de reume, ou alteré par quelque autre mauvaise constitution, le vin nous semple meilleur, à mesme que nous avons ouvert et lavé nos pores. Aumoins il ne m'advient guere, que pour la premiere fois j'en prenne bien le goust.*
32. See Diogenes Laertius, *Life of Anacharsis.*
33. See Plato, *Laws*, book II.
34. See Diogenes Laertius, *Life of Stilpo.*
35. See Idem, *Life of Arcesilaus.*
36. Cf. Seneca, *Epistle* 83.
37.   *Si munitæ adhibet vim sapientiæ.*
                              —Horace, *Odes*, III, 28.4.
38. See Crinitus, *Life of Lucretius.*
39.   *Sudoresque ita et pallorem exsistere toto*
      Corpore, et infringi linguam vocemque aboriri,

Of Drunkenness

Caligare oculos, sonere auris, succidere artus;
Denique concidere, ex animi terrore videmus.
—Lucretius, III, 154.

40. That is, the sage.

41. *Humani a se nihil alienum putet.*
—Terence, *Heautontimoroumenos*, I, 1.25.
Montaigne gives the familiar text a meaning to suit his purpose.

42. *Sic fatur lachrymans, classique immittit habenas.*
—Virgil, *Æneid*, VI, 1.

43. See Plutarch, *Life of Publicola*.

44. The Stoics.

45. The Epicureans.

46. *Occupavi te, Fortuna, atque cepi; omnesque aditus tuos interclusi, ut ad me aspirare non posses.*—Cicero, *Tusc. Disp.*, V, 9.

47. *Un vesseau de pierre.*

48. *Que vous pilez.* See Diogenes Laertius, *Life of Anaxarchus*.

49. Prudentius, *Of Crowns*; the words are attributed to St. Lawrence.

50. *Lache belistre.*

51. See Josephus, *History of the Maccabees*, VIII.

52. Μανείειν μᾶλλον ἢ ἡθείειν;
—A saying of Antisthenes. See Aulus Gellius, IX, 5; Diogenes Laertius, *Life of Antisthenes*.

53. *Entreprend de se faire mignarder à la goute.* Cf. Seneca, *Epistles* 66, 67, 92, *passim*.

54. *Spumantemque dari, pecora inter inertia, votis*
     Optat aprum, aut fulvum descendere monte
          leonem. —Virgil, *Æneid*, IV, 158.

Notes and Comments

55. *Ardeur et manie.*

56. This whole passage, from "Our soul could not attain," is taken from Seneca, *De Tranquillitate Vitæ*, XV. The opinion of Plato is found in *Io* and that of Aristotle in *Problems*, 30.

57. See Plato, *Timæus*.

CHAPTER III

A Usage of the Island of Cea

A. THE COMMENT BY MISS NORTON

THE occasion for this title does not appear till the last page of the Essay, and it is then found to be inaccurate. It is not a *custom* of Cea that suggested these pages, but an incident that occurred there when the Consul Sextus Pompeius was passing through the island. The narrative of the voluntary death by poison, with Socratic calmness, of a woman of ninety "of great position," in the presence of the consul, which Montaigne gives here, he took from Valerius Maximus, who was in the consul's suite.

The many preceding pages are a discussion of the causes and the justifications of voluntary death, with full recognition of the cowardice that may be shown in the desertion of life and the fortitude that may be shown in enduring it; the

A Usage of the Island of Cea

writer points out on one side what fantastic and foolish humours have induced the act, and on the other, some diseases which give a man good right to destroy himself, chief among them the stone. Some seven or eight years after Montaigne wrote of this disease, he was himself attacked by it, and it is to be remembered that he bore his sufferings heroically, as is testified by his *Journal de Voyage*.

Page after page here is taken up by individual cases of suicide, of those who from one cause and another have taken refuge in death; some more or less publicly, some with more or less solemn display. Other pages are given to descriptions of the self-destruction of whole cities when besieged. Still other pages note deaths sought from eagerness for the life to come.

The last words are, "Physical pain and the fear of a worse death seem to me the most excusable incitements."

In the literary style of this Essay is evident a method that M. Villey thus describes (*Les Sources*, etc., II, 44):

"Montaigne is wont to use the form of ending off what he is saying with phrases or eloquent expressions gathered here or there from the works of the ancients, mingling them with illustrative examples which sometimes he has taken the trouble to collect himself, but which sometimes he has found brought together by his forerunners. The citations that are in verse retain their Latin form; they especially please him because, as he says (in Book I, chapter 26): 'Just as the voice, when confined within the narrow channel of a trumpet, comes forth more penetratingly and more strongly, so it seems to me that the phrase compressed within the metrical forms of verse darts forth with more sudden force, and strikes with a livelier impact!'

Notes and Comments

"Those that are in prose he generally translates, or he imitates them; almost all of them he borrows from Seneca, because the style of Seneca is more terse and impressive than any other. Transitions, of course, lead from one citation to another, bind them together, smelt them, so to speak, into the substance of the topic; but Montaigne makes these transitions of little length because they enfeeble and lessen the force of the citation."

In this Essay there are nearly forty "stories"! It is one of the Essays that offended Pascal; and it is one of the boldest, which fact explains the precautions of the opening.

B. THE NOTES BY MR. IVES

1. *Coustume.*
2. *Niaser et fantastiquer.*
3. *Au cathedrant.*
4. See Plutarch, *Apothegms of the Lacedæmonians.*
5. See *Ibid.*
6. See Plutarch, *Apothegms of the Lacedæmonians.*
7. See *Ibid.*
8. See Cicero, *Tusc. Disp.*, V, 14.
9. See Seneca, *Epistle* 70.
10. *La clef des champs.* See *Ibid.*
11. See *Ibid.*
12. See Tacitus, *Annals*, XIII, 56.
13. See Seneca, *Epistle* 70.
14.   *Ubique mors est; optime hoc cavit Deus,*
    Eripere vitam nemo non homini potest;
    At nemo mortem; mille ad hanc aditus patent.
        —Seneca, *Thebaïs (Phœnissæ)*, I, 1, 151.
15. See Seneca, *Epistle* 78.

A Usage of the Island of Cea

16. See *Epistle* 70.
17. See *Epistle* 69.
18. See *Epistle* 77. Cf. Book I, chap. 20: *Où que votre vie finisse, elle y est toute.*
19. See *Epistle* 69. *Bella res est mori sua morte.*
20. See *Epistle* 70.
21. See *Epistle* 77.
22. See Suetonius, *Lives of Eminent Grammarians.*
23. See Seneca, *Epistle* 58.
24. See *Cicero, De Fin.,* III, 18.
25. See Diogenes Laertius, *Life of Aristippus.*
26. See Idem, *Life of Speusippus.*
27. See St. Augustine, *De Civ. Dei,* I, 22, and Vivès's *Commentary* thereon.
28. *Proxima deinde tenent mœsti loca, qui sibi lætum*
    Insontes peperere manu, lucemque perosi
    Projecere animas. —Virgil, *Æneid,* VI, 434.
29. *Duris ut ilex tonsa bipennibus*
    Nigræ feraci frondis in Algido,
    Per damna, per cædes, ab ipso
    Ducit opes animumque ferro.
    —Horace, *Odes,* IV, 4.57.
30. *Non est, ut putas, virtus, pater,*
    Timere vitam, sed malis ingentibus
    Obstare, nec se vertere ac retro dare.
    —Seneca, *Thebaïs,* I, 190.
31. *Rebus in adversis facile est contemnere mortem:*
    Fortius ille facit qui miser esse potest.
    —Martial, XI, 56.15.
32. That is, courage.

1749

Notes and Comments

33.　　　*Si fractus illabatur orbis,*
　　　　　　Impavidam ferient ruinæ.
　　　　　　　　　　　　—Horace, *Odes*, III, 3.7.

34.　　　*Hic, rogo, non furor est, ne moriare, mori?*
　　　　　　　　　　　　—Martial, II, 80.2.

35.　　　　　　　*Multos in summa pericula misit*
　　　Venturi timor ipse mali; fortissimus ille est,
　　　Qui promptus metuenda pati, si cominus
　　　　　instent,
　　　Et differre potest.　　　　—Lucan, VII, 104.

36.　　　　　　*Usque adeo, mortis formidine, vitæ*
　　　Percipit humanos odium, lucisque videndæ,
　　　Ut sibi consciscant mærenti pectore letum,
　　　Obliti fontem curarum hunc esse timorem.

37. See Plato, *Laws*, book IX.

38.　　　*Debet enim, misere cui forte ægreque futurum*
　　　　　est,
　　　Ipse quoque esse in eo tum tempore cum male
　　　　　possit
　　　Accidere.　　　　　　—Lucretius, III, 862.

39. That is, who recommend suicide.

40. εὔλογον ἐξαγωγήν.　　　　—Diogenes Laertius, *Life of Zeno*.

41. See Seneca, *Epistle* 77.

42. See Book I, chap. 14, p. 60.

43. See Plutarch, *Of the virtuous deeds of women*.

44. See Plutarch, *Lives of Agis and Cleomenes*.

45.　　　*Sperat et in sæva victus gladiator arena,*
　　　　Sit licet infesto pollice turba minax.
—Attributed to Pentadius, in Justus Lipsius, *Saturnalium Sermonum Libri*.

1750

A Usage of the Island of Cea

46. See Seneca, *Epistle* 70.
47. See Josephus, *De Vita Sua*, 28.
48. April 14, 1544.
49. This sentence is not in the *Édition Municipale;* it was added in 1595.
50. *Aliquis carnifici suo superstes fuit.*—Seneca, *Epistle* 13.11.
51.   *Multa dies variusque labor mutabilis ævi*
    Rettulit in melius; multos alterna revisens
    Lusit, et in solido rursus fortuna locavit.
                  —Virgil, *Æneid*, XI, 425.
52. See Pliny, *Natural History*, XXV, 3. Editions of 1580 to 1588 add: *la seconde, la douleur d'estomach; la tierce, la douleur de teste.*
53. See Seneca, *Epistle* 58.36.
54. See Livy, XXXVII, 46.
55. See Idem, XLV, 26.
56. See G. Paradin, *Histoire de nostre Temps*, etc.; Villey, *Livres de l'Histoire Moderne*, etc., pp. 139, 140.
57. See Josephus, *History of the Maccabees.*
58. *Aposterent.*
59. *Pour leur en faire curée.* See Seneca, *Epistle* 70.
60. See II *Maccabees* (Apocrypha), XIV, 37-46.
61. See *Commentary* of Vivès on St. Augustine, *De Civ. Dei*, I, 26.
62. In the epigram, *De Oui et Nenny.*
63. See Tacitus, *Annals*, VI, 48.
64. Tacitus, *Annals*, XV, 71.
65. See Herodotus, I, 213.
66. See Herodotus, VII, 107; Plutarch, *Life of Cimon.*
67. See Goulard, *Histoire du Portugal*, IX, 27.

Notes and Comments

68. See Tacitus, *Annals*, VI, 29.
69. See *Ibid.*, 26.
70. See Plutarch, *Of talking overmuch*.
71. Capua.
72. That is, the Capuan.
73. See Livy, XXVI, 13-15.
74. See Livy, XXVI, 15.
75. See Quintus Curtius, IX, 4. M. Villey, who discovered this passage in Quintus Curtius, points out that the reference to Diodorus Siculus, hitherto generally adopted by commentators, is not satisfactory.
76. See Livy, XXVIII, 22, 23.
77. *Qu'ils avoient diversement condamnez au feu et au naufrage.*
78. *Qui eut pouvoir sur soi.* See Livy, XXXI, 18.
79. See Tacitus, *Annals*, VI, 29.
80. *Philippians*, I, 23. In the Vulgate the passage reads: "Desiderium habens dissolvi, et esse cum Christo"; in the Authorised Version, "having a desire to depart and be with Christ."
81. *Romans*, VII, 24. Vulgate: "Quis me liberabit de corporis mortis hujus?" Authorised Version: "Who shall deliver me from the body of this death?"
82. See Cicero, *Tusc. Disp.*, I, 34.
83. See Prince de Joinville, *Mémoires*, LI.
84. See G. de Mendoza, *History of the Kingdom of China*.
85. *En amusant une partie.*
86. See Valerius Maximus, II, 6, 7.
87. See Valerius Maximus, II, 6, *ext.* 8.
88. See Pliny, *Natural History*, IV, 12.

CHAPTER IV

Business To-morrow

A. THE COMMENT BY MISS NORTON

THIS little Essay is the simple jotting down of the reflections that came to Montaigne on reading in Plutarch (in the treatise, *Of Curiosity*) two stories, one of a certain Rusticus who, while listening to a public speech that Plutarch was making, received a missive from the emperor, which, out of courtesy to the speaker, he delayed to open; and the other of a tyrant of Thebes who, receiving a communication which would have warned him of plots against him, laid it carelessly aside, being at supper, saying, "Business to-morrow," a phrase "which became a proverb in Greece"—and which gives the title to our Essay.

Montaigne thinks by no means that "business to-morrow" is good counsel; for a man in public office it is inexcusable not to be ready to interrupt his dinner, or even his sleep.

The last sentence of the Essay is the wisest one in it; and the first page—a eulogy of Amyot, the translator of Plutarch—the most interesting page.

The paragraph beginning "I have never opened [a letter]" is a curious indication of the *doings* of those days.

1753

Notes and Comments

B. THE NOTES BY MR. IVES

1. *Epineux et ferré.*
2. At this time there was no French translation of the complete works of Xenophon.
3. *Chez soi.*
4. See Plutarch, *Of Curiosity.*
5. See Plutarch, *Life of Cæsar.*
6. See Plutarch, *Of the Familiar Demon of Socrates.*
7. See Plutarch, *Table-Talk.* Editions of 1580 to 1588 add: *ou pour luy donner quelque avertissement à l'oreille.*

CHAPTER V

Of the Conscience

A. THE COMMENT BY MISS NORTON

THIS Essay is, very simply, a study (in stories) of the external manifestations of men's consciences. Like the preceding one, its subject is derived from the *Œuvres morales* (Amyot's translation) of Plutarch.

The Essay opens with an amusing description of the extreme timidity of "a gentleman of agreeable demeanour," whom Montaigne and his brother met one day when travelling. In this passage occurs the mention (for which Mon-

Of the Conscience

taigne has been absurdly criticised) of the death of his Italian page, an incident interestingly illustrative of the conditions of that day.

B. THE NOTES BY MR. IVES

1. *De sa cazaque.*
2.   *Occultum quatiens animo tortore flagellum.*
   —Juvenal, *Satires*, XIII, 195.
3. *De gayeté de cœur.*
4. See Plutarch, *Of the delays of divine justice.*
5. See *Ibid.*
6. See Seneca, *Epistle* 105.
7.   *Malum consilium consultori pessimum.*
   —Aulus Gellius, IV, 5.
8. See Plutarch, *Of the delays of divine justice.*
9.   *Vitasque in vulnere ponunt.*
   —Virgil, *Georgics*, IV, 238.
10. See Plutarch, *Of the delays of divine justice.*
11.   *Quippe ubi se multi per somnia sæpe loquentes,*
    Aut morbo delirantes, protraxe ferantur,
    Et celata diu in medium peccata dedisse.
    —Lucretius, V, 1158.
12. See Plutarch, *Of the delays of divine justice.*
13. See Seneca, *Epistle* 97.
14.   *Prima est hæc ultio, quod se*
    Judice nemo nocens absolvitur.
    —Juvenal, *Satires*, XIII, 2.
15.   *Conscia mens ut cuique sua est, ita concipit intra*
    Pectora pro facto spemque metumque suo.
    —Ovid, *Fasti*, I, 485.

Notes and Comments

16. See Plutarch, *How a man may praise himself.*
17. See Aulus Gellius, IV, 18; Valerius Maximus, III.
18. *Au greffe.*
19. See Aulus Gellius, IV, 18.
20. *Cauterizée.*
21. See Livy, XXXVIII, 52.
22.   *Etiam innocentes cogit mentiri dolor.*
                                        —Publius Syrus.
23. See St. Augustine, *De Civ. Dei*, XIX, 6.
24. *En ont chargé leur teste.*
25. See Quintus Curtius, end of book XVII.
26. *D'autant qu'elle seroit coupable de son accusation.*
27. See Froissart, IV, 87 (anno 1397). The general was Bajazet I.

CHAPTER VI

Of Experience

A. THE COMMENT BY MISS NORTON

THE title of this Essay in the original French is *De l'Exercitation,* a word that has almost passed out of the French language, and after receiving some half-dozen significations, is becoming obsolete in English. It is used here by Montaigne not quite in its Latin sense (one of its senses) of *practice,* but, rather, to signify the result of "prac-

Of Experience

tice"—*experience*. And he did not propose to write of "experience" in general, but of the experience of death. I have already pointed out how constantly Montaigne's mind was occupied with the idea of death,—in youth as in old age, in old age as in youth,—and at the same time how greatly his mood about it, his way of regarding it, changed. This Essay stands almost midway between his earlier and his later expressions. Later, he does not speak of death as "the greatest deed we have to accomplish"; earlier, he does not say humorously, "We can not test it more than once. We are all apprentices when we come to it."

Stories of death-beds always had a peculiar interest for Montaigne, and it is a striking one that he tells here, or, rather, his own comment is striking when he says that his old Roman philosopher wished "that his own death might be of service to him as a lesson."

It seems to Montaigne that if we can not *learn* death, we have at least experiences that resemble it; that by sleep, Nature, "while we are living, presents to us the everlasting condition she holds for us after this life, thus accustoming us to it and taking from us fear of it."

Moreover, it is not death itself, but the forerunners of death, that we have reason to fear; and these do come into our *experience*, and against these we can strengthen ourselves by *practice*, especially since our imagination pictures many things to us as more painful than they are in reality. The paragraph in which he develops this thought is of great personal interest, and the unconscious expression of the strength of his sympathies (and this is only one of many similar relations) should silence those who talk of his egotism. How many men in comfort by their fireside are "dis-

Notes and Comments

mayed and distressed" for those exposed to the storm outside—especially when they have learned by experience that it is not as bad as it seems!

As sleep resembles death, so conditions of extreme weakness resemble our last moments; and Montaigne had learned from experience how painless these may be, by the consequences of a fall from his horse, of which he tells the story at length. In speaking of his opinions on this point, it is touching to see how his memory brings to mind talks he had with his dead friend on these subjects.

The Essay originally ended a very few sentences after the close of his story, with the words, "this is not to teach another, it is what I am learning myself," and the subsequent pages have nothing to do with death. They are another Essay—and a most admirable and interesting one, in his very latest "manner." It is a most vigorous justification, an eloquent explanation, of his study of his own nature.

B. THE NOTES BY MR. IVES

1. *De l'Exercitation.*
2. An allusion to Crates. Cf. Book 1, chap. 14: *Tel, pour arriver à la pauvretè, jetta ses escuz en cette mesme mer que tant d'autres fouillent de toutes pars pour y pescher des richesses* (Vol. I, p. 81); and Book I, chap. 39: *D'anticiper aussi les accidens de fortune, se priver des commoditez qui nous sont en main . . . jetter ses richesses emmy la riviere,* etc. (Vol. I, p. 322).
3. Cf. the second passage cited in the preceding note.
4.   *Nemo expergitus exstat.*
    Frigida quem semel est vitai pausa sequuta.
                            —Lucretius, III, 929.

Of Experience

5. *Maraut;* in 1580 to 1588: *monstre.*
6. See Seneca, *De Tranquillitate Vitæ*, XIV, 4-9.
7. *Jus hoc animi morientis habebat.*—Lucan, VIII, 636.
8. That is, with death.
9. Cf. Cicero, *Tusc. Disp.*, I, 38.
10. That is, death's.
11. *Bouillante.*
12. Cf. Book I, chap. 20: *Je trouve que j'ay bien plus affaire à digerer cette resolution à mourir quand je suis en vigueur et en pleine santé que je n'ay quand je suis malade* (Vol. 1, p. 118).
13. *Roussin.*
14. *Pas*—an entirely uncertain measure.
15.   *Perche, dubbiosa anchor del suo ritorno,*
        Non s'assecura attonita la mente.
            —Tasso, *Gierusalemme Liberata*, XII, 74.
16. *Si pres du naturel.*
17.   *Come uel ch'or apre or chiude*
        Gli occhi, mezzo tra'l sonno è l'esser desto.
            —Tasso, *Ibid.*, VIII, 26. (Added in 1582.)
18.   *Vi morbi sæpe coactus*
        Ante oculos aliquis nostros, ut fulminis ictu,
        Concidit, et spumas agit, ingemit, et fremit
            artus;
        Desipit, extentat nervos, torquetur, anhelat
        Inconstanter, et in jactando membra fatigat.
                            —Lucretius, III, 487.
19.   *Vivit, et est vitæ nescius ipse suæ.*
                            —Ovid, *Tristia*, I, 3.12.
20. This whole addition of 1588 is difficult of connection with what precedes and what follows.

Notes and Comments

21.   *Hunc ego Diti*
Sacrum jussa fero, teque isto corpore solvo.
—Virgil, *Æneid*, IV, 702.

22. *A belles ongles.*

23. *Semianimesque micant digiti ferrumque retractant.* —Virgil, *Æneid*, X, 396.

24. *Falciferos memorant currus abscindere membra,*
Ut tremere in terra videatur ab artubus id quod
Decidit abscisum, cum mens tamen atque hominis vis
Mobilitate mali non quit sentire dolorem.
—Lucretius, III, 642, 644-646.

25. *Par l'escorce.*

26. *De chez moi.*

27. *Lechée.* Cf. Book II, chap. 12: *Comme les ours façonnent leurs petits en les lechant à loisir.*

28. *Ut tandem sensus convaluere mei.*
—Ovid, *Tristia*, I, 3.14.

29. In 1580: *quatre ans apres.*

30. See Pliny, *Natural History*, XXII, 24.

31. *Ce n'est pas ici ma doctrine, c'est mon estude; et n'est pas la leçon d'autruy, c'est la mienne.*

32. *Tant de menus airs.*

33. *Se testonner.*

34. *Au lieu qu'on doit moucher l'enfant, cela s'apelle l'enaser.*

35. *In vitium ducit culpæ fuga.*
—Horace, *Ars Poetica*, 31.
Literally, "avoidance of an error leads to a fault"; but the free rendering alone fits Montaigne's thought.

36. That is, forbidding one to talk about oneself.

1760

37. *Ce sont brides a veaux* [literally, "bridles for calves"] *des quelles ny les Saincts . . . ne se brident.* The play upon words is impossible of reproduction in English.

38. *S'ils n'en escrivent à point nommé* (= *de parti pris*).

39. *De se jetter bien avant sur le trotoir.*

40. That is, the Protestants.

41. *Qui ne peut tumber en production ouvragiere.*

42. *D'une montre particuliere.*

43. That is, in his writings.

44. This sentence is so nearly unintelligible to the translator, that the French text is given entire: *L'effaict de la toux en produisoit une partie; l'effaict de la pallur ou battemant de cœur, un'autre, et doubteusement.*

45. See *Nicomachæan Ethics*, IV, 7.

46. That is, of presumption.

47. Of censure.

CHAPTER VII

Marks of Honour

A. THE COMMENT BY MISS NORTON

THERE is excellent good sense in this Essay; but it is a good sense so remote from modern conditions of life that it seems almost useless to us, and our interest conse-

Notes and Comments

quently centres on the mention in it of the historic "order" of Saint-Michel, because of Montaigne's personal interest in that. On a later page (chapter 12) he says: "I asked of fortune, as eagerly as any thing, the order of Saint-Michel in my youth"; but when it was bestowed on him, it was no longer of much value to him, it had been made so common.

It was in 1571 that Montaigne received the *cordon de Saint Michel* from Charles IX through the hands of his friend Gaston de Foix, marquis de Trans, the father-in-law of Madame Diane de Foix (to whom the Essay on the Education of Children is addressed).

Brantôme has a foolish page about this: "We have seen councillors issue forth from the halls of parliament, drop the gown and the square cap, and undertake to wear a sword and to put on immediately this collar, without any other indication of having known war; as did the sieur de Montaigne, whose more fitting course would have been to continue to make use of his pen in writing essays than to put on a sword which did not so well become him."—*Discours sur les capitaines illustres*, Article "Tavanne."

B. THE NOTES BY MR. IVES

1. *Des Recompenses d'Honneur.*
2. *Des pures recompenses d'honneur.* The word *recompense* is translated by varying words, because no one English word covers so much ground.
3. *Toutes les recompenses militaires.*
4. *Gens de qualité.* In early editions, *Gens d'honneur.*
5. *Et grande apparence.*
6. Editions 1580 to 1588 add: *c'est une monnoye à toute espèce de marchandise.*

Marks of Honour

7. *Le parler.* How we recompense "speaking" with money is not clear.

8. *Cui malus est nemo, quis bonus esse potest.*
—Martial, XII, 82.

9. "We remark," understood.

10. Virtue.

11. That is to say, I call *vaillance* (valour) a virtue.

12. That is, valour *(vaillance)*.

13. *Neque enim eædem militares et imperatoriæ artes sunt.*—Livy, XXV, 19. The citation would fit much better after "guerdon" above.

14. The Ordre du Saint-Esprit, established by Henry III, in 1578.

15. In 1580 to 1588 we read here: *et nous estant si familier par l'air Français qu'on luy a donné si parfaict et si plaisant*, referring to Amyot's translation.

16. *Un homme qui vaut beaucoup, ou un homme de bien.*

17. *La force*, that is, *virtus.* Cf. Book I, chap. 20, pp. 104, 105.

CHAPTER VIII

Of the Affection of Fathers for Their Children

A. THE COMMENT BY MISS NORTON

THE lover of Montaigne perhaps "loves" this Essay as much as any; but he has no very logical reasons to assign for this preference. If you ask him why it charms him, he can only answer: "Because it is Montaigne." There is no higher, deeper, stronger feeling in it than other men have expressed on this same subject; it has no special wit or wisdom; but no other man has ever expressed himself with just this *manner*, of which one never wearies. It is "as pure as water and as good as bread." What Madame de Sévigné said is echoed by every reader—she is writing from Livry: "I have found entertainment in a volume of Montaigne that I did not think I had brought with me. Ah! the charming man! What good company he is! He is an old friend of mine, but by dint of being old, he is new to me. I can not read without tears what the maréchal de Montluc says of the regret that he felt in not having imparted himself to his son, and in having left him in ignorance of the tenderness he felt for him. Read this page, I beg you, and tell me what you find in it. It is in a letter to Madame d'Estissac about the love of fathers to their children. Mon Dieu! how full this book is of good sense!"

1764

Of the Affection of Fathers

This Essay is one to which several long additions were made, and of which several passages were *réfondu*.

In the first edition (1580) the praises of Madame d'Estissac were more warmly expressed than in the later editions. Originally Montaigne spoke of *l'honneur et reverence singuliere que j'ay tousjours rendu à vos merites et à vos vertuz;* and, in the same sentence, of *vos aultres grandes qualités.*

In 1588, these phrases were omitted or altered. One feels a little gossiping curiosity about the change. But she could not complain—with the delightful eulogium of her *affection maternelle* that was left.

Just before the publication of 1580, this lady—after fifteen years of widowhood—had remarried. Her son was the Monsieur d'Estissac who, in 1580, accompanied Montaigne on his travels. In her youth she had been the mistress of Cardinal Bourbon.

B. THE NOTES BY MR. IVES

1. Cf. Book II, chap. 6, p. 501.
2. In 1580-1588: *et reverence singuliere.*
3. *Qu'en vous reconnaissant pour telle;* that is, "as the most devoted of mothers"(?).
4. See Aristotle, *Nicomachæan Ethics*, IX, 7.
5. *S'ils sont autres;* that is, if they are unworthy.
6. In 1580-1588; *pour le plaisir que nous en recevions, non pour eux mesmes.*
7. That is, avarice.
8. See *Nicomachæan Ethics*, I, 57.
9.   *Et errat longe, mea quidem sententia,*
  Qui imperium credat esse gravius aut stabilius

1765

Notes and Comments

*Vi quod fit, quam illud quod amicitia
     adjungitur.* —Terence, *Adelphi*, I, 1.40.
10. *Malitieusement opiniastres.*
11. See Plutarch, *Of Avarice.*
12. *Nullum scelus rationem habet.*—Livy, XXVIII. 28.1.
13. *Car ailleurs, où la vie est questuere, la pluralitè et compaignie des enfans, c'est un agencement de mesnage.*
14. September 23, 1565.
15. See Aristotle, *Politics*, VII, 16.9. Aristotle says 37.
16. See Plato, *Republic*, book V.
17. See Diogenes Laertius, *Life of Thales;* Plutarch, *Table-Talk.*
18. See Cæsar, *De Bello Gallico*, VI, 21, where this is said of the Germans.
19. *Ma hor congiunto à giovinetta sposa,
     Lieto homai de' figli, era invilito
     Ne gli affetti di padre e di marito.*
            —Tasso, *Jerusalem Delivered*, X, 39.
20. See Plato, *Laws*, book VIII.
21. Muley-Hassan.
22. See Paulus Jovius, *History of his own Time*, XXXIII.
23. See de Gomara, *Histoire générale des Indes*, II, 12.
24. In 1580: *et de ses riches atours.*
25. *Solve senescentem mature sanus equum, ne
     Peccet ad extremum ridendus, et ilia ducat.*
            —Horace, *Epistles*, I, 1.8.
26. Cf. Book I, chap. 57, pp. 436-437.
27. The editions of 1580-1588 add: *De produire librement ce qui me vient en la bouche.*

1766

Of the Affection of Fathers

28. *La subjection.* In 1580, *l'obligation;* in 1588, *l'importunité;* in 1595, *l'obligation.*
29. *Le plus en parade.*
30. Jean d'Estissac, died 1576.
31. In 1580, *santé.*
32. *Obstiné au demeurant de mourir en cette démarche.*
33. That is, "monsieur."
34. This sentence appears in 1595, but not in the *Édition Municipale.*
35. *Vrais espouvantails de cheneviere.*
36. *Un bastelage.*
37. *Ille solus nescit omnia.*
—Terence, *Adelphi,* IV, 2.9.
38. See Seneca, *Epistle* 47.5.
39. *Volonté.*
40. *Volonté.*
41. *De me produire et de me presenter.*
42. See Cæsar, *De Bello Gallico,* VI, 18.
43. *Debonnaires.*
44. *Sans nous;* that is, if we make no disposition of it.
45. *Heureux qui se trouve à point pour leur oindre la volonté sur ce dernier passage!*
46. Cf. Book II, chap. 17.
47. *Fera honneur à.*
48. See Plato, *Laws,* book XI.
49. The Salic Law.
50. See Herodotus, IV, 180: "The children . . . are assigned to those whom they most resemble." (Rawlinson's translation.) Montaigne's source is Saliat's French translation.
51. In 1580-1588: *chair de nostre chair et os de nos os.*

Notes and Comments

52. *Les enfantements de nostre esprit, de nostre courage et suffisance.*

53. See Plato, *Phædrus*. Plato has Darius instead of Minos.

54. Tricca. See Nicephorus Callistus, *Ecclesiastical History.*

55. That is, his book, Αἰθιόπικα, commonly known as *Theagenes and Chariclea.*

56. *Goderonnée* = beruffled.

57. *Des humeurs paternelles.*

58. See Seneca, *Controversia.*

59. See Tacitus, *Annals*, IV, 34. His name was Cremutius Cordus.

60. See *Ibid.*, XV, 70.

61. See Diogenes Laertius, *Epicurus;* Cicero, *De Fin.,* II, 35.

62. In 1580-1588: *de France.*

63. See Aristotle, *Ethics*, IX, 7.

64. Leuctra and Mantinea.

65. See Diodorus Siculus, XV, 23. Cornelius Nepos *(Epaminondas)* mentions but one "daughter."

66.   *Tentatum mollescit ebur, positoque rigore
        Subsidit digitis.*   —Ovid, *Metam.*, X, 283:

CHAPTER IX

Of the Armour of the Parthians

A. THE COMMENT BY MISS NORTON

THIS is an Essay much overlooked, little noticed usually by the readers and critics of Montaigne; and yet it has its peculiar importance as confirming the impression received from other Essays, and from scattered, much-disregarded passages, of Montaigne's strong personal interest in military matters, in the things belonging to the life and conditions of a soldier. It shows that, when reading the Roman historians, his attention was attracted by their descriptions of the arms of the Romans and of those of the nations which they subjected; and that his own knowledge of the arms and armour in use by his countrymen and contemporaries—and, it may be believed, by himself—greatly stimulated his curiosity in the comparison of bodily means of defence in different ages and countries.

B. THE NOTES BY MR. IVES

1. That is, because they (the servants) are carrying their arms.
2. *Intolerantissima laboris corpora vix arma humeris gerebant*—Livy, XXVII, 48.
3. *Tegmina queis capitum raptus de subere cortex.* —Virgil, *Æneid*, VII, 742.
4. See Quintus Curtius, IX, 6, and IV, 13.

Notes and Comments

5. See Tacitus, *Annals*, III, 43, 46.
6. See Plutarch, *Life of Lucullus*.
7. See Plutarch, *Apothegms of Kings*, etc.; Valerius Maximus, III, 7.2.
8. See Plutarch, *Apothegms of Kings*, etc.
9. *L'husbergo in dosso haveano, e l'elmo in testa,*
   Dui di quelli guerrier, de i quali io canto.
   Ne notte o di, doppo ch'entraro in questa
   Stanza, gli haveano mai mesi da canto,
   Che facile a portar come la vesta
   Era lor, perche in uso l'havean tanto.
   —Ariosto, *Orlando Furioso*, XII, 30.
10. See Xiphilin, *Life of Caracalla*.
11. *Arma enim membra milites esse dicunt.*—Cicero, *Tusc. Disp.*, II, 16.
12. See Plutarch, *Apothegms of Kings*, etc.
13. In 1580 to 1588: *Or par ce qu'elle me semble bien fort approchante de la nostre, j'ay voulu retirer ce passage de son autheur, ayant pris autresfois la peine de dire bien amplement, ce que je sçavois sur la comparaison de nos armes aux armes romaines; mais ce lopin de mes brouillards m'ayant este desrobé avec plusieurs autres, par un homme qui me servoit, je ne le priverai point du profit qu'il en espere faire; aussi me seroit-il bien malaisé de remascher deux fois une mesme viande.*
14. That is, mail-coats.
15. *Roides.*
16. See Ammianus Marcellinus, XXIV, 7, XXV, 1.
17. See Plutarch, *Life of Demetrius*.

CHAPTER X

Of Books

A. THE COMMENT BY MISS NORTON

OF this long and delightful Essay there is little to be said. It is perhaps the one that would best introduce the general reader to Montaigne. It has nothing of his deepest and most original quality of thought, but it is entirely charming in the easy flow of its admirable literary criticisms, made doubly interesting by their personal note. As Montaigne says of Terence, so may we say of Montaigne: "I can not read him so often that I do not find in him some new beauty and charm."

Monsieur Villey has pointed out a singular and important *lapsus calami*, which, very strangely, has not before been noted. It is unquestionable that it was Seneca who in Montaigne's eyes was the most *uniforme et constant*, Plutarch more *ondoyans et divers*.

B. THE NOTES BY MR. IVES

1. *L'essay*.
2. *De mes discours*.
3. In 1580 to 1588: *ce que je pense*. "Excutienda damus præcordia" (Persius, *Satires*, V, 20). The quotation was placed here in 1588, but in 1595 was transferred to the Essay, *De la Vanité*, Book III, chap. 9.
4. Cf. Book I, chap. 26 (p. 193); chap. 40 (p. 333).

Notes and Comments

5. *Non à ma teste, mais à ma suite* (not in *Édition Municipale*).
6. *De mon sens.*
7. That is, not in Latin.
8. *Sergent de bande.*
9. *Mes pieces.*
10. *Has meus ad metas sudet oportet equus.*
 —Propertius, IV, 1.70.
11. *Primsautier.*
12. *Et que je l'y remette à secousses.*
13. *D'une puerile et aprantise intelligence.* In 1580 to 1588: *par ce que mon jugement ne se satisfaict pas d'une moyenne intelligence.*
14. That is, in the category of "modern" ones, though the *Basia* are written in Latin, *moderne* signifying written in French.
15. In 1580 to 1588: *Ce que j'en opine, ce n'est pas aussi pour etablir la grandeur et mesure des choses, mais pour faire connoistre la mesure et force de ma veue.*
16. Not usually attributed to Plato.
17. In 1580 to 1588: *Autres meilleurs jugemens, ny ne se donne temerairement la loy de les pouvoir accuser.*
18. *Ceux qui les mythologisent.*
19. *Eut donné encore quelque tour de pigne.*
20. Cf. what Montaigne says of Terence near the beginning of chap. 40 of Book I, p. 334.
21. *Bestise barbaresque.*
22. *O seclum insapiens et infacetum!*
 —Catullus, XLIII, 8.
23. Cicero. Cf. Book II, chap. 31, *infra: Que Cicero, père d'eloquence,* etc.

Of Books

24. Horace on Plautus. See the *Ars Poetica*, 270.
25. *Liquidus puroque simillimus amni.*
 —Horace, *Epistles*, II, 2.120.
26. *Pointes.*
27. *Minus illi ingenio laborandum fuit, in cujus locum materia successerat.*—Martial, Preface to book VIII.
28. *Excursusque breves tentat.*
 —Virgil, *Georgics*, IV, 194.
29. That is, since Amyot translated him.
30. Plutarch to Hadrian, Seneca to Nero.
31. In 1580 to 1588: *Leurs creances sont des meilleures de toute la philosophie, et traictées.*
32. *Plus ondoyant et divers.* See Miss Norton's Comment.
33. See Seneca, *De Beneficiis*, II, 20.
34. That is, to my feast of reading.
35. Plutarch and Seneca.
36. See Book II, chap. 31.
37. *Les hommes gras et gosseurs.*
38. The editions of 1580-1588 add: *Si est-ce qu'il n'a pas en cela franchi si net son advantage comme Vergile a faict en la poesie: car bien tost après luy il s'en est trouvé plusieurs qui l'ont pensé égaler et surmonter, quoy que ce fust à bien fauces enseignes; mais à Vergile nul encore depuis luy n'a osé se comparer, et à ce propos j'en veux icy adjouter une histoire.*
39. *Comme on se fourre souvent.*
40. See Seneca, *Suasoriæ*, VIII.
41. Tacitus, *De Oratoribus*, XVIII.
42. *Esse videatur.*—*Ibid.*, XXIII.
43. *Ego vero me minus diu senem esse mallem, quam*

Notes and Comments

esse senem, antequam essem.—Cicero, *De Senectute*, X.

44. Montaigne probably here has in mind the game of tennis *(paume)* in which a ball that comes on the right side of the player is much more easily dealt with than one that comes on his left side. In 1580 to 1588 the sentence read: *Historiens sont le vray gibier de mon estude.*

45. In 1580-1588 this passage read (after "at the same time"): *la consideration des natures et conditions de divers hommes, les coustumes des nations differentes, c'est le vray suject de la science morale.*

46. *Qu'il ne soit ou plus estandu ou plus entandu.* He refers to Diogenes Laertius.

47. See Cicero, *Brutus*, LXXV.

48. *Qu'il n'y soit allé beaucoup plus du sien qu'il n'y en met.*

49. *Ils veulent nous mascher les morceaux.*

50. The early editions add: *Ceux-la sont aussi bien plus recommandables historiens, qui connoissent les choses dequoy ils escrivent, ou pour avoir esté de la partie à les faire, ou privez avec ceux qui les ont conduites.*

51. See Suetonius, *Life of Cæsar.*

52. Jean Bodin, *Methodus ad facilem historiarum cognitionem.*

53. Francesco Guicciardini, Italian historian.

54. *Et sentant un peu au caquet scholastique.*

55. That is, his point of view.

56. Martin du Bellay and Guillaume de Langey.

57. Anne de Pisseleu, duchesse d'Estampes, mistress of Francis I.

58. *Discours non vulgaires.*

CHAPTER XI

Of Cruelty

A. THE COMMENT BY MISS NORTON

THIS Essay might quite as well—and better, one would think—have been entitled "Of Virtue," for it says more (and more interestingly) about virtue in general than about the vice of cruelty. Indeed, even when it reaches in mid-stretch this its nominal subject, it is still chiefly the virtue of compassion that it dwells on. This is delightfully characteristic of Montaigne: he never turns our attention, save momentarily, to the common, or uncommon, vices of mankind, but brings before us the habitual excellences and possible superiorities of human nature. There is interest in comparing the admirable conception of virtue in the opening sentences with the more "romantic" one, written later than this, in the "Education of Children."

This is one of the charmingly conversation-like Essays, as we feel when we come across the sudden, almost humorous, confession of an unthought-of difficulty in his argument. It occurs to him that the *best* men after all do not find virtue difficult, but he soon discovers (just as in talk—a Platonic talk) that there may be considered to be three degrees of virtue: the first is "being simply endowed with an easy and kindly nature"; a higher is "preventing by active strength the progress of vice"; and highest of all is "pre-

Notes and Comments

venting the birth of temptations." In the course of this discussion he makes use of the noble examples of the death of Socrates and that of the younger Cato, bestowing on the latter an enthusiasm of admiration that jars a little on modern sensibilities; and one is glad to have him recognise that that of Socrates is "the more beautiful."

In one of the very last Essays, that on Physiognomy, Montaigne recurs again to a comparison of these two great men. In that passage, and in a later one of the same Essay, he gives clear evidence of ranking the character of Socrates as much the higher.

Continuing his course, and observing that men are often praised for what rather deserves blame in them, he says "one word about myself," and describes himself with his wonted simplicity and truthfulness; and in so doing he is led to say, "I cruelly hate cruelty," adding (after a digression on the "violent pleasure" of "hunting"), "I feel very tenderly compassionate about the sufferings of others"; and from this he passes to admirable counsels regarding the forms of capital punishment.

A passage often referred to as indicating one of the points where Montaigne's thought was far in advance of the general tone of his times is thus phrased: "All that is beyond mere death seems to me pure cruelty." This is repeated in the Essay, "Cowardice the Mother of Cruelty." It was one of the points for which he was reprimanded at Rome, and which he defended, saying, of it and other like things, "that this was my opinion and that these things I had uttered, not considering them to be errors." It was only a very few of his contemporaries who had reached this height in their conception of the proper manner of dealing

Of Cruelty

with criminals. This passage connects itself with that in "Of the Conscience," where he condemns more at length the use of torture.

What he says of the incredible cruelty of his own times is of frightful force, and assists our imaginations in seeing his own life, truly, as far other than that of a recluse student—a man of letters.

In the other Essay on cruelty, referred to above, he says: "I have seen some of the most cruel men weeping easily and for trifling causes." (It is only this generation of Montaigne's American readers that has seen many "cruel men.")

He, in fact, had beheld at many different times and in many different scenes men "dying in agony"—from the cruelty of their fellows. We should never forget, in reading Montaigne, that, as Sainte-Beuve says, "he lived in an age which a man who had passed through the Terror [M. Daunou] could call the most tragic age of all history."

From cruelty to men he passes to cruelty to animals, and thence to the transmigration of souls; and closes with a lovely passage about a general duty of humanity not to animals only, but even to trees and to plants.

B. THE NOTES BY MR. IVES

1. *Les ames reglées d'elles mesmes et bien nées.*
2. See Diogenes Laertius, *Life of Arcesilaus.*
3. *Contournans ses paroles à gauche.*
4. *Et en ses meurs.*
5. *Et ii qui* φιλήδονοι *vocantur, sunt* φιλόκαλοι *et* φιλοδίχαιοι, *omnesque virtutes et colunt et retinent.*—Cicero, *Epistulæ ad Familiares*, XV, 19. This is a letter

Notes and Comments

which was written to Cicero by C. Cassius.

6. *Multum sibi adjicit virtus lacessita.*—Seneca, *Epistle* 13.3.

7. The Pythagorean. See Cicero, *De Off.*, I, 44.

8. See Plutarch, *Of the Familiar Spirit of Socrates.*

9. See Plutarch, *How one can derive benefit from one's enemies.*

10. See Plutarch, *Life of Marius.*

11. Cf. the very different conception of virtue which Montaigne sets forth in Book I, chap. 26, p. 193, in a passage written after 1588.

12. *A une vertu si eslevée que la sienne, je ne puis rien mettre en teste.*

13. *Volupté.*

14. *Pour son object necessaire.*

15. *Trop de gaillardise et de verdeur.*

16. *Sic abiit e vita ut causam moriendi nactum se esse gauderet.*—Cicero, *Tusc. Disp.*, I, 30.

17. Julius Cæsar.

18. *Et d'une volupté virile.*

19. *Deliberata morte ferocior.*
—Horace, *Odes*, I, 37.29.

20. Cf. Book I, chap. 37, p. 307: *Qui plus est, nos jugemens sont encore malades et suyvent la depravation de nos meurs,* etc.

21. *Catoni cum incredibilem natura tribuisset gravitatem, eamque ipse perpetua constantia roboravisset, semperque in proposito consilio permansisset, moriendum potius quam tyranni vultus aspiciendus erat.*—Cicero, *De Off.*, I, 31.

22. Cf. the opening sentence of Book II, chap. 13, p.

Of Cruelty

817; also the last sentence of Book I, chap. 19, p. 102: *Au jugement de la vie d'autruy, je regarde tousjours comment s'en est porté le bout.*

23. An allusion to the *Phædo* of Plato.
24. *Pour estre desenforgée des incommoditez passées.*
25. Montaigne recurs to this comparison between the deaths of Cato and Socrates, in Book III, chap. 12.
26. See Diogenes Laertius, *Life of Aristippus.*
27. *Plus grossiers.*
28.   *Haud ignarus quantum nova gloria in armis,*
    Et prædulce decus primo certamine possit.
                    —Virgil, *Æneid*, XI, 154.
29. *Je se sçay point nourrir des querelles et du debat chez moy.*
30.   *Si vitiis mediocribus et mea paucis*
    Mendosa est natura, alioqui recta, velut si
    Egregio inspersos reprehendas corpore nævos.
                    —Horace, *Satires*, I, 6.65.
31. *D'une race fameuse en preud'homie.*
32.   *Seu libra, seu me scorpius aspicit*
    Formidolosus, pars violentior
      Natalis horæ, seu tyrannus
      Hesperiæ Capricornus undæ.
                    —Horace, *Odes*, II, 17.17.
33. See Diogenes Laertius, *Life of Antisthenes.*
34. *Semble s'arreter à cette image.*
35. *Et ma concupiscence moins desbauchée que ma raison.*
36. See Diogenes Laertius, *Life of Aristippus.*
37. See *Ibid.*
38. See Diogenes Laertius, *Life of Epicurus.*

Notes and Comments

39.   *Nec ultra errorem foveo.* —Juvenal, VIII, 164.
40. See Plutarch, *Contradictions of the Stoic Philosophers.*
41. *Toutes les humeurs.*
42. See Diogenes Laertius, *Life of Aristotle.*
43. See Cicero, *Tusc. Disp.*, IV, 37.
44. See Cicero, *De Fato*, V.
45. *La volupté.*
46.   *Cum jam præsagit gaudia corpus,*
Atque in eo est venus ut muliebria conserat arva. —Lucretius, IV, 1106.
47. The passage, "while there . . . encounter" was substituted in 1595 for the following passage of 1580-1588: *auquel il semble qu'il y ait plus de ravissement; non pas, à mon advis, que le plaisir soit si grande de soy, mais parce qu'il ne nous donne pas tant de loisir de nous bander et preparer au contraire, et qu'il nous surprend.*
48.   *Quis non malarum, quas amor curas habet,*
    Hæc inter obliviscitur?
—Horace, *Epodes*, II, 37.
49. In 1580-1588: *C'est ici un fagotage de pieces decousus; je me suis detourné de ma voye, pour dire ce mot de la chasse. Mais—*
50. *Ou feintes ou peintes.*
51. Cf. Book I, chap. 31, p. 281.
52. See Suetonius, *Life of Julius Cæsar.*
53. That is, the effect on the people.
54. *Qui corpus occidunt, et postea non habent quod faciant.*—St. Luke, XII, 4.
55.   *Heu! relliquias semiassi regis, denudatis ossibus,*

Of Cruelty

Per terram sanie delibutas fœde divexarier.
—Ennius, in Cicero, *Tusc. Disp.*, I, 44.

56. The last two sentences were added in 1582.
57. *Contre l'escorce.*
58. See Plutarch, *Apothegms of Kings*, etc.
59. See Herodotus, II, 47.
60. *En peinture et en ombrage.*
61. *Ut homo hominem, non iratus, non timens, tantum spectaturus occidat.*—Seneca, *Epistle* 90.45.
62. *Quæstuque cruentus
Atque imploranti similis.*
—Virgil, *Æneid*, VII, 501.
63. See Plutarch, *Table-Talk*.
64. *Primoque a cæde ferarum
Incaluisse puto maculatum sanguine ferrum.*
—Ovid, *Metam.*, XV, 106.
65. *Morte carent animæ; semperque, priore relicta
Sede, novis domibus vivunt, habitantque
receptæ.* —Ovid, *Metam*, XV, 158.
66. See Cæsar, *De Bello Gallico*, VI, 14.
67. *Muta ferarum
Cogit vincla pati, truculentos ingerit ursis,
Prædonesque lupis, fallaces volpibus addit;
Atque ubi per varios annos per mille figuras
Egit, lethæo purgatos flumine, tandem
Rursus ad humanæ revocat primordia formæ.*
—Claudian, *In Rufinum*, II, 482.
68. *Ipse ego, nam memini, Trojani tempore belli
Panthoïdes Euphorbus eram.*
—Ovid, *Metam.*, XV, 160.
69. See Plutarch, *Of Isis and Osiris*.

Notes and Comments

70. *Belluæ a barbaris propter beneficium consecratæ.*
—Cicero, *De Nat. Deor.*, I, 36.
71. *Crocodilon adorat
Pars hæc, illa pavet saturam serpentibus Ibin;
Effigies sacri hic nitet aurea cercopitheci.*

. . . .

*. . . hic piscem fluminis, illic
Oppida tota canem venerantur.*
—Juvenal, XV, 2-4, 6, 7.
72. See Plutarch, *Of Isis and Osiris.*
73. See Plutarch, *Roman Questions;* Cicero, *Pro Roscio,* XX; Livy, V, 47; Pliny, *Natural History,* X, 22.
74. *Les mules et mulets.*
75. See Plutarch, *Life of Cato the Censor.*
76. See Diodorus Siculus, XIII, 82.
77. See Herodotus, II, 66-69.
78. See Plutarch, *Life of Cato the Censor;* Herodotus, VI, 103.
79. The headland of the dog's burial. See Plutarch, *Life of Cato the Censor.*
80. See *Ibid.*

CHAPTER XII

Apology for Raimond Sebond

A. THE COMMENT BY MISS NORTON

It will be observed that this Introduction differs from the others in retaining the original form of the French quotations. This has been necessary, partly because this Essay has a peculiar interest from its relation to the *Pensées* of Pascal, and the original words of each author need to be compared.

This is by far the longest of Montaigne's Essays, and one of the most noted. It scarcely deserves the reputation it has gained, either for ability or as an expression of irreligion, and the point of view which regards it as peculiarly, though obscurely, expressive of Montaigne's character is open to question. In a sense it is almost out of place in the collection of Essays. It was a comparatively early piece of writing, and while nominally an "apology" for a certain author, it is, in fact, the formless, diffuse outpouring of Montaigne's opinions on many philosophical and religious matters with which his mind was not particularly fitted to deal, and to which his attention seems to have been accidentally turned. It is thus of a different quality from all the other Essays. Its interest to a reader to-day lies almost solely in its characteristic sincerity and in the remarkably modern nature of some of the opinions expressed in it,—also often characteristic of Montaigne's thought,—and in a few noble passages of religious feeling, which give proof of the deep foundations of Montaigne's morality. Its fate has been peculiar. It has been much misunderstood, greatly misrepresented, and warmly argued against.

The first thinker of importance who declared himself as an opponent of the thoughts of Montaigne in this Essay and elsewhere was Pascal, who was so familiar with them that they had become blood of his blood and bone of his bone, and that he reproduces them when arguing against them.

Pascal's opposition to Montaigne was, however, balanced by open admiration of him. But the associates of Pascal, the Port Royalists and their followers, echoing Pascal's cry of dismay at the absence in Montaigne of any religious emotion akin to their own high-strung consecration of their lives to asceticism and self-sacrifice, added to the note of dismay a note of indignant contempt, and uttered the epithet "Atheist," which was caught up and repeated generation after generation by those who did not themselves read Montaigne's writings, and knew him only by this deceptive hearsay.

Sixty years ago this report of him was renewed and affirmed by a man whom it is strange to find regarding him in this light, the admirable writer and thinker, Sainte-Beuve. When writing his great history of the Port Royalists, Sainte-Beuve—almost overmastered by the power of intellectual comprehension and moral sympathy that in later years obediently served him—looked at the world, as it were, through the windows of Port Royal; and through that distorting medium to see Montaigne truly or even dis-

Apology for Raimond Sebond

tinctly was impossible; so that the vigour and ability with which Sainte-Beuve then depicted his figure served to present an image as incorrect as it was striking.

Afterwards, the opinions of the eminent critic greatly changed; and though he never openly retracted his previous judgement, he showed an appreciation of the essayist so different as to amount to a practical recantation of it. But the impression of his earlier assertions on the reading public was not wholly corrected. Within the last few years, however, the defenders and admirers of Montaigne have been so numerous and so able that the legend of his irreligion and immorality is vanishing.

Emerson's designation of Montaigne, among his Representative Men, as the Sceptic, is likely to mislead those unfamiliar with the true sense of that word, but they will be set right by his definition of the type: "The ground occupied by the sceptic is the vestibule of the temple. Scepticism is the attitude assumed by the student in relation to the particulars which society adores, but which he sees to be reverend only in their tendency and spirit." This definition may be accepted as not inappropriate to the position of Montaigne.

In this Essay,—the "Apologie,"—which was considered by Sainte-Beuve as an arsenal of weapons forged to war upon Religion, collected and wielded by a hypocritical, friendly-seeming enemy, to other minds there appears strong evidence, strongly confirmed by other portions of his writings, that, while Montaigne was far from being himself constantly guided by strictly religious principles, he did not question their essential validity, and, possessing a simple devoutness and reverence of feeling, he sincerely

Notes and Comments

believed in the authority of the Church. It is to be observed that the Church itself never took offence at this Essay. Immediately after the publication of the first edition of the Essays—in 1580—Montaigne went to Rome, and while he was there his book was censured; but censured only for his use of the word "fortune," for his praises of the Emperor Julian the Apostate, and for his admiration of the heretic Théodore de Bèze as a poet, and other minor points. Nothing was said of the "Apologie" or of his opinions in general. And even these censures were soon withdrawn, and the authorities assured him that "they honoured his intentions and his affection for the Church and his ability."

The Essay before us is connected with the fact that Monhibitorum till 1676.)

The Essay before us is connected with the fact that Montaigne had been induced to make a translation of the work of which he styles himself the apologist, by circumstances which he narrates in the opening pages of the Essay. The book was so warmly approved by his father that he begged Michel to translate it. No man—not even so affectionate a son as Montaigne—is likely to translate a volume of one thousand solid pages merely to please his father; and it is fair to suppose that he also admired the book and sympathised with the author's object, which, he says, was "*par raisons humaines et naturelles, d'establir et verifier contre les atheistes tous les articles de la religion chretienne.*"

But the first clause of Montaigne's praise, where he says, "*Sa fin est hardie et courageuse,*" may be revised into a criticism, and one which is forced home to the reader of the "Apologie" far more distinctly than it was to Montaigne's own mind. The boldness of such attempts as that of Se-

1786

Apology for Raimond Sebond

bond appears nowadays as rashness; to Montaigne it seemed courageous only.

Montaigne was no logician, and consequently he was not perturbed by the immense assumptions with which Sebond starts, or by the colossal leaps his argument makes in reaching his conclusions. But he was a competent judge of honesty of purpose, and the heartfelt piety of the book, which the elder Montaigne had thought might make it a barrier against Lutheranism, inspired the translator with a respect that made him its apologist. But the whole situation was curious. It shows the perversity of even intelligent minds, that Lutheranism should have been regarded as one with atheism; Sebond's argument, composed in the middle of the fifteenth century, was in reality not opposed to the Reformation; and, had it been so, its force was greatly diminished by its apologist in the heat of his sympathetic admiration for it. The conditions are confused; it may be well to examine them in detail.

The two points that Montaigne felt called upon to answer in the objections made to the book were: first, that Christian belief is conceived by faith, and can not rest on reasoning, but comes from divine grace; and second, that Sebond's arguments are feeble and easily overthrown.

These two points together, really, it may be seen, cover the whole contents of the volume, the value of which the translator had it at heart to maintain; but Montaigne was too unskilled a dialectician to perceive this, and believed himself to be concerned only with minor matters.

The first point (where he maintains that Christianity—or rather religious truth—can be at least supported by reason) becomes, if one treats as synonymous, as he does, the

1787

Notes and Comments

terms Truth and Faith, the matter one would think most needed defence against its opponents. But Montaigne seems to have considered it the most easy of defence, or, perhaps, we may believe he was less interested by the discussion of it than by that of the more personal question of his author's ability; for he devotes but about six times as many pages to the second point as to the first. But long before the last page one feels that he is not discussing, but simply discoursing.

It is to be remarked that throughout this Essay the corrections and additions of the later editions are not of a character to affect the thought; yet his point of view had become very different from that of Sebond. His mind had run itself clear by the very process of expression; but it can easily be believed that he never cared to review his conclusions—all the more, because they took no formal or formulated shape to him. He did not himself know—if, indeed, he cared to know—what he believed. Belief, or faith, seemed to him above reason, but none the less to rest on that; inspired from above, it could derive strength from below.

In his discussion of his first point, he lays less stress on the connection between faith and reason than on the irreligion of his fellow Christians, eloquently maintaining that irreligion is irreverence to God; and declaring that this irreligion is because "we" accept our religion only from worldly motives, not with faith, whereas the knot that should join us to our Creator should be a divine and supernatural bond.

Then he makes one of his odd "turns," and goes on to say that not only our heart and soul but our brains should be at the service of our faith, and that, if a man will but look

Apology for Raimond Sebond

around him, he will find that the structure of the world bears imprints of the hand of the Great Architect; and that, if reasonings like those of Sebond be illumined by faith, they are capable of serving as guides in the right path.

When Montaigne comes to the second point, he seems to confuse somewhat those who declare the arguments of Sebond to be weak, with those who feel at liberty to fight against Christianity with merely human weapons; and he seems to think that he is answering the former as well as the latter (as indeed in one sense he is), by demonstrating the weakness of all human reason. And this is, in truth, the thesis of all the many following pages, in which it is set forth by every variety of illustration. Man, it is averred, has in his power no arguments stronger than those of Sebond; it is also averred that he can arrive at no certainty through reasoning. Montaigne does not perceive that this conclusion is fatal to Sebond's work.

The essayist begins by considering man in himself alone, man deprived of divine grace, and in an impressive passage he depicts *"cette misérable et chétive creature,"* this quintessence of dust, and asks who has persuaded him that the glories of the universe, the mighty forces of nature which he can understand so little, and can command not at all, are for his sole advantage? At this early stage of the discussion Montaigne forsakes the path of Sebond, carried away, it would seem, by the force of his own thought and the power of his expression; for to his ironical questioning, who has persuaded man that he is of such immense importance? the immediate, natural answer of the reader of Sebond would be: Sebond has at least done his best to prove that the whole creation is for the benefit of man.

Notes and Comments

Montaigne even passes here into a fantastic consideration of the powers of the heavenly bodies, and in view of their influences and their incorruptible life he questions why we do not attribute to them a reasonable soul.

He then enters on an argument (if it may be so called by courtesy), which extends over many pages, to prove that it is only man's presumption that makes him count himself the superior of other creatures. He supports, or thinks he supports, his opinions by all sorts of illogical deductions from the stories in Plutarch's treatise on water and land animals, in Pliny's *Natural History*, in Herodotus, and other ancient authors. He is not to be blamed for not being wiser than his age on the matters he here treats of; but the fact that he was not deprives this part of the Essay of all interest but that of curiosity, for the modern "enlightened" reader.

As he draws to the close of these anecdotes, he remarks that, while we attribute to ourselves imaginary advantages —future and absent advantages—and the fictitious advantages of reason, learning, and honour, we recognise that beasts have the essential advantages of peace, security, innocence, and health. We have for our share the mass of human weaknesses and passions. And of what avail is learning against our human miseries?

His thought now becoming deeper, Montaigne questions what gain there is in intellectual attainments. Learning (*"la science,"* philosophy) only by indirection brings us to the same ends that ignorance reaches directly, and ignorance is the more comfortable condition; witness the maladies caused and increased by the imagination, and the readiness with which the higher movements of the soul pass

Apology for Raimond Sebond

into madness. The sovereign good is tranquillity; absence of ill, the best man can hope for; and to this *la simplesse* leads us, and learning itself throws us into the arms of ignorance by unavailing counsels of forgetfulness.

La simplesse renders life not only easier, but better; and knowledge is the root of evil; "*la simplicité [est] la meilleure sagesse.*" He here interpolates the consideration that, from the inadequacy of our powers to conceive the heights of the divine, it comes to pass that those works of our Creator which most fully express his nature are those which we least understand; and consequently an incredible thing is an occasion for belief: it is all the more according to reason as it is opposed to reason.

This leads to an interesting and modern passage—an expression of agnosticism: *c'est à Dieu seul de se cognoistre.*

Whatever knowledge we have of truth, it is not by ourselves that we have acquired it; our faith is a pure gift, and it is through our ignorance more than our learning that we are wise with this divine wisdom.

Recurring to the comparison of learning with ignorance, he declares that all the wisdom of the ages affirms the ignorance that is the wise child of learning: *Le plus sage homme qui fut oncques, quand on luy demanda ce qu'il sçavoit, respondit, Qu'il sçavoit cela, qu'il ne sçavoit rien.*

All philosophers may be divided into three schools: those who think they have discovered the truth; those who think it can not be discovered; those who are still looking for it. The Peripatetics, Epicureans, Stoics, and others—the Dogmatists, the Aristotelians—have believed it found; the Academicians and others have judged that it could not be attained by us; Pyrrho and other Sceptics have persisted in

1791

Notes and Comments

the search, using doubt for their instrument of investigation. Nothing in human invention has contained so much truthfulness and usefulness. Even the Dogmatists are forced at times to adopt Pyrrhonism and to distrust learning. The Academicians are sometimes "dogmatists," sometimes "doubters."

From this presentation of the schools of philosophy, Montaigne passes to the contemplation of the pleasure of study, even when vain, as useless knowledge is, and thence to the uselessness of the inventions of philosophers; or rather their vanity, since in the end truth must bend to the utility of action—to *la loy civile*.

In the course of these remarks, Montaigne quotes *un ancien*, who reproached for making profession of philosophy when in truth he did not hold it in great account, answered, *"que cela c'etoit vrayment philosopher."* Pascal echoes this phrase in a form that makes it applicable to Montaigne himself: *Se moquer de la philosophie, c'est vraiment philosopher.*

He turns a little aside to consider the attitude of philosophers regarding religion: *Platon dit tout destroussement en sa Republique, que, pour le profit des hommes il est souvent besoin de les piper.* But it appears to Montaigne that among the vain labours of the human understanding are the various conceptions of God; and he enters on a long enumeration of them; and reaches the conclusion that all other imaginations regarding the divine nature are less to be censured than those which represent it as resembling our own. When—*comme l'ancienneté*—we make to ourselves gods like ourselves, it is a marvellous madness. All his remarks on this subject are noble and interesting, and we

Apology for Raimond Sebond

have now reached a part of the Essay as interesting at one age of the world as another, since it is concerned with the unknowable.

Questioning whether philosophers of old could have been in earnest in what they said of their gods, Montaigne easily passes to the same question regarding what they said of the immortality awaiting us hereafter, and recognises at the same time that it is one in philosophic character with Christian beliefs. The pages on the impossibility of the union of the human and the divine might have been written yesterday, to-day, or to-morrow. Those who are in sympathy with them will always accept them; those whose minds have a different bent will always reject them with a certain regretful disapproval.

A very striking passage is that where he questions by what right the gods can punish or reward man hereafter if his conduct here is caused by them. The discussion of free will was in the air, though the question was as old as Epicurus, and it is evident that Montaigne had forgotten the premise, derived from Sebond, that incomprehensibility is the sustaining atmosphere of faith.

Recurring to heathen beliefs, he dwells on the strangeness of the fancy that divine benevolence can be pleased by our sufferings, and here as elsewhere one recognises that in criticising ancient customs he criticises the religion of his own day.

Carried along on the wings of his subject from one mountain top to another, so that it is impossible to follow him closely by the footpath of logical sequence, Montaigne next flies to the point he has already touched upon, that, because of the infinite difference between the divine nature

Notes and Comments

and human nature, we can have no knowledge of the conditions of the universe. We prescribe rules to Nature though we know but a small portion of her operations, and even these rules of our making are infringed by many things that we see and that we call miraculous. Rather we should call every thing miraculous, since it is beyond comprehension.

There is, he declares, much reckless irreverence in the definiteness of many religious phrases. But language is full of weakness and inadequacy and lends itself easily to falsity and incomprehensibility. This passage about language is but a long parenthesis, though an important one; and Montaigne recurs to the impossibility of our understanding God, and of the folly of considering him akin to ourselves. These pages are made very confused by the insertion of a long addition, the close of which has no real connection with the text as originally printed. And there immediately follows a passage several pages long, added in 1588, which very much cumbers the ground. It treats of ancient deifications, and the limitations of the powers of the gods and the consequent degradation of the idea of divinity, emphasising again man's presumption in thinking that all things are for his sake, and the rashness of understanding.

This again is followed by an incongruous addition made in 1595, after which the Essay reverts to its controlling thought—that of the insufficiency of learning. *"La philosophie n'est qu'une poësie sophistiquée,"* and has created unreasonable complications in the study of nature and man.

At the best it is difficult to know ourselves. Have those who find the reasoning of Sebond weak, and who themselves know every thing, have they never, busy with their

Apology for Raimond Sebond

books, discovered this difficulty? We receive ancient beliefs, and do not examine common opinions: presuppositions lead to mistakes; and philosophy fails to explain the perceptions of the senses.

Let us see if philosophy—reason—can tell us any thing of the soul. No; *ignoratur enim, quæ sit natura animai.*

In a digression on the vanity of philosophical enquiries in which he comments on the "man" of Plato, Montaigne refers to the "atoms" of the Epicureans, and classes the arguments regarding them as examples *"non d'arguments faux seulement mais ineptes."*

Returning to the philosophical study of the soul, after considerations regarding its preëxistence come those regarding its immortality. He remarks: *Ils* [les philosophes] *ont ce dilemme tousjours en la bouche pour consoler nostre mortelle condition: "Ou l'ame est mortelle ou immortelle: si mortelle elle sera sans peine; si immortelle, elle ira en amendant." Ils ne touchent jamais l'autre branche: "Quoy, si elle va en empirant?"*

Reason, it is evident, can not convince us of the immortality of the soul. But, though reason is feeble, man is presumptuous, and Montaigne exclaims: *Ce saint* [Augustine] *m'a faict grand plaisir: Ipsa utilitatis occultatio aut humilitatis exercitatio est aut elationis adtritio.*

Reason knows no more about the corporeal than the spiritual part of man; philosophers can not agree regarding human generation.

But if we know not ourselves, what can we know?

A paragraph now occurs that has almost the nature of an *envoi*. Montaigne here warns some one, individually addressed, against making use in the defence of Sebond of

Notes and Comments

this "*dernier tour d'escrime*" which Montaigne has himself employed—this assertion of the feebleness, the incompetency, of human reason: *Nous secouons icy les limites et dernieres clostures des sciences, ausquelles l'extremite est vicieuse, comme en la vertu.*

(An unquestioned tradition has existed for two hundred years and more that this warning was addressed to Marguerite de Valois, the wife of Henri IV. But there is no evidence in support of this tradition, and there is little likelihood of its truth. On the contrary, there is reason to believe that the Essay was presented to the sister of Henri IV, Catherine de Bourbon.)

The next paragraph might be the opening of an Essay entitled "De l'insuffisance de nos propres moyens pour saisir la vérité," since it deals with the uncertainties, not of our reason alone, but also of our senses. In the pages that follow there is one allusion to Sebond, and the style differs from the preceding pages in the constant occurrence of that personal note so characteristic of Montaigne's usual writing. He here goes over part of the same ground just traversed, but in a more interesting and vigorous manner, and these pages are free from the mass of untrustworthy, and often almost puerile, borrowed matter that crowds and clogs those that go before. They take up again the question of the limits of human knowledge, opening with the assertion that if the soul (reason) knows neither itself nor its body, it knows nothing with certainty.

This is followed by a fresh account of the sects of the philosophers, the Academicians and the wiser Pyrrhonists. But soon we leave *cette infinie confusion d'opinions qui se void entre les philosophes mesmes,* and enter on the con-

Apology for Raimond Sebond

sideration of the uncertainty that every man perceives in himself. Truth is the direct gift of God: it can not be conveyed from man to man.

It is certain that the faculties of the soul are affected by the conditions of the body, and the consequent inequalities of a man's state. Even the state of the weather changes our conditions, as says that verse in Cicero from the Greek:

> Tales sunt hominum mentes, quali pater ipse
> Juppiter auctifera lustravit lampade terras.

The reason—*c'est un instrument de plomb et de cire, alongeable, ployable;* and the weakness of the judgement is shown again by the power that mere assertion, even by oneself, has over one's mind.

The fact that our passions often inspire noble actions beyond reason impels us to ask (Montaigne implies) if such actions in which our judgement has no part are more excellent than its dictates, what advantage do we derive from the judgement?

The passion of love is a familiar example of the intoxication of the judgement: and who shall say whether the lover or the same man when he is not in love sees things most truly?

These considerations have led Montaigne, he says, to be slow to embrace new opinions; we have great reason to distrust them. *Je me tiens en l'assiette ou Dieu m'a mis. Ainsi me suis-je, par la grace de Dieu, conservé pur et entier sans agitation et trouble de conscience, aux anciennes creances de nostre religion, au travers de tant de sectes et de divisions que nostre siecle a produittes* (1588).

The truths of geometry, he goes on, subvert the truths

Notes and Comments

of experience; but many things formerly held as truths of cosmography are on the other hand subverted by the truths of experience.

A long passage was here inserted in 1595, about the various opinions regarding the world, which confuses, as usual, the train of thought, all the more that it is inserted in a passage which very irrelevantly concerns itself with the idea of Epicurus that similar opinions to those that exist in this world exist also in other worlds. Montaigne thinks Epicurus would have been the more convinced of this had he seen the similarities of belief to be found in the New World and the Old; which he goes on to point out. All this was written after the first publication of the Essay, and before the (so-called) fifth edition, that is, between 1580 and 1588.

After the interruption of this insertion we return to *autres tesmoignages de nostre imbecillité;* one of which is the variableness of man's desires; he himself had wanted the Order of Saint-Michel.

Then, after some questioning regarding the sovereign good of man, and the opinions of philosophers about it, a point *duquel par le calcul de Varro nasquirent deux cents quatre vingt sectes*, he remarks that from this diversity of opinion regarding the sovereign good arises the universal confusion in customs and laws, and that the most reasonable course, *c'est generalement à chacun d'obeir aux lois de son pays*. Yet what does this mean—save that duty has but a fortuitous rule?

We now come to a passage of considerable length about laws, one of the many interesting evidences in the Essays of how seriously Montaigne's mind had been given to the significance and the authority of human laws—his atten-

1798

Apology for Raimond Sebond

tion, perhaps, having been especially directed to the subject by his avocations as *conseiller*.

The consideration of the varyingness and changeableness of laws of nations leads him to consider the question of natural laws inherent in human nature, and to argue against their existence, at least against their present existence, even if man has been subjected to them in the past, as other creatures are now.

The next pages in the "Apologie" recur again to the confusion of judgements, and connect with this the fact that there may be a thousand interpretations of the same words; from which Montaigne slips, by way, again, of differences of judgements, into *la consideration des sens*, the concluding topic of the Essay.

He dwells first on his doubt whether man *soit pourveu de tout sens naturels;* and then on the recognised *incertitude et faiblesse de nos sens*, in spite of which *la force et l'effect des sens* is all powerful.

A passage added here in 1595, and another previously added in 1588, confuse the connection. But *cette mesme piperie que les sens apportent à nostre entendement, ils le recoivent à leur tour; nostre ame par fois s'en revenche de mesme: ils mentent et se trompent à l'envy.*

In fine, we sleep when we wake, and wake when we sleep. *Ceux qui ont apparié nostre vie à un songe ont eu de la raison à l'advanture plus qu'ils ne pensaient.*

He then suggests that there is probably great difference between our senses and those of animals; and that to judge of our senses we ought to know more about these differences and those that it is probable exist between different human beings; also it is to be noted that our different senses

Notes and Comments

bear different testimony of the same objects. And who can judge of all these differences?

Though *toute cognoissance s'achemine en nous par les sens,* yet such is their uncertainty that it *rend incertain tout ce qu'ils produisent . . . et nous, et nostre jugement et toutes choses mortelles, vont coulant et roulant sans cesse.*

In truth we have no communication with any constant existence—*nous n'avons aucune communication à l'estre;* and at the close of the Essay is a long quotation from Plutarch on the incessant progressive changes of Nature, one thing becoming always another, so that God alone is. Montaigne, as his last words, comments on the saying of Seneca: "*O la vile chose et abjecte, que l'homme, s'il ne s'esleve au dessus de l'humanite.*" Man can not of himself, says Montaigne in effect, rise above himself and humanity, but he may be uplifted by the hand of God; and it is Christian faith, not stoical virtue, that works this miracle.

A careful study of these pages makes it almost certain that a considerable portion of its substance was composed as early as 1572, seven or eight years before it was first printed in 1580, and it is to be seen that between the edition of that year and the edition of 1588 Montaigne still made additions, interposing them here and there among the earlier portions. From this the important fact results that this "Apologie" is not a whole, conceived at once, in which the parts were naturally united and closely dependent on each other, but rather a large frame in which Montaigne placed from time to time his successive ideas regarding the weakness of human reason.

When he wrote the latest words, he was on a higher plane than when he entered on the subject.

1800

Apology for Raimond Sebond

The Credulity of Montaigne

It is curious to observe the great confidence that Montaigne places in human testimony. There is, however, nothing contradictory in this to his general mental attitude of suspense of judgement, and it is fully explained in the Essay on the folly of considering our knowledge as a measure of the true and false. It was part of his perpetual *Que sçais-je?* which made it not difficult to him to look at the impossible as possible. To-day even, the limits for the impossible are very vague to untrained minds; and in Montaigne's day of scientific ignorance there can have been no fixed limits to a thinker who, like Montaigne, had emancipated himself from dependence on the evidence of the senses, or on his personal experience. That he did not reject the inexplicable is never more apparent than in view of the credulity with which he listened to the voice of history. The degree of his belief varied, not according to the character of the facts, but according to the character of the witnesses. Froissart and "our annals" did not seem to him witnesses of sufficient weight to control our judgement and to take from us freedom of question—*pour nous tenir en bride;* but when Plutarch affirms as of his certain knowledge that a battle lost in Germany two hundred and fifty leagues from Rome was known of in Rome the same day, and when Cæsar declared that an incident is often forerun by knowledge by it, "Shall we say," asks Montaigne, "that these honest folk [*ces simples gents*] were deceived and were not as clear-sighted as we?" And when St. Augustine testifies to miracles seen by himself, and brings forward two holy bishops as also witnesses to them, "Shall we accuse them," he asks again, "of ignorance, stupidity, carelessness, or of cunning and imposture? Is there any man of these days so impudently conceited as to think of himself comparable to them in virtue and piety, or in learning, judgement, and ability?" He writes thus of Tacitus: "He may be thought bold in the statements he makes: as when he declares that a soldier bearing a load of wood had his hands so stiffened with cold and so glued to his burden that they remained fastened there and dead, having separated from the arms. I am wont to bow before the authority of so weighty a witness."

Montaigne's mind was balanced between credulity and scepticism. By nature he inclined, or was not always disinclined, to believe; by intelligence he learned to distrust. The contrast in this respect of his later thought with his earlier is marked in one of the last Essays, that entitled "Des Boiteux," of which Voltaire said: *Qui veut apprendre à douter doit lire ce chapitre de Montaigne, le moins méthodique des philosophes, mais le plus sage et le plus aimable.* Here Montaigne remarks that men are generally more ready to seek the cause of an alleged fact than to question its truth: *Ils commencent ordinairement ainsi: "Comment est ce que cela se faict?" "Mais se faict il?" faudrait il dire.* He goes on: *J'ay veu la naissance de plusieurs miracles de mon temps. Encore qu'ils s'estoufent en naissant, nous ne laissons pas de prevoir le train qu'ils eussent pris s'ils eussent vescu leur aage.* And, speaking of sorcerers reported to be seen one day in the East and the next day in the West: *Certes, je ne m'en croirais pas moymesme;* it is much more likely that two men lie than that another flies like the wind.

But if we turn back to the early Essay already quoted from, we find him saying, not less wisely, that it is foolish

Apology for Raimond Sebond

presumption but a common vice in those who think they have better brains than most, to judge that to be false which does not seem to them probable. "I used to be so minded myself," he says, "and if I heard some one talk of spirits returning, or of prognostications of future things, of enchantments, or sorceries, or tell some other tale of which I could make nothing,—

> Somnia, terrores magicos, miracula, sagas,
> Nocturnos lemures, portentaque Thessala,—

I felt compassion for the poor people deceived by such follies. And now I think that I was at least as much to be pitied myself; not that experience has since then shewn me any thing beyond my former beliefs . . . but reason has taught me that to condemn a thing so positively as false and impossible is to assume the advantage of knowing the boundaries and limits of the will of God and of the power of our mother Nature, and that there is no more notable foolishness than to measure these by our capacity and intelligence."

Bacon agreed with him. "Neither," says he, "am I of opinion in this history of marvels that superstitious narratives of sorceries, witchcrafts, charms, dreams, divinations, and the like, where there is an assurance and clear evidence of the fact, should be altogether excluded. For it is not yet known in what cases, and how far, effects attributed to superstition participate of natural causes."

B. THE NOTES BY MR. IVES

1. Montaigne published in 1569 a translation of the work he here treats of *(Theologie Naturelle)*, which, he says, he made at his father's request. The author's name

1803

Notes and Comments

appears as Sebon, Sebeyde, Sabonde, and de Sebonde; the date of his birth is not known; he died in 1432 at Toulouse, where he had professed medicine and theology.

2. See Diogenes Laertius, *Life of Herillus;* Cicero, *Academica*, II, 42 and *De Fin.*, II, 13.

3. One of the ablest Ciceronians of the sixteenth century (1499-1546). His visit to the Chateau de Montaigne was probably in 1544.

4. Montaigne *père*.

5. In 1580 to 1588: *(et tout le monde est quasi de ce genre)*.

6. *Nam cupide concultatur nimis ante metutum.*
—Lucretius, V, 1140.

7. *Il [le vulgaire] nait interposé son decret.*

8. The phrase *quelques jours* is one of the countless illustrations of how little Montaigne's indications of the lapse of time can be taken literally; for a few lines farther on he speaks of the great pleasure his father took in the accomplishment of his work; and the translation of a thousand octavo pages could not be achieved—least of all, by Montaigne—in "a few days."

9. In 1580-1588: *avec la nonchalance qu'on void, par l'infini nombre des fautes, que l'imprimeur y laissa, qui en eust la conduite, luy seul.*

10. Another of Montaigne's bad inaccuracies about time. It was only some 140 years. There were only 90 years between the publication of Sebond's work and that of Montaigne's translation.

11. That is, political opinions.

12. *Illisos fluctus rupes ut vasta refundit,*
Et varias circum latrantes dissipat undas

Apology for Raimond Sebond

Mole sua. —An imitation (author unknown) of Virgil, *Æneid*, VII, 587, in a poem *In laudem Ronsardi*.

13. That is, Christianity.
14. *Evenements.* This word seems out of place in this list.
15. That is, of the truth of our religion.
16. Cf. *Mémoires de Joinville*, XIX.
17. See Boccaccio, *Decameron*, First Day, *Novella* 2.
18. See *Matthew*, 17, 20.
19. *Brevis est institutio vitæ honestæ beatæque, si credas.*—Quintilian, XII, 11.
20. *Doibt* in all editions except that of Lyons, 1595, which has *promist*, which is clearly the meaning.
21. That is, piety.
22. That is, in the wars of that time.
23. That is, belief in divine guidance.
24. *De quoi nous pelotons.*
25. "This passage must have been written in the last half of 1589 or in 1590. In the lifetime of King Henri III, who was assassinated May 31, 1589, it was the Protestants who asserted the right to take arms against the king, and the Catholics denied that theory. After the death of Henri III, when a Protestant, Henri IV, succeeded him on the throne, the positions were reversed."—M. Villey.
26. *De l'armée, mesmes legitime:* that is, even the army of the King. In 1580-1588: *de nos armées.*
27. *Progrez* = advance forward.
28. *Il n'est point d'hostilité excellante comme la chrestiene.*
29. *Il ne va ny de pied n'y d'aile.*
30. Mock at.

Notes and Comments

31. That is, immortal glory.
32. See Diognes Laertius, *Life of Antisthenes*.
33. See Idem, *Life of Diogenes*.
34. *Non jam se moriens dissolvi conquereretur;*
Sed magis ire foras, vestemque relinquere, ut anguis,
Gauderet, prælonga senex aut cornua cervus.
—Lucretius, III, 613.
35. See Philippians, 'I, 23. The Vulgate reads: *desiderium habens dissolvi, et esse cum Christo.*
36. *The Phædo.* The allusion is to the story of Cleombrotus, who killed himself after reading the *Phædo.* See Book II, chap. 3, p. 478 of this volume.
37. *Liaisons.*
38. See Plato, *Republic*, book I.
39. *Et la persuasion.*
40. See Plato, *Republic*, book III.
41. See Diogenes Laertius, *Life of Bion*.
42. *Par contenance.*
43. *Pour l'avoir plantée en leur conscience pourtant.*
44. *L'erreur.*
45. *Estreindre.*
46. *Estreinte.*
47. That is, the world's frame.
48. See Plutarch, *Of the tranquillity of the soul*.
49. See *Romans*, I, 20. The Vulgate text reads: *Invisibilia enim ipsius a creatura mundi, per ea quæ facta sunt, intellecta conspiciuntur; sempiterna quoque ejus virtus, et divinitas.*
50. *Atque adeo faciem cœli non invidet orbi*
Ipse Deus, vultusque suos corpusque recludit

Apology for Raimond Sebond

*Semper volvendo; seque ipsum inculcat et
   offert,
Ut bene cognosci possit, doceatque videndo
Qualis eat, doceatque suas attendere leges.*
                    —Manilius, *Astronomica*, IV, 907.

51. In 1580 to 1588, the following sentence came immediately after the lines from Manilius: *Si mon imprimeur estoit si amoureux de ces prefaces questées et empruntées, dequoy par l'humeur de ce siècle il n'est pas livre de bonne maison, s'il n'en a le front garny, il se devoit servir de tels vers que ceux-cy, qui sont de meilleure et plus ancienne race que ceux qu'il y est allé planter.*

52. That is, of faith.

53.   *Se melius quid habes, accerse, vel imperium fer.*
                    —Horace, *Epistles*, I, 5.6.

54. *On couche volontiers les sens des escris d'autrui.*

55. Οὐ γὰρ ἐᾷ φρονέειν ὁ θεός μέγα ἄλλον ἢ ἑαυτόν.
                    —Herodotus, VII, 10.
Montaigne took it from Stobæus's *Anthology* (Sermon 22). It was inscribed on the walls of his library.

56. That is, the Evil One.

57. *Deus superbi resisti; humilibus autem dat gratiam.*
                    —I Peter, V, 5.

58. See Plato, *Timæus*.

59. *Experiences.*

60. See St. Augustine, *De Civ. Dei*, XXI, 5.

61. *Nulle facilité* = no way of comprehension?

62. See *Colossians*, II, 8: *Videte ne quis vos decipiet per philosophiam vinanem et fallaciam, secundum traditionem hominum, secundum elementos mundi, non secundum Christum.*

Notes and Comments

63. See I *Corinthians*, III, 19: *Sapientia enim hujus mundi stultitia est apud Deum.*

64. See *Ibid.*, VIII, 2: *Si quis autem se existemat scire aliquid, nondum cognovit quemadmodum oporteat cum scire.*

65. See *Galatians*, VI, 3: *Nam si quis existemat se aliquid esse, cum nihil sit, ipse se seducit.*

66. That is, those who believe in *la philosophie mondaine.*

67. *Cette miserable et chetive creature qui n'est pas seulement maistresse de soy, exposée aux offences de toutes choses, se die maistresse et Emperiere de l'univers.* It is to be regretted that it is impossible to express the bitterly ironic effect of this description of man as of the feminine gender, made possible in French by the fact that *creature* is feminine.

68. Cf. Cicero, *De Nat. Deor.*, I, 9.

69. *Quorum igitur causa quis dixerit effectum esse mundum? Eorum scilicet animantium quæ ratione utuntur. Hi sunt dii et homines, quibus profecto nihil est melius.*—Cicero, *De Nat. Deor.*, II, 54.

70.   *Cum suspicimus magni cœlestia mundi Templa super stellisque micantibus Æthere fixum, Et venit in mentem lunæ solisque viarum.*
    —Lucretius, V, 1204.

71.   *Facta etenim et vitas hominum suspendit ab astris.*
    —Manilius, *Astronomica*, III, 58.

72.   *Speculataque longe Deprendit tacitis dominantia legibus astra,*

Apology for Raimond Sebond

*Et totum alterna mundum ratione moveri,
Fatorumque vices certis discernere signis.*
—*Ibid.*, I, 60.

73. *Au branle.*
74. *Quantaque quam parvi faciant discrimina
    motus;
    Tantum est hoc regnum, quod regibus imperat
    ipsis!*
    —Manilius, *Astronomica*, I, 55 and IV, 93.
75. *furit alter amore,
    Et pontum tranare potest et vertere Trojam;
    Alterius sors est scribendis legibus apta;
    Ecce patrem nati perimunt, natosque parentes,
    Mutuaque armati coeunt in vulnera fratres;
    Non nostrum hoc bellum est; coguntur tanta
    movere,
    Inque suas ferri pœnas lacerandaque membra;
    Hoc quoque fatale est, sic ipsum expendere
    fatum.* —*Ibid.*, IV, 79-85, 118.

76. *Distribution du ciel;* that is, from the disposition of the heavenly bodies in a certain order.

77. *Quæ molitio, quæ ferramenta, qui vectes, quæ machinæ, qui ministri tanti operis fuerunt?*—Cicero, *De Nat. Deor.*, I, 8.

78. *Quæ sunt tantæ animi angustiæ!*—Cicero, *De Nat. Deor.*, I, 31.

79. See Plutarch, *Of the face in the moon.*

80. See Diogenes Laertius, *Life of Anaxagoras.*

81. *Inter cætera mortalitatis incommoda te hoc est, caligo mentium, nec tantum necessitas errandi sed errorum amor.*—Seneca, *De Ira*, II, 9.

1809

Notes and Comments

82. *Corruptibile corpus aggravat animam, et deprimit terrena inhabitatio sensum multa cogitantem.—Book of Wisdom*, IX, 15; St. Augustine, *De Civ. Dei*, XII, 15.

83. See Pliny, *Nat. Hist.*; the Latin sentence is quoted at the end of chap. 14 (vol. 3).

84. Those that crawl, distinguished from those that fly and swim.

85. The edition of 1595 adds: *Nous nous entretenons de singeries reciproques; si j'ay mon heure de commencer ou de refuser, aussi a elle la sienne.*

86. That is, man.

87. See Plato, *Statesman*.

88. See Idem, *Timæus*.

89. That is, the beasts.

90. This sentence first appeared in the edition of 1582, but only Apollonius "and others" were included. The other three names were added in 1588.

91. See Pliny, *Nat. Hist.*, VI, 35; Plutarch, *Common conceptions of the Stoics.*

92.   *Et mutæ pecudes et denique secla ferarum*
    Dissimiles fuerunt voces variasque cluere,
    Cum metus aut dolor est, aut cum jam gaudia
       gliscunt.   —Lucretius, V, 1059.

93.   *Non alia longe ratione atque ipsa videtur*
    Protrahere ad gestum pueros infantia linguæ.
               —Idem, 1030.

94.   *E'l silentio ancor suole*
    Haver prieghi e parole.
              —Tasso, *Aminta*, II, 34.

95. See Quintilian, book XI.

96. See Pliny, *Nat. Hist.*, VI, 35.

97. See Plutarch, *Apothegms of the Lacedæmonians*.
98. That is, in the power of producing effects.
99.   *His quidam signis atque hæc exempla sequuti,*
     Esse apibus partem divinæ mentis et haustus
     Æthereos dixere.
                        —Virgil, *Georgics*, IV, 219.

100. *Plustost d'une figure quarrée que de la ronde.*—Here Montaigne so clearly says the opposite of what he means, that the terms are transposed in the translation.
101. Of the clay.
102. For this whole passage, from the verses from the *Georgics*, see Plutarch, *What animals are the most cunning*.
103. That is, other creatures.
104. *Servile.*
105. That is, the government of the world.
106. See Seneca, *Epistle* 90.
107. An allusion to Pliny, *Nat. Hist.*, beginning of book VII.
108.   *Tum porro puer, ut sævis projectus ab undis*
     Navita, nudus humi jacet, infans, indigus omni
     Vitali auxilio, tum primum in luminis oras
     Nixibus ex alvo matris natura profudit;
     Vagituque locum lugubri complet, ut æquum
         est
     Cui tantum in vita restet transire malorum.
     At variæ crescunt pecudes, armenta, feræque,
     Nec crepitacula eis opus est, nec cuiquam
         adhibenda est
     Almæ nutricis blanda atque infracta loquela;
     Nec varias quærunt vestes pro tempore cœli;

Notes and Comments

Denique non armis opus est, non mœnibus altis,
Queis sua tutentur, quando omnibus omnia large
Tellus ipsa parit naturaque dædala rerum.
—Lucretius, V, 222.

109. In 1580 to 1588: *la foiblesse de nostre naissance se trouve à peu pres, en la naissance des autres creatures.*
110. *Au vent et à l'air.*
111. See Plutarch, *Life of Lycurgus.*
112. *Sentit enim vim quisque suam quam possit abuti.* —Lucretius, V, 1033.
113. *Sans soing et sans façon.*
114. *Et tellus nitidas fruges vinetaque læta*
Sponte sua primum mortalibus ipsa creavit;
Ipsa dedit dulces fœtus et pabula læta;
Quæ nunc vix nostro grandescunt aucta labore,
Conterimusque boves et vires agricolarum.
—Lucretius, II, 1157.
115. That is, that this is a natural instinct in us.
116. See Plutarch, *What animals are the most cunning.*
117. *Et nous changeons d'idiome selon l'espece.*
118. *Cosi per entro loro schiera bruna*
S'ammusa l'una con l'altra formica
Forse à spiar lor via, et lor fortuna.
—Dante, *Purgatory*, XXVI, 34.
119. See Lactantius, *Divine Institutions*, III, 10.
120. See Aristotle, *History of Animals*, IV, 9.9.
121. *Variæque volucres*
Longe alias alio jaciunt in tempore voces,
Et partim mutant cum tempestatibus una

1812

Apology for Raimond Sebond

      Raucisonos cantus.   —Lucretius, V, 1078—84.
122. That is, that the child would talk in some way.
123. See Book I, chap. 36, p. 302.
124. *Indupedita suis fatalibus omnia vinclis.*
                                —Lucretius, V, 876.
125.   *Res quæque suo ritu procedit, et omnes*
     Fœdere naturæ certo discrimina servant.
                                —Lucretius, V, 923.
126. *Goust.*
127. *Une plus belle recommendation.*
128. See Plutarch, *What animals are the most cunning.*
129. See Plutarch, *How to tell a flatterer from a friend.*
130. See Herodotus, V, 5.
131. See Cæsar, *De Bello Gallico*, III, 22.
132. *En cette rude escole des escrimeurs à outrance.*
133. See Justus Lipsius, *Saturnalium sermonum*, II, 5.
134.   *Ure meum, si vis flamma caput, et pete ferro*
     Corpus, et intorto verbere terga seca.
                                —Tibullus, I, 9.21.
135. See Herodotus, IV, 71, 72.
136. See Diogenes Laertius, *Life of Diogenes.*
137. See Plutarch, *That wild beasts make use of reason.*
138.   *Serpente ciconia pullos*
    Nutrit, et inventa per devia rura lacerta,
    Et leporem aut capream famulæ Jovis, et
        generosæ
    In saltu venantur aves.
                      —Juvenal, XIV, 74, 75, 81, 82.
139. See Pliny, *Nat. Hist.*, X, 8.
140. The Sea of Azof.
141. See *Ibid.*

Notes and Comments

142. *Colliers* = *collets*.
143. *Ligne:* fishing-line(?)
144. See Plutarch, *What animals are the most cunning*.
145. See Idem, *Life of Sylla*.
146. For this and the following examples, See Plutarch, *What animals are the most cunning*.
147. See *Ibid.*; also, *Life of Alexander*.
148. In 1580: *qu'ils ne font mal ne douleur quelconque*—Plutarch's words as rendered by Amyot; changed in 1588 to *que nous ne le sçaurions faire avec si peu de douleur:* "No longer having the text before him," says M. Villey, "Montaigne makes his statement less emphatic."
149. A Greek philosopher, about 280 B.C.
150. See Plutarch, *What animals are the most cunning;* Sextus Empiricus, *Hypotyposes*, I, 14. Montaigne's version of the story does not follow absolutely either text.
151. The *sufficiens enumeratio partium* was one of the essential qualities of a syllogism according to the old scholastic logic.
152. Georgius Trapezuntius (George of Trebizond), 1396-1486.
153. See Plutarch, *What animals are the most cunning*, for this and the following examples.
154. See Pliny, *Nat. Hist.*, X, 29.
155. See Arrianus (not Arrius), *History of India*, XIV.
156. See Plutarch, *What animals are the most cunning*.
157. See *Ibid*.
158. See Plutarch, *What animals are the most cunning*.
159. Barbary.
160. See *Ibid*.
161. Cf. Book I, chap. 42, p. 345.

Apology for Raimond Sebond

162. See Plutarch, *What animals are the most cunning.*
163. The keepers. See *Ibid.*
164. *Siquidem Tyrio servire solebant
Annibali, et nostris ducibus, regique Molosso,
Horum majores, et dorso ferre cohortes,
Partem aliquam belli et euntem in prœlia
turmam.* —Juvenal, XII, 107.
165. See de Gomara, *Histoire Générale des Indes.*
166. In 1580 to 1588: *Nous vivons, et eux et nous, sous mesme tect et humons une mesme air: il y a, sauf le plus et le moins, entre nous une perpetuelle ressemblance.*
167. *Inclinations serpentées.*
168. See Plutarch, *What animals are the most cunning.*
169. *Nomen habent, et ad magistri
Vocem quisque sui venit citatus.*
—Martial, IV, 29.6.
170. *Precepte* = authoritative command. See Plutarch, *What animals are the most cunning;* Pliny, *Nat. Hist.,* VIII, 1.
171. See Plutarch, *What animals are the most cunning.*
172. That is, many authors.
173. *Galere capitanesse.*
174. See Pliny, *Nat. Hist.,* XXXII, 1.
175. That is, astrologer, the Latin *mathematicus.*
176. See Plutarch, *What animals are the most cunning.*
177. See *Ibid.*
178. *Par l'effect de la souffrance.*
179. *Jaunisse* (jaundice).
180. *Car c'est prester à la lettre.*
181. *Au travers des filets et de la scene.* See *Ibid.*
182. In 1580 to 1588: *Car à nos enfans il est certain*

Notes and Comments

que bien avant en l'aage, nous n'y découvrons rien sauf la forme corporelle, par où nous en puissions faire triage.

183. *Leurs causes motrices.*

184.   *More ferarum*
Quadrupedumque magis ritu, plerumque
        putantur
Concipere uxores; quia sic loca sumere possunt,
Pectoribus positis, sublatis semina lumbis.
—Lucretius, IV, 1264; the sense is given in the text.

185. *Nam mulier prohibet se concipere atque*
        repugnat,
Clunibus ipsa viri venerem si læta retractet,
Atque exossato ciet omni pectore fluctus.
Ejicit enim sulcum recta regione viaque
Vomerem, atque locis avertit seminis ictum.
                —Idem, IV, 1269.

186. See Plutarch, *What animals are the most cunning.*
187. That is, Pyrrhus. See *Ibid.*
188. See Plutarch, *That beasts make use of reason.*
189. *Les apprests à nos cuisines ne touchent pas son ordonnance.*

190.   *Neque illa*
Magno prognatum deposcit consule cunnum.
                —Horace, *Satires*, I, 2.69.

191.   *Nec habetur turpe juvencæ*
Ferre patrem tergo; fit equo sua filia conjux;
Quasque creavit init pecudes caper; ipsaque
        cujus
Semine concepta est, ex illo concipit ales.
                —Ovid, *Metam.*, X, 325.

192. See Plutarch, *What animals are the most cunning.*

Apology for Raimond Sebond

193. See *Ibid*.

194.   *Quando leoni*
Fortior eripuit vitam leo? quo nemore unquam
Expiravit aper majoris dentibus apri?
                                   —Juvenal, XV, 160.

195.   *Sæpe duobus*
Regibus incessit magno discordia motu,
Continuoque animos vulgi et trepidantia bello
Corda licet longe præsciscere.
                         —Virgil, *Georgics*, IV, 67.

196. *Fulgur ibi ad cœlum se tollit, totaque circum*
Ære renidescit tellus, subterque virum vi
Excitur pedibus sonitus, clamoreque montes
Icti rejectant voces ad sidera mundi.
                              —Lucretius, II, 325.

197.   *Paridis propter narratur amorem*
Græcia Barbariæ diro collisa duello.
                           —Horace, *Epistles*, I, 2.6.

198. *Qui ne devroient esmouvoir deux harangeres à s'esgratigner.*

199. For Anthony is fired with Glaphyre's charms
Fain would his Fulvia tempt me to her arms,
If Anthony be false, what then? Must I
Be slave to Fulvia's lustful tyranny?
Declare for love or war, she said, and frowned,
'No love I'll grant, so let the trumpets sound!'
                              —Martial, XI, 21.3.

Said to have been written by Augustus.

200. Some princess; probably Catherine de Bourbon, sister of Henri IV.

Notes and Comments

201. *Quam multi Lybico voluuntur marmore fluctus,*
Sævus ubi Orion hybernis conditur undis,
Vel cum sole novo densæ torrentur aristæ,
Aut Hermi campo, aut Lyciæ flaventibus arvis,
Scuta sonant, pulsuque pedum tremit excita
tellus. —Virgil, *Æneid*, VII, 718.
202. See Seneca, *Natural Questions*, Preface.
203. *It nigrum campis agmen.*
—Virgil, *Æneid*, IV, 404.
204. That is, dust. See Plutarch, *Life of Sertorius*.
205. See Idem, *Life of Eumenes*.
206. See Idem, *Life of Marcus Crassus*.
207. *Hi motus animorum atque hæc certamina tanta*
Pulveris exigui jactu compressa quiescent.
—Virgil, *Georgics*, IV, 86.
208. *Qu'on descouple mesmes de nos mouches apres.*
209. Of the bees. See Goulard, *History of Portugal*.
210. *Menez et ramenez.*
211. *Ils veulent aussi legierement que nous, mais ils peuvent plus.*
212. This paragraph is an addition of 1582.
213. See Plutarch, *What animals are the most cunning*, for this and the following examples relating to dogs.
214. *Il leur faisoit feste de la queue.*
215. *S'enquerans des nouvelles du poil de ce chien.*
216. Montaigne took this story almost verbatim from Aulus Gellius, *Noctes Atticæ*, V, 14.
217. Androcles.
218. *Ayant r'asseuré sa veue pour le considerer et reconnoistre.*
219. *Post, bellator equus, positis insignibus, Æthon*

1818

Apology for Raimond Sebond

*It lachrymans, guttisque humectat grandibus
    ora.* —Virgil, *Æneid*, XI, 89.

220. See Plutarch, *What animals are the most cunning.*

221. In 1580 and 1582: *pour le service de sa vie, de certains animaux ou des hommes.*

222. See Plutarch, *What animals are the most cunning.*

223. See *Ibid.*

224. See Plutarch, *What animals are the most cunning.*

225. That is, the practical application of astronomy, as an art, to human uses.

226. *Clos et environné tout à lentour.*

227. See Plutarch, *Ibid.*

228. See *Ibid.*

229. See Arrian of Nicomedia. Montaigne read Arrian in a translation (1581), called *Les faits et les conquestes d'Alexandre le Grand.*

230. See Plutarch, *What animals are the most cunning.*

231. *Le vous estreinct et vous le serre.*

232. See Plutarch, *What animals are the most cunning;* Pliny, *Nat. Hist.*, X, 32.

233. Cf. *supra*, p. 622: *Elles [les bestes] produisent en encores d'autres qui surpassent de bien loin nostre capacité, ausquelles il s'en faut tant que nous puissions arriver par imitation que par imagination mesme nous ne les pouvons concevoir.*

234. *Quippe videbis equos fortes, cum membra
        jacebunt
    In somnis, sudare tamen, spirareque sæpe,
    Et quasi de palma summas contendere vires.*
        —Lucretius, IV, 987.

235. *Venantumque canes in molli sæpe quiete*

Notes and Comments

*Jactant crura tamen subito, vocesque repente
Mittunt, et crebras reducunt naribus auras,
Ut vestigia si teneant inventa ferarum,
Experge factique sequuntur inania sæpe
Cervorum simulacra, fugæ quasi dedita cernant;
Donec discussis redeant erroribus ad se.*
—Idem, IV, 991.

236. *Spirituel.*

237. *Consueta domi catulorum blanda propago
Degere, sæpe levem ex oculis volucremque soporem
Discutere, et corpus de terra corripere instant,
Proinde quasi ignotas facies atque ora tuantur.*
—Lucretius, IV, 998.

The second line is not found in modern texts.

238. *Turpis Romano Belgicus ore color.*
—Propertius, II, 18.26.

239. See Gomara, *Histoire Générale des Indes.*
240. See *Ibid.*
241. See Gasparo Balbi, *Travels in India.*
242. See Gomara, *ubi sup.*
243. See Pliny, *Nat. Hist.*, VI, 13.
244. See Gomara, *ubi sup.*
245. This sentence refers back to the statement as to the Peruvians' preference for large ears (p. 642), the intervening passages having been added in 1588 or 1595.
246. *Qui y demande de la mignardise et de la douceur.*
247. See Cicero, *De Nat. Deor.*, I, 10. Cicero refers to a passage in the *Timæus.*
248. See *Ibid.*

Apology for Raimond Sebond

249. That is, in the matter of beauty.
250. *A multis animalibus decore vincimur.*—Seneca, *Epistle* 124.22.
251. *Qui ne peut tumber en proportion.*
252. *Vers le ciel son origine*—a puzzling phrase.
253. *Pronaque cum spectent animalia cætera terram,*
Os homini sublime dedit, cœlumque videre
Jussit, et erectos ad sidera tollere vultus.
—Ovid, *Metam.*, I, 84.
254. See Plato, *Timæus, passim;* Cicero, *De Nat. Deor.*, II, 53 *et seq.*
255. *Simia quam similis, turpissima bestia, nobis!*
—Ennius, in Cicero, *De Nat. Deor.*, I, 35.
256. *Ille quod obscœnas in aperto corpore partes*
Viderat, in cursu qui fuit, hæsit amor.
—Ovid, *De Remedio Amoris*, 429.
257. *Nec veneres nostras hoc fallit; quo magis ipsæ,*
Omnia summo opere hos vitæ post scænia celant,
Quos retinere volunt adstrictosque esse in
amore. —Lucretius, IV, 1185.
258. That is, to animals.
259. See Plutarch, *Common conceptions against the Stoics.*
260. *Ce masque corporel.*
261. *N'est rien qui vaille.*
262. *Ut vinum ægrotis, quia prodest raro, nocet sæpissime, melius est non adhibere omnino, quam, spe dubiæ salutis, in apertam perniciem incurrere; sic haud scio an melius fuerit humano generi motum istum celerem cogitationis, acumen, solertiam, quam rationem vocamus, quoniam pestifera sint multis, admodum paucis salutaria, non*

Notes and Comments

dari omnino, quam tam munifice et tam large dari.—Cicero, *De Nat. Deor.*, III, 27.

263. *Sont ils entrez en composition de la mort.*

264. In 1580 to 1588: *en quelques republiques.*

265. See Cornelius Agrippa, *Of the uncertainty and vanity of learning.*

266. *Illiterati num minus nervi rigent?*
—Horace, *Epodes*, VIII, 17.

267. *Scilicet et morbis et debilitate carebis,*
Et luctum et curam effugies, et tempora vitæ
Longa tibi post hæc fato meliore dabuntur.

268. *La doctrine.*

269. *La gloire.* In 1580 to 1588: *La doctrine est encores moins necessaire au service de la vie que n'est la gloire.*

270. *Et ce neantmoins.*

271. *Ce discours.*

272. *Qui peut effectuer un homme de bien.*

273. *A son discours.*

274. See Plutarch, *Against Colotes the Epicurean.* Coste suggested this source. If Montaigne had it in mind, his memory betrayed him, for Plutarch's words have a different sense, and according to him, it was Colotes, not Epicurus, who said it.

275. *Où l'homme n'eust rien à connoistre et à causer.*

276. *Eritis sicut dii, scientes bonum et malum.*—*Genesis*, III, 5.

277. See Cicero, *De Fin.*, V, 18, alluding to *Odyssey*, XII, 188.

278. *Cavete ne quis vos decipiat per philosophiam et inanes seductiones secundum elementa mundi.*—*Colossians*, II, 8.

1822

Apology for Raimond Sebond

279. *Ad summum, sapiens uno minor est Jove; dives,*
Liber, honoratus, pulcher, rex denique regum
Præcipue sanus, nisi cum pituita molesta est.
—Horace, *Epistles*, I, 1.106.

280. *Usage = manière d'user quelque chose.*

281. See Stobæus, *Sermon* 21. The passage of Epictetus referred to is in the *Enchiridion*, XI.

282. See Plutarch, *Common conceptions against the Stoics.*

283. See Cicero, *Tusc. Disp.*, V, 36. Cicero is speaking of *philosophia.*

284. *Sans desplaisir et sans offence.* See *Ibid.*, I, 26.

285.   *Deus ille fuit, Deus, inclute Memmi,*
Qui princeps vitæ rationem invenit eam, quæ
Nunc appellatur sapientia, quique per artem
Fluctibus e tantis vitam tantisque tenebris
In tam tranquillo et tam clara luce locavit.
—Lucretius, V, 8.

286. Lucretius.

287. Epicurus.

288. See Cicero, *Academica*, II, 23.

289. See Idem, *De Fin.*, II, 13.

290. See Plutarch, *Common conceptions against the Stoics.*

291. See Seneca, *Epistle* 22.17.

292. *In virtute vere gloriamur; quod non contingeret, si id donum a deo, non a nobis haberemus.*—Cicero, *De Nat. Deor.*, III, 36.

293. See Seneca, *Epistle* 53.

294. *Bien faire la figue à la douleur.* See Cicero, *Tusc. Disp.*, II, 25.

Notes and Comments

295. In 1580 to 1588: *Ce n'est que vent et paroles.*
296. *Re succumbere non oportebat verbis gloriantem.*—Cicero, *Tusc. Disp.*, II, 13.
297. See Cicero, *De Fin.*, V, 31.
298. See *Ibid.*
299. See Diogenes Laertius, *Life of Pyrrho.*
300. That is, learning.
301. *A present;* added in 1588.
302. The soul.
303. Torquato Tasso was confined in a hospital at Ferrara from 1579 to 1586.
304. *Tendue.*
305. *On a mis en lumiere.*
306. *Tant à desirer qu'à craindre.*
307. *Segnius homines bona quam mala sentiunt.*—Livy, XXX, 21.
308.   *Pungit*
  In cute vix summa violatum plagula corpus,
  Quando valere nihil quemquam movet. Hoc juvat unum,
  Quod me non torquet latus aut pes; cætera quisquam
  Vix queat aut sanum sese, aut sentire valentem.
                              —La Boëtie.
309. *A la seule indolence.*
310. *Nimium boni est, cui nihil est mali.*
              —Quoted in Cicero, *De Fin.*, II, 13.
311. *Ce mesme chatouillement et esguisement.*
312. See Cicero, *Tusc. Disp.*, III, 6.
313. *Istud nihil dolere, non sine magna mercede contingit immanitatis in animo, stuporis in corpore.*—*Ibid.*

314. This is the doctrine of Epicurus. See Cicero, *Tusc. Disp.*, III, 16, and *De Fin.*, II, 30 and 32.

315. *Levationes ægritudinum in avocatione a cogitanda molestia et revocatione ad contemplandas voluptates ponit.* —Idem, *Tusc. Disp.*, III, 15.

316. *Ce feroit plutost luy empirer son marché.*

317. *Che ricordarsi il ben doppia la noia.*
    —A refashioning of the *Inferno*, IV, 121.

318. This again is Epicurean doctrine. See Cicero, *De Fin.*, II, 32.

319. *Suavis est laborum præteritorum memoria.*
—Euripides *(Andromeda)*, in Cicero, *De Fin.*, II, 32.

320. *Est situm in nobis, ut et adversa quasi perpetua oblivione obruamus et secunda jucunde et suaviter meminerimus.*—Cicero, *De Fin.*, I, 17.

321. *Memini etiam quæ nolo, oblivisci non possum quæ volo.*—*Ibid.*, II, 32. Words attributed by Cicero to Themistocles.

322. *Qui se unus sapientem profiteri sit ausus.*—*Ibid*, II, 3 (Epicurus).

323. *Qui genus humanum ingenio superavit, et omnes*
Præstrinxit, stellas exortus ut ætherius sol.
    —Lucretius, III, 1043.

324. *Iners malorum remedium ignorantia est.*—Seneca, *Œdipus*, III, 7.

325. *Apparences frivoles.*

326.   *Potare et spargere flores*
Incipiam, patiarque vel inconsultus haberi.
    —Horace, *Epistles*, I, 5.14.

327. *Cette humeur peccante.*

Notes and Comments

328. In the *Adages* of Erasmus, the examples of Lycas and Thrasilaus, the Greek verse, and the quotations from *Ecclesiastes* are found under *Fortunata stultitia*.

329.
>   *Pol! me occidistis, amici,*
>   *Non servastis, ait, cui six extorta voluptas*
>   *Et demptus per vim mentis gratissimus error.*
>   —Horace, *Epistles*, II, 2.138.

330. See Athenæus, book XII.

331. Ἐν τῷ φρονεῖν γὰρ μηδὲν ἥδιστος βίος.
>   —Sophocles, *Ajax*, 552.

332. See *Ecclesiastes*, I, 18. Montaigne, of course, used the Vulgate.

333. *Placet? pare. Non placet? quacunque vis, exi.*—Seneca, *Epistle* 70. The original reads: *Placet? vive. Non placet? licet eo reverti unde venisti.*

334. *Pungit dolor? Vel fodiat sane. Si nudus es, da jugulum; sin tectus armis Vulcaniis, id est fortitudine, resiste.* —Cicero, *Tusc. Disp.*, II, 14.

335. *Aut bibat, aut abeat.*—*Ibid.*, V, 41.

336.
>   *Vivere si recte nescis, decede peritis;*
>   *Lusisti satis, edisti satis atque bibisti;*
>   *Tempus abire tibi est, ne potum largius æquo*
>   *Rideat et pulset lasciva decentius ætas.*
>   —Horace, *Epistles*, II, 2.213.

337. That is, philosophy's.

338.
>   *Democritum postquam matura vetustas*
>   *Admonuit memorem motus languescere mentis,*
>   *Sponte sua leto caput obvius obtulit ipse.*
>   —Lucretius, III, 1039.

339. See Plutarch, *Common conceptions against the Stoics.*

Apology for Raimond Sebond

340. *Par la hart.* See Diogenes Laertius, *Life of Crates.*

341. See Plutarch, *Of progress in virtue;* Seneca, *Epistles* 59, 62, 64, 98, 108.

342. There is no such passage in the New Testament. See C. Agrippa, *Of the uncertainty and vanity of learning.*

343. Valentinianus. There was no Emperor Valentianus. The mistake is Agrippa's. See *Ibid.*

344. *Di cittatorie piene e di libelli,*
D'esamine e di carte, di procure,
Hanno le mani e il seno, e gran fastelli
Di chiose, di consigli e di letture:
Per cui le faculta de poverelli
Non sono mai ne le citta sicure;
Hanno dietro e dinanzi, e d'ambi ilati,
Notai, procuratori e advocati.
—Ariosto, *Orlando Furioso*, XIV, 84.

345. Says M. Villey: "Cette allégation est peut-être une déformation d'un mot de Varron qui a été rapporté par Nonius au mot *cepe.* Je n'ai pas retrouvé la source de Montaigne."

346. *Preud'hommie.*

347. *Regent.*

348. ἡ δεισιδαιμονία καθάπερ πατρὶ τῷ τυφῷ πείτεται.—Stobæus, *Sermon* 22; attributed to Socrates.

349. See Plato, *Apology.*

350. See *Ecclesiasticus*, X, 9. The Latin is *Quid superbit terra et cinis?* By changing the third person of the verb to the second, Montaigne achieves an admirable rhetorical effect. The sentence was one of those written on the beams of his library.

351. This sentence, too, was written in Latin on the

Notes and Comments

beams of the library, and credited to "Eccl. VII." But it is not to be found in *Ecclesiastes*, and M. Villey suggests that it was written by Montaigne himself, or that he borrowed it from some author who deceived him as to its origin.

352. *Ce n'est rien à la verité que de nous.*

353. *Melius scitur Deus nesciendo.*—De Ordine, II, 16.

354. *Sanctius est ac reverentius de actis deorum credere quam scire.*—Germania, XXXIV.

355. See *Laws*, book VII.

356. *Atque illum quidem parentem hujus universitatis invenire difficile; et, quum jam inveneris, indicare in vulgus, nefas.*—Cicero, translation of Plato, *Timæus*, II.

357. *Immortalia mortali sermone notantes.*
—Lucretius, V, 121.

358. *Pour s'avaler.*

359. *Arriver aus apparentes.*

360. See Cicero, *De Nat. Deor.*, III, 15.

361. See *Nicomachæan Ethics*, VII, 1.1.

362. *Neque gratia, neque ira teneri potest, quod quæ talia essent, imbecilla essent omnia.*—Cicero, *De Nat. Deor.*, I, 17. (Part of a quotation from Epicurus.)

363. That is, the scribe.

364. *Par la vanité de la predication.* See *I Corinthians*, I, 19-21.

365. See Plutarch, *Of the progress of virtue.*

366. See Cicero, *De Nat. Deor.*, I, 17.

367. See Diogenes Laertius, *Life of Pherecides.*

368. Socrates. In 1580 to 1588: *(et qui n'eust autre plus juste occasion d'estre appellé sage que cette sienne sentence).*

Apology for Raimond Sebond

369. See Cicero, *Academica*, I, 4; Plato, *Apology*, etc.

370. See the *Politicus*.

371. *Omnes pene veteres nihil cognosci, nihil percipi, nihil sciri posse dixerunt; angustos sensus, imbecillos animos, brevia curricula vitæ.*—Cicero, *Academica*, I, 12.

372. Montaigne took this from Cornelius Agrippa (*Of the uncertainty and vanity of learning*), who mistakenly refers to Valerius Maximus.

373. *Dicendum est, sed ita ut nihil affirmem, quæram omnia, dubitans plerumque et mihi diffidens.*—Cicero, De Div., II, 3.

374. *Qui vigilans stertit . . .*
Mortua cui vita est prope jam vivo atque videnti.
—Lucretius, III, 1048, 1046.

375. *Meurs (mœurs).*

376. *Ils se sont tenus.* In 1580 to 1588, *ils se sont resolus.*

377. *Collège.*

378. *La fin de ceux-cy, c'est la foiblesse.*

379. See Sextus Empiricus, *Hypotyposes*, I, 1.1.

380. See Diogenes Laertius, *Life of Pyrrho*.

381. *Nil sciri quisquis putat, id quoque nescit*
An sciri possit quo se nil scire fatetur.
—Lucretius, IV, 469.

382. *La consentante.*

383. *C'estoit apparence.* Cicero's word is *visum*.

384. See Cicero, *Academica*, IV, 47.

385. *Droicte.*

386. See Sextus Empiricus, *Hypot.*, I, 12.

387. *La revenche.*

388. See *Ibid.*, I, 13.

Notes and Comments

389. *Par certain jugement.*

390. *Ad quamcunque disciplinam velut tempestate delati, ad eam tanquam ad saxum adhærescunt.*—Cicero, *Academica*, II, 3.

391. *Hoc liberiores et solutiores quod integra illis est judicandi potestas.*—*Ibid.*

392. See *Ibid.*, 43.

393. See Cicero, *Academica*, II, 33. Panætius did not give his assent to the general belief of his (the Stoic) sect.

394. *De se couvrir.*

395. *Ut, quum in eadem re paria contrariis in partibus momenta inveniuntur, facilius ab utraque parte assertio sustineatur.*—Cicero, *Academica*, I, 12.

396. *Pour quoi une chose soit fauce, que non pas qu'elle soit vraie.*

397. See Sextus Empiricus, *Hypot.*, I, 22; 19; 23. "Most of the Sceptic aphorisms were written in Greek on the beams of Montaigne's library."—M. Villey.

398. Cf. the opening words of Book I, chap. 47: *C'est bien ce que dict ce vers:*

Ἐπέων δε πολὺς νόμος ἔνθα καὶ ἔνθα.

(*Iliad*, XX, 249.) "*Il y a prou loy de parler par tout, et pour et contre.*" This sentence was on the library beams.

399. Another remark of Sextus, which was carved on the library beams.

400. *Voyla leurs refreins.*

401. See Sextus Empiricus, *Hypot.*, I, 11.

402. *Non enim nos Deus ista scire, sed tantummodo uti voluit.*—Cicero, *De Div.*, I, 18.

403. In 1580 to 1588: *ce que* [Diogenes] *Laertius dict de la vie de Pyrrho, et à quoy Lucianus, Aulus Gellius,*

Apology for Raimond Sebond

et autres semblent s'encliner.

404. This whole passage, down to "touchstone" p. 675, line 11, is a translation of portions of Cicero, *Academica*, II, 31, 33, and 34.

405. *Et se plie à ce que.*

406. *D'expresse contrariete.*

407. That is, the Pyrrhonian philosophy (taking up the thread broken by the addition of the *Édition Municipale*).

408. *Telles formes.*

409. There is no such sentence in *Ecclesiastes*.

410. *Dominus novit cogitationes hominum, quoniam vanæ sunt.*—Psalm XCIV, 11.

411. *Quam docti fingunt, magis quam norunt.*— Source not known.

412. See Plato, *Timæus*.

413. *Ut potero, explicabo; nec tamen, ut Pythius Apollo, certa ut sint et fixa, quæ dixero; sed, ut homunculus, probabilia conjectura sequens.*—Cicero, *Tusc. Disp.*, I, 9.

414. *Discours naturel et populere.*

415. *Si forte, de deorum natura ortuque mundi disserentes, minus id quod habemus animo consequimur, haud erit mirum. Æquum est enim meminisse et me qui disseram, hominem esse, et vos qui judicetis; ut, si probabilia dicentur, nihil ultra requiratis.*—Cicero, in his translation of Plato, *Timæus*, III.

416. Aristotle.

417. See Plutarch, *Table-Talk*.

418. In 1580 to 1588: *(comme pour exemple sur le propos de l'immortalité de l'ame).*

419. *C'est par effect un Pyrrhonisme soubs une forme resolutive.* In 1580 to 1588: *Pyrrhonisme qu'il represente*

Notes and Comments

soubs la forme de parler qu'il a entreprise.

420. *Qui requirunt quid de quaque re ipsi sentiamus, curiosius id faciunt quam necesse est. Hæc in philosophia ratio contra omnia disserendi nullamque rem aperte judicandi, profecta a Socrate, repetita ab Arcesila, confirmata a Carneade, usque ad nostram viget ætatem. Hi sumus qui omnibus veris falsa quædam adjuncta esse dicamus, tanta similitudine ut in iis nulla insit certe judicandi et assentiendi nota.*—Cicero, *De Nat. Deor.*, I, 5.

421. In 1588: *pour en voiler leurs opinions.*

422. See Cicero, *Academica*, II, 45.

423. In 1588: *Pourquoi a crainct Epicurus qu'on l'entendit.*

424. Obscure. See Cicero, *De Fin.*, II, 5.

425.   *Clarus ob obscuram linguam magis inter inanes,*
    Omnia enim stolidi magis admirantur amantque
    Inversis quæ sub verbis latitantia cernunt.
                   —Lucretius, I, 639, 641, 642.

Lucretius is talking about Heraclitus.

426. See Cicero, *De Off.*, I, 6.

427. See Diogenes Laertius, *Life of Aristippus*.

428. See Idem, *Life of Zeno*.

429. Possibly an erroneous reminiscence of a passage in Plutarch, *Contradictions of the Stoic philosophers*.

430. See Plutarch, *Life of Alexander*.

431. The form of this passage, from "Chrysippus," p. 274, was somewhat different in 1580 to 1588.

432. *Estimant toute autre aprantissage subsecutif à celuyla et supernumerere.*

1832

Apology for Raimond Sebond

433. *Parum mihi placeant eæ litteræ quæ ad virtutem doctoribus nihil profuerunt.*—Sallust, *Jugurtha*, LXXXV, 32. The text of Sallust differs from Montaigne's version, which he took from the *Politics* of Justus Lipsius. Marius is speaking of the Greek language.

434. That is, the philosophers.

435. See Sextus Empiricus, *Hypot.*, I, 33.

436. *Leur autheur.*

437. See Seneca, *Epistle* 88.

438. See Diogenes Laertius, *Life of Plato*, at the end.

439. *Sages femmes.*

440. *Sage homme.* The play upon words is Montaigne's, not Plato's.

441. *En son amour virile et mentale.*

442. See Plato, *Theætetus.*

443. That is, the Dogmatists.

444. See Cicero, *Academica*, II, 5.

445. *Douteuse en substance et un dessein enquirant plustost.* These first few lines are slightly different in form in 1580 to 1588.

446. In 1588: *Car, au bout de ses discours, il venoit s'escrier.*

447. See Cicero, *Academica*, II, 5.

448. *Cogitationes mortalium timidæ, et incertæ adinventiones nostræ et providentiæ.*—Wisdom of Solomon, IX, 14.

449. See Seneca, *Epistle* 88.

450. See Plutarch, *Table-Talk.*

451. *Satius est supervacua discere quam nihil.*—Seneca, *Epistle* 88.

452. *En toute pasture.*

Notes and Comments

453. See Cicero, *Academica*, II, 41.
454. In 1588: *Comme fut Phæton.* See Plutarch, *That one can not live happily according to the doctrine of the Stoics.*
455. *Unicuique ista pro ingenio finguntur, non ex scientiæ vi.*—Seneca, *Suasoriæ*, 4.
456. In 1580 to 1588: *car il n'est deffendu de faire nostre profit de la mensonge mesme, s'il est besoing.*
457. *Espelucher au vif.*
458. See Diogenes Laertius, *Life of Plato.*
459. See Plato, *Republic*, end of book II and beginning of book III.
460. See *Ibid.*, book V.
461. *Non tam id sensisse quod dicerent, quam exercere ingenia materiæ difficultate videntur voluisse.*—Source not known.
462. In 1580 to 1588: *Car les deitez, ausquelles l'homme de sa propre invention a voulu donner une forme, elles sont injurieuses, pleines d'erreurs et d'impieté.*
463. *Jupiter omnipotens rerum, regumque deumque*
      Progenitor genitrixque.
      —Verses of Valerius Soranus, quoted twice by St. Augustine, *De Civ. Dei*, VII, 9 and 11.
464. *Daignant à l'avanture fomenter.*
465. See *Acts*, XVII, 23.
466. *Sans prescription, sans declaration.* See Plutarch, *Life of Numa.*
467. *Mouvemens ceremonieuses.*
468. "Manifestly," says M. Villey, "in this whole passage, Montaigne criticises Protestantism."
469. Ronsard, *Remontrances au peuple de France.*

Apology for Raimond Sebond

470. This and the following theories of philosophers are taken from Cicero, *De Nat. Deor.*, I, 10-15.

471. *Les quatre natures.*

472. Montaigne uses *images* to translate Cicero's word *imagines*, which, in its turn, is a translation of Democritus's *eidolon*—a word for which no language since his time has found an exact equivalent. He attempted to express by it something that is *not* the "object" itself, but is, as it were, thrown off from the thing and preserves its characteristics. Lucretius, like Cicero, employs for this the word *imagines*, and his translators have used indiscriminately the words "images," "idols," "scales," and "phantoms."

473. That is, in the various books of the *Laws*.

474. *L'ardeur du ciel.*

475. *Laquelle loy est un animant.* This is not an accurate statement of Zeno's doctrine, but is derived from Cicero's comment: *Quam legem quomodo efficiat animantem, intelligere non possumus.*

476. This sentence is placed by Montaigne in a different connection from that in which it is placed in Cicero's enumeration. Cicero's words are *Aer quo Diogenes Apolloniates utitur deo.* Montaigne, in transplanting them, carelessly miswrote *l'aage* for *l'air*, and this error has been perpetuated to this day.

477. See Diogenes Laertius, *Life of Diogenes*. Cicero's report of the doctrine of Xenophanes is quite different.

478. *La chaleur supreme.*

479. *Contoit, entre mille formes de dieus qu'il faict.*

480. See Cicero, *De Nat. Deor.*, I, 23.

481. *Luisans, transparans, et perflables.*

482. See Cicero, *De Div.*, II, 17.

Notes and Comments

483. *Ego deum genus esse semper duxi, et dicam*
cœlitum;
Sed eos non curare opinor, quid agat humanum
genus. —Ennius, in *Ibid.*, II, 50.

484. *Le trouble des formes mondaines.*

485. *Les divers meurs et fantasies aus mienes.*

486. This sentence is found only on the Bordeaux copy of 1588, and evidently should have been inserted, as a parenthesis, after "so much as they instruct me," just above.

487. *Foiblesse de discours.*

488. That is, the Egyptians; see Plutarch, *Of Isis and Osiris.*

489. *Quæ procul usque adeo divino ab numine*
distant,
Inque Deum numero quæ sint indigna videri.
—Lucretius, V, 122.

490. *Formæ, ætates, vestitus, ornatus noti sunt; genera, conjugia, cognationes, omniaque traducta ad similitudinem imbecillitatis humanæ; nam et perturbatis animis inducuntur; accipimus enim deorum cupiditates, ægritudines, iracundias.*—Cicero, *De Nat. Deor.*, II, 28; taken by Montaigne from St. Augustine, *De Civ. Dei*, IV, 30.

491. See Cicero, *De Nat. Deor.*, II, 23; St. Augustine, *De Civ. Dei*, IV, 30, and Vivès's *Commentary.*

492. *Quid juvat hoc, templis nostros inducere mores?*
O curvæ in terris animæ et cælestium inanes!
—Persius, II, 62, 61.

493. *Sur peine de la hart.*

494. See St. Augustine, *De Civ. Dei*, XVIII, 5.

495. See Cicero, *Tusc. Disp.*, I, 26.

496. See the *Gorgias* near the end, and *Republic*, book

Apology for Raimond Sebond

X; also Plutarch, *Of the face in the moon.*
497.   *Secreti celant calles, et myrtea circum*
           Sylva tegit; curæ non ipsa in morte relinquunt.
                               —Virgil, *Æneid*, VI, 443.
498.   "The divine Plato."
499.   *S'il y a quelque chose du mien.*
500.   *Commoditez.*
501.   See *I Corinthians*, II, 9, after *Isaiah*, LXIV, 4.
502.   See Plutarch, *Of the face in the moon.*
503.   *Hector erat tunc cum bello certabat; at ille,*
           Tractus ab Æmonio, non erat Hector, equo.
                               —Ovid, *Tristia*, III, 11, 27.
504.   *Quod mutatur, enim dissolvitur; interit ergo;*
           Trajiciuntur enim partes atque ordine migrant.
                               —Lucretius, III, 756.
505.   In 1580 to 1588: *et qu'il souffre pour luy.*
506.   The reference is to Porphyrus. See St. Augustine, *De Civ. Dei*, X, 30, 621.
507.   See Pliny, *Nat. Hist.*, X, 2.
508.   *Nec si materiam nostram collegerit ætas*
           Post obitum, rursumque redegerit, ut sita
               nunc est,
           Atque iterum nobis fuerint data lumina vitæ,
           Pertineat quidquam tamen ad nos id quoque
               factum,
           Interrupta semel cum sit repetentia nostra.
                               —Lucretius, III, 847.
509.   See Plutarch, *Of the face in the moon.*
510.   *Scilicet, avolsis radicibus, ut nequit ullam*
           Dispicere ipse oculus rem, seorsum corpore toto.
                               —Lucretius, III, 563.

1837

Notes and Comments

511. *Inter enim jacta est vitai pausa, vageque
 Deerrarunt passim motus ab sensibus omnes.*
—Lucretius, III, 860.
It is difficult so to translate these words as equally to correspond with the thought in the mind of Lucretius and the meaning given to them by Montaigne. Lucretius is speaking of the possibility that these very same seeds of which we now are formed have often before been placed in the same order in which they now are; and yet we can not recover this in memory. Montaigne is declaring that the separation of soul and body is the death of our personality. "For a cessation of life is thrown between these states, and on every side all the motions of sense wander pell-mell."

512. *Et nihil hoc ad nos, qui coitu conjugioque
 Corporis atque animæ consistimus uniter apti.*
—Lucretius, III, 845.

513. *D'un seul clin.*

514. That is, the reason.

515. See Plutarch, *Why divine justice sometimes delays the punishment of evil doing.*

516. *Flatant sa justice d'une.*

517. See Livy, XLI, 16.

518. See Idem, XLV, 33.

519. See Arrian, *Anabasis*, VI, 19, 5; Diodorus Siculus, XVII, 104.1.

520.   *Sulmone creatos
 Quattuor hic juvenes, totidem quos educat
  Ufens,
 Viventes rapit, inferias quos immolet umbris.*
—Virgil, *Æneid*, X, 517.

521. See Herodotus, IV, 94.

Apology for Raimond Sebond

522. See Plutarch, *Of Superstition;* Herodotus, VII, 114.

523. *Tantum religio potuit suadere malorum!*
—Lucretius, I, 101.

524. See Plutarch, *Of Superstition.*

525. *Qui mignardoient leur Diane.*

526. See Plutarch, *Apothegms of the Lacedæmonians.*

527. *Et casta inceste, nubendi tempore in ipso,*
Hostia concideret mactatu mæsta parentis.
—Lucretius, I, 98.

528. In 1588: *et que Decius, . . . se brulast tout vif en holocauste à Saturne, entre les deux armées.*

529. *Quæ fuit tanta deorum iniquitas, ut placari populo Romano non possent, nisi tales viri occidissent?*—Cicero, *De Nat. Deor.,* III, 6.

530. See Herodotus, III, 41, 42.

531. *Tantus est perturbatæ mentis et sedibus suis pulsæ furor, ut sic dii placentur, quemadmodum ne homines quidem sæviunt.*—St. Augustine, *De Civ. Dei,* VI, 10.

532. That is, the human body.

533. *Ubi iratos deos timent, qui sic propitios habere merentur? In regiæ libidinis voluptatem castrati sunt quidam; sed nemo sibi, ne vir esset, jubente domino, manus intulit.*—St. Augustine, *De Civ. Dei,* after Seneca.

534. *Sæpius olim*
Religio peperit scelerosa atqui impia facta.
—Lucretius, I, 82.

Modern texts read *illa* for *olim.*

535. *Infirmum dei fortius est hominibus, et stultum dei sapientius est hominibus.*—*I Corinthians,* I, 25.

536. See Diogenes Laertius, *Life of Stilpo.*

Notes and Comments

537. That is, "the divine nature." The thread is broken by the 1595 interpolation.

538. *Formes = conceptions mentales.*

539. *Omnia cum cœlo terraque marique*
Nil sunt ad summam summaï totius omnem.
—Lucretius, VI, 678.

540. *Le contrerolle.*

541. *C'est pour toy.* It may be observed that each of the sentences immediately following contains a transparent allusion to some passage in the Scriptures.

542. *Terramque, et solem, lunam, mare, cætera quæ sunt,*
Non esse unica, sed numero magis innumerali.
—Lucretius, II, 1085.

543. *Cum in summa res nulla sit una,*
Unica quæ gignatur, et unica solaque crescat.
—Ibid., 1077.

544. *Sans compaignon.*

545. *Quare etiam atque etiam tales fateare necesse est*
Esse alios alibi congressus materiaï,
Qualis hic est avido complexu quem tenet æther. —Ibid, 1064.

546. See Plutarch, *Of the opinions of philosophers.*

547. In the *Timæus;* but Montaigne, doubtless, took it from St. Augustine, *De Civ. Dei*, X, 29.

548. See St. Augustine, *Ibid*, XIII, 16. Origen, especially, is referred to.

549. In 1580 to 1588: *Plato.* See Diogenes Laertius, *Life of Democritus.*

550. See Diogenes Laertius, *Life of Epicurus.* Epicurus

Apology for Raimond Sebond

thought that some were spherical, some elliptical, etc.

551. The pseudo-facts that Montaigne here narrates are to be found in Herodotus (IV, 191; III, 116; IV, 27; III, 101), and in Pliny (*Natural History*, VII, 2; VIII, 22); but Pliny disavows belief in them, and Montaigne very probably took them second-hand from other works.

552. See Plutarch, *Of the face in the moon.*

553. That is, man—men like this.

554. That is, able to laugh.

555. Cf. Book I, chap. 27, pp. 240, 241; Book II, chap 30, at the end.

556. *Monstreux et desordonné.*

557. See Cicero, *Academica*, II, 23 and 31.

558. See *Ibid.*

559. Montaigne himself translates before quoting. This was one of the passages inscribed in his library. The verses are found, in slightly different form, in Sextus Empiricus, Diogenes Laertius *(Pyrrho)*, in the *Gorgias* of Plato, and in Stobæus, *Sermons* 121 and 122; in the latter Stobæus cites the passage of the *Gorgias* which ascribes this thought to Euripides.

560. See Plato, *Theætetus:* " 'That alone is unmoved which is named the universe.' This is the language of Parmenides, Melissus and their followers, who stoutly maintain that all being is one and self-contained, and has no place in which to move." (Jowett's translation.) See also Diogenes Laertius, *Life of Melissus:* "Placuit autem si universum infinitum esse, et immutabile atque immobile et unum sibi ipsi simile ac plenum. Motumque non esse, verum videri esse."

561. In 1588: *Je ne sçay si la doctrine ecclesiastique*

Notes and Comments

en juge autrement, et me soubmets en tout et part tout à son ordonnance.

562. See Seneca, *Epistle* 88. Seneca's words as to Parmenides may help to elucidate the obscurity: *Parmenides ait, "ex his, quæ videntur, nihil esse ab uno diversum." ... Si Parmenidi [credo], nihil est præter unum.*

563. See Plato, *Parmenides*.

564. See Seneca, *Epistle* 88: *Tota rerum natura umbra est, aut inanis, aut fallax.*

565. *Soubs les lois de nostre parolle.*

566. Cf. Book III, chap. 13, near the beginning: *Pourquoy est-ce que nostre langage commun, si aisé à tout autre usage, devient obscur et non intelligible en un contract et testament?* etc.

567. The first word in the consecration of the sacrament of the Eucharist: *Hoc est corpus meus*. Montaigne refers to the great quarrel concerning Transubstantiation.

568. See Cicero, *Academica*, II, 29.

569. See Diogenes Laertius, *Life of Pyrrho*.

570. In 1580 to 1588: *ce moqueur de Pline*. See Pliny, *Nat. Hist.*, II, 5 (7).

571. Pliny.

572.
>   *Cras vel atra*
> *Nube polum pater occupato,*
> *Vel sole puro; non tamen irritum*
> *Quodcumque retro est, efficiet, neque*
> *Diffinget infectumque reddet*
> *Quod fugiens semel hora vexit.*
>   —Horace, *Odes*, III, 29.43.

573. *De son poix*. In 1580 to 1588: *de sa suffisance*.

574. *Mirum quo procedat improbitas cordis humani,*

1842

parvulo aliquo invitata successu.—Pliny, *Nat. Hist.*, II, 23.

575. See Seneca, *Epistle* 92.27.

576. Tertullian.

577. *Magna dii curant, parva negligunt.*—Cicero, *De Nat. Deor.*, II, 66.

578. *Nec in regnis quidem reges omnia minima curant.*—*Ibid.*, III, 35.

579. *Nos mouvemens et nos mesures ne le touchent pas.*

580. *Deus ita artifex magnus in magnis, ut minor non sit in parvis.*—St. Augustine, *De Civ. Dei*, XI, 22.

581. *De ses pois et mouvemens.*

582. See Cicero, *Academica*, II, 38.

583. *Quod beatum æternumque sit, id nec habere negotii quicquam, nec exhibere alteri.*—Idem, *De Nat. Deor.*, I, 17.

584. See *Ibid.*, I, 19.

585. See Cicero, *De Div.*, I, 57.

586. See *Romans*, I, 22, 23.

587. *Enterrement* (burial)—an odd word to be used in this connection.

588. See Herodian, book IV.

589. *Quod finxere, timent.*   —Lucan, I, 486.

590. *Quasi quicquam infelicius sit homine cui sua figmenta dominantur.*—Source unknown.

591. See St. Augustine, *De Civ. Dei*, VIII, 23, 24.

592. See Plutarch, *Apothegms of the Lacedæmonians*.

593. In a marginal addition on the Bordeaux copy Montaigne wrote, then erased, the original text of St. Augustine (*De Civ. Dei*, VIII, 24), which he here translates.

594. *Nosse cui divos et cœli numina soli,*
    Aut soli nescire, datum: —Lucan, I, 452.

Notes and Comments

The original text is: *Solis nosse divos et cœli numina vobis.*

595. See Cicero, *De Nat. Deor.*, III, 13, 14.
596. *Voyla pas triomfe!*
597. See Cicero, *De Nat. Deor.*, II, 6, 8.
598. See *Ibid.*, 16.
599. *Parquoy nous voila compaignons.*
600. *Non, si te ruperis, inquit.*
—Horace, *Satires*, II, 3.319. The reference is to the fable of the frog and the ox.

601. *Profecto non Deum, quem cogitare non possunt, sed semet ipsos pro illo cogitantes, non illum sed se ipsos non illi sed sibi comparant.*—St. Augustine, *De Civ. Dei*, XII, 18.

602. That is, the Divinity.
603. *Consultez en, pour voir, avec vostre astrolabe.*
604. See Josephus, *Antiquities of the Jews*, XVIII, 4. The god named in the tale is Anubis, not Serapis.
605. See St. Augustine, *De Civ. Dei*, VI, 7. The story is told somewhat differently by Plutarch in the *Life of Romulus*.
606. See Diogenes Laertius, Life of Plato.
607. *En la religion de Mahomet, il se treuve, par le creance de ce peuple.*
608. See Guillaume Postel, *Histoire des Turcs.*
609. See Cicero, *De Nat. Deor.*, I, 27.
610. *Hors de ce raport et de ce principe.*
611. See *Ibid.*, I, 18.
612. *Ita est informatum, anticipatum mentibus nostris ut homini, cum de deo cogitet, forma occurrat humana.*—*Ibid.*, 27.
613. See Eusebius, *Evangelical Preparation*, XIII, 13.

Apology for Raimond Sebond

614. *Tam blanda conciliatrix et tam sui est lena ipsa natura!*—Cicero, *De Nat. Deor.*, I, 27.

615. *Domitosque Herculea manu*
   Telluris juvenes, unde periculum
      Fulgens contremuit domus
   Saturni veteris. —Horace, *Odes*, II, 12.6.

616. *Neptunus muros magnoque emota tridenti*
   Fundamenta quatit, totamque a sedibus urbem
   Eruit. Hic Juno Scæas sævissima portas
   Prima tenet. —Virgil, *Æneid*, II, 610.

617. See Herodotus, I, 172.

618. *Adeo minimis etiam rebus prava religio inserit deos.*—Livy, XXVII, 23.

619. *Hic illius arma,*
   Hic currus fuit. —Virgil, *Æneid*, I, 16.

620. *O sancte Apollo, qui umbilicum certum terrarum obtines!*—Cicero, *De Div.*, II, 56.

621. *Pallada Cecropidæ, Minoïa Creta Dianam,*
   Vulcanum tellus Hipsipilea colit,
   Junonem Sparte Pelopeiadesque Mycenæ;
   Pinigerum Fauni Mænalis ora caput;
   Mars Latio venerandus.
                    —Ovid, *Fasti*, III, 81.

622. *Junctaque sunt magno templa nepotis avo.*
                    —*Ibid.*, I, 294.

623. *Populaires.*

624. See St. Augustine, *De Civ. Dei.*, IV, 8.

625. See *Ibid.*, and VI, 7.

626. See St. Augustine, *De Civ. Dei*, IV, *passim*.

627. *Aucuns certeins.* See *Ibid.*, III, 12.

628. *Quos quoniam cœli nondum dignamur honore,*

Notes and Comments

Quas dedimus certe terras habitare sinamus.
—Ovid, *Metam.*, I, 194.

629. Civils. See St. Augustine, *De Civ. Dei*, VI, 5.
630. In 1588: *Il en est de jeunes et fleurissans.*
631. See Plutarch, *Common conceptions against the Stoics.*
632. *Jovis incunabula Creten.*
—Ovid, *Metam.*, VIII, 99.
633. See St. Augustine, *De Civ. Dei*, IV, 31 and 27.
634. *Cum veritatem qua liberetur, inquirat, credatur ei expedire quod fallitur.*—See *Ibid.*, 31.
635. See Xenophon, *Memorabilia*, IV, 7.7.
636. See Cicero, *De Nat. Deor.*, II, 22.
637. *Inevitable necessité.*
638. See Xenophon, *Memorabilia*, IV, 7.2.
639. See Cicero, *Academica*, II, 33.
640. See Xenophon, *Memorabilia*, IV, 7.7.
641. See Plato, *Timæus.*
642. *Temo aureus, aurea summæ Curvatura rotæ, radiorum argenteus ordo.*
—Ovid, *Metam.*, II, 107.
643. See Plato, *Republic*, book X.
644. *Mundus domus est maxima rerum, Quam quinque altitonæ fragmine zonæ Cingunt, perquam limbus pictus bis sex signis Stellimicantibus, altus in obliquo æthere, lunæ Bigas acceptat.*
—Verses of Varro, quoted by Valerius Probus in his notes on Virgil's Sixth *Eclogue*.
645. See Plato, *Second Alcibiades.*
646. *Latent ista omnia crassis occultata et circumfusa*

1846

tenebris, ut nulla acies humani ingenii tanta sit, quæ penetrare in cœlum, terram intrare possit.—Cicero, *Academica*, II, 39.

647. Of philosophy.
648. *Un poete descousu.*
649. See Diogenes Laertius, *Life of Plato*. In place of this last sentence, 1595 has: *Toutes les sciences sur-humaines s'accoustrent du stile poetique.*
650. *Des cuisses.*
651. *De l'embonpoinct.*
652. That is, learning.
653. See Plato, *Timæus*. These sentences follow a passage concerning the nature of the soul, about a third from the end.
654. That is, philosophy.
655. *Ravissement = ravisement.*
656. That is, the philosophers.
657. That is, Microcosmos.
658. *Tant ils ont employé de pieces et de visage à le maçonner et bastir.*
659. Imitated from Plato, *Critias*.
660. See Plato, *Theætetus;* Diogenes Laertius, *Life of Thales*.
661. *Quod est ante pedes, nemo spectat; cœli*
       scrutantur plagas.
—Quoted by Cicero, *De Div.*, II, 13, from a tragedy of Ennius. Montaigne mistakes the meaning of the passage: it is not Democritus who says this; but Cicero is blaming Democritus for wasting time on insoluble questions.
662. See Plato, *Theætetus*.

Notes and Comments

663. *Quæ mare compescant causæ; quid temperet annum;*
Stellæ sponte sua jussæve vagentur et errent;
Quid premat obscurum Lunæ, quid proferat orbem;
Quid velit et possit rerum concordia discors.
—Horace, *Epistles*, I, 12.16.

664. The last three words were omitted in the *Édition Municipale* and in 1595.

665. *Omnia incerta ratione et in naturæ majestate abdita.*—Pliny, *Nat. Hist.*, II, 37.

666. *Modus quo corporibus adhærent spiritus, omnino mirus est, nec comprehendi ab homine potest; et hoc ipse homo est.*—St. Augustine, *De Civ. Dei*, XXI, 10.

667. *Comme un jargon.*

668. Diogenes Apolloniates. See *supra*, note 476.

669. *De quelle humeur.*

670. See Cornelius Agrippa, *Of the uncertainty and vanity of learning*.

671. In 1580 to 1588: *la principale foiblesse et fausseté*.

672. See C. Agrippa, *Of the uncertainty and vanity of learning*.

673. *Or n'y peut avoir des principes aux hommes.*

674. That is, in their eyes.

675. That is, those who love their own opinions. See Plato, *Republic*, end of book V.

676. That is, philosophers.

677. *De cette-cy feroient capables.*

678. That is, philosophers.

679. That is, of the reason.

Apology for Raimond Sebond

680. See Diogenes Laertius, *Life of Thales*.
681. *Ignoratur enim quæ sit natura animaï,*
Nata sit, an contra nascentibus insinuetur,
Et simul intereat nobiscum morte dirempta,
An tenebras Orci visat vastasque lacunas,
An pecudes alias divinitus insinuet se.
—Lucretius, I, 112.

682. The following opinions come for the most part from Sextus Empiricus (*Hypot.*), Cicero (*Academica*, and, especially, *Tusc. Disp.*, I, 10), Plutarch (*The Opinions of Philosophers*), Lactantius, etc. But Montaigne certainly took them at second-hand from lists in the works of his contemporaries.

683. *Sanguineam vomit ille animam.*
—Virgil, *Æneid*, IX, 349.

The original is: *Purpuream vomit ille animam et cum sanguine mixta, Vina refert moriens*—describing the death of Rhetus. It is difficult to perceive the aptness of this quotation, in any sense.

684. *Igneus est ollis vigor, et cœlestis origo.*
—*Ibid.*, VI, 730.

685. *Habitum quemdam vitalem corporis esse,*
Harmoniam Græci quam dicunt.
—Lucretius, III, 99.

686. *Harum sententiarum quæ vera sit, deus aliquis viderit.*—Cicero, *Tusc. Disp.*, I, 11.

687. See St. Bernard, *Liber de anima*.
688. *Dæmons*.
689. See Diogenes Laertius, *Life of Heraclitus*.
690. *Ut bona sæpe valetudo cum dicitur esse*

Notes and Comments

Corporis, et non est tamen hæc pars ulla valentis.
—Lucretius, III, 102.

691. *Hic exultat enim pavor ac metus, hæc loca circum*
Lætitiæ mulcent. —*Ibid.,* 141.

692. For all these opinions see, in addition to the sources mentioned in note 680, C. Agrippa, *Of the uncertainty and vanity of learning.*

693. *Qua facie quidem sit animus, aut ubi habitet, ne quærendum quidem est.*—*Tusc. Disp.,* I, 28.

694. *Peu roides et peu ignorees.*

695. See Galen, *De placitis Hippocratis et Platonis.*

696. See Seneca, *Epistle* 57.7.

697. This was the opinion of Origen, which Montaigne took from St. Augustine, *De Civ. Dei,* XI, 23, and especially from the *Commentary* of Vivès.

698. *Come dict Plutarque de la teste des histoires.*

699. See Plutarch, *Life of Theseus.*

700. *S'abismant en.*

701. *Se tiennent en pareille bestise.*

702. *Voyes chez lui le jargon des dieux.*

703. *L'homme de Platon.* See Diogenes Laertius, *Life of Diogenes.*

704. "Pour toute cette critique de la physique épicurienne, cf. le *De Fin.,* I, et le *Commentaire* de Lucrèce par Lambin, *passim.*"—M. Villey.

705. The Epicureans.

706. See Cicero, *De Nat. Deor.,* II, 37.

707. See *Ibid.,* III, 9.

708. This whole passage is taken (many sentences literally) from the *De Nat. Deor.,* II, 37, III, 9, and II, 8.

Apology for Raimond Sebond

709. In 1580 to 1588: *comme il s'en voit infinis chez Plutarque, contre les Epicuriens et Stoiciens, et en Seneque contre les Peripateticiens.*

710. In 1580 to 1588: *Combien de fois leur voyons nous dire des choses diverses et contraires?*

711. See Plato, *First Alcibiades*.

712. *A cette resolution de leur irresolution.*

713. *Nihil tam absurde dici potest quod non dicatur ab aliquo philosophorum.*—Cicero, De Div., II, 58.

714. *Mes meurs.*

715. *Regimant.*

716. In 1580 to 1588: *(car j'ay choisi ce seul exemple pour le plus commode à tesmoigner nostre foiblesse et vanité.)*

717. See Plato, *Timæus;* Diogenes Laertius, *Life of Plato*. But it is probable that Montaigne took it from the first of the *Dialogues* of Guy de Brués *contre les nouveaux académiciens.*

718.   *Medium non deserit unquam*
   Cœli Phœbus iter; radiis tamen omnia lustrat,
—Claudian, *De Sexto Consulatu Honorii*, V, 411.

719.   *Cætera pars animæ per totum dissita corpus*
    Paret, et ad numen mentis nomenque movetur.
                      —Lucretius, III, 143.

720. *Matière.* The scholastic use of the word.

721.   *Deum namque ire per omnes*
   Terrasque tractusque maris cœlumque
      profundum;
   Hinc pecudes, armenta, viros, genus omne
      ferarum,
   Quemque sibi tenues nascentem arcessere vitas;

Notes and Comments

*Scilicet huc reddi deinde, ac resoluta referri
Omnia; nec morti esse locum.*
—Virgil, *Georgics*, IV, 221.

722. *Aucuns, de toute ancienneté.*
723. *Du rond de la lune.*
724. *Instillata patris virtus tibi.*—Source unknown.
725. *Fortes creantur fortibus et bonis.*
—Horace, *Odes*, IV, 4.29.
726. *Denique cur acris violentia triste leonum
Seminium sequitur; dolus vulpibus, et fuga cervis
A patribus datur, et patrius pavor incitat artus;
Si non, certa suo quia semine seminioque
Vis animi pariter crescit cum corpore toto?*
—Lucretius, III, 741-743, 746, 747.
727. See Plutarch, *Why divine justice sometimes postpones the punishment of evil deeds.*
728. *Si in corpus nascentibus insinuatur,
Cur superante actam ætatem meminisse nequimus,
Nec vestigia gestarum rerum ulla tenemus?*
—Lucretius, III, 671.
729. *Comme nous voulons.*
730. See Plato, *Phædo*, XVIII.
731. That is, while in the body.
732. *Outre l'aprentissage.*
733. *Le vice.*
734. *Nam, si tantopere est animi mutata potestas
Omnis ut actarum exciderit retinentia rerum,
Non, ut opinor, ea ab leto jam longior errat.*
—Lucretius, III, 674.

Apology for Raimond Sebond

735. See Plato, *Republic*, book X.
736. *Ces bonnes apparences.*
737. *Gigni pariter cum corpore, et una*
     Crescere sentimus, pariterque senescere
     mentem. —Lucretius, III, 445.
738. That is, the philosophers.
739. *Mentem sanari, corpus ut ægrum*
     Cernimus, et flecti medicina posse videmus.
     —Lucretius, III, 510.
740. *Corpoream naturam animi esse necesse est,*
     Corporeis quoniam telis ictuque laborat.
     —*Ibid.*, 175.
741. *Vis . . . animaï*
     Conturbatur et . . . divisa seorsum
     Disjectatur, eodem illo distracta veneno.
     —*Ibid.*, 499.
742. *Vis morbi distracta per artus*
     Turbat agens animam, spumantes æquore salso
     Ventorum ut validis fervescunt viribus undæ.
     —Lucretius, III, 492.
743. In 1580 to 1588: *de la vie.*
744. *Morbis in corporis, avius errat*
     Sæpe animus; dementit enim, deliraque fatur;
     Interdumque gravi lethargo fertur in altum
     Æternumque soporem, oculis nutuque cadenti.
     —Lucretius, III, 463.
745. *Ils se donnent un beau jeu.*
746. For example, in Cicero, *Tusc. Disp.*, I, 11.
747. *Le goust.*
748. *Quippe etenim mortale æterno jungere, et una*
     Consentire putare, et fungi mutua posse.

1853

Notes and Comments

*Desipere est. Quid enim diversius esse
putandum est,
Aut magis inter se disjunctum discrepitansque,
Quam mortale quod est, immortali atque
perenni
Junctum, in concilio sævas tolerare procellas?*
—Lucretius, III, 800.

749. *Simul ævo fessa fatiscit.* —*Ibid.*, 458.

750. *Contrahi animum et quasi labi putat atque concidere.*—Cicero, *De Div.*, II, 58.

751. *Non alio pacto quam si, pes cum dolet ægri,
In nullo caput interea sit forte dolore.*
—Lucretius, III, 110.

752. See the *Metaphysics*, II, 1.

753. See Cicero, *Tusc. Disp.*, I, 16.

754. See C. Agrippa, *Of the uncertainty and vanity of learning.*

755. *Rem gratissimam promittentium magis quam probantium.*—Seneca, *Epistle* 102.

756. *Of the immortality of the soul.*

757. See Plato, *Laws*, book X. "But it was not the text of Plato that suggested these words to Montaigne."—M. Villey.

758. Cf. Cicero, *Tusc. Disp.*, I, 14, 15.

759. *Courts.*

760. *Somnia sunt non docentis, sed optantis.*—Cicero, *Academica*, II, 38.

761. *Némbrot.*

762. *Perdam sapientiam sapientium, et prudentiam prudentium reprobabo.*—*I Corinthians*, I, 19.

763. *Idiomes.*

Apology for Raimond Sebond

764. Augustine; the passage quoted is in the *De Civ. Dei*, XI, 22.

765. *Ipsa utilitatis occultatio aut humilitatis exercitatio est, aut elationis attritio.*

766. That is, "All things arrived at by our own reasoning," etc. (p. 742).

767. *Et qui retentera son estre et ses forces . . . sans ce privilege divin* [of immortality].

768. *Cum de animorum æternitate disserimus, non leve momentum apud nos habet consensus hominum aut timentium inferos, aut colentium. Utor hac publica persuasione.*—Seneca, *Epistle* 117.6.

769. *Usuram nobis largiuntur tanquam cornicibus; diu mansuros aiunt animos; semper, negant.*—Cicero, *Tusc. Disp.*, I, 31.

770. In 1580 to 1588: *Socrates, Platon, et quasi tous ceux qui ont voulu croire l'immortalité des ames, se sont laissez emporter à cette invention, et plusieurs nations, comme entre autres la nostre* [*et nos Druides*]. The last three words were dropped in 1588.

771. See Diogenes Laertius, *Life of Pythagoras*; Seneca, *Epistle* 108.19. And cf. Book II, chap. 11, p. 575.

772. See Plutarch, *On the face in the moon*.

773.   *O pater, anne aliquas ad cœlum hinc ire*
        putandum est
Sublimes animas iterumque ad tarda reverti
Corpora? Quæ lucis miseris tam dira cupido?
            —Virgil, *Æneid*, VI, 719.

774. See St. Augustine, *De Civ. Dei*, XXI, 16.

775. See *Ibid.*, XXII, 28.

776. See *Ibid.*

Notes and Comments

777. See Plato, *Meno.*

778. *Elementaire*; that is, belonging to earth, air, fire, and water.

779. See Plato, *Timæus.*

780. *Denique connubia ad Veneris partusque ferarum*
Esse animas præsto deridiculum esse videtur,
Et spectare immortales mortalia membra
Innumero numero, certareque præproperanter
Inter se, quæ prima potissimaque insinuetur.
—Lucretius, III, 776.

781. An allusion to Lucretius, III, 718 ff.

782. *Cognoissance.*

783. See Vivès's *Commentary* on St. Augustine, *De Civ. Dei*, IX, 11.

784. *Non par aucune ordonnance civile.*

785. See Plutarch, *Life of Romulus.* This quotation is copied textually by Montaigne from Amyot's translation.

786. *Si haute.*

787. See Diogenes Laertius, *Life of Archelaus.*

788. *Nous l'avons proposé luy mesmes à soy.*

789. *Quasi vero mensuram ullius rei possit agere qui sui nesciat.*—Pliny, *Nat. Hist.*, II, 1.

790. *Nous en contoit des belles.*

791. See Cicero, *Academica*, II, 46; Plato, *Cratylus.*

792. *La neantise du compas et du compassur.*

793. See Diogenes Laertius, *Life of Thales.*

794. *D'estendre un si long corps.*

795. Gobrias.

796. See Plutarch, *How to know a flatterer from a friend*; Herodotus, III, 78.

Apology for Raimond Sebond

797. See Goulard, *History of Portugal*, XII, 23.

798. Cf. Book I, chap. 15, p. 86: *La vaillance a ses limites comme les autres vertus, lesquels franchis et outrepassez, on se trouve dans le train du vice.*

799. *Chi troppo s'assottiglia si scavezza.*—Petrarch, *Canzone* XXII, 48.

800. In 1580 to 1588: *et qui se fut servy, à faire son amas, d'autres que de nostre Plutarque.*

801. See Plutarch, *Against Colotes*.

802. *A deux doigts près.* See Plato, *Laws*, book IX.

803. *Il luy faut tailler par art.*

804. *Qui certis quibusdam destinatisque sententiis addicti et consecrati sunt, ut etiam quæ non probant, cogantur defendere*—Cicero, *Tusc. Disp.*, II, 2.

805. That is, the *trivium* and *quadrivium*, or course of seven sciences. Hence the "faculty of arts," and the degrees of Bachelor and Master of Arts.

806. *L'approbation et le cours.*

807. *On ne plaide pas de l'alloy, mais de l'usage.*

808. That is, *liaisons de mariages = nouements d'aiguillete.*

809. An astrological term, signifying the division of the sky into twelve parts, called "houses," corresponding to the signs of the Zodiac.

810. *Quand la mensale coupe le tubercle de l'enseigneur.*

811. See C. Agrippa, *Of the uncertainty and vanity of learning*.

812. *Par gens de composition.*

813. This image is found in Aulus Gellius, and is frequent in sixteenth-century writers, *e. g.*, Rabelais, Du Bel-

Notes and Comments

lay, Estienne Pasquier, who apply it to the most diverse subjects.

814.   *Ut hymettia sole
Cera remollescit, tractataque pollice, multas
Vertitur in facies, ipsoque fit utilis usu.*
                                 —Ovid, Metam., X, 284.

815. That is, some things are impossible for man to know.

816. *Des principes.*

817. *Les principes.*

818. *Non potest aliud alio magis minusve comprehendi quoniam omnium rerum una est definitio comprehendendi.*—Cicero, Academica, II, 41.

819.   *Mulciber in Troiam, pro Troia stabat Apollo.*
                                —Ovid, Tristia, I, 2.5.

820. *Nous nous sommes plus voisins.*

821. *Trop crud.*

822. This figure was used by Democritus, and Cicero employs it twice (*Academica*, I, 12, and II, 10). Montaigne has it again in Book III, chap. 8.

823. In 1580 to 1588: *beaucoup plus veritable et plus ferme.*

824. *Il la verroit entiere aussi bien que demie, naissante et imperfecte.*

825. *Si elles ne font que floter et vanter* [venter?].

826. *Inter visa vera aut falsa ad animi assensum nihil interest.*—Cicero, Academica, II, 28.

827. *J'y suis tout entier, j'y suis voyrement.*

828.   *Posterior . . . res illa reperta,
Perdit, et immutat sensus ad pristina quæque.*
                                 —Lucretius, V, 1414.

Apology for Raimond Sebond

829. *Nos moyens.*
830. See Plutarch, *Apothegms of the Lacedæmonians.*
831. *Les jugemens.*
832. *Tales sunt hominum mentes, quali pater ipse Juppiter auctifera lustravit lampade terras.*
—These lines are a translation by Cicero (among his *Fragmenta*) of the *Odyssey*, XVIII, 135. They are cited by St. Augustine, *De Civ. Dei*, V, 28. Montaigne has already cited them once before in Book II, chap. 1, near the beginning.
833. *Ressorts;* that is, impelling forces.
834. *Cette apparence de discours.*
835. *A tous biais.*
836.   *Quis sub Arcto*
Rex gelidæ metuatur oræ,
Quid Tyridatem terreat, unice
   Securus.   —Horace, *Odes*, I, 26.3.
837. *Si aysé à croler et si prest au branle.*
838. *Me voila honneste homme.*
839. *Une mesme forme.*
840.   *Velut minuta magno*
Deprensa navis in mari vesaniente vento.
              —Catullus, XXV, 12.
841. See Plutarch, *Of Moral Courage.*
842. *Semper Ajax fortis, fortissimus tamen in furore.*
            —Cicero, *Tusc. Disp.*, IV, 23.
The following sentences are directly inspired by *Ibid.*, 19.
843. In 1580 to 1588: *Au moins cecy ne sçavons nous que trop, que les passions produisent infinies et perpetuelles mutations en nostre ame, et la tyrannisent merveilleusement. Le jugement d'un homme corroucé, ou de celuy qui*

Notes and Comments

est en crainte, est-ce le jugement qu'il aura tantost, quand il sera rassis?

844. *Ut maris tranquillitas intelligitur, nulla, ne minima quidem, aura fluctus commovente; sic animi quietus et placatus status cernitur, quum perturbatio nulla est qua moveri queat.*—Cicero, *Tusc. Disp.*, V, 6.

845. The judgement? See the next sentence.

846. See Cicero, *De Div.*, I, 57, and II, 48; Plato, *Phædrus* and *Timæus*.

847. *Qualis ubi alterno procurrens gurgite pontus*
      Nunc ruit ad terras, scopulisque superjacit
          undam,
      Spumeus, extremamque sinu perfundit arenam,
      Nunc rapidus retro atque æstu revoluta
          resorbens
      Saxa fugit, littusque vado labente relinquit.
                —Virgil, *Æneid*, XI, 624.

848. *Le plus roide.*

849. See Plutarch, *Of the face in the moon.*

850. In 1580 to 1588: *jusques à ce qu'il y a environ 18. cent ans, quelqu'un.* See Cicero, *Academica*, II, 39.

851. *Sic volvenda ætas commutat tempora rerum;*
      Quod fuit in pretio, fit nullo denique honore;
      Porro aliud succedit, et e contemptibus exit,
      Inque dies magis appetitur, floretque repertum
      Laudibus, et miro est mortales inter honore.
                —Lucretius, V, 1276.

852. In 1580 to 1588: *de Matiere, Forme, et Privation.*

853. *Exempts du boute-hors.*

854. *Combien y a-t-il que la medecine est au monde?*

Apology for Raimond Sebond

855. *Un homme de cette profession de nouvelletez et de reformations physiques.*

856. *Nam quod adest præsto, . . .*
. . . placet, et pollere videtur.
—Lucretius, V, 1412, 1413.

857. In 1580 to 1588: *Aristote dict que toutes les opinions humaines ont est par le passé, et feront à l'advenir, infinies autres fois; Platon, qu'elles ont a renouveller et revenir en estre, apres trente six mille ans.*

858. See Plato, *Politics*.

859. See Herodotus, II, 142, 143.

860. Origen. Montaigne took this from Vivès's *Commentary* on St. Augustine, *De Civ. Dei*, XII, 13.

861. *Createur sans creature.*

862. *Qu'il s'est desdict de son oisiveté.*

863. That of Plato; see the *Timæus, passim.*

864. See Diogenes Laertius, *Life of Heraclitus.*

865. *Sigillatim mortales, cunctim perpetui.*—Apuleius, *De Deo Socratis*. Montaigne took this from St. Augustine, *De Civ. Dei*, XII, 10.

866. *Leurs monumans.* See *Ibid.*, VIII, 5, and XII, 10.

867. See St. Augustine, *De Civ. Dei*, XII, 10 (Vivès's *Commentary*).

868. *Discours.*

869. Very many of these "facts" are taken from Gomara's *Histoire Générale des Indes*.

870. That is, the discoverers.

871. *Penitentiers.*

872. This item, added in 1595, is taken from Osorio, *Histoire du Roi Emmanuel des Portuguais.*

873. That is, the natives.

Notes and Comments

874. *Subsides tyranniques.*
875. That is, hieroglyphics.
876. *Leur revolution.*
877. *Nous touchons à la main.*
878. *Et plaga cœli non solum ad robur corporum, sed etiam animorum facit.*—Vegetius, I, 2. Montaigne took this citation from the *Politics* of J. Lipsius.
879. *Athenis tenue cœlum, ex quo etiam acutiores putantur Attici; crassum Thebis, itaque pingues Thebani et valentes.*—Cicero, *De Fato*, IV.
880. See Plutarch, *Apothegms of Kings*, etc., and Herodotus, IX, 122.
881. *Tailler et coudre.*
882.   *Quid enim ratione timemus*
 Aut cupimus? quid tam dextro pede concipis,
  ut te
 Conatus non pœniteat votique peracti?
        —Juvenal, X, 4
883. See Xenophon, *Memorabilia*, I, 3.2.
884. See Plato, *Second Alcibiades*.
885. *Conjugium petimus partumque uxoris; at illi*
 Notum qui pueri qualisque futura sit uxor.
        —Juvenal, X, 352.
886. *Attonitus novitate mali, divesque miserque*
 Effugere optat opes, et quæ modo voverat, odit.
      —Ovid, *Metam.*, XI, 128.
887. See Chap. 7, pp. 505 ff.
888. See Cicero, *Tusc. Disp.*, I, 47: Herodotus, I, 31; Plutarch, *Consolation to Apollonius.*
889. *Virga tua et baculus tuus ipsa me consolata sunt.*—Psalm XXIII, 4.

1862

Apology for Raimond Sebond

890.   *Si consilium vis*
Permittes ipsis expendere numinibus, quid
Conveniat nobis, rebusque sit utile nostris;
Charior est illis homo quam sibi.
—Juvenal X, 346-348, 350.

891. That is, from the divine powers.

892. See Xenophon, *Memorabilia*, I, 3.2.

893. See St. Augustine, *De Civ. Dei*, XIX, 2.

894. *Qui autem de summo bono dissenti, de tota philosophiæ ratione dissentit.*—Cicero, *De Fin.*, V, 5.

895.   *Tres mihi conviviæ prope dissentire videntur,*
Poscentes vario multum diversa palato;
Quid dem? quid non dem? Renuis tu quod
    jubet alter;
Quod petis, id sane est invisum acidumque
    duobus. —Horace, *Epistles*, II, 2.61.

896. See Plutarch, *Of Hearing*.

897.   *Nil admirari prope res est una, Numaci,*
Solaque quæ possit facere et servare beatum.
—Horace, *Epistles*, I, 6.1
The true reading is "Numici."

898. That is, loftiness of soul. See Aristotle, *Ethics*, IV.

899. *Les soustenemens.*

900. *Les consentements et appliances.* See Sextus Empiricus, *Hypot.*, I, 33.

901. *Bransle de leur ame.*

902. See Book I, chap. 25, p. 185.

903. In 1580 to 1588: *comme l'oracle de Socrates luy avoit apris, que exactement faire devoir de pieté n'est autre chose que servir Dieu selon l'usage de sa nation.* See Xenophon, *Memorabilia*, I, 3.1.

1863

Notes and Comments

904. In 1534 Henry VIII and his successors were recognized by Parliament as sole heads of the English Church; 1553, accession of Queen Mary; 1558, accession of Queen Elizabeth.

905. Guyenne belonged to England from 1152 to 1453.

906. *En ma maison.*

907. That is, the Reformed faith.

908. Apollo. See Xenophon, *Memorabilia*, I, 3.1.

909. *Pour avoir desniaise nostre creance de.*

910. In 1580 to 1588: *qui en l'espace d'un jour a peu recevoir un si estrange changement, d'estre devenu vice.* It is evident, from the difference in expression between the early texts and 1595, that Montaigne rewrote this sentence after reading a page of Erasmus in the *Querela Pacis:* "Ceu rerum veritas commutetur, ita quædam scita non trajiciunt mare, quædam non superant Alpes, quædam non tranant Rhenum."

911. See Plato, *Republic*, book I.

912.   *Gentes esse feruntur*
In quibus et nato genitrix et nata parenti
Jungitur, et pietas geminato crescit amore.
                             —Ovid, *Metam.*, X, 331.

913. *Nihil itaque amplius nostrum est; quod nostrum dico, artis est.*—Cicero, *De Fin.*, V, 21. The original text reads: *Sed virtutem ipsam nihil amplius. Itaque nostrum est, etc.*

914. See Book I, chap. 23, p. 152.

915. See Plutarch, *Life of Lycurgus*.

916. *Damasquinée.*

917. *Corrompre un chaste courage.* See Sextus Empiri-

1864

Apology for Raimond Sebond

cus, *Hypot.*, III, 24; Diogenes Laertius, *Life of Aristippus*.

918. See Diogenes Laertius, *Ibid*.

919. See *Ibid*.

920. *Voyla comant la raison fournit d'apparance à divers effects.* In 1580 to 1588: *Voyla comme ils avoyent tous deux raison de divers effects* (that is, both were right).

921. *Bellum, O terra hospita, portas;*
Bello armantur equi, bellum hæc armenta
  minantur.
Sed tamen iidem olim curru succedere sueti
Quadrupedes, et frena jugo concordia ferre;
Spes est pacis.
  —Virgil, *Æneid*, III, 539.

922. See Diogenes Laertius, *Life of Solon*.

923. See Idem, *Life of Socrates*.

924. See Sextus Empiricus, *Hypot.*, III, 24.

925. See *Ibid.*, I, 14; III, 24.

926. *Inde furor vulgi, quod numina vicinorum*
Odit quisque locus, cum solos credat habendos
Esse deos quos ipse colit.
  —Juvenal, XV, 37.

927. Two eminent Italian jurisconsults of the fourteenth century.

928. *Et d'un subject si arbitraire;* that is, depending on the discretion of the judge.

929. See Plutarch, *Rules concerning health*.

930. *Et obscœnas voluptates, si natura requirit, non genere, aut loco, aut ordine, sed forma, ætate, figura metiendas Epicurus putat.*—Cicero, *Tusc. Disp.*, V, 33.

931. *Ne amores quidem sanctos a sapiente alienos esse arbitrantur.*—Idem., *De Fin.*, III, 20.

Notes and Comments

932. *Quæramus ad quam usque ætatem juvenes amandi sint.*—Seneca, *Epistle* 123.15.

933. See Cicero, *Tusc. Disp.*, IV, 34.

934. That is, few of the philosophers of old times.

935. In 1580 to 1588: *Ils refusoient et desdaignoient la pluspart de nos ceremonies. Chacun a ouy parler de la deshontée façon de vivre des philosophes Cyniques.*

936. Perhaps an inexact memory of a passage in Plutarch, *Contradictions of the Stoics:* "He [Chrysippus] says that he will turn three somersaults if some one will give him a talent."

937. See Herodotus, VI, 129.

938. See Diogenes Laertius, *Life of Metrocles.*

939. *Mœchus es Aufidiæ, qui vir, Corvine, fuisti;*
      Rivalis fuerat qui tuus, ille vir est.
      Cur aliena placet tibi, quæ tua non placet uxor?
      Nunquid securus non potes arrigere?
                                            —Martial, III, 70.

940. *Nullus in urbe fuit tota qui tangere vellet*
      Uxorem gratis, Cæciliane, tuam,
      Dum licuit; sed nunc, positis custodibus, ingens
      Turba fututorum est. Ingeniosus homo es.
                                            —Martial, I, 74.

941. This last sentence was omitted here in 1595, to be inserted later, in Book III, chap. 5. It is derived from C. Agrippa, *Of the uncertainty and vanity of learning.*

942. *A l'election.*

943. See Sextus Empiricus, *Hypot.*, I, 29 and 32.

944. *Et par consequent rien en aucune; car rien n'est ou tout est.*

945. "Landit" was the name of a great fair, formerly

Apology for Raimond Sebond

held, in June, near St. Denis, lasting fifteen days. The salaries of the professors of the University were paid by the scholars on the first day, with a public ceremony.

946. Plato's belief is summarised from the *Phædo* and the *Theætetus*.

947.
*Via qua munita fidei
Proxima fert humanum in pectus templaque
   mentis.* —Lucretius, V, 102.

948. *Invenies primis ab sensibus esse creatam
Notitiam veri, neque sensus posse refelli.
Quid majore fide porro quam sensus haberi
Debet?*
—Lucretius, IV, 478, 479, 482, 483.

949. The substance of the next few pages was suggested by Sextus Empiricus, *Hypot.*, I, 14.

950. *An poterunt oculos aures reprehendere, an
   aures
Tactus? an hunc porro tactum sapor arguet
   oris,
An confutabunt nares, oculive revincent?*
—Lucretius, IV, 486.

951. *Seorsum cuique potestas
Divisa est, sua vis cuique est.*
—*Ibid.*, 489.

952 That is, the schools of philosophy.

953. *Quicquid id est, nihilo fertur majore figura
Quam nostris oculis quam cernimus, esse
   videtur.* —Lucretius, V, 577.

954. *Nec tamen hic oculis falli concedimus hilum
Proinde animi vitium hoc oculis adfingere noli.*
—*Idem.*, IV, 379, 386.

Notes and Comments

955. *Proinde quod in quoque est his visum tempore,*
　　　　verum est.
　　　Et, si non potuit ratio dissolvere causam,
　　　Cur ea quæ fuerint juxtim quadrata, procul sint
　　　Visa rotunda, tamen præstat rationis egentem
　　　Reddere mendose causas utriusque figuræ,
　　　Quam manibus manifesta suis emittere
　　　　quoquam,
　　　Et violare fidem primam, et convellere tota
　　　Fundamenta quibus nixatur vita salusque.
　　　Non modo enim ratio ruat omnis, vita quoque
　　　　ipsa
　　　Concidat extemplo, nisi credere sensibus ausis,
　　　Præcipitesque locos vitare, et cætera quæ sint
　　　In genere hoc fugienda. —Lucretius, IV, 499.

956. *Extantesque procul medio de gurgite montes*
　　　　Iidem apparent longe diversi licet.
　　　Et fugere ad puppim colles campique videntur
　　　Quos agimus propter navem . . .
　　　. . . ubi in medio nobis equus acer obhæsit
　　　Flumine, equi corpus transversum ferre videtur
　　　Vis, et in adversum flumen contrudere raptim.
　　　　　　—Lucretius, IV, 397, 389, 390, 420.

The lines are given as they appear in the *Édition Municipale*. There is a different arrangement in 1588 and 1595.

957. A mason.

958. That is, that really belongs to "the person."

959. *Auferimur cultu; gemmis auroque teguntur*
　　　　Crimina: pars minima est ipsa puella sui.
　　　Sæpe ubi sit quod ames inter tam multa
　　　　requiras;

1868

Apology for Raimond Sebond

Decipit hac oculos Ægide dives amor.
—Ovid, *Remedia Amoris*, I, 343.

960. *Cunctaque miratur, quibus est mirabilis ipse;*
Se cupit imprudens; et qui probat, ipse
probatur;
Dumque petit, petitur; pariterque accendit et
ardet. —Idem, *Metam.*, III, 424.

961. *Oscula dat reddique putat, sequiturque*
tenetque,
Et credit tactis digitos insidere membris;
Et metuit pressos veniat ne livor in artus.
—*Ibid.*, X, 256.

962. *Ut despici sine vertigine simul oculorum animique non possit.*—Livy, XLIV, 6.

963. *Fit etiam sæpe specie quadam, sæpe vocum gravitate et cantibus, ut pellantur animi vehementius; sæpe etiam cura et timore.*—Cicero, *De Divin.*, I, 37.

964. *Et solem geminum, et duplices se ostendere*
Thebas. —Virgil, *Æneid*, IV, 470.

965. *Multimodis igitur pravas turpesque videmus*
Esse in delitiis, summoque in honore vigere.
—Lucretius, IV, 1155.

966. *In rebus quoque apertis noscere possis,*
Si non advertas animum, proinde esse, quasi
omni
Tempore semotæ fuerint, longeque remotæ.
—Lucretius, IV, 811.

967. *Tantaque in his rebus distantia differitasque*
est,
Ut quod alis cibus est, aliis fuat acre venenum.
Sæpe etenim serpens, hominis contacta saliva,

Notes and Comments

>*Disperit, ac sese mandendo conficit ipsa.*
>—Lucretius, IV, 636.

968. *Lievres marins (lepus marinus).*

969. See Sextus Empiricus, *Hypot.*, I, 14, for this and the statements following the quotation.

970. >*Lurida præterea fiunt quæcunque tuentur Arquati.* —Lucretius, IV, 332.

971. >*Bina lucernarum florentia lumina flammis,*
>*Et duplices hominum facies, et corpora bina.*
>—Lucretius, IV, 450, 452.

972. >*Et vulgo faciunt id lutea russaque vela*
>*Et furruginea, cum magnis intenta theatris,*
>*Per malos volgata trabesque trementia pendent;*
>*Namque ibi consessum caveaï subter, et omnem*
>*Scenaï speciem, patrum, matrumque, deorum*
>*Inficiunt, coguntque suo volitare colore.*
>—Lucretius, IV, 75.

973. This sentence—"Sick people . . . but"—was in the texts of 1580 to 1588, but was omitted in 1595.

974. >*Ut cibus, in membra atque artus cum diditur omnes,*
>*Disperit, atque aliam naturam sufficit ex se.*
>—Lucretius, III, 703.

975. >*Denique ut in fabrica, si prava est regula prima,*
>*Normaque si fallax rectis regionibus exit,*
>*Et libella aliqua si ex parte claudicat hilum,*
>*Omnia mendose fieri atque obstipa necessum est,*
>*Prava, cubantia, prona, supina, atque absona tecta,*
>*Jam ruere ut quædam videantur velle, ruantque*

Apology for Raimond Sebond

> *Prodita judiciis fallacibus omnia primis.*
> *Hic igitur ratio tibi rerum prava necesse est*
> *Falsaque sit, falsis quæcumque a sensibus orta*
>   *est.* —Lucretius, IV, 513.

976. *Le subject.*

977. All this is from Sextus Empiricus, *Hypot.*, II, 7.

978. This and the following pages are taken almost literally from Plutarch, *Of the meaning of the word Ei.*

979. Sextus Empiricus (*Hypot.*, I, 32) ascribes this belief to Protagoras.

980. See Plutarch, *Common conceptions against the Stoics.*

981. The persons. See Plutarch, *Why divine justice sometimes postpones the punishment of evil-doers.*

982. The transcription from Amyot's translation of Plutarch's treatise *Of the meaning of the word Ei* continues hence almost to the end (with many omissions), except the quotation from Lucretius.

983. *Mutat enim mundi naturam totius ætas,*
    Ex alioque alius status excipere omnia debet.
    Nec manet ulla sui similis res; omnia migrant,
    Omnia commutat natura et vertere cogit.
              —Lucretius, V, 826.

984. That is, the reason.

CHAPTER XIII

Of Judging the Death of Others

A. THE COMMENT BY MISS NORTON

THIS is one of the Essays that is injured by its *story-telling*. The first four or five pages are worth reading again and again. The second half is scarcely read with interest even once, because the *fifteen* narratives in those pages are not in themselves of much value, and they are not very illustrative of the real argument. Some of them are, to be sure, instances of calmness in facing death; but they are all concerned with *self-given* deaths.

B. THE NOTES BY MR. IVES

1. That is, "our vision."
2. *Provehimur portu, terræque urbesque recedunt.*
—Virgil, *Æneid*, III, 72.
3. *Jamque acput quassans grandis suspirat arator,*
Et cum tempora temporibus præsentia confert
Præteritis, laudat fortunas sæpe parentis,
Et crepat antiquum genus ut pietate repletum.
—Lucretius, II, 1164, 1166-68.
4. *Tot circa unum caput tumultuantes deos.*—Seneca, *Suasoriæ*, I, 4.
5. *Italiam si, cœlo authore, recusas,*
Me pete; sola tibi causa hæc est justa timoris,

Of Judging the Death of Others

      Vectorem non nosse tuum; perrumpe procellas,
      Tutela secure mei.   —Lucan, V, 579.

6.   *Credit jam digna pericula Cæsar*
      Fatis esse suis. Tantusque evertere, dixit,
      Me superis labor est, parva quem puppe sedentem
      Tam magno petiere mari?   —Idem, V, 653.

7.   *Ille etiam, extincto miseratus Cæsare Romam,*
      Cum caput obscura nitidum ferrugine texit.
                                   —Virgil, *Georgics*, I, 466.

8. In 1580 to 1588: *que le pois de nos interests altere aussi le ciel, et qu'un grand Roy lui couste plus à tuer qu'une puce.*

9. *Non tanta cœlo societas nobiscum est, ut nostro fato mortalis sit ille quoque siderum fulgor.*—Pliny, *Nat. Hist.*, II, 8.

10. That is, regarding their "resolution and firmness." He seems, for the moment, to have forgotten La Boëtie.

11. These were common illustrations, in Montaigne's day, of cruelty. The first is reported by Suetonius of Caligula, the second, of Tiberius.

12.   *Vidimus et toto quamvis in corpore cæso*
      Nil animæ letale datum, moremque nefandæ
      Durum sævitiæ pereuntis parcere morti.
                                   —Lucan, IV, 178.

13. See Lampridius, *Life of Heliogabalus.*

14.   *Impiger et fortis virtute coacta.*
                                   —Lucan, IV, 798.

15. *Que le nez lui eut saigné, qui l'en eut mis au propre.*

16. See Plutarch, *Life of Cæsar.* The text has *la Prusse*, which is evidently a misprint for *l'Abruzze.* In his *Journal*

Notes and Comments

de Voyage, Montaigne wrote *Brusse*.

17. See Tacitus, *Annals*, IV, 22.

18. See *Ibid.*, VI, 48.

19. *Le capitaine Demosthenes.* See Plutarch, *Life of Nicias*.

20. See Appian, *De Bello Mithridatico*.

21. See Tacitus, *Annals*, XVI, 15.

22. *Qui n'a le gosier ferré à glace* (rough-shod).

23. See Xiphilin, *Life of Adrianus*.

24. See Suetonius, *Life of Cæsar;* Plutarch, *Apothegms of Kings*, etc.

25. See the *Nat. Hist.*, VII, 53.

26. That is, to men.

27. *Qui craint à la marchander.* Littré interprets this: *qui se hate de mourir*.

28.   *Emori nolo, sed me esse mortuum nihili æstimo.*
    —Cicero, *Tusc. Disp.*, I, 8.

29. See Book II, chap. 6, pp. 490-492.

30. See Xenophon, *Memorabilia*, IV, 8.

31. See Cornelius Nepos, *Life of Atticus*, XXII.

32. See Diogenes Laertius, *Life of Cleanthes*.

33.   *Invitum qui servat idem, facit occidenti.*
    —Horace, *Ars Poetica*, 467.

34. See Seneca, *Epistle* 77.5-9.

35. See Plutarch, *Life of Cato of Utica;* Seneca, *De Providentia*, II.

CHAPTER XIV

How Our Mind is Hindered by Itself

A. THE COMMENT BY MISS NORTON

THIS Essay opens with the presentation of the sophism known as "Buridan's Ass," which was a sort of example that was made use of for a very long time in the Schools. Buridan was one of the most renowned philosophers of the fourteenth century, but what exactly his ass originally was, is uncertain; it may possibly in his own day have been connected either with the Pons Asinorum of the logicians, or with some other ancient quibble. Bayle, one of the most competent authorities, declares that he could never find any one who could explain it. His guesses about it are founded on the belief that has long prevailed, that "Buridan's Ass" represented precisely the state of mind described by Montaigne—"a mind exactly balanced between two similar desires."

The way in which Montaigne extricates us from the difficulty begs the question with delightful and characteristic common sense; but how annoying his so cutting the knot must have been to Pascal, who revenged himself by calling his reference, a few lines farther on, to the squaring of the circle, "ignorant"!

1875

Notes and Comments

B. THE NOTES BY MR. IVES

1. See Plutarch, *Contradictions of the Stoics*.
2. *Il est impossible de toute impossibilité.*
3. *La faucée.*
4. *Solum certum nihil esse certi, et homine nihil miserius aut superbius.*—Pliny, *Nat. Hist.*, II, 7.

CHAPTER XV

That Desire is Increased in Us by Difficulty

A. THE COMMENT BY MISS NORTON

THIS is one of the Essays which even a familiar reader of Montaigne would find it difficult to give a résumé of, from memory; and perhaps a safe inference from this is that it is one of the least important. There is one interesting passage in it, the last two pages—autobiographical—added in 1595. The rest is fifteen years or more older in date. It keeps very close to the outline of its title; and the subject, an interesting one from the psychological point of view, is but little so when considered only superficially and anecdotically.

1876

Desire is Increased by Difficulty

B. THE NOTES BY MR. IVES

1. That is, the Pyrrhonians. See Sextus Empiricus, *Hypot.*, I, 6.

2. See Seneca, *Epistle* 4.6.

3. *In æquo est dolor amissæ rei, et timor amittendæ.*—Idem, *Epistle* 98.6.

4. *Si nunquam Danaën habuisset ahenea turris,*
   Non esset Danaë de Jove facta parens,
   —Ovid, *Amores*, II, 19.27.

5. *Omnium rerum voluptas ipso quo debet fugare periculo crescit.*—Seneca, *De Beneficiis*, VII, 9.

6. *Galla, nega; satiatur amor, nisi gaudia torquent.*
   —Martial, IV, 37.

7. Horace, *Epodes*, XI, 9.

8. Lucretius, IV, 1079, 1080, 1082, 1083.

9. That is, to Saint James of Compostella, in Galicia.

10. Spa, near Liége.

11. "What Montaigne says here with regard to the transaction of Cato's wife, Marcia, becoming, with his consent, the wife of Hortensius, and his receiving her later again as his own wife, would seem to be merely a personal opinion. Plutarch in his *Life of Cato* says nothing to suggest this view. Cæsar, in his attack on Cato, accused him of this being a matter of avarice."—Grace Norton, *Le Plutarque de Montaigne*, p. 127.

12. *Transvolat in medio posita, et fugientia captat.*
    —Horace, *Satires*, I, 2.108.

13. *Nisi tu servare puellam*
    Incipis, incipiet desinere esse mea.
    —Ovid, *Amores*, II, 19.47.

Notes and Comments

14. *Tibi quod superest, mihi quod desit, dolet.*
—Terence, *Phormio*, I, 4.10.

15. The text from this point to "drowsy passion" is an addition of 1582.

16. *Si qua volet regnare diu, contemnat amantem.*
—Ovid, *Amores*, II, 19.33.

17. *Contemnite, amantes,*
Sic hodie veniet, si qua negavit heri.
—Propertius, II, 14.19.

18. Virgil, *Eclogues*, III, 65.
19. Propertius, II, 15.6.
20. This paragraph was added in 1582.
21. See Valerius Maximus, II, 1.4; Aulus Gellius, IV, 3.
22. *Quod licet, ingratum est; quod non licet, acrius urit.* —Ovid, *Amores*, II, 19.3.
23. See Seneca, *De Clementia*, I, 23.
24. *Latius excisæ pestis contagia serpunt.*
—Rutilius, *Itinerarium*, I, 397.
25. That is, whether it is a fact, an essential truth.
26. That is, by punishments.
27. The Essay ended here in 1580.
28. See Herodotus, IV, 23.
29. See Lopez de Gomara, *Histoire Générale des Indes*.
30. The Essay ended here in 1588.
31. *Furem signata sollicitant. . . . Aperta effractarius præterit.*—Seneca, *Epistle* 68.4.
32. *L'estate de ma perte ne seroit de guere pire.* That is, it would hardly be worse [for me?] to be ruined myself than to have the common people ruined.
33. Since the beginning of the civil commotions in 1560-1562. These concluding sentences have sometimes

Of Fame

been taken to refer to Montaigne's age (he was born in 1533); but, as they were added after 1588, they undoubtedly mean that he had "continued" to live in an undefended house throughout the troublous period.

CHAPTER XVI

Of Fame

A. THE COMMENT BY MISS NORTON

THIS is one of the Emerson-like Essays, in which there is little or nothing to be commented on, every thing to be accepted; few pages that make one exclaim, "How admirable!" many that make one feel, "How wise!" The text of the whole is in the first page: "There is nothing so remote from reason, as for us to go in quest" of glory and honour; let us rather provide ourselves with more necessary possessions. It is true that there are advantages accompanying them; and even Epicurus himself, in the teeth of his own philosophy, could not but somewhat desire it, in the shape of after-death fame. Other philosophers have ranked it high; so high that they have maintained that "virtue itself is desirable only for the glory that always follows after it." How false an opinion! Let us receive from ourselves the law of well-doing. "Virtue is a very empty and valueless thing if it derives its recommendation from fame," especial-

1879

ly since fame is the most fortuitous of things; "it is fate that confers fame on us."

The first paragraph after "True and wise greatness of soul" (page 841) is one of the *personal* touches inserted in 1595, and breaks the connection.

The rest of the page is interesting from its *military* note, and the next pages for their high feeling and vigorous expression.

Not only is reputation a mere matter of chance, but the voice of the multitude is the voice of ignorance, injustice, and inconstancy. Every man likes praise, but it is but outward wealth. Even the folly of liking to be talked of, no matter in what tone, is common. But what profits it? If public approbation served to make men or nations or rulers better, then, indeed, might the love of fame be cherished by legislators as other false opinions are; but—?

The Essay closes with a word addressed to women, counselling them to distinguish, in this matter of reputation, the shadow from the substance (or, as he phrases it in the opening sentence of the Essay, the name from the thing), and to hold their virtue rather than their honour the protection of their chastity.

In fine, all persons of honour must feel that "the actions of virtue are too noble in themselves to seek other reward than from their own worth; and especially to seek it in the vanity of human judgements."

B. THE NOTES BY MR. IVES

1. *De la Gloire.*
2. *Gloria in excelsis Deo, et in terra pax hominibus.*—Luke, II, 14.

1880

Of Fame

3. Montaigne probably had in mind Cicero, *De Fin.*, III, 17, as he repeats Cicero's words a little later.

4.   *Deça vers nous, deça, O treslouable Ulisse,*
    Et le plus grand honneur dont la Grece fleurisse.
—A translation—whose, is not known—of the Odyssey, XII, 184.

5. See Cicero, *De Fin.*, III, 17.

6.   *Gloria quantalibet quid erit, si gloria tantum est?*   —Juvenal, VII, 81.

7. See Plutarch, *Whether it were rightly said, Live concealed.*

8. See Seneca, Epistle 21. 3, 4.

9. See Cicero, *De Fin.*, II, 30. Diogenes Laertius (*Life of Epicurus*) gives the same letter as addressed to Idomeneus.

10. See Cicero, *De Fin.*, II, 31.

11. See *Ibid.*, III, 17.

12. See the *Nicomachæan Ethics*, II, 7.

13. See Cicero, *De Fin.*, II, 15.

14.   *Paulum sepultæ distat inertiæ*
    Celata virtus.   —Horace, *Odes*, IV, 9.29.

15. See Cicero, *De Fin.*, II, 18.

16. See Cicero, *De Fin.*, II, 17. Caius had deposited with Sextus a legacy for his wife. On the death of Caius, Sextus went to the widow, who knew nothing of the transaction, and handed the legacy over to her.

17. See *Ibid*. Quintus Fadius Gallus left his property to Publius Sextilius Rufus, stating in his will that he desired that the entire inheritance should pass through Sextilius to his (Fadius's) daughter. The Voconian laws excluded daughters from inheriting largely from their fathers. Sex-

Notes and Comments

tilius denied that there was any such request, and added that he did not dare to disobey the Voconian law.

18. *Pour certeines quotites.*

19. See Cicero, *De Off.*, III, 18.

20. *Meminerint deum se habere testem, id est (ut ego arbitror) mentem suam.—Ibid.*, III, 10.

21. *Profecto fortuna in omni re dominatur; ea res cunctas ex libidine magis quam ex vero celebrat obscuratque.*—Sallust, *Catiline*, VIII, 1.

22. See Cicero, *Tusc. Disp.*, I, 45.

23. That is, glory.

24. *La noblesse;* in 1580 to 1588, *nos gens de guerre.*

25. *Quasi non sit honestum quod nobilitatum non sit.*—Cicero, *De Off.*, I, 4. The original is: *honestum, quod etiamsi nobilitatum non sit, tamen honestum sit.*

26. *Vera et sapiens animi magnitudo honestum illud quod maxime naturam sequitur, in factis positum, non in gloria, judicat.—Ibid.*, I, 19.

27. *Qui fut bonne en commun.*

28. That is, Cæsar's and Alexander's.

29. "But of Hannibal," etc., was omitted in 1595.

30. *Contre un poullaillier.*

31. *Gloria nostra est testimonium conscientiæ nostræ.*—II *Corinthians*, I, 12.

32.   *Credo che'l resto di quel verno cose*
      Facesse degne di tenerne conto;
      Ma fur sin' a quel tempo si nascose,
      Che non è colpa mia s'hor' non le conto;
      Perche Orlando a far opre virtuose,
      Piu ch'a narrarle poi, sempre era pronto,
      Ne mai fu alcun' de li suoi fatti espresso,

1882

Of Fame

Senon quando hebbe i testimonii apresso.
—Ariosto, *Orlando Furioso*, XI, 81.

33. *Virtus, repulsæ nescia sordidæ,*
Intaminatis fulget honoribus,
Nec sumit aut ponit secures
Arbitrio popularis auræ.
—Horace, *Odes*, III, 2.17.

34. *Non emolumento aliquo, sed ipsius honestatis decore.*—Cicero, *De Fin.*, I, 10.

35. See Cicero, *De Fin.*, II, 15.

36. *An quidquam stultius quam quos singulos contemnas, eos aliquid putare esse universos?*—Idem, *Tusc. Disp.*, V, 36.

37. *C'est une bute qui n'a ny forme ny prise.*

38. *Nihil tam inæstimabile est quam animi multitudinis.*—Livy, XXXI, 34.

39. See Seneca, *Epistle* 91.19.

40. *Ego hoc judico, si quando turpe non sit tamen non esse non turpe, quum id a multitudine laudetur.*—Cicero, *De Fin.*, II, 15.

41. *Dedit hoc providentia hominibus munus, ut honesta magis juvarent.*—Quintilian, *Institutio Oratoria*, I, 12.19.

42. Cf. Seneca, *Epistle* 85.33: *Qui hoc potuit dicere, "Neptune, nunquam hanc navem nisi rectam," arti satisfecit;* see also Idem, *Consolatio ad Marciam*, VI.

43. *Hommes, soupples, mestis, ambigus.*

44. *Risi successu posse carere dolos.*
—Ovid, *Heroides*, I, 18.

45. See Livy, XLIV, 22.

46. See *Ibid.*

Notes and Comments

47. *Laudari haud metuam, neque enim mihi cornea
fibra est;
Sed recti finemque extremumque esse recuso
Euge tuum et belle.* —Persius, I, 47.

48. The ring of Gyges. See Plato, *Republic*, book II; Cicero, *De Off.*, III, 9.

49. *Falsus honor juvat, et mendax infamia terret
Quem, nisi mendosum et mendacem?*
—Horace, *Epistles*, I, 16.39.

50. *Goujats.* This and the next sentence were added in 1582.

51. *Non, quicquid turbida Roma
Elevet, accedas, examenque improbum in illa
Castiges trutina; nec te quæsiveris extra.*
—Persius, I, 5.

52. Herostratus: this is not in Trogus Pompeius, but in Valerius Maximus, VIII, 5, *ext.* 14. Manlius Capitolinus: see Livy, VI, 2. Montaigne took the sentence from the preface to Bodin, *Methodus ad facilem historiarum cognitionem*.

53. It = "the cognisance of my friends."

54. *Meslera nos fusées.*

55. *Nunc levior cyppus non imprimit ossa?
Laudat posteritas; nunc non e manibus illis,
Nunc non e tumulo fortunataque favilla
Nascuntur violæ?* —Persius, I, 37.
The original *laudant convivæ* beginning the second line.

56. In Book I, chap. 46, p. 371.

57. *Casus multis hic cognitus ac jam
Tritus, et e medio fortunæ ductus acervo.*
—Juvenal, XIII, 9.

1884

Of Fame

58. *Ad nos vix tenius famæ perlabitur aura.*
—Virgil, *Æneid*, VII, 646.
59. See Plutarch, *Apothegms of the Lacedæmonians*.
60. *Quos fama obscura recondit.*
—Virgil, *Æneid*, V, 302.
61. *Recte facti, fecisse merces est.*—Seneca, *Epistle* 81.19.
62. *Officii fructus ipsum officium est.*—Cicero, *De Fin.*, II, 22.
63. *Ce grand pendart.*
64. See Plato, *Laws*, book XII.
65. Plato and Socrates.
66. *Ut tragici poetæ confugiunt ad deum, cum explicare argumenti exitum non possunt.*—Cicero, *De Nat. Deor.*, I, 20.
67. See Diogenes Laertius, *Life of Plato*.
68. *Opinion* = public opinion.
69. See Plutarch, *Life of Numa* and *Life of Sertorius*.
70. *Histoire de Saint-Louis*, LVI.
71. *In ferrum mens prona viris, animæque capaces*
 Mortis, et ignavum est redituræ parcere vitæ.
—Lucan, I, 461.
72. *Ut enim consuetudo loquitur, id solum dicitur honestum quod est populari fama gloriosum.*—Cicero, *De Fin.*, II, 15.
73. *Quæ, quia non liceat, non facit, illa facit.*
—Ovid, *Amores*, III, 4.4.

1885

CHAPTER XVII

Of Presumption

A. THE COMMENT BY MISS NORTON

AN abridgement of this Essay might be entitled, "Montaigne judged by himself"; and its chief interest lies in the simplicity with which in the course of its easy pages he depicts himself. The portrait is of such intimacy that no man could so portray another; but it is as free from *arrangement*, as little *composed*, as if taken unawares. In the modern phrase, *il se regardait vivre;* but this doubling of himself into the observed and the observer he accomplished with no trace of modern morbid self-introspection, and no modern morbid exaggeration of qualities and defects into virtues and vices. All is characteristically moderate in tone.

The Essay opens with a reference to the preceding one, and it was perhaps its opening sentence that suggested its title; but it soon passes into a justification of talking about oneself, and then into autobiography.

The subsequent pages need no analysis, but it is only after many readings and re-readings of them in many different lights that one fully recognises the value to one's own mind of familiarity with this natural, *sane* intelligence, an intelligence whose native veracity, strengthened by conscious will, rendered it capable of *weighing itself* and calmly proclaiming what it found indicated.

1886

Of Presumption

Montaigne divides the vice of "presumption" into two: the esteeming oneself too highly, and the esteeming another not highly enough. It is the presence or absence of the first defect that he studies in himself for many pages; but he then enters on the other part, and this leads to some very interesting remarks on the men he had known (notably La Boëtie) and the mistakes made in education in that day; from which he passes to an enumeration of the most remarkable men of the time,—soldiers, statesmen, poets,— and then to the praises of Marie de Gournay, which last passage was not printed till 1595.

It is noteworthy as evincing an interesting trait in her character that in the edition of the Essays which she published in 1635 and dedicated to Cardinal Richelieu, this passage is suppressed.

Most of the Essay was written in 1573 and 1574, but it was much "variated" in the edition of 1595.

B. THE NOTES BY MR. IVES

1. *Ille velut fidis arcana sodalibus olim*
   Credebat libris, neque, si male cesserat, usquam
   Decurrens alio, neque si bene; quo fit ut omnis
   Votiva pateat veluti descripta tabella
   Vita senis. —Horace, *Satires*, II, 1.30.
2. *Nec id Rutilio et Scauro citra fidem aut obtrectationi fuit.*—Tacitus, *Agricola*, I.
3. *Pas inconvenient.*
4. See Plutarch, *How to distinguish a flatterer from a friend.*
5. See Plutarch, *Life of Alcibiades.*
6. The last clause was omitted in 1595.

1887

Notes and Comments

7. See Plutarch, *Life of Cæsar.*
8. *Entre les contenances desreglées.*
9. See Ammianus Marcellinus, XXI, 16. It was Constantius II.
10. That is, unconscious.
11. *Gloire:* the word here has a different meaning from that in which it is used as the subject of the last Essay.
12. The last clause was omitted in 1595.
13. *Je n'ay point mes moyens en proposition et par estat.*
14. *En l'eschole mesme de la sapience.*
15. This is a translation of a sentence inscribed on the beams of Montaigne's library: *Cognoscendi studium homini dedit Deus epis torquendi gratia. Eccl. I.* "This thought," says Miss Norton (*Studies in Montaigne,* p. 167), "is to be found in *Ecclesiastes* I, 13: *Et proposui in animo mea quærere et investigare sapienter de omnibus quæ fiunt sub sole. Hanc occupationem pessimam dedit Deus filiis hominum ut occuparentur in ea.*"
16. See Seneca, *Epistle* 71.31, and *Epistle* 110.
17. This sentence was omitted in 1595.
18.   *Mediocribus esse poetis*
Non dii, non homines, non concessere columnæ.
                            —Horace, *Ars Poetica,* 372.
19.   *Verum*
Nil securius est malo Poeta.
                                —Martial, XII, 63.13.
20. *Que n'avons nous de tels peuples!*
21. See Diodorus Siculus, XIV, 28.
22. See Diodorus Siculus, XV, 20.
23. This was the name of the festival (of Bacchus), not

Of Presumption

of the tragedy; but the error was made by Amyot, in his translation, and repeated by Montaigne.

24. See Diodorus Siculus, *ubi supra*. When Montaigne wrote in the second chapter of Book I (Vol. I) that Dionysius the Tyrant "died of joy," his authority was the elder Pliny. It was after reading Diodorus, says M. Villey, that he toned down his statement.

25. *En foule et en chambre.*

26. *Cum relego, scripsisse pudet, quia plurima
    cerno,
    Me quoque qui feci judice, digna lini.*
    —Ovid, *Ex Ponto*, I, 5.15.

27. See Plutarch, *Marriage Precepts*, XXVI.

28. *Si quid enim placet,
    Si quid dulce hominum sensibus influit,
    Debentur lepidis omnia gratiis.*
    —Source unknown.

29. See Cicero, *Academica*, I, 2.

30. This sentence of 1580 to 1588 was omitted in 1595.

31. See his translation of the *Timæus* of Plato, II.

32. *Je me prens à la conclusion.*

33. *Facile et poli; il est aspre et desdeigneus.* In 1580: *doux et fluide, il est sec et espineux.* In 1588: *facile et fluide; il est aspre.*

34. *Brevis esse laboro,
    Obscurus fio.* —Horace, *Ars Poetica*, 25.

35. See *Politicus, Laws* (book X), and the last part of the *Phædo*.

36. *Comme à faire.* In the edition of 1595, *faire* was misprinted *taire*, and the error was repeated in many later

Notes and Comments

editions, and by Florio in his translation: "As well in *silence* as in speech," etc.

37. *Brusquement.* In 1580: *toujours avec vehemence.*
38. See Tacitus, *Dialogus de Oratoribus*, 39.
39. *Des contrées en deça;* that is, *en deça la Charente,* the limit of the *langue d'Oc.*
40. *Qui ne sentit evidemment son ramage.*
41. *Quelque signerie contrefaicte.*
42. *De toutes les sectes la plus civilisee, attribue à la sagesse.*
43.
> *Agros divisere atque dedere*
> *Pro facie cujusque et viribus ingenioque;*
> *Nam facies multum valuit viresque vigebant.*
> —Lucretius, V, 1110.

44. Vegetius, I, 5. But Montaigne's source was the *Politiques* of Justus Lipsius, V, 12.
45. Referring to *Il Cortegiano*, by Baldasarre Castiglione, I, 20.
46. *Qui le face montrer au doigt.*
47. That is, as Castiglione does.
48. See Aristotle, *Nicomachæan Ethics*, IV, 7.
49. Aristotle, *Politics*, IV, 44. But Montaigne took this from the Commentary of Loys le Roy, who translated the *Politics* of Aristotle in 1568.
50.
> *Ipse inter primos præstanti corpore Turnus*
> *Vertitur, arma tenens, et toto vertice supra est.*
> —Virgil, *Æneid*, VII, 783.

51. *Speciosus forma præ filiis hominum.*—Psalm XLV.
52. See the *Republic*, book VII.
53. This is the text of 1580. In 1588 the name was changed to Philopœmen, and the parenthesis was dropped.

Of Presumption

54. See Plutarch, *Life of Philopœmen*.

55. *Ny l'epesseur bien unie d'une barbe brune à escorce de chataigne, ny le poil relevé.*

56. *Inclinant un peu sur la grossesse* (1580; omitted in 1588 and 1595).

57. The phrases in italics were added in 1588.

58. *Unde rigent setis mihi crura, et pectora villis.*
—Martial, II, 36.5.

59. The last clause was omitted in 1588 and 1595.

60. *Minutatim vires et robur adultum*
Frangit, et in partem pejorem liquitur ætas.
—Lucretius, II, 1131.

61. *Singula de nobis anni prædantur euntes.*
—Horace, *Epistles*, II, 2.55.

62. *Un père très dispost.* In 1580 to 1588: *le plus dispost qui se vid de son temps.* As to his father's activity, see Book II, chap 2, p. 455.

63. Cf. Book I, chap. 40, p. 339.

64. *Molliter austerum studio fallente laborem.*
—Horace, *Satires*, II, 2.12.

65. *Tanti mihi non sit opaci*
Omnis arena Tagi, quodque in mare volvitur aurum.
—Juvenal, III, 54.

66. About a friend's affairs, or public affairs?

67. In 1595 is substituted for this last clause: *une occasion pourtant, que mille autres de ma cognoissance eussent prinse, pour planche plutost, à se passer à la queste, à l'agitation et inquietude.*

68. *Non agimur tumidis velis Aquilone secundo;*
Non tamen adversis ætatem ducimus austris;
Viribus, ingenio, specie, virtute, loco, re,

Notes and Comments

Extremi primorum, extremis usque priores.
—Horace, *Epistles*, II, 2.201.

69. In this paragraph the text of 1580 to 1588 is rearranged, without substantial change.

70. *Hæc nempe supersunt,*
Quæ dominum fallant, quæ prosint furibus.
—Horace, *Epistles*, I, 6.45.

By slightly changing the text, Montaigne precisely reverses the sense.

71. *Quand j'y demeurerois.*
72. *Dubia plus torquent mala.*
—Seneca, *Agamemnon*, III, 1.29.
73. *C'est la siege de la constance.*
74. *Spem pretio non emo.*
—Terence, *Adelphi*, II, 2.11.
75. *Alter remus aquas, alter tibi radat arenas.*
—Propertius, III, 3.23.
76. *Capienda rebus in malis præceps via est.*
—Seneca, *Agamemnon*, II, 1.47.
77. *Cui sit conditio dulcis sine pulvere palmæ.*
—Horace, *Epistles*, I, 1.51.
78. *Turpe est, quod nequeas, capiti committere*
pondus,
Et pressum inflexo mox dare terga genu.
—Propertius, III, 9.5.
79. *La facilité de mes meurs.*
80. *Nunc, si depositum non inficiatur amicus,*
Si reddat veterem cum tota ærugine follem
Prodigiosa fides et Tuscis digna libellis,
Quæque coronata lustrari debeat agna.
—Juvenal, XIII, 60.

Of Presumption

81. *Estouffe sa recommendation.*
82. *Nihil est tam populare quam bonitas.*—Cicero, *Pro-Ligario*, 10.
83. *Plustost lairrois je rompre le col aux affaires.*
84. The last clause *(Édition Municipale)* was omitted in 1595.
85. The last clause *(Édition Municipale)* was omitted in 1595.
86. See Aristotle, *Nicomachæan Ethics*, IV, 8.
87. See Apollonius, *Letters*, 83. This sentence was added in 1582.
88. Charles VIII. See G. Corrozet, *Propos Memorables.*
89. See Aurelius Victor, *De Viris Illustribus*, LXVI.
90. *Quo quis versutior et callidior est, hoc invisior et suspectior, detracta opinione probitatis.*—Cicero, *De Off.*, II, 9.
91. See Tacitus, *Annals*, I, 11.
92. An allusion to Machiavelli, whose *Prince* was then the subject of much controversy.
93. These facts came originally from Paulus Jovius, *Historiarum sui temporis libri*, but Montaigne took them from Machiavelli's *Thesoro Politico*, II, 5.
94. *Et que je m'eschauffe par l'opposition du respect.*
95. That is, what seems to be a truth.
96. See Diogenes Laertius, *Life of Aristippus.*
97. Montaigne has much to say on the subject of his poor memory in Book I, chap. 9, pp. 37ff.
98. That is, the memory.
99. *Entre les libreries de village.*
100. In 1580: *car il m'est impossible.*

Notes and Comments

101. See Pliny, *Nat. Hist.*, VII, 24, where it is said simply that he forgot his own name.

102. *Memoria certe non modo philosophiam, sed omnis vitæ usum omnesque artes una maxime continet.*—Cicero, *Academica*, II, 7.

103. *Plenus rimarum sum, hac atque illac effluo.*
—Terence, *Eunuchus*, I, 2.25.

104. See *De Senectute*, VII: *Nec vero quemquam senum audivi oblitum quo loco thesaurum obruisset.*

105. *Tardif et mousse; le moindre nuage luy arreste sa pointe.*

106. "Costé refers to *Epistle* 3. I doubt if Montaigne alludes to that letter, but I have found no better source to suggest."—M. Villey.

107. *Si chetive.*

108. In 1580-1588: *c'est à mon advis une bien lourde faute.*

109. Abdera. It was Democritus who drew this conclusion from what he saw Protagoras doing. See Aulus Gellius, V, 3.

110. The last clauses, of the text of 1580, from "I greatly doubt," were omitted in all the later editions.

111. *Nasutus sis usque licet, sis denique nasus,*
Quantum noluerit ferre rogatus Athlas,
Et possis ipsum tu deridere Latinum,
Non potes in nugas dicere plura meas,
Ipse ego quam dixi; quid dentem dente juvabit
Rodere? carne opus est, si satur esse velis.
Ne perdas operam; qui se mirantur, in illos
Virus habe; nos hæc novimus esse nihil.
—Martial, XIII, 2.1.

Of Presumption

112. In September, 1559.
113. *Ne si, ne no, nel cor mi suona intero.*
—Petrarch, *Sonnet* 135.
114. See Diogenes Laertius, *Life of Chrysippus.*
115. *Dum in dubio est animus, paulo moment huc atque illuc impellitur.*
—Terence, *Andria*, I, 6.32.
116. *Sors cecidit super Mathiam.*—*Acts*, I, 26.
117. *Ipsa consuetudo assentiendi periculosa esse videtur et lubrica.*—Cicero, *Academica*, II, 21.
118. *Justa pari premitur veluti cum pondere libra Prona, nec hac plus parte sedet, nec surgit ab illa.*
—Tibullus, IV, 1.40.
119. *Cædimur, et totidem plagis consumimus hostem.*
—Horace, *Epistles*, II, 2.97.
120. *Principes trop grossiers et apparens.*
121. *Nunquam adeo fœdis adeoque pudendis Utimur exemplis ut non pejora supersint.*
—Juvenal, VIII, 183.
122. *Es ouvrages estrangers.*
123. The edition of 1595 and all subsequent editions based upon it add at this point: *Et qui verroit bien à clair la hauteur d'un jugement estranger, il y arriveroit, et y porteroit le sien.*
124. That is, good sense.
125. That is, the scholars, and the common and uncultured souls.
126. *A qui vous tombez en partage.*
127. That is, my opinions.
128. *Mihi nempe valere et vivere doctus.*
—Lucretius, V, 961.

Notes and Comments

129. *Nemo in sese tentat descendere.*
—Persius, IV, 23.

130. *Omnino, si quidquam est decorum, nihil est profecto magis quam æquabilitas universæ vitæ, tum singularum actionum; quam conservare non possis, si, aliorum naturam imitans, omittas tuam.*—Cicero, *De Off.*, I, 31.

131. That is, *s'estimer trop.*

132. *L'adresse.*

133. *Le mieux.*

134. That is, Jerome.

135. Which he has already discussed at great length in Book I, chap. 26.

136. *Par jargon et par cœur.*

137. That is, virtue.

138. That is, our education.

139. See Diogenes Laertius, *Life of Polemo;* Valerius Maximus, VI, 9, *ext.* 1.

140. *Faciasne quod olim*
 Mutatus Polemon? ponas insignia morbi,
 Fasciolas, cubital, focalia, potus ut ille
 Dicitur ex collo furtim carpsisse coronas,
 Postquam est impransi correptus voce magistri?
—Horace, *Satires*, II, 3.253.

141. *Plus sapit vulgus, quia tantum quantum opus est, sapit.*—Lactantius, *Institutiones Divinæ*, III, 5.

142. *Pour gens suffisans.*

143. In Latin, Auratus; in French, Dorat or Daurat.

144. *Ma fille d'alliance.*

145. This passage does not appear on the Bordeaux copy of 1588, but was added in 1595. See the Introduction to this chapter.

CHAPTER XVIII

Of Giving the Lie

A. THE COMMENT BY MISS NORTON

IT is not easy to say why this Essay is entitled "Of Giving the Lie" rather than "Of Lying." Be that as it may, the introduction to the subject is longer than the treatment of the subject itself, and is more interesting.

We come to the matter of lying only after three or four previous pages filled with a charming plea of excuse for writing about himself, which is like an echo—a reverberating echo—of the *avant-propos* of the book, "The author to the reader." There is a delightful passage about his interest in the modes of living, the actions, the looks and words of his ancestors, and a droll gibe at his posterity, if it be different in this respect from himself.

Just following this is a passage, added in 1595, of peculiar interest as a piece of mental biography: "Modelling this figure after myself," and what follows.

And then we reach the point that he has been slowly approaching, and he questions: Who can be believed, nowadays, about himself, when so few men can be believed about any thing?

The passage is a fine one,—Montaigne is always eloquent and forcible in his praises of truth,—and in conclusion he touches on the special point of the Essay, without enlarging on it, and promises to return to it—which he failed to do.

1897

Notes and Comments

A comparison of this Essay with that "Of Liars" (Book I, chapter 9) shows how much Montaigne had gained in vigour of thought and fineness of expression.

B. THE NOTES BY MR. IVES

1. *Non recito cuiquam, nisi amicis, idque rogatus,*
   Non ubivis, coramve quibuslibet. In medio qui
   Scripta foro recitent, sunt multi, quique lavantes.
   —Horace, *Satires*, I, 4.73.

2. *Non equidem hoc studeo, bullatis ut mihi nugis*
   Pagina turgescat. . . .
   Secreti loquimur. —Persius, V, 19.

3. The last sentence is translated from the text of 1580 to 1588; in 1595 is added that he preserves *l'escriture, le seing, des heures et une espée peculiere.*

4. *Paterna vestis et annulus tanto charior est posteris, quanto erga parentes major affectus.*—St. Augustine, *De Civ. Dei*, I, 13.

5. This means that printing is better than copies made by hand.

6. *Ne toga cordyllis, ne penula desit olivis.*
   —Martial, XIII, 1.1.

7. *Et laxas scombris sæpe dabo tunicas.*
   —Catullus, XCIV, 8.

8. *Pour m'extraire.*

9. That is, concerned only with me.

10. *Zon dessus l'œil, zon sur le groin,*
    Zon sur le dos de Sagoin!
    —Clement Marot, *Fripelippes, valet de Marot, à Sagon.*

11. *Effleurer.*

1898

12. See Plutarch, *Life of Marius.*
13. See the *Republic*, book III.
14. *Qui est loyalle.*
15. See his *De Gubernatione Dei*, I, 14.
16. See Plutarch, *Life of Lysander.*
17. Lysander. See Plutarch, *Life of Lysander.*
18. *De leur devoir.*
19. See Plutarch, *Life of Pompey* and *Life of Cato of Utica.*

CHAPTER XIX

Of Liberty of Conscience

A. THE COMMENT BY MISS NORTON

THE subject of this Essay is the Emperor Julian. The title arises from the consideration (in the last paragraph) of the policy of Julian in employing general tolerance—liberty of conscience—in the hope that this freedom would increase, to his gain, the dissensions of the people; a policy employed in Montaigne's own time by the kings of France (with regard to the Protestants), from precisely opposite intentions and hopes—at least, so Montaigne states.

Montaigne's view of the emperor is interesting, but has no peculiar value.

1899

Notes and Comments

The first paragraph—concerning the moral conditions of those engaged in the civil wars of France—is perhaps as noteworthy as any; and the very first sentence is a characteristic expression of moral good sense.

B. THE NOTES BY MR. IVES

1. See Flavius Vopiscus, *Life of the Emperor Tacitus;* Bodin, *Methodus ad facilem historiarum cognitionem.*
2. That is, the Christians.
3. See Ammianus Marcellinus, XXIV, 4.27.
4. See Idem, XXV, 3.23.
5. See Idem, XXII, 10.1.
6. See Idem, XXV, 4.20.
7. See Idem, XXII, 10.7.
8. Julian.
9. Marcellinus.
10. Julian.
11. See Zonaras, *Chroniques, etc.;* cf. also Sozomenes, *Histoire Ecclésiastique.*
12. See Eutropius, X, 8. At this point, in 1580, is the following passage, which was omitted altogether in 1588, and was inserted on a later page in 1595. *Aussi ce que plusieurs disent de luy, qu'estant blessé à mort d'un coup de traict, il s'ecria, "Tu as vaincu"; ou, comme disent les autres, "Contente toy, Nazarien," n'est non plus vraysemblable. Car ceux qui estoint presens à sa mort, et qui nous en recitent toutes les particulieres circonstances, les contenances mesmes et les parolles, n'en disent rien; non plus que de je ne sçay quels miracles que d'autres y meslent.*
13. See Ammianus Marcellinus, XXII, 3.
14. See Idem, XXV, 4.4.

1900

Of Liberty of Conscience

15. That is, the power of going without sleep (keeping vigil).
16. See Idem, XVI, 5.4.
17. See Idem, XXV, 4.
18. See Idem, XVI, 5.
19. See *Ibid*.
20. That is, Julian.
21. See Ammianus Marcellinus, XXV, 3.
22. See Idem, XXV, 3.
23. See Idem, XXV, 5.
24. See Idem, XXV, 4
25. See Idem, XXV, 3.
26. See Idem, XX, 5.
27. See Idem, XXV, 2.
28. See Theodoretus, III, 20.
29. See Zonaras, *Chroniques*, etc.
30. This addition of 1595 is a shortened version of the passage of 1580 quoted above (p. 906, note 12).
31. See Ammianus Marcellinus, XXI, 2.
32. *Le peuple decousu avec les prelats de l'Eglise Chrestienne divisez.*
33. See Ammianus Marcellinus, XXII, 5.
34. Ammianus's.

CHAPTER XX

We have no Experience of Any Simple Thing

A. THE COMMENT BY MISS NORTON

NO good, Montaigne declares, is free from ill. This Essay is the development of this thought. And, as physical pains and pleasures are intermingled and interdependent, so are moral good and evil mingled together in the soul. The justest laws have something unjust, and the wisest men are sometimes fools. The two most interesting paragraphs are the personal one of his self-examination, and the following one, full of sound sense on the conduct of affairs, especially public affairs.

B. THE NOTES BY MR. IVES

1. *Nous ne goustons rien de pur.*
2. *Medio de fonte leporum Surgit amari aliquid, quod in ipsis floribus angat.*
—Lucretius, IV, 1133.
3. *Ipsa felicitas, se nisi temperat, premit.*—Seneca, Epistle 74.18.
4. Referring back to what he said immediately before the verses of Lucretius, added in 1588.
5. Attributed to Epicharmus by Xenophon (*Memorabilia*, II, 1.20):

πόνων πωλοῆσιν ἡμῖν πάντα ταγαθὰ θεοί.

We have no Experience of any Simple Thing

6. See Plato, *Phædo*. Montaigne refers again to this passage in the last Essay of all. The Latin text that he used (Ficino's) translates the last clause: *in unum saltem eorum apices conjunxisse;* and Jowett: "he fastened their heads together."

7. M. Villey remarks that Seneca (*Epistle* 99) *consacre un long paragraphe à combattre cette idée, qui le scandalise. Montaigne prend parti contre le stoicien Senèque, dont la psychologie lui parait trop raide, pour l'épicurien Metrodore, qui lui parait plus réaliste.*

8. Cf. Seneca, *Epistle* 99.

9. *Est quædam flere voluptas.*
—Ovid, *Tristia*, IV, 3.27.

10. See Seneca, *Epistle* 63.5.

11. *Minister vetuli, puer, falerni,
Ingere mi calices amariores.*—Catullus, XXVII.

12. *Nullum sine auctoramento malum est.*—Seneca, *Epistle* 69.4.

13. *Plus verte.* In 1580 to 1588: *plus nette.*

14. See the *Republic*, book IV. This and the quotation following, Montaigne took from Bodin's *Methodus ad facilem historiarum cognitionem.*

15. *Omne magnum exemplum habet aliquid ex iniquo, quod contra singulos utilitate publica rependitur.*—*Annals*, XIV, 44. The Essay ended here in 1580.

16. *Les esprits communs et moins tendus.*

17. *Volutantibus res inter se pugnantes obtorpuerant animi.*—Livy, XXXII, 20.

18. See Cicero, *De Nat. Deor.*, I, 22. The question was, what God was.

19. *Un engin moyen.*

1903

CHAPTER XXI

Against Slothfulness

A. THE COMMENT BY MISS NORTON

THIS Essay is not so much against slothfulness in general as "the slothfulness of princes"—"*les rois fainéants*"; and, as we are not princes, and are not inconvenienced nowadays by "*rois fainéants*," the interest of Montaigne's remarks is more historical than personal. They have also in themselves rather *too* historical a flavour. The emperors Vespasian and Hadrian and Julian, Selim I, Bajazet II, Amurath III, Edward III of England and Charles V of France, the kings of Castile and Portugal, and Moley Moluch, King of Fez, were unquestionably important personages, but somehow we are not very much interested about them; at least, by any thing that can be said in a few lines.

But one becomes interested when one puts oneself into Montaigne's skin, and sees one's prince weakly occupy himself in "feeble and frivolous occupations." There is little question that there is a reference here to Henri III, who, when he was duc d'Anjou, was remarkable for brilliant valour, but after he became king never appeared in the field. The "one prince" of whom Montaigne speaks on the same page—"I know one prince . . ."—is evidently Henri IV.

The thought with which the Essay opens and concludes, that the noblest death is to die "standing," is a favourite one with Montaigne. He spoke of this saying in the Essay,

Against Slothfulness

"That to think as a philosopher is to learn to die."

It is to be observed that this Essay consisted in 1580 and also in 1588 of merely the first and third paragraphs—"*L'empereur Vespasian*," "*L'empereur Julian*." All the rest was added in 1595.

B. THE NOTES BY MR. IVES

1. No text has been found which narrates this saying of Vespasian. Montaigne's memory evidently played him false.

2. See Spartianus, *Life of Ælius Verus*, where Hadrian is reported as saying: *Sanum principem mori debere, non debilem.*

3. Probably an allusion to King Henri IV.

4. See Froissart, I, 123.

5. That is, their generals.

6. *Respirer.* See Zonaras, *Life of Julian.*

7. See the *Cyropædeia*, I, 2.16.

8. See Seneca, *Epistle* 88.19.

9. *Victor, Marce Fabi, revertar ex acie: Jovem patrem Gradivumque Martem aliosque iratos invoco deos.*—Livy, II, 45.

10. See Goulard, *Histoire du Portugal.*

11. See Diodorus Siculus, XVI, 6. This long passage, from "Fortune" (28 lines above), is found in 1595, but not in the *Édition Municipale.*

12. The battle of Alcazar, in 1578.

13. *Coacervanturque non solum cæde, sed etiam fuga.*—Livy, II, 4.7.

14. See Jeronimo de Franchi Conestaggio, *Dell'unione del regno di Portogallo alla corona di Castiglia.*

15. Cf. Book I, chap. 20, pp. 105, 106.

CHAPTER XXII

Of Posting

A. THE COMMENT BY MISS NORTON

THESE two pages about riding post—after the first two sentences they are but a string of facts—show what an admirable collaborator for an encyclopædia Montaigne would have been.

The first sentence is one of those that make the unfading strokes in the portrait of him created by the Essays. The second sentence suggests the picture of the moment of conception of this Essay, when, laying down the volume of Xenophon, he let his thoughts dwell, as he walked about his circular library, on what he had been reading.

B. THE NOTES BY MR. IVES

1. *Mais j'en quitte le mestier.* These four lines first appeared in the edition of 1588.
2. See Xenophon, *Cyropædeia*, VIII, 6.9.
3. *De Bello Civili*, III, 2.
4. Cæsar. See Suetonius, *Life of Cæsar.*
5. See Pliny, *Nat. Hist.*, VII, 20.
6. *Per dispositos equos prope incredibili celeritate ab Amphissa tertio die Pellam pervenit.*—Livy, XXXVII, 7.
7. See Pliny, *Nat. Hist.*, X, 24. This and the next two examples Montaigne took from Justus Lipsius, *Saturnalium Sermonum Libri*, II, 26.

8. See Pliny, *Nat. Hist.*, X, 37.
9. *A tout de portoires.*
10. See Gomara, *Histoire Générale des Indes*, V, 7.
11. See Chalcondylas, XIII, 14.
12. The last sentence is found in 1595, but is not in the *Édition Municipale*.

CHAPTER XXIII

Of Bad Means Employed

for a Good End

A. THE COMMENT BY MISS NORTON

THE opening of this Essay is not very interesting from any point of view. It treats of the resemblance of states and individuals in plethoric conditions; but in the course of it we have one of the personal expressions about the public affairs of the day which are always of interest. The consideration of the gain that may come from the evil of war leads to general examples of the use of bad means for a good end—uninteresting again.

B. THE NOTES BY MR. IVES

1. *Et patimur longæ pacis mala; sævior armis,*
 Luxuria incumbit. —Juvenal, VI, 291.

1907

Notes and Comments

2. *Foisonnant en trop de gaillardise.*
3. *Aus affaires de deça.* See Froissart, I, 213.
4. *En sa gendarmerie.* No source for this statement has ever been found. Philip Augustus sent his son on an expedition into England (1215); but the son's name was Louis, not Jean, and it is nowhere stated that the purpose of the expedition was to get rid of the troops who were overrunning France.
5. *Nil mihi tam valde placeat, Rhamnusia virgo,*
Quod temere invitis suscipiatur heris.
—Catullus, LXVIII, 77.
6. See Plutarch, *Life of Lycurgus.*
7. *Escrimeurs à outrance.*
8. *Quid vesani aliud sibi vult ars impia ludi,*
Quid mortes juvenum, quid sanguine pasta voluptas?
—Prudentius, *Contra Symmachum*, II, 672.
9. This whole passage, to the end of the Essay, the quotations included, is taken from Justus Lipsius, *Saturnalium Sermonum Libri,* books I and II.
10. *Arripe dilatam tua, dux, in tempora famam,*
Quodque patris superest, successor laudis habeto.
Nullus in urbe cadat cujus sit pœna voluptas.
Jam solis contenta feris infamis arena,
Nulla cruentatis homicidia ludat in armis.
—Prudentius, *Contra Symmachum*, II, 643.
11. *Consurgit ad ictus;*
Et quoties victor ferrum jugulo inserit, illa
Delitias ait esse suas, pectusque jacentis
Virgo modesta jubet converso pollice rumpi.
—*Ibid.,* II, 617.

1908

12. *Nunc caput in mortem vendunt, et funus arenæ,*
Atque hostem sibi quisque parat, cum bella quiescunt.
—Manilius, *Astronomica*, IV, 225.

13. *Hos inter fremitus novosque lusus,*
Stat sexus rudis insciusque ferri,
Et pugnas capit improbus viriles.
—Statius, *Sylvæ*, I, 6.51.

CHAPTER XXIV

Of the Roman Grandeur

A. THE COMMENT BY MISS NORTON

I FANCY that this Essay was built up round the story about C. Popilius, which comes near the middle. Perhaps Montaigne laid down his "Tite-Live," open at this page, to take up his pen, or to dictate to his secretary as he walked about his library. These desultory pages are like five minutes' talk with Montaigne—or from him—on one of the subjects most familiar to his thought. All that concerned Rome and the Romans was peculiarly interesting to him. He was more at home with them than with his own countrymen.

1909

Notes and Comments

B. THE NOTES BY MR. IVES

1. See Cicero, *Epistulæ ad Familiares*, VII, 5.2.
2. See Idem, *De Div.*, II, 37.
3. Suetonius says, "*Prope sex millier talentorum.*" Montaigne found the equivalent in French money in a note to his edition of Suetonius.
4. Such a sum for Galatia; for so much, Pontus; for so much, Lydia.—Claudian, *In Eutropium*, I, 203.
5. See Plutarch, *Life of Antony*.
6. It was from 130 to 140 years. "It" = Rome.
7. That is, of one kingdom.
8. The king.
9. See Livy, XLV, 12, 13.
10. That is, the authority of Rome.
11. Tacitus, *Agricola*, XIV.
12. The last clause is not in the *Édition Municipale*.

CHAPTER XXV

Of Not Counterfeiting Sickness

A. THE COMMENT BY MISS NORTON

I THINK that it was some hot summer, when he could not take the physical exercise which he says was always necessary to stir his brain, that Montaigne, sitting in his cool

Of Thumbs

tower, wrote the dozen short chapters that precede and follow and include this. They may have served *pour passer le temps* for himself, but they do not afford the reader any great pleasure. They have little life in them. All the entertainment in them is borrowed, and *réchauffé* stories are a kind of diet which one soon wearies of.

B. THE NOTES BY MR. IVES

1. *Tantum cura potest et ars doloris,*
   Desiit fingere Cœlius podagram.
   —Martial, VII, 39.8.
2. See Appian, IV, 6.41.
3. *De m'en sejourner.*
4. See Pliny, *Nat. Hist.*, VII, 50.
5. In Book I, chap. 21, pp. 124ff.
6. *Nul ne connoit estre avare, nul convoiteux.* Seneca's words are: *Nemo se avarum esse intelligit, nemo cupidum.*
7. See Seneca, *Epistle* 50.2.

CHAPTER XXVI

Of Thumbs

A. THE COMMENT BY MISS NORTON

TWO pages of historical and etymological facts about thumbs; their bare simplicity is their only merit. In the hands of a modern magazine writer they could be padded

Notes and Comments

with rhetoric to make twenty pages of worthless entertainment. And in a modern scientific journal they would become learned praises of the thumb as an element of civilisation. With only the rudimentary thumb of the anthropoid ape, man would have remained a harmless monkey.

B. THE NOTES BY MR. IVES

1. This fact is reported by Tacitus (*Annals*, XII, 47), but M. Villey has made it clear that Montaigne took it from Beroald's Commentary on Suetonius's *Life of Augustus*, XXIV, where he found also the substance of the next paragraph.

2. The last clause, from "pollere" (1580 to 1588), was omitted in 1595. See Macrobius, *Saturnalia*, VII, 13.

3. *Sed nec vocibus excitata blandis,*
   Molli pollice nec rogata, surgit.
   —Martial, XII, 97.8.

4. *Fautor utroque tuum laudabit pollice ludum.*
   —Horace, *Epistles*, I, 18.66.

5. *Converso pollice vulgi*
   Quemlibet occidunt populariter.
   —Juvenal, III, 36.

6. See Suetonius, *Life of Augustus*, XXIV, and Beroald's Commentary.

7. See Valerius Maximus, VI, 3.3. Taken by Montaigne from Beroald's Commentary on Suetonius.

8. Perhaps a mistaken reminiscence of Philocles, in Plutarch, *Life of Lysander*.

9. See Cicero, *De Off.*, III, 11; Valerius Maximus, IX, 2, *ext.* 8.

10. See Plutarch, *Life of Lycurgus*.

CHAPTER XXVII

Cowardice the Mother of Cruelty

A. THE COMMENT BY MISS NORTON

A LONG Essay of Montaigne's is sure to be interesting; one may almost say, the longer, the more interesting. It always contains not merely *actually* more, but *in proportion* more of Montaigne's thought; and, I believe, the thought, the more there is of it, always, invariably, becomes richer in quality, deeper as well as wider. The short and long Essays may be compared to shrubs and trees; the shrubby ones often are covered with flowers and fruitage of erudition, but the tree-like ones do not need such adornments.

This chapter is of medium length and medium interest. The somewhat commonplace thesis (perhaps not so commonplace before his day as in later times) receives vitality from the note of *personal observation:* "I have seen extremely cruel men who—." Few of Montaigne's present readers have seen many cruel men. The note of personal observation passes into the note of personal meditation on the conditions of his time—always most interesting from his pen.

The pages about Publius Rutilius, the Emperor Maurice, and Herodicus are a little too antique to touch us much; but following them is an important passage for the estimation of the character of Montaigne's opinions; and it is one often referred to: "All [punishment or revenge] that goes be-

1913

Notes and Comments

yond simple death seems to me pure cruelty." This same expression is used by him in the other Essay on cruelty, and it is one of the points for which he was reprimanded at Rome by the "Maestro del sacro palasso."

B. THE NOTES BY MR. IVES

1. See Plutarch, *Life of Pelopidas.*
2. *Nec nisi bellantis gaudet cervice juvenci.*
 —Claudian, *Epistula ad Hadrianum,* 30.
3. *S'aguerrit et se gendarme.*
4. *Et lupus et turpes instant morientibus ursi,*
Et quæcunque minor nobilitate fera est,
 —Ovid, *Tristia,* III, 5.35.
5. See Plutarch, *Of Hearing.*
6. See Plutarch, *On the delays of divine justice.*
7. See Goulard, *Histoire du Portugal,* IV, 12.
8. See Pliny, *Natural History,* Preface. Montaigne undoubtedly took it from Vivès's Commentary on St. Augustine, *De Civ. Dei,* V, 27.
9. *C'estoit faire la figue à un aveugle et dire des pouilles à un sourd.*
10. See Diogenes Laertius, *Life of Aristotle.*
11. *Cum in se cuique minimum fiduciæ esset.*—Source unknown.
12. See Monstrelet, I, 9.
13. See Herodotus, I, 82.
14. See Livy, I, 24.
15. That is, the sieur de Matecolom.
16. *Nostre apprentissage.*
17. *Primitiæ juvenum miseræ, bellique futuri*
Dura rudimenta. —Virgil, *Æneid,* XI, 156.

18. See Livy, XXVIII, 21. The princes were Corbis and Orsua.

19.   *Non schivar, non parar, non ritirarsi*
Voglion costor, ne qui destrezza ha parte.
non danno i' colpi finti hor pieni, hor scarsi;
Toglie l'ira e il furor l'uso de l'arte.
Odi le spade horribilmente urtarsi
'A mezzo il ferro; il pie d'orma non parte;
Sempre è il pie fermo, è la man sempre in moto;
Ne scende taglio in van, ne punta à voto.
         —Tasso, *Jerusalem Delivered*, XII, 55.

20. See Valerius Maximus, II, 3.2.
21. *Escrime populere et civile.*
22. See Plutarch, *Life of Cæsar*.
23. See Idem, *Life of Philopœmen*.
24. That is, in fencing.
25. See Plato, *Laches*.
26. See Idem, *Laws*, book VII.
27. See Zonaras, III; Gentillet, *Discours sur le moyens de bien gouverner*, III, 8. The son-in-law's name was Philippicus.
28.   *Cuncta ferit, dum cuncta timet.*
         —Claudian, *In Eutropium*, I, 182.
29. *Tant de fusees à demesler.*
30. See Livy, XL, 3.
31. *Les belles matieres tiennent tousjours leur ranc, en quelque place qu'on les seme.*
32. The edition of 1595 adds: *Quand elles sont si riches de leur propre beauté, et se peuvent seules trop soustenir, je me contente du bout d'un poil, pour les joindre à mon propos.*

Notes and Comments

33. See Livy, XL, 4.
34. See Josephus, *Autobiography*, near the end.
35. See Chalcondylas, X, 2.
36. Mohammed.
37. See J. de Lavardin, *Histoire de Scanderbeg*.
38. See Plutarch, *Of the malignity of Herodotus*.
39. See Paulus Jovius, *Historiarum sui Temporis Libri*, XIII.

CHAPTER XXVIII

All Things Have Their Season

A. THE COMMENT BY MISS NORTON

I SAID in connection with the last chapter that the longer the Essay, the greater, almost always, its interest. But this short Essay is peculiarly delightful. Its mingling of personal and impersonal reflections, of admirable citations and of original expressions, makes every line of value.

B. THE NOTES BY MR. IVES

1. In 1580 to 1588 the sentence ends thus: *font à mon opinion grand honneur au premier; car je les trouve eslongnez d'une extreme distance.*
2. See Plutarch, *Life of Cato the Censor*.
3. Cf. Book I, chap. 56, p. 423.

1916

All Things have their Season

4. See Plutarch, *Parallel between Flaminius and Philopœmen.*
5. *Imponit finem sapiens et rebus honestis.*
—Juvenal, VI, 444.
6. See Plutarch, *Apothegms of the Lacedæmonians.*
7. See Idem, *Life of Philopœmen.*
8. See Seneca, *Epistle* 36.4.
9. See Idem, *Epistles* 13.17 and 23.9.
10. *Tu secunda marmora*
    Locas sub ipsum funus, et sepulchri
    Immemor, struis domos.
—Horace, *Odes*, II, 18.17.
11. *Olim jam nec perit quicquam mihi nec acquiritur.
... Plus superest viatici quam viæ.*—Seneca, *Epistle* 77.3.
12. *Vixi, et quem dederat cursum fortuna peregi.*
—Virgil, *Æneid*, IV, 653.
13. In 1580 to 1588: *lorsqu'il faut apprendre à mourir.*
14. See Seneca, *Epistle* 36.4.
15. *Diversos diversa juvant, non omnibus annis*
    Omnia conveniunt.
—Maximianus (Pseudo-Gallus), I, 104.
16. See Seneca, *Epistle* 68.14.
17. See Plutarch, *Life of Cato of Utica.*
18. See Seneca, *Epistle* 71.11.

CHAPTER XXIX

Of Vigour

A. THE COMMENT BY MISS NORTON

THE admirably expressed page of good sense with which this Essay opens, in which Montaigne says that he thinks that transient exhibitions of *vertu* (which word to him meant strength of mind—*vigour*—rather than our "virtue"), powerful *flights*, are possible to many men, and that nothing but justness of judgement and steadiness of purpose, that is, an ordered life, unfailingly denotes a superior character—this page sounds the same note as the fine lines of Ben Jonson (to Lucy, Countess of Bedford) about

> The manly soul that should, with even powers,
> The rock, the spindle and the shears control
> Of destiny, and spin its own free hours.

Montaigne adduces Pyrrho as one who strove to make his life harmonise with his beliefs; and then brings forward various instances, near and distant, of men and women who, for motives more or less trivial, more or less serious, more or less sudden, more or less meditated, found the strength to mutilate or destroy themselves.

On a later page he turns to the conception of fate, and to the strength, the courage, which comes from a belief in fate: a courage quite lacking in his fellow countrymen, but testified to as existing in other days and other nations. Two ex-

1918

Of Vigour

ceptions—two believers in fate—among his contemporaries whom he mentions, one would like to fit names to. The last I suppose to be Henri IV.

B. THE NOTES BY MR. IVES

1. See Idem, *De Providentia*, VI; cf. *Epistle* 53. 11.12.
2. *Par secousse.*
3. Cf. Book II, chap. 2, pp. 459, 460.
4. *C'eust esté choquer ses propositions, qui ostoient au sens mesmes.*
5. See Diogenes Laertius, *Life of Pyrrho.*
6. See *Ibid.*
7.   *Non viriliter
Iners senile penis extulerat caput.
          —Tibullus, De Inertia Inguinis.*
8. Bergerac.
9. See Cicero, *Tusc. Disp.*, V, 27; Ælian, *Varia Historia*, VII, 18.
10.   *Ubi mortifero jacta est fax ultima lecto,
    Uxorum fusis stat pia turba comis;
Et certamen habent lethi, quæ viva sequatur
    Conjugium; pudor est non licuisse mori.
Ardent victrices, et flammæ pectora præbent
    Imponuntque suis ora perusta viris.
          —Propertius, III, 13.17.*
11. *Brasses:* a measure of which the length is not now known.
12. See Plutarch, *Life of Alexander.*
13. See Joinville, *Vie de Saint Louis*, XXX.
14. See Commines, VIII, 9; Gentillet, *Discours sur les moyens de bien gouverner*, II, 9.

1919

Notes and Comments

15. See Chalcondylas, VII, 8.
16. See *Ibid.*
17. In 1595 is added: *Soit qu'il la croye, soit qu'il la prenne pour excuse à se hazarder extraordinairement, pourveu que fortune*, etc.
18. William the Silent. The two men were Jehan de Jeaureguy (1582) and Balthazar Gérard (1584).
19. The assassination of the duc de Guise by Poltrot de Méré, in 1563.
20. Balthazar Gérard, the assassin of the Prince of Orange.
21. See du Haillant, *Histoire des Rois de France*. The text of 1595 adds: *pendant nos entreprinses de la guerre saincte; et pareillement Conrad, marquis de Mont-Ferrat, les meurtriers conduits au supplice, tous enflez et fiers d'un si beau chef d'œuvre.*

CHAPTER XXX

Of a Child Monster

A. THE COMMENT BY MISS NORTON

THIS chapter demands but few words, and the last paragraph, added in 1595, is the only one that need be read twice, or even once. But the *c'est à croire* suggestion

Of Anger

there is extremely interesting in its *modernness;* and the quotation from Cicero may well be pondered.

B. THE NOTES BY MR. IVES

1. *D'une forme commune.*
2. Henri III.
3. *Ut quum facta sunt, tum ad conjecturam aliqua interpretatione revocantur.*—Cicero, *De Div.*, II, 31.
4. See Aristotle, *Rhetoric*, III, 12.
5. *Quod crebro videt, non miratur, etiam si cur fiat nescit. Quod ante non vidit, id, si evenerit, ostentum esse censet.*—Cicero, *De Div.*, II, 27.

CHAPTER XXXI

Of Anger

A. THE COMMENT BY MISS NORTON

FOR ages it has been recognised that parents are not always the wisest guardians of their own children. The ancients considered chiefly those results of mistakes in education that concern the State; modern thinkers, those chiefly that concern the child itself. Montaigne was a modern in this as in so many other respects; and he takes his first illustrations of the sin of anger from its cruel effects on children, then touches on its injustice toward inferiors; and, after a

Notes and Comments

digression on the difference between saying and doing, he dwells on a story of Plutarch's treatment of a slave, which, he says, was the occasion of this Essay. (At least, I so interpret the sentence, though I confess the phrase *à quartier* is puzzling.)

The story about Plutarch only enforces the note already struck, that chastisement should never be inflicted by one in anger. Then follow other considerations of anger, and other illustrations: the anger of women, and the feminine-like anger of the orator Celius, etc. One would like to know who *le plus cholere homme de France* may have been, or the "other" to whom Montaigne gave such sage counsel about not being *too* calm. "Sage" I call it a little ironically, for it is surely open to question whether Montaigne's theory is true that *on incorpere la cholere en la cachant*. It is the theory of a Gascon, and, as he himself says, of a not very choleric Gascon; for surely the unrestrained expression of anger, as of any passion, makes it, with most men, blaze the more hotly and the more frequently. But perhaps he has Shakespeare on his side:

> Anger is like
> A full hot horse who, being allowed his way,
> Self-mettle tires him.

But, on the other hand, in the splendid Alcibiades scene in *Timon of Athens*, it is in praise of his friend that Alcibiades says:

> And with such sober and unnoted passion
> He did behave his anger, ere 't was spent,
> As if he had but prov'd an argument.

It is amusing counsel that Montaigne reports himself as

Of Anger

giving his family, and all the "personalities" that follow are very entertaining. It is a charming sentence with which the passage closes: "As advancing age sharpens my temper, I study to correct it; and I shall so manage, if I can, that I shall be henceforth so much the less peevish and hard to please as I shall have more excuse and inclination to be so."

B. THE NOTES BY MR. IVES

1. See *Nicomachæan Ethics*, X, 9.
2. That of childhood.
3.   *Rabie jecur incendente, feruntur*
Præcipites ut saxa jugis abrupta, quibus mons
Subtrahitur, clivoque latus pendente recedit.
                      —Juvenal, VI, 647.
4. See Plutarch, *How to Restrain Anger*.
5.   *Gratum est quod patriæ civem populoque*
dedisti,
Si facis ut patriæ sit idoneus, utilis agris,
Utilis et bellorum et pacis rebus agendis.
                      —Juvenal, XIV, 70.
6. See Seneca, *De Ira*, I, 5.
7. See *Ibid.*, III, 32.
8. See Plutarch, *How to Restrain Anger*.
9. See *Ibid.*
10.   *Ora tument ira, nigrescunt sanguine venæ,*
Lumina Gorgoneo sævius igne micant.
                —Ovid, *De Arte Amandi*, III, 503.
11. The name was changed to *Caius Rabirius* in 1595. See Suetonius, *Life of Cæsar*, XII.
12. *Ceux-là se sont donnez beau jeu.*
13. That is, other than the character of her ministers.

1923

Notes and Comments

14. See Plutarch, *Apothegms of the Lacedæmonians*.
15. See *Ibid*.
16. Cf. Seneca, *Epistle* 64.3: *Non faciunt animum, quia non habent.*
17. See Plutarch, *Of Hearing*.
18. *Me suis jetté en ce discours à quartier.*
19. See Aulus Gellius, I, 26.40.
20. See Plutarch, *On the bringing up of children* and *On the delays of divine justice;* also, Cicero, *Tusc. Disp.*, IV, 36.
21. See Plutarch, *ubi supra;* Valerius Maximus, IV, 1.
22. See Plutarch, *Apothegms of Kings*, etc., and *Apothegms of the Lacedæmonians*.
23. See Seneca, *De Ira*, I, 16.
24. See Seneca, *De Ira*, III, 8.
25. That is, women.
26. See Plutarch, *Political Precepts*.
27. See Seneca, *De Ira*, I, for an opposite conclusion.
28. *C'est le plus patient homme que je cognoisse.*
29.   *Magno veluti cum flamma sonore*
Virgea suggeritur costis undantis aheni,
Exultantque æstu latices; furit intus aquaï
Fumidus atque alte spumis exuberat amnis;
Nec jam se capit unda; volat vapor ater ad auras.
—Virgil, *Æneid*, VII, 462.
30. See Diogenes Laertius, *Life of Diogenes*.
31. *Omnia vitia in aperto leviora sunt; et tunc perniciosissima cum simulata sanitate subsidunt.*—Seneca, *Epistle* 56.10.
32.   *Et secum petulans amentia certat.*
—Claudian, *In Eutropium*, I, 237.

.1924

33. *Mugitus veluti cum prima in prœlia taurus*
Terrificos ciet atque irasci in cornua tentat,
Arboris obnixus trunco, ventosque lecessit
Ictibus, et sparsa ad pugnam proludit arena.
—Virgil, *Æneid*, XII, 103.

34. *Si que j'aille jettant à l'abandon et sans chois toute sorte de parolles injurieuses.*

35. *Justes.*

36. That is, great occasions.

37. *Elles me mettent en cervelle.*

38. See Seneca, *De Ira*, I, 16, alluding to Aristotle, *Nicomachæan Ethics*, III, 8.

CHAPTER XXXII

Defence of Seneca and Plutarch

A. THE COMMENT BY MISS NORTON

THIS is a charming Essay, one of the *talking* ones; but there is the least possible to be said about it. One can remark that the judgement, on the next page, of the cardinal de Lorraine is very interesting, and that the terrible story beginning, "I have seen a peasant," contains a whole volume of historical information regarding the times, and of personal picturing regarding Montaigne's life; but the thing to do with this Essay is to *read* it!

1925

Notes and Comments

B. THE NOTES BY MR. IVES

1. See Dion Cassius, LXI, 10, 12, 20, etc.
2. See *Annals*, XIII, 1; XIV, 53, 54, 55; XV, 60, 64; Suetonius, *Life of Nero*.
3. See Bodin, *Methodus ad facilem historiarum cognitionem*, IV.
4. See *Ibid*.
5. In 1580 to 1588: *je ne me fusse pas mis en peine de le defendre*.
6. See Bodin, *ubi supra*; the fact is taken from Plutarch's *Life of Lycurgus*.
7. That is, regarding the bodily powers.
8. See Plutarch, *Life of Pyrrhus*.
9. See Cicero, *Tusc. Disp.*, II, 14; Plutarch, *Life of Lycurgus*.
10. Not Plutarch, but Valerius Maximus, III, 3, *ext.* 1, of a *Macedonian* child.
11. Plutarch's.
12. *A ce prix*.
13. See Ammianus Marcellinus, XXII, 16. 23.
14. Montaigne now passes to examples of endurance in general, and, thence, of obstinacy.
15. See Tacitus, *Annals*, IV, 45.
16. See *Ibid.*, XV, 57.
17. This tale is told in Poggi's *Facezie*, and is mentioned by Castiglione in the *Courtier*, III, 22.
18. In Book I, chap. 27, pp. 239-244.
19. The edition of 1595 adds: *Luy propose l'on quelque chose des actions ou facultez d'un autre? La premiere chose qu'il appelle à la consultation de son jugement, c'est son*

exemple; selon qu'il en va chez luy, selon cela va l'ordre du monde.

20. *Je vois bien le tour que celles là se donnent.*
21. Bodin.
22. See the *Methodus ad facilem historiarum cognitionem*.
23. See *Ibid.*
24. That is, of those with whom Plutarch compares them.
25. Bodin's.
26. *Plus enflez, glorieux, et pompeus.*
27. In 1580 to 1588: *et Scipion encore à Epaminondas, qui estoyent aussi de son rolle.*
28. That is, with Pompeius. See Plutarch, *Parallel between Pompeius and Agesilaus.*
29. See Plutarch, *Parallel between Sylla and Lysander.*
30. *Pour les avoir simplement presentez aux Grecs.*

CHAPTER XXXIII

The Story of Spurina

A. THE COMMENT BY MISS NORTON

THIS is less the story of Spurina—"a young man of Tuscany," who does not appear till the last pages—than the story of the passion of love, with personal illustra-

1927

Notes and Comments

tions, derived from the experience of princes, philosophers, and potentates, chiefly from the life of Julius Cæsar, whose character is also considered in others of its aspects: so that this Essay may almost be considered as a prologue to the next one—on Cæsar as a *chef de guerre*.

The last two paragraphs are among the finest expressions of Montaigne's *beautiful* "good sense." They were added in 1595.

B. THE NOTES BY MR. IVES

1. *A gener leurs reins.*
2. *Et que les haires ne rendent pas tousjours heres ceux qui les portent.*
3. *Lascifs.*
4. See Suetonius, *Life of Cæsar.*
5. See *Ibid.*
6. See Plutarch, *Life of Cæsar.*
7. See Suetonius, *Life of Cæsar.*
8. See *Ibid.*
9. See *Ibid.*, Beroald's *Commentary.*
10. See *Ibid.* Ægisthus was the lover of Clytemnestra and murderer of Agamemnon.
11. See *Ibid.*, Beroald's *Commentary.*
12. Mohammed II.
13. *Une haute entreprise.*
14. See Chalcondylas, V, 11. The same anecdote is found in several historical works of the time: Lavardin's *Histoire de Scanderbeg*, the History of Paul Jovius, etc.; but Montaigne's version was probably from Chalcondylas.
15. Ambition.
16. *N'estimoit luy devoir guere en cette partie.*

1928

The Story of Spurina

17. See Plutarch, *Life of Cæsar*.
18. See Suetonius, *Life of Cæsar*.
19. See *Ibid*.
20. See *Ibid*.
21. See Plutarch, *Life of Cato of Utica*.
22. Cf. Book I, chap. 24, p. 174.
23. See Cæsar, *De Bello Civili*, I, 24; III, 10.
24. Cæsar.
25. See Suetonius, *Life of Cæsar*.
26. Plutarch says this expressly of Labienus, in the *Life of Cæsar*.
27. See Suetonius, *Life of Cæsar*.
28. This sentence appears, almost word for word, on the fly-leaf of Montaigne's copy of Cæsar.
29. See Suetonius, *Life of Cæsar*, for this example and all those that follow, down to the anecdote of Spurina.
30. *Pour me remettre sur mes brisées.*
31. *Qualis gemma micat, fulvum quæ dividit aurum,*
 Aut collo decus aut capiti, vel quale, per artem
 Inclusum buxo aut Oricia terebintho,
 Lucet ebur. —Virgil, *Æneid*, X, 134.
32. See Valerius Maximus, IV, 5, *ext.* 1.
33. *Font ... une belle espargne.*
34. That is, the life of Diogenes.

1929

CHAPTER XXXIV

Observations on Julius Cæsar's Method of Making War

A. THE COMMENT BY MISS NORTON

WE have had in the preceding chapter some expression of Montaigne's ardent and very interesting admiration for Julius Cæsar. This admiration is another proof, I think, of an excitable love of action dormant in Montaigne himself, checked and chilled all his life by a certain physical indolence, and by the subtlety of his intellectual judgements and the elevation of his spiritual moods; or, in a word, by the absence in his nature of any ambition for *power*. Of his unfailing admiration for men of action there is evidence again, and very convincing, in chapter 36 of this book—the Essay, "Of the Most Eminent Men." If he does not admit Cæsar to be as great as Alexander, and consequently one of the three greatest men in the world, he says that he could hardly *not* do so, and that the balance was heavier on the side of Alexander solely because the final result of the ambition of Cæsar was the ruin of his country. This seemed to Montaigne more a fatal misfortune than the fault of Cæsar, but still fatal to his supreme glory.

The present Essay is again of interest as one of those that evince Montaigne's familiarity with military affairs, and his interest in them. It can not be too often repeated that Mon-

Cæsar's Method of Making War

taigne was not, primarily, a "man of letters." *Je suis moins faiseur de livres, que de nulle aultre besogne,* he himself says.

B. THE NOTES BY MR. IVES

1. Cf. Book II, chap. 36, p. 1018.
2. See Cicero, *Tusc. Disp.*, II, 26.
3. See Plutarch, *Life of Brutus*.
4. See Bodin, *Methodus ad facilem historiarum cognitionem*, Prœmium.
5. Cæsar.
6. See Suetonius, *Life of Cæsar*.
7. See *Ibid.*, Beroald's *Commentary;* Xenophon, *Cyropædeia*, VI, 3.
8. See Suetonius, *Life of Cæsar*.
9. See *Ibid*.
10. See *Ibid*.
11. Cæsar.
12. See Suetonius, *Life of Augustus*.
13.   *Rheni mihi Cæsar in undis*
   Dux erat, hic socius; facinus quos inquinat,
     æquat.   —Lucan, V, 289.
14. *Trop rabaissée.*
15. See Suetonius, *Life of Cæsar*.
16. See Cæsar, *De Bello Gallico*, IV, 17.
17. Cf. Book I, chap. 17, p. 90.
18. The Nervi. See Cæsar, *De Bello Gallico*, II, 21.
19. See Plutarch, *Life of Cæsar*.
20. *Quand on ne feroit qu'aller.*
21.   *Ocior et cœli flammis et tigride fœta.*
                —Lucan, V, 405.

Notes and Comments

22. *Ac veluti montis saxum de vertice præceps*
    Cum ruit avulsum vento, seu turbidus imber
    Proluit, aut annis solvit sublapsa vetustas,
    Fertur in abruptum magno mons improbus
        actu,
    Exultatque solo, silvas, armenta virosque
        Involvens secum.   —Virgil, *Æneid*, XII, 684.
23. See Cæsar, *De Bello Gallico*, VII, 24.
24. See Suetonius, *Life of Cæsar.*
25. *Il fut le premier à sonder le gué.* See *Ibid.*
26. See Cæsar, *De Bello Gallico*, I, 72.
27.   *Rapuitque ruens in prœlia miles,*
    Quod fugiens timuisset, iter; mox uda receptis
    Membra fovent armis, gelidosque a gurgite,
        cursu.
    Restituunt artus.   —Lucan, IV, 151.
28. *Sic tauri-formis volvitur Aufidus,*
    Qui regna Dauni perfluit Appuli,
        Dum sævit, horrendamque cultis
            Diluviem meditatur agris.
                    —Horace, *Odes*, IV, 14.25.
29. See Suetonius, *Life of Cæsar.*
30. See Cæsar, *De Bello Gallico*, II, 25.
31. See Suetonius, *Life of Cæsar.*
32. See *Ibid.*; Plutarch, *Life of Cæsar;* Appian, *Civil War*, II; Dion Cassius, XLI, 46; Lucan, V, 519.
33. See Plutarch, *Apothegms of Kings*, etc.
34. See Suetonius, *Life of Cæsar.*
35. Cæsar wrote 8000: *Coactus equitum IIX millibus et peditum circa CCXL.* See *De Bello Gallico*, VII, 76.
36. See Plutarch, *Life of Lucullus.*

1932

Caesar's Method of Making War

37. See Cæsar, *De Bello Gallico*, VII, 75.
38. See Xenophon, *Cyropædeia*, II, 2.
39. See Chalcondylas, III, 11.
40. See Lavardin, *Histoire de Scanderbeg*.
41. That is, of the two "extraordinary occurrences."
42. See Cæsar, *De Bello Gallico*, VII, 68.
43. *Ne se doit jamais engager.*
44. See Suetonius, *Life of Cæsar*.
45. That is, Cæsar.
46. *Cette religion.*
47. See Cæsar, *De Bello Gallico*, I, 46.
48. See Suetonius, *Life of Cæsar*.
49. See *Ibid*.
50. *Pas.* Cotgrave defines *pas* as "a measure of two and a half feet; or (as in some places) three and a half; or (as among the Romans) five."
51. *Trainant à belles dents.*
52. See Suetonius, *Life of Cæsar*.
53. See Suetonius, *Life of Cæsar*.
54. Gaspard de Coligny, assassinated in the Massacre of Saint Bartholomew, 1572.
55. That is, *dans le camp des catholiques* (M. Villey).
56. See Livy, XXIV, 18.
57. Cæsar.
58. See Suetonius, *Life of Cæsar*.
59. See *Ibid*.
60. See *Ibid*.
61. Cæsar's. See *Ibid*.
62. See Plutarch, *Life of Cæsar*.
63. *Corps de garde.*
64. See Cæsar, *De Bello Civili*, III, 9.

CHAPTER XXXV

Of Three Good Women

A. THE COMMENT BY MISS NORTON

THIS Essay concerns itself with a nameless Italian bourgeoise; with the Arria who, dying, murmured: *Pæte, non dolet;* and with Pompeia Paulina, a young and very noble Roman lady, who married Seneca in his extreme old age. They were all wives whose devotion to their husbands proved itself by the sacrifice of life; and their honourable stories are beautiful, narrated by Montaigne. His tone of tender respect toward them is artistically heightened by the shrewd and gay irony of the introductory paragraph about wives in general.

The accounts of the first two he takes from Pliny's *Letters;* the last from Tacitus.

It may be observed, as with the preceding Essay, that this one underwent scarcely more than a few verbal changes in 1595; and evidently from the same cause, that is, because the matter is not for the most part original thought, but transcription.

B. THE NOTES BY MR. IVES

1. The literal translation of this title, which seems necessary, is not the true rendering of its meaning: it should rather be, "Of Three Devoted Wives."

1934

Of Three Good Women

2. *Volonté.*
3. *Y ont prou affaire.*
4. *La vie est pleine de combustion; le trespas, d'amour et de courtoisie.*
5. *Ce mistere.*
6. *Jactantius mœrent, quæ minus dolent.*—Tacitus, *Annals*, II, 77.
7. *C'est par là qu'elle parle françois.*
8. *Pour ne disconvenir du tout à nostre usage.*
9. See Pliny, *Epistles*, VI, 24.
10.   *Extrema per illos*
    Justitia excedens terris vestigia fecit.
                      —Virgil, *Georgics*, II, 473.
11. *Vous avez beau faire, vous me pouvez bien faire plus mal mourir.*
12. *Vertu.*
13. See Pliny, *Epistles*, III, 16.
14.   *Casta suo gladium cum traderet Arria Pæto,*
     Quem de visceribus traxerat ipsa suis:
  Si qua fides, vulnus quod feci non dolet, inquit;
  Sed quod tu facies, id mihi, Pæte, dolet.
                     —Martial, I, 14.1.
15. That is, her own words are much more alive than those of Martial.
16. *Exemples.*
17. See Tacitus, *Annals*, XV, 61-64.
18. In 1580: *Ou comme Ariosto a rengé en une suite.*
19. *Il faut arrester l'ame entre les dents.*
20. *Irresoluement.* Montaigne uses this word in the sense of *sans fermeté.*
21. See Seneca, *Epistle* 104.1-5.

1935

CHAPTER XXXVI

Of the Most Eminent Men

A. THE COMMENT BY MISS NORTON

THE three *plus excellens hommes*—the three greatest men—of all time, in Montaigne's judgement, when he wrote this Essay, were Homer, Alexander, and Epaminondas; and as I have remarked (in considering the Essay on Cæsar's wars), this selection indicates Montaigne's admiration for men of action. Homer is great in his eyes, not because of his learning and his art, but because "his words are the only words that have movement and action, are the only *substantial* words"; because he was a master in military discipline, and his work is the best counsellor in military affairs; because all those who since his day have established governments have looked to him for guidance; because, in fine, in an ideal sense, if not literally, he was busied with *affairs*—with *things done*, not *things thought*. Therefore he is greater than the philosophers; greater than Aristotle, greater than Socrates.

Alexander is greater than Cæsar because his glory was unstained by ruin wrought to his country. And Epaminondas is the greatest of all men, because his glory, lesser than that of the others, was stainless, his "innocence" was *maistresse, constante, uniforme, incorruptible*. And, in truth, *glory* "is not a part of the substance of the thing [excel-

Of the most Eminent Men

lence]." The proof of his greatness, in sharpest contrast with Cæsar's, was that "the prosperity of his country died when he died, even as it was born with him." For another eulogy of Epaminondas see the first chapter of Book III.

The notice of Alcibiades toward the end of this Essay, and what just precedes, were added in 1595.

In later years Montaigne thought Socrates "the man most deserving to be known, and to be set before the world as an example." (See Book III, chapter 12.)

B. THE NOTES BY MR. IVES

1. *Des plus excellens hommes.*
2. Virgil.
3. *Tale facit carmen docta testudine, quale*
   Cynthius impositis temperat articulis.
   —Propertius, II, 34.79.
4. *Qui, quid sit pulchrum, quid turpe, quid utile, quid non,*
   Plenius ac melius Chrysippo ac Crantore dicit.
   —Horace, *Epistles*, I, 2.3.
5. *A quo, ceu fonte perenni,*
   Vatum Pyeriis labra rigantur aquis.
   —Ovid, *Amores*, III, 9.25.
6. *Adde Heliconiadum comites, quorum unus Homerus*
   Sceptra potitus. —Lucretius, III, 1037.
7. *Cujusque ex ore profuso*
   Omnis posteritas latices in carmina duxit,
   Amnemque in tenues ausa est deducere rivos,
   Unius fœcunda bonis.
   —Manilius, *Astronomica*, II, 8.

Notes and Comments

8. See Bodin, *Methodus ad facilem historiarum cognitionem*, IV, 74, quoting Vellius Paterculus, I, 5.

9. See Plutarch, *Oracles of the Pythian Prophetess;* Aristotle, *Poetics*, XXIV.

10. See Plutarch, *Life of Alexander;* Pliny, *Nat. Hist.*, V, 29.

11. See Plutarch, *Apothegms of the Lacedæmonians*.

12. See Idem, *Of Garrulity*.

13. See Idem, *Apothegms of Kings*, etc., and *Life of Alcibiades*.

14. See Idem, *Apothegms of Kings*, etc.

15. See Cicero, *Tusc. Disp.*, I, 32.

16. See Gentillet, *Discours sur les moyens de bien gouverner*.

17. *Farce*.

18. That is, as audience.

19. Translation of a Greek verse, quoted by Aulus Gellius, III, 11.

20. That is, another of "the most eminent men."

21.   *Impellens quicquid sibi summa petenti*
    Obstaret, gaudensque viam fecisse ruina.
—Lucan, I, 149.

22. See Plutarch, *Life of Alexander;* Quintus Curtius, I, 11.

23. For all these, see Plutarch, *Life of Alexander*.

24. See Quintus Curtius, VIII, 1.

25. *Cette action*.

26. See Idem, X, 5. Montaigne took this from Conestaggio, *Unione del regno*, etc.

27. See Plutarch, *Life of Alexander:* "This notwithstanding, before he departed from those parts, he put forth

Of the most Eminent Men

many vain and false devices to make his name immortal among that people. He made armours of greater proportion than his own, and mangers for horses, higher than the common sort; moreover, he made bits also far heavier than the common sort, and made them to be thrown and scattered abroad in every place."—North's translation of Amyot. Cf. Diodorus Siculus, XVII, 95; Quintus Curtius, IX, 3.

28. See Arrian, VII, near the end.

29. The original source of this is Livy, XXXV, 14, and one of Lucian's *Dialogues of the Dead*.

30. In 1580 only: *Car on tient entre autres choses que sa sueur produisoit une tres douce et souefve odeur.*

31. *Qualis, ubi Oceani perfusus Lucifer unda,*
Quem Venus ante alios astrorum diligit ignes,
Extulit os sacrum cœlo, tenebrasque resolvit.
—Virgil, *Æneid*, VIII, 589.

32. See G. Postel, *Histoire des Turcs*.

33. Cf. Book II, chap. 34, pp. 998, 999.

34. *Et velut immissi diversis partibus ignes*
Arentem in silvam et virgulta sonantia lauro;
Aut ubi decursu rapido de montibus altis
Dant sonitum spumosi amnes et in æquora currunt.
Quisque suum populatus iter.
—Virgil, *Æneid*, XII, 521.

35. Cf. Book III, chap. 1, p. 1085.

36. Cf. the opening paragraph of Book II, chap. 16.

37. *Ny si enflez.*

38. *D'estre aussi poisants, et roides.*

39. See Diodorus Siculus, XV, 24; Pausanias, VIII, 11; Cicero, *De Oratore*, III, 34.

Notes and Comments

40. See Plutarch, *Of the dæmon of Socrates*, and *Of Hearing*.

41. See Diodorus Siculus, XV, 10; Cicero, *De Off.*, I, 44.

42. See Diodorus Siculus, XV, 24.

43. Epaminondas.

44. See Plutarch, *Of the dæmon of Socrates*.

45. Plutarch is supposed to have written a "parallel" between the lives of Scipio and Epaminondas, which has never been recovered.

46. *Mais galant home qu'ils nomment, de meurs civiles et communes.*

47. See Plutarch, *That it is not possible to live happily according to the teaching of Epicurus*, and *Life of Coriolanus*.

48. *Il couche de beaucoup.*

49. *Sans connoissance de cause.* See Plutarch, *Of the dæmon of Socrates*.

50. See *Ibid.*

51. *De leur avoir passé sur le ventre.*

52. That is, the Bœotians'.

53. See Diodorus Siculus, XV, 19.

54. See *Ibid.*, XV, 24; C. Nepos, *Life of Epaminondas*.

1940

CHAPTER XXXVII

Of the Resemblance of Children to Their Fathers

A. THE COMMENT BY MISS NORTON

THIS is one of the *conversational* Essays; indeed, it is of a completely irregular character, since a letter to Madame de Duras is interpolated in the middle of it. But the beginning of it always seems to me as if it had been *talked* in his tower-room to some friend—Pierre de Brach, perhaps, or Charron—to whom he had just been showing the pile of unprinted manuscripts which a year later were to be published. (This date is fixed by the first line of the second paragraph of the next page, if, as is natural, we assign the time of his *retreat*—1571—as the time of his beginning to write the Essays.)

This is the last Essay of the second book, that is, the last of those which appeared in 1580; and it is the longest but two ("Of the Education of Children," and "Of Presumption") in the two books (not counting the "Apology," always to be considered by itself). In this respect of its length, and still more in the freedom of its movement, it foretells the superior quality of the third book. But, because of its subject, it can not take rank with the *great* Essays. Its subject is now out of date and consequently lacking in interest;

1941

Notes and Comments

for it is not *la ressemblance des enfants aux pères* that this Essay treats of, but the imperfections of the science of medicine, and the mistakes of medical men. The imperfections and mistakes of that age are so obvious to us now, that it demands some effort to recognise how much intelligence was needed to perceive them in their own day; and the careless reader is likely to accept Montaigne's truths as truisms and to find them dull because they are such familiar truths to us; or else to misinterpret them, fancying foolishly that Montaigne would hold the same views to-day.

He is led to discourse of medicine by speaking of the incomprehensible characters of inherited bodily conditions—*la ressemblance* [in a sense] *des enfants aux pères;* and he is led to speak of these inherited conditions by what he has been saying about his sufferings from the stone, a malady he inherited from his father.

The first part of the *talk* is the communication, as to a friend, of how these Essays—that he is now thinking of printing—have come into being, and of the changes wrought in himself during the years he has been writing them; especially, during the last eighteen months, the unpleasant change to *un vivre choliqueux*.

The quibblers about Montaigne's sincerity and truthfulness sometimes point critically to the passage here where he says: *Je ne corrige point mes premieres imaginations, peu les secondes*, and cry, "Look at the differences in the different editions!" But they do not observe that the differences are of the slightest (except in the way of *additions*) till fifteen years later, in the posthumous edition; and even then there is no correction of *opinions*, only of language, and only trivial "takings away."

1942

Of the Resemblance of Children

B. THE NOTES BY MR. IVES

1. Cf. Book II, chap. 9, near the end (text of 1588).
2. *La cholique pierreuse:* "A paine like the cholicke, but comming of a stone in the kidneys."—Cotgrave.
3. That is, the years.
4.   *Debilem facito manu,*
    Debilem pede, coxa,
    Lubricos quate dentes;
    Vita dum superest, bene est.
                    —Seneca, *Epistle* 101.
5. See Chalcondylas, III, 10.
6. See Diogenes Laertius, *Life of Antisthenes.*
7. Cf. Book II, chap. 6, pp. 492, 493.
8.   *Summum nec metuas diem, nec optes.*
                    —Martial, X, 47.13.
9. Passions.
10. *Le vif et les effects.*
11. *Ny cordiale, ny stomacale.*
12. In 1580 to 1588: *C'est bien assez que nous soyons tels, que avons nous accoustumé en nos pensées et actions principales.*
13. See Laurent Joubert, *Erreurs populaires au faict de la médecine.*
14. See Diogenes Laertius, *Life of Epicurus.* Henri Estienne, in his Latin translation, has: *Cum tamen cruciatur et ingemiscet et ejulabit*, but the modern texts give a precisely opposite sense.
15. *Pugiles etiam, cum feriunt in jactandis cœstibus, ingemiscunt, quia profundenda voce omne corpus intenditur, venitque plaga vehementior.*—Cicero, *Tusc. Disp.*, II, 23.

Notes and Comments

Cicero wrote: *ingemiscunt; non quid doleant, animove succumbant, sed quia*, etc.

16. *Ejulatu, questu, gemitu, fremitibus*
Resonando multum flebiles voces refert.
—Attius, *Philoctetes*, quoted by Cicero, *De Fin.*, II, 29, and *Tusc. Disp.*, II, 14.

17. *Laborum*
Nulla mihi nova nunc facies inopinaque surgit:
Omnia præcepi atque animo mecum ante peregi.
—Virgil, *Æneid*, VI, 103.

18. See Pliny, *Nat. Hist.*, VII, 12.
19. See Plutarch, *On the delays of divine justice.*
20. See the *Politics*, II, 2 (Le Roy's translation). Herodotus (IV, 180) says that this custom prevails among the Auseans, a tribe of Libya.
21. *De ce progres.*
22. *Un doctrine.*
23. *De leur doctrine.*
24. That is, physicians.
25. Montaigne slightly misrepresents the facts: his great-grandfather, Ramon Eyquem, purchased *le maison noble de Montaigne* in 1477, when his son, Montaigne's grandfather, was already born.
26. Another mistake in reckoning: Montaigne's great-grandfather was born in 1402; his father died in 1568, or two hundred years, lacking *thirty-four*, later.
27. This is the reading of 1580 to 1588; the posthumous edition reads: *d'avoir vescu* sain *quarante-sept ans;* the inserted word *(sain)* would seem to be there by mistake; the difference of date is the difference between the writing and the publication of the Essay.

1944

Of the Resemblance of Children

28. See Cicero, *Tusc. Disp.*, V, 33; Diogenes Laertius, *Life of Epicurus*.

29. *Toute cette marchandise.*

30. In 1580: *Mais je dy que ce qui s'en void en practique, il y a grand dangier que ce soit pure imposture, j'en croy leurs confraires, Fioravant et Paracelse.*

31. See Plutarch, *Banquet of the seven Sages*.

32. *La pastissage.*

33. Presumably, he means his *general* health.

34. Physicians.

35. The same idea is found in Cornelius Agrippa. *Of the uncertainty and vanity of the sciences*, LXXXIII; as are also many of those in the following pages.

36. See Pliny, *Nat. Hist.*, XXIX, 1.

37. But Pliny says that the (Greek) physicians were not banished until long after Cato's death. Montaigne doubtless got his idea from the treatise of Agrippa just cited.

38. See Plutarch, *Life of Cato the Censor*.

39. See Pliny, *Nat. Hist.*, XXV, 53; copied textually by C. Agrippa, *ubi supra*.

40. See Herodotus, IV, 187.

41. See Plato, *Timæus*.

42. *On va troublant et esveillant le mal par oppositions contreres.*

43. A Gascon term, from *via foras*. "A word or voice wherewith French carters hasten on their horses."—Cotgrave.

44. See Seneca, *Epistles* 107 and 77.15.

45. See Cornelius Agrippa, *ubi supra*.

46. See *Ibid*. Agrippa took it from Xiphilin, *Life of Hadrian*.

Notes and Comments

47. See Diogenes Laertius, *Life of Diogenes*.

48. See the *Collection of the Monks Antonius and Maximus* (CXLVI), printed at the end of Stobæus.

49. The physicians.

50.   *Rhedarum transitus arcto*
    Vicorum inflexu.   —Juvenal, III, 236.

51. *De requerir du malade une application de creance favorable.*

52. See Plato, *Republic*, book III. Montaigne makes the curious mistake of taking literally a sentence in which Plato uses the words *medicamentum* and *medicus* metaphorically; as is made evident by the next sentence: "The rulers of the state are the only persons who should have the privilege of lying . . . they may be allowed to lie for the good of the state."

53. Physicians. See *Fable* 13, "The Sick Man and the Physician." Cf. what Montaigne says of Æsop's fables in Book II, chap. 10 (p. 545).

54. See Cornelius Agrippa, *ubi supra*.

55. The accepted myth is that it was Hyppolytus who was resuscitated by Æsculapius. The name of Helen would seem to have been suggested by Pliny's phrase: *Quoniam Tyndareum revocavisset in vitam* (*Nat. Hist.*, XXIX, 1). Montaigne corrected it before 1595, and "Hippolitus" is substituted in the later editions.

56.   *Nam pater omnipotens, aliquem indignatus ab umbris*
    Mortalem infernis ad lumina surgere vitæ,
    Ipse repertorem medicinæ talis et artis
    Fulmine Phœbigenam stygias detrusit ad undas.
                —Virgil, *Æneid*, VII, 770.

1946

Of the Resemblance of Children

57. *C'est mon.*

58. See the *Collection of the Monks Antonius and Maximus.*

59. See Pliny, *Nat. Hist.*, XXIX, 1.

60. *Ut si quis medicus imperet ut sumat.*
—Cicero, *De Div.*, II, 64.
Cicero adds: *Potius quam hominum more cochleam dicere:* "Instead of saying, like everybody else, a snail."

61. See Pliny, *Nat. Hist.*, XXIX, 1.

62. See Cornelius Agrippa, *ubi supra.*

63. *Le mestier.*

64. See *Ibid.*

65. All these opinions are taken from the same treatise of Agrippa.

66. *Aux esprits.*

67. See Pliny, *Nat. Hist.*, XXIX, 1. Pliny's words are: *Mirum et indignum protinus fuit, nullam Artium Medicina inconstantiorem fuisse, et etiamnum sæpius mutari quum sit fructiosior nulla.* But he uses *fructiosior* in the sense of "lucrative."

68. This whole history of medicine is taken from the chapter of Pliny's *Natural History* frequently cited above.

69. *Latineurs.*

70. It is not known to whom Montaigne refers.

71. *La drogue.*

72. In 1580 to 1588: *si elle nous est inconnue, si elle ne vient d'outre mer, et ne nous est apportée de quelque lointaine region, elle n'a point de force.*

73. Paracelsus, 1493-1541; Fioravanti died in 1588; Argenterius,—Jean Argentier de Quiers,—1513-1572.

74. See *Fable 76,* "The Ethiopian."

Notes and Comments

75. That is, physicians.
76. *Pour affuter justement son dessein.*
77. *Pour en engendrer une parfaicte symmetrie.*
78. *De prendre martre pour renard.*
79. For the stone.
80. See Cornelius Agrippa, *ubi supra.*
81. *Ethiquetes.*
82. That is, the apothecary's.
83. See Herodotus, II, 84.
84. That is, our physicians.
85. *Indigestible.*
86. La Boëtie, who died of dysentery in 1563.
87. The following pages, down to "everywhere else in that art" (page 1053), were mostly added in 1582. The text of 1580 reads: *Somme ilz n'ont nul discours, qui ne soit capable de telles oppositions. Quant au jugement de l'operation des drogues, il est autant ou plus incertain. J'ay esté deux fois boyre des eaus chaudes de noz montaignes; et m'y suis rangé, par ce que c'est une potion naturelle, simple, et non mixtionnée, qui au moins n'est point dangereuse, si elle est vaine; et qui de fortune s'est rencontrée n'estre aucunement ennemi de mon goust (il est vray que je la prens selon mes regles, non selon celles des medecins) outre ce que le plaisir des visites de plusieurs parens et amis, que j'ay en chemin, et des compaignies qui s'y rendent, et de la beauté de l'assiette du pais, m'y attire. Ces eaux la ne font nul miracle sans doute, et tous les effectz estranges qu'on en rapporte je ne les croy pas; car pendant que j'y ay esté, il s'est semé plusieurs telz bruits que j'ay decouvers faus m'en informant un peu curieusement. Mais le monde se pipe aiséement de ce qu'il desire. Il ne leur faut pas oster aussi qu'elles*

Of the Resemblance of Children

n'esveillent l'appetit et ne facilitent la digestion, et ne nous prestent quelque nouvelle alegresse, si on n'y va du tout abatu de forces. Mais moy je n'y ay esté ny ne suis deliberé d'y aller que sain et avecques plaisir. Or quant à ce que je dis de la difficulté, qui se presente au jugement de l'operation, en voycy l'exemple. Je fus premierement à Aiguescaudes, de celles la je n'en sentis nul effet, nulle purgation apparente; mais je fus un an entier aprez en estre revenu sans aucun ressentiment de colique, pour laquelle j'y estoy allé. Depuis je fus à Banieres, celles-cy me firent vuyder force sable, et me tindrent le ventre long temps apres fort lache. Mais elles ne me garantirent ma santé que deux mois: car apres cela j'ay esté tresmal traicté de mon mal. Je demanderois sur ce tesmoignage, ausquelles mon medecin est d'avis que je me fie le plus, ayant ces divers argumentz et circonstances pour les unes et pour les autres. Qu'on ne crie pas donc plus apres ceux, qui en cete incertitude se laissent gouverner à leur appetit et au simple conseil de nature. Or ainsi, quand ils nous conseillent une chose plus tost qu'une autre, quand ils nous ordonnent les choses aperitivez, comme sont les eaux chaudes, ou qu'ils nous les deffendent, ils le font d'une pareille incertitude, et remettent sans doubte à la mercy de la fortune l'evenement de leur conseil: n'estant en leur puissance ny de leur art de se respondre de la mesure des corps sableus, qui se couvent en noz reins; là où une bien legiere differance de leur grandeur peut produire en l'effet de nostre santé des conclusions contradictoires. Par cet exemple l'on peut juger de la forme de leurs discours. Mais pour les presser plus vivement, il ne fauldroit pas un homme si ignorant come je suis de leur art.

    88. Illustrations of Montaigne's remarks here and below

1949

Notes and Comments

may be found in his *Journal de Voyage*, where he describes his sojourn at the baths of La Villa.

89. That is, the use of medicinal springs.
90. *Sont à grenouiller.*
91. *Ont de particulier de se faire generallement tous corneter et vantouser avec scarification.*
92.   *Alcon hesterno signum Jovis attigit. Ille,*
   Quamvis marmoreus, vim patitur medici.
  Ecce hodie, jussus transferri ex æde vetusta,
   Effertur, quamvis sit Deus atque lapis.
       —Ausonius, *Epigram* 74.
93.   *Lotus nobiscum est hilaris, cœnavit et idem,*
   Inventus mane est mortuus Andragoras.
  Tam subitæ mortis causam, Faustine, requiris?
   In somnis medicum viderat Hermocratem.
       —Martial, VI, 53.
94. That is to say, a lawyer.
95. *Devenu grand;* in 1580 to 1588, *devenu monsieur.*
96. *Qu'on le retire.*
97. See *Ecclesiasticus*, XXXVIII, 1.
98. See *II Chronicles*, XVI, 12.
99. Physicians.
100. *Si molle.*
101. The original form of this clause is uncertain; the editors of 1595 give it the exact opposite of the above meaning.
102. *Civilité.*
103. See Herodotus, I, 197.
104. See Diogenes Laertius, *Life of Plato*. For Homer, see *Odyssey*, IV, 231.
105. *Quinte essence.*

1950

Of the Resemblance of Children

106. *Une conduite vray-semblable à cette experience.*

107. *Des autres experiences.*

108. *Le sens humain y perd son latin.*

109. As some liberty has been taken with the text, to make it more intelligible, the original words are given: *et avant qu'il ait trouvé parmy cette infinité de choses que c'est cette corne; parmy cette infinité de maladies, l'epilepsie; tant de complexions, au melancholique; tant de saisons, en hyver; tant de nations, au François: tant d'aages, en la vieillesse; tant de mutations celestes, en la conjonction de Venus et de Saturne; tant de parties du corps, au doigt.*

110. Marguerite d'Aure de Gramont, the widow of Jean de Durfort, Seigneur de Duras.

111. See Tacitus, *Annals*, VI, 46.

112. *Desrobera à.*

113. That is, physicians.

114. See Pliny, *Nat. Hist.*, XXIX, 1.

115. The edition of 1580 adds: *Les Montaignes ou elles sont assises ne tonent et ne retentissent rien que Gramont.*

116. See Plutarch, *Life of Pericles*.

117. A *chanson de geste* of the twelfth century (printed at the end of the fifteenth), entitled *Les quatre fils d'Aymon*, narrated the adventures of the sons of a prince of Ardennes, who were knighted by Charlemagne. The brothers constantly appear in old French and Italian romances and poems, together with their famous horse, Bayard.

118. See Cicero, *Academica*, II, 26.

BOOK THREE

CHAPTER I

Of the Useful and the Honourable

A. THE COMMENT BY MISS NORTON

WE enter now the Third Book, written during the years between the forty-seventh and fifty-seventh of Montaigne's life, and we pass, one may say in general, from the Montaigne who *in doctorum virginum sinu recessit*—the inscription of 1571 in his tower—to the Montaigne who, sure of acceptance and appreciation, finds pleasure in representing himself to his friends in a manner to recall himself to their memories, as he says, *au naturel*. In his preface to his first publication he speaks as if this had been his purpose from the beginning; but I think this preface was written at the moment of publication, and that then, this intention being fully formed in his mind, he forgot how little some of the Essays in the first two books conform to it. The first two books are indeed *essays;* the thirteen long chapters of the last book are *memoirs*, autobiographical memoirs, of the man, not of the accidents of his life. "I" and "me," "my" and "mine" are, rightly, to be found in every line; and those persons who talk of Montaigne's "egotism" are incapable of understanding the charm of his writings, and still less their permanent value. He was interesting to himself not as a personality but as a man among men. If he says (in the Essay, "Of Repentance") that he wishes to present

1952

Of the Useful and the Honourable

himself as Michel de Montaigne, it is because that name signifies his *estre universel*, and implies no qualities of an external character. He found himself interesting because he recognised that the study of the individual, the dissection of "a specimen," is the only way to learn the laws of life; that to know oneself is the source of the highest wisdom. He had the scientific sense, also, to perceive that, in dissecting the whole being, nothing is unimportant; mental weaknesses mean as much as intellectual abilities; bodily capacities and physical tastes must all be noted, and the circumstances of the being, the *milieu* by which it is influenced, must not be neglected.

Thus it is that what are called Montaigne's "trivialities" justify themselves. They show Montaigne to have been too much of a philosopher to pretend that he was one every moment.

How far, too, they are justified by a simply human emotion—but not the emotion of egotism—is a question each reader must answer after his own heart. For my part, while Montaigne's vigorous and accurate delineation of human nature from observation of himself seems to me the most remarkable part of his production, the vivifying force of his affections renders the details of his self-portraiture infinitely touching to me. If he paints for his friends,—his personal look, his personal tastes,—it is in part because of his tender longing to be remembered, to be loved, after death; to be remembered and loved as he remembered and loved La Boëtie. Montaigne will never be justly estimated till his enthusiastic, one may even say his passionate, power of attachment, and his lifelong feeling of loneliness, are recognised as amongst his most marked traits.

1953

Notes and Comments

Not only are the Essays of this Third Book, of later date, in general much longer than the earlier ones, but most of them contain still more conscious and intimate revelations of the writer's *moi*. In some of them he enables us to follow him in his usual occupations, to see the domestic annoyances of his private life, to recognise the character of his public life in the midst of the civil troubles of the day, to witness his differences with his neighbours, to accompany him on his travels; the pages impregnate us with his impressions, his reflections, his personal bearing, and we arrive at a delightful familiarity with him.

The style of these later writings also partakes of the increased *largeness;* it has greater freedom in its flow. Of no writer is it more true than of Montaigne that the reader who gives time and thought to his pages, who becomes familiar with them, is rewarded by finding in them a far deeper wisdom than is perceived at first glance. The charm of style becomes subordinate to the charm of character; the book is endowed, as it were, with the personality of a friend, full of good counsel, at once serious and humorous.

And a hundred questions arise, both entertaining and instructive, before the eyes of a student of the Essays; some of them regarding human nature, in considering Montaigne's personal qualities; some of them regarding the modes of human expression, in considering his special method of presenting his thought.

Almost the most interesting of these questions are those that resolve themselves into a consideration of Montaigne's individual manner; of the meaning, not merely of his words, but of the way in which he develops his thoughts. That this has been greatly misunderstood is, perhaps, not surprising,

Of the Useful and the Honourable

since the study of other authors affords little aid in the study of Montaigne. Shakespeare, for example, was preceded and followed by kindred spirits; in a certain sense he belongs to a group, however much he towers above them. No spirit kindred to that of Montaigne is known in literature.

In studying some of Montaigne's Essays, questions about his manner present themselves which are unanswerable, which could have been answered only by himself—and perhaps not even by him. The reader may amuse himself with forming what hypotheses he pleases.

This first chapter is not a particularly interesting one except *for its personalities;* and even these are more interesting biographically than didactically. For the "useful" and "honourable" of which the Essay treats are the usefulness that may be thought—erroneously—to belong to perfidy and treason, and the honourableness that forbids them. And perfidy and treason—does our age know what they are? Our age, perhaps, but not ourselves. And one reads this chapter with the same sense of remoteness with which one reads Macchiavelli's *Il Principe,* to which this seems, in fact, almost an intentional counterblast. But we must not forget that under such kings as Charles IX and Henri III the highest nobles thought it no shame to be traitors, or to make use of assassination; and that it is a splendid moral innovation when Montaigne suggests with bitter irony that, if the public good requires treachery and lying, and massacres, these actions should be committed to the hands of citizens forced to sacrifice their honour and their conscience, as in other times they would sacrifice their lives, to save their country.

Montaigne's belief is that treason can never be excusable except when it is employed to *"trahir la trahison."*

1955

Notes and Comments

About a fifth of this Essay was added in 1595; one long passage of two or three pages, beginning with "Timoleon," and many shorter ones; and all the nine *prose* Latin quotations and one of the five in verse.

B. THE NOTES BY MR. IVES

1. *Curieusement.*
2. *Næ iste magno conatu magnas nugas dixerit.*
   —Terence, *Heautontimoroumenos*, III, 5.8.
3. Tiberius.
4. See Tacitus, *Annals,* II, 88.
5. *Un affronteur.*
6. *Profession.*
7. *Suave, mari magno, turbantibus æquora ventis, E terra magnum alterius spectare laborem.*
   —Lucretius, II, 1.
8. *A la cousture de nostre liaison.*
9. The reference may be to the negotiations between the duc de Guise and the King of Navarre with which Montaigne was entrusted when Henri was at the French court, about 1572; or to the later negotiations, in 1584 or 1585, when hostilities between the League and the Protestant party were renewed after the rupture of the peace of Fleix.—M. Villey.
10. *Et s'enferrassent en mon masque.*
11. Of negotiators.
12. *Leur opportunité et leur mise.*
13. See Plutarch, *How to distinguish a flatterer from a friend.*
14. *Simplement legitime et civile.*
15. *Utatur motu animi qui uti ratione non potest.*—

Of the Useful and the Honourable

Cicero, *Tusc. Disp.*, IV, 25. This quotation is found in 1595, but not in the *Édition Municipale*.

16. *Jusques au feu, mais exclusivement si je puis.*
17. *Autant que mon devoir me donne de corde.*
18. See Cornelius Nepos, *Life of Atticus*, VI.
19. *De se tenir chancelant et mestis.*
20. *Ea non media, sed nulla via est, velut eventum expectantium quo fortunæ consilia sua applicent.*—Livy, XXXII, 21. The original reads. *Ea non media, sed nulla via est; etenim præterquam quod aut accipienda, aut aspernanda vobis Romana societas est; quid aliud quam nusquam gratia stabili, xelut qui eventum expectaverimus, ut fortunæ applicaremus nostra consilia?*
21. See Herodotus, VII, 163.
22. Jean de Morvilliers (1506-1577), Keeper of the Seals in 1568, took part in negotiating the treaty of Cateau-Cambresis, and in the Council of Trent. For a Catholic, he seems to have shown much moderation toward the Protestants.—M. Villey.
23. The prince.
24. Of the two enemies.
25. Cf. Book II, chap. 2, p. 450 ff., where Montaigne dwells at length on this effect of drunkenness.
26. See Plutarch, *Of Curiosity*.
27. *Superiorité.*
28. Than those he trod in his youth.
29. That is, his fortune.
30. *Engin.*
31. See Æsop, *Fable* 293; imitated by La Fontaine, IV.
32. *Id maxime quemque decet quod est cujusque suum maxime.*—Cicero, *De Off.*, I, 31.

1957

Notes and Comments

33. *Veri juris germanæque justitiæ solidam et expressam effigiem nullam tenemus; umbra et imaginibus utimur.*—*Ibid.*, III, 17.

34. See Plutarch, *Life of Alexander*.

35. *Ex senatusconsultis plebisque scitis scelera exercentur.*—Seneca, *Epistle* 95.

36. Tiberius.

37. See Tacitus, *Annals*, II, 64-67. The pretenders were Rhescuporis and Cotys, brother and son of the king of Thrace.

38. *Leur meilleur effect.*

39. *Du Palais et des plaids.*

40. That is, of keeping the records.

41. See Plutarch, *How to distinguish a flatterer from a friend.*

42. That is, the kings. See Plutarch, *Apothegms of Kings*, etc.

43. That is, to lie, to betray, etc.

44. The well-known story is that the physician of Pyrrhus offered to Fabricius to poison his master; Fabricius informed Pyrrhus of his treachery, and sent the man back in chains. See Cicero, *De Off.*, III, 22; Plutarch, *Apothegms of Kings*, etc.

45. The Hungarian.

46. See H. Fulstin, *Histoire des roys de Pologne* (French translation by Baudouin, 1573), book III.

47. That is, the soldiers.

48. See Plutarch, *Life of Eumenes.*

49. See Florus, *Epitome* of Livy, XXVII.

50. That is, those who are served by such methods.

51. *Ils les font pendre avec la bourse de leur paiement*

Of the Useful and the Honourable

au col. Aiant satisfaict à leur seconde foi et speciale, ils satisfont à la generale et premiere. In the edition of 1595, the next sentence with the anecdote of King Clovis, is placed *before* this general remark.

52. The brother.
53. Mahomet.
54. See Lavardin, *Histoire de Scanderbeg;* and cf. Chalcondylas, VII, 11.
55. See du Haillant, *Histoire des roys de France.*
56. *Qui les leur reprochent.*
57. *Car il touche la malignité de vostre courage par vos mains, sans desadveu, sans object.*
58. *Les hommes perdus.*
59. See Tacitus, *Annals*, V, 9.
60. See Chalcondylas, I, 10.
61. The source of this illustration has not been found.
62. *Car il a quitté sa raison à une plus universelle et puissante raison.*
63. *Sed videat ne quæratur latebra perjurio.*—Cicero, *De Off.*, III, 29.
64. *Ainsi comme ainsi.*
65. See Plutarch, *Life of Timoleon.* Cf. Book I, chap. 38, p. 316.
66. *Leur arrest prenderoit party à la faveur du liberatur de son pais, ou à la desfaveur du meurtrier de son frere.* See Diodorus Siculus, XVI, 29.
67. See Cicero, *De Off.*, III, 22.
68. It is probably Cicero whom Montaigne here criticises: see *De Off.*, I, 10, and III, 29; but the discussion of this fundamental question was everywhere in the air, from the days of Machiavelli and Bodin. The Council of Con-

Notes and Comments

stance (1414) declared that there was no obligation to keep faith with the enemies of the faith.

69. *Quasi vero forti viro vis possit adhiberi.*—Cicero, *De Off.*, III, 30.

70. See Book II, chap. 36, p. 1022.

71. As those of Epaminondas.

72. Pompeius. See Plutarch, *Life of Pompeius*.

73. Cæsar. See Idem, *Life of Cæsar*.

74. Marius. See Idem, *Life of Marius*.

75. Epaminondas.

76. *La civilité*.

77. See Plutarch, *Apothegms of the Lacedæmonians*.

78. Cf. what Seneca says of Fabricius in *Epistle* 120.

79. *Manente memoria, etiam in dissidio publicorum fœderum privati juris.*—Livy, XXV, 18.

80. *Et nulla potentia vires*
Præstandi, ne quid peccet amicus, habet.
—Ovid, *De Ponto*, I, 7.37.

81. *Non enim patria præstat omnibus officiis, et ipsi conducit pios habere cives in parentes.*—Cicero, *De Off.*, III, 23.

82. *Nous n'avons que faire de durcir nos courages par ces lames de fer.*

83. *Dum tela micant, non vos pietatis imago*
Ulla, nec adversa conspecti fronte parentes
Commoveant; vultus gladio turbate verendos.
—Lucan, VII, 320.

84. See Tacitus, *History*, III, 51.

85. See *Ibid*.

86. *Omnia non pariter rerum sunt omnibus apta.*
—Propertius, III, 9.7.

CHAPTER II

Of Repenting

A. THE COMMENT BY MISS NORTON

AFTER an exordium of a kind that now becomes more or less habitual with him, expressing his manner of writing and thinking, Montaigne comes quickly to the present point,—that he rarely *repents*,—and then goes on to show why this is so; and, further, what repentance is, or should be. But this can not be done without such discussion of the general nature of man that the thought touches now this point, now that, and any abridgement of the Essay would be foolishness.

The sketch of himself which, without writing the name beneath, he gives on one page, has the special interest of the touch about his military life (which I am persuaded was of greater extent than is generally supposed)—*non plus en guerre qu'en paix*.

This Essay was considerably added to and somewhat changed in 1595; all the four *prose* Latin quotations were added, and several longish passages—about a quarter of the whole.

B. THE NOTES BY MR. IVES

1. *Je le recite.*
2. *Mes-huy c'est fait.*

Notes and Comments

3. *D'une ivresse naturelle.*

4. With this change to the first person, he identifies himself as his "subject."

5. See Plutarch, *Life of Demosthenes.*

6. *Je ne m'essaierois pas, je me resoudrois.*

7. Here begins the subject of the Essay; the preceding pages are only a prologue.

8. See Seneca, *Epistle* 81.22: *Malitia ipsa maximam partem veneni sui bibit.*

9. See Plutarch, *Of the tranquillity of the mind.*

10. *Quæ fuerant vitia, mores sunt.*—Seneca, *Epistle* 39.6.

11. *De me chapitrer et mercurialiser à cœur ouvert.*

12. *Que je n'eusse guere failli, de faillir.*

13. *Tuo tibi judicio est utendum.*—Cicero, *Tusc. Disp.,* I, 23.

14. *Virtutis et vitiorum grave ipsius conscientiæ pondus est; qua sublata, jacent omnia.*—Idem, *De Nat. Deor.,* III, 35.

15. *Le peché qui est en son haut appareil, qui loge en nous.*

16. Ligurinus, to whom the following lines are addressed.

17.   *Quæ mens est hodie, cur eadem non puero fuit?*
    Vel cur his animis incolumes non redeunt genæ?
                 —Horace, *Odes,* IV, 10.7.

18. See Plutarch, *Banquet of the seven wise men.*

19. See Idem, *Political Precepts.*

20. *Les églises.* See Idem, *Life of Agesilaus.*

21. Cf. Plutarch, *Life of Pericles.*

22. See *Nicomachæan Ethics,* X, 7.

1962

Of Repenting

23. *Sic ubi desuetæ silvis in carcere clausæ*
Mansuevere feræ, et vultus posuere minaces,
Atque hominem didicere pati, si torrida parvus
Venit in ora cruor, redeunt rabiesque furorque,
Admonitæque tument gustato sanguine fauces;
Fervet, et a trepido vix abstinet ira magistro.
— Lucan, IV, 237.

24. For the way in which Montaigne was taught Latin, see Book I, chap. 26, pp. 231, 232.

25. *Une forme sienne.*

26. *L'institution.*

27. *Si je ne suis chez moi.*

28. That is, the pleasure.

29. *Je fay coustumierement entier ce que je fay, et marche tout d'une piece.*

30. See Seneca, *Epistle* 94.

31. That is, those who boast of repentance, etc.

32. In 1588: *d'en estre marris et desplaisants.*

33. *Ma forme universelle.*

34. *Resistance.* The suggested meaning is conjectural.

35. See Plutarch, *Apothegms of Kings*, etc.

36. *Selon moy, ce ne sont que mouches et atomes qui promeinent ma volonté.*

37. That is, of the Stoic conception of causes.

38. *Nec tam aversa unquam videbitur ab opere suo providentia, ut debilitas inter optima inventa sit.*—Quintilian, *Inst. Orat.*, V, 12.19.

39. See Diogenes Laertius, *Life of Antisthenes.*

40. Montaigne's name for stone in the bladder.

41. *Lors on me donnoit de mon menton par le nez.*

42. *Ne sentent à l'aigre et au moisi.*

1963

CHAPTER III

Of Three Sorts of Intercourse

A. THE COMMENT BY MISS NORTON

THIS is one of the Essays that do much to create that affectionate respect for its author which becomes the dominant feeling with the admirers of Montaigne. The great pleasure to be had—the first pleasure in becoming acquainted with him—from the way he says things, soon passes into far deeper pleasure from the things he says, and the affection excited by his personal charm is blended with the respect excited by his wisdom.

There is another element still in this complex emotion, an element springing partly from the affection, partly from the respect—the element of *compassion;* not of pity, pity is not for a good, great man, but of sympathy for what was lacking to his enjoyment of life, the feeling precisely of "compassion." One needs to know Montaigne intimately to have the intelligent appreciation of his circumstances and conditions which justify this note of *tenderness* toward him; but when it has once been struck in the reader's heart, it sounds often and at unexpected moments. When Montaigne exclaims, in the midst of cheerful, sensible conversation with us: "Good God! what a great service wisdom does those whose desires it limits to their power!" and quotes, as full of meaning, Socrates' phrase: *Selon qu'on peult,* we feel that he himself could not what he would. And the page in

Of Three Sorts of Intercourse

this Essay about friendship and about "the difficulties and sensitiveness of social intercourse" is touched with a perhaps unconscious sadness.

But the Essay as a whole is amongst those of the most cheerful, the most conscious, the most delightful egotism, or rather—for there must be a new word invented for Montaigne's kind of egotism—the most charming I-ism,—the *ism* of a philosophic and poetic I, which does honour to the listener by speaking of itself.

Montaigne's self-delineations became more frequent now, in these later Essays, than before. He does not "confide in the public"—a foolish phrase for a foolish thing; but he has confidence in the public: he had become assured, by the way in which the first two books of the Essays had been received, that he could trust his readers to take a serious interest in the study that so seriously and nobly interested him —the study of Michel de Montaigne. And henceforth he does not hesitate to represent himself—as he would have been glad to do from the first—"wholly and nakedly"; not an heroic figure, as he himself well knew, but a figure, more than he thought, to be honoured, and the contemplation of whose friendly face makes us more intelligent and more serene.

This special Essay perhaps particularly gives evidence of the largeness of the field of his "intelligence." It can scarcely be questioned that no one else could ever have written of the three so diverse worlds of men, of women, and of books, with the intimacy of knowledge and the fineness of perception and the mastery of expression that Montaigne here manifests.

The first half of this Essay is characteristically "incoherent"; but one of its sentences might be its epigraph: "A soul well-endowed and accustomed to dealing with men becomes of itself agreeable. Art [the art of expression] is nothing else than the examination and record of what such souls bring forth."

B. THE NOTES BY MR. IVES

1. *Huic versatile ingenium sic pariter ad omnia fuit, ut natum ad id unum diceres, quodcumque ageret.*—Livy, XXXIX, 40.
2. *A cette heure;* that is, at this time of my life.
3. *Une penible occupation.*
4. *Vitia otii negotio discutienda sunt.*—Seneca, *Epistle* 56.
5. *Quibus vivere est cogitare.*—Cicero, *Tusc. Disp.*, V, 38.
6. See the *Nicomachæan Ethics*, X, 8. Cf. Cicero, *De Fin.*, V, 4.
7. *Discours.*
8. This sentence of 1588 is not found in 1595. Cf. Book III, chap. 8: *La plus part des hommes sont riches d'une suffisance estrangere.*
9. *Propos de contenance.*
10. These lines have an apparent, but not a real, inconsistency with what Montaigne says elsewhere about his great sociability.
11. *Il me les faut trier sur le volet.*
12. *Les plus desliées.*
13. Cf. Seneca, *Epistles* 14 and 103.
14. This is with the "humble and ordinary."
15. See Xenophon, *Memorabilia*, I, 3.3.

Of Three Sorts of Intercourse

16. *Beste de compaignie, mais non pas de troupe.* See Plutarch, *Of the plurality of friends.*

17. *Qu'il ne se peut parler du monde.*

18. *Qui sçache et se tendre et se desmonter.*

19. See Plato, *Laws*, book VI.

20. *Les autres s'estudient à eslancer et guinder leur esprit; moy, à le baisser et coucher.*

21.   *Narras, et genus Æaci,*
Et pugnata sacro bella sub Ilio;
    Quo Chium pretio cadum
Mercemur, quis aquam temperet ignibus,
    Quo præbente domum, et quota,
Pelignis caream frigoribus, taces.
        —Horace, *Odes*, III, 19.3.

22. See Plutarch, *How to restrain anger.*

23. *De faire l'entendu.*

24. *Favellar in punta di forchetta.* That is, to speak in subtle and carefully chosen words.

25. *Trainez-vous au demeurant à terre, s'ils veulent.*

26. That is, the ladies.

27.   *Hoc sermone pavent, hoc iram, gaudia, curas,*
    Hoc cuncta effundunt animi secreta; quid ultra?
    Concumbunt docte.   —Juvenal, VI, 189.

28. *De capsula totæ.*—Seneca, *Epistle* 115. The original text has *totos*.

29. *De farder le fard.*

30. *Elles commandent à baguette, et regentent les regens et l'eschole.*

31. *Parlier.*

32. *D'assistance et convoiemens.*

33. *Y entretient qui veut ses pensées.*

Notes and Comments

34. *Substitutions.* The meaning of this word is not at all clear. It has been suggested that it refers here to subjects that have "weight and depth."

35. See Plutarch, *Life of Dion.* Hippomachus was a teacher of wrestling and fencing.

36. *Nam nos quoque oculos eruditos habemus.*—Cicero, *Paradoxa,* V, 2.

37. *Quicunque Argolica de classe Capharea fugit,*
   Semper ab Euboicis vela retorquet aquis.
   —Ovid, *Tristia,* I, 1.83.

38. *Sans obligation de volonté.* He is speaking of a more than external relation with women.

39. *Neque affectui suo aut alieno obnoxiæ.*—Tacitus, *Annals,* XIII, 45.

40. In the *Phædrus,* near the beginning. Lysias is not speaking of women.

41. *Qu'elles ont entre elles des accointances de longue bienveuillance.*

42. See G. Postel, *Histoire des Turcs.*

43. That is, intercourse with men and with women.

44. *Ils me destournent facilement à eux et me la desrobent.*

45. See Olivier de la Marché, *Mémoires* (1562).

46. The library.

47. The library.

48. *C'est là mon siege.*

49. *Magna servitus est magna fortuna.*—Seneca, *Consolatio ad Polybium,* XXVI.

50. *Ils n'ont pas seulement leur retraict pour retraitte.*

51. *Pour le quest;* that is, for the sake of more learning.

CHAPTER IV

Of Distraction

A. THE COMMENT BY MISS NORTON

THE word and the thought were both unfamiliar in the sixteenth century. Pasquier remarks on the use of the word, and says he does not well understand what it signified in Montaigne's mouth; if he was in doubt about that, he certainly did not well understand what the chapter was about. It would hardly seem to require more brains than Pasquier had to see that Montaigne used the word simply in its Latin sense, and that the Essay tells us how our thoughts are *turned away* from one path to another, from one object of contemplation to another; the ease with which this can be done by ourselves or others being sometimes good-fortune, sometimes ill-fortune.

He himself has succeeded in consoling for the moment a sorrowing lady (whom I fancy to be Diane de Foix, after the death of her young husband and his two brothers on the same day in battle)—in consoling her by gently turning her thoughts from her grief.

And he has lately "diverted" from thoughts of vengeance a young prince, not by preaching Christian forgiveness, or presenting the poetic tragedies of revenge, but by turning him round with his back to this passion and fixing his ambition's eyes on the honour to be gained from clemency. From power of distraction over the passion of ven-

Notes and Comments

geance, he passes to its power over the passion of love, and also over the passion of sorrow. Then, to its being the great medicine of Time. And then, with Alcibiades, to its value in giving the change to Rumour.

On a later page the subject turns from the effects of *diversion* to the triviality of the things that divert us from the core of the matter and fix our attention on its surface. And, even, we are affected by merely a surface, as if there *were* a core—witness "the sorrows of Dido and of Ariadne." And our imagination can not fully conceive a sorrow, save when aided by the eyes and ears. Even the eyes and ears alone can create the emotion of sorrow.

Returning to methods of *diversion*, he speaks of the manner by which the women in "a district near our mountains" divert themselves from grief for the loss of their husbands. The inserted passage that follows is admirable. And indeed we need no true cause to divert, to agitate, our senses: it may be done by "a vague imagination." There is nothing in nature but man "over which inanity [that which has no substance] has power." Yet the soul exults over the weakness of the body!

B. THE NOTES BY MR. IVES

1. *De la diversion.*
2. *Uberibus semper lachrimis, semperque paratis
   In statione sua, atque expectantibus illam,
   Quo jubeat manare modo.* —Juvenal, VI, 272.
3. See Cicero, *Tusc. Disp.*, III, 31, for these "methods."
4. See Book II, chap. 33.
5. Cf. Plutarch, *Life of Pericles*, XXII. If Montaigne had this passage in mind, his memory was at fault.

Of Distraction

6. *Gaigna le jour.* See Commines, II, 3.
7. That is, in the category of crafty devices.
8. *La deesse tutrisse de cette amoureuse ardeur.*
9.   *Obstupuit virgo, nitidique cupidine pomi*
    Declinat cursus, aurumque volubile tollit.
                      —Ovid, *Metam.*, X, 666.
10. *Fourvoyement et divertissement.*
11. Montaigne probably took the story from Ovid.
12. *Catarre;* formerly the term for apoplexy.
13. *Abducendus etiam nonnunquam animus est ad alia studia, solicitudines, curas, negotia; loci denique mutatione, tanquam ægroti non convalescentes, sæpe curandus est.*—Cicero, *Tusc. Disp.*, IV, 35.
14. To make it confront ills directly.
15. See Cicero, *Tusc. Disp.*, I, 34; Valerius Maximus, VIII, 9, *ext.* 3.
16. *Ils courent, ils visent à un estre nouveau.*
17. Niger was to cut off his head. See Tacitus, *Annals*, XV, 67.
18. *Un honneste homme.*
19.   *Spero equidem mediis, si quid pia numina*
        possunt,
    Supplicia hausurum scopulis, et nomine Dido
    Sæpe vocaturum....
    Audiam, et hæc manes veniet mihi fama sub
       imos.
                 —Virgil, *Æneid*, IV, 382-384, 387.
20. See Valerius Maximus, IV, 10, *ext.* 2; Diogenes Lærtius, *Life of Xenophon.*
21. See Cicero, *De Fin.*, II, 30; Diogenes Lærtius, *Life of Epicurus.* And see Book II, chap. 16, pp. 838, 839,

Notes and Comments

where Montaigne quotes the letter of Epicurus referred to.

22. *Omnes clari et nobilitati labores fiunt tolerabiles.*—Cicero, *Tusc. Disp.*, II, 24.

23. See Cicero, *Tusc. Disp.*, II, 26.

24. See *Ibid.*, II, 24.

25. *Hæc sunt solatia, hæc fomenta summorum dolorum.*—*Ibid.*

26. *Surintendante.*

27. See Seneca, *Epistle* 82.

28. See Idem, *Epistle* 83.

29. *Ce sont toujours bien lourdement des hommes.*

30. *Cum moroso vago singultiet inguine vena,*
—Persius, VI, 73.

31. *Conjicito humorem collectum in corpora quæque.* —Lucretius, IV, 1065.

32. *Si non prima novis conturbes vulnera plagis,*
Volgivagaque vagus venere ante recentia cures.
—*Ibid.*, 1070.

33. *Je fourvoye.*

34. *Un sage.* The first publication of this Essay (1588) was just five and twenty years after La Boëtie's death.

35. See Cicero, *Tusc. Disp.*, III, 15.

36. See Idem, *Life of Alcibiades.*

37. That is, the lovers.

38. *Serviteur aposté* (literally, posted for a bad purpose).

39. *Folliculos ut nunc teretes æstatae cicadæ*
Linquunt. —Lucretius, V, 803.

40. See Plutarch, *Letter of consolation to his wife.*

41. See Idem, *Life of Antony.*

42. *His se stimulis dolor ipse lacessit.*—Lucan, II, 42.

43. Tiberius. See Suetonius, *Life of Tiberius.*

Of Distraction

44. See the *Æneid*, IV; and Catullus, *Epithalamium Pelei et Thetidos*.

45. See Diogenes Lærtius, *Life of Polemo*.

46. The text of this difficult sentence is: *Et nulle sagesse ne va si avant de concevoir la cause d'une tristesse si vive et entiere par jugement, qu'elle ne souffre accession par la presence, quand les yeux et les oreilles y ont part, parties qui ne peuvent estre agitées que par vains accidens.*

47. *Qu'ils s'esbranlent en forme empruntée.*

48. Philibert, comte de Grammont et de Guiche, was the husband of "La belle Corisande," to whom Montaigne dedicated the chapter that originally contained the 29 sonnets of La Boëtie (Book I, chap. 29). When Montaigne left Paris for his journey to Italy he went first to the siege of La Fère (1580), where M. de Grammont was killed. A note in his handwriting, under date of August 6, in the *Ephemerides*, records the death and the fact that he was present.

49. See Quintilian, *Inst. Orat.*, VI, 2.

50. A proverbial expression founded on the tale of a priest named Martin, who acted both as priest and acolyte in saying mass.

51. See Herodotus, III, 30; Plutarch, *Of Brotherly Love*.

52. See Plutarch, *Of Superstition*.

53. See *Ibid*.

54.   *O prima infelix fingenti terra Prometheo!*
     Ille parum cauti pectoris egit opus.
   Corpora disponens, mentem non vidit in arte;
     Recta animi primum debuit esse via.
                     —Propertius, III, 5.7.

CHAPTER V

On Certain Verses of Virgil

A. THE COMMENT BY MISS NORTON

VIRGIL'S lines, though so hidden away in the body of it, are in every sense the heart of this *flux de caquet, flux impetueux par fois et nuisible* (Montaigne's own words); or, if not *nuisible,* at least indelicate—lacking in the open reserve that wisely avoids speech concerning "the sacred secrets known to all."

The emotion that led Montaigne to "free" speech here and elsewhere (an emotion, I think, entirely removed from personal coarseness of nature—almost indeed the result of the opposite) was the mistaken belief that, as he says in Latin, *non pudet dicere, quod non pudet sentire.* He did not recognise—and perhaps his constant contact with heathen conceptions of the relations of man and woman somewhat stood in the way of his recognising—that the greatest mystery of human nature, the blending of the spiritual and the physical in sexual intercourse, the workings of the angel and the animal, that this mystery of human nature is but the environment of the divine mystery of the creation of life. Montaigne's eyes were attracted by the splendid parti-coloured clouds of the environment; he seems never to have gazed long at the central sun, that "alma Venus" of which Lucretius so magnificently sang.

1974

On Certain Verses of Virgil

Quæ, quoniam rerum naturam sola gubernas
Nec sine te quidquam divas in luminis oras
Exoritur, neque fit lætum, neque amabile
    quidquam.

(Quoted by Montaigne with some changes. "Since thou then art sole mistress of the nature of things and without thee nothing rises up into the divine borders of light, nothing grows up to be glad or lovely.")

Montaigne's constant contemplation of the coming of death seems never to have turned his thoughts, as it well might have done, to the preceding coming of life. He had no intimations of immortality from perceiving any trailing clouds of glory about himself; and it was simply *man* here—man neither before nor after his earthly birth and death—that interested him.

With all his conviction that we can know nothing with certainty, it was what we can (imperfectly) *know* that was his object of study. "Mysteries" were outside the scope of his consideration, and when his way was blocked by the great and awful mysteries that do exist, he simply took another path: *Je gauchis tout doucement*.

This renders his treatment, always, of the subject of these *vers de Virgile* trivial and uninteresting, exaggerated and paradoxical; but it is never gross, never repulsive, save in the licentiousness of his illustrations and especially his quotations, for which his times, more than he, may be blamed.

He handles with neither strength nor delicacy the whole question of the *place* of women in the world; and nevertheless from his own day to ours, women have been his warmest friends; because, I think, they value, more than any high

1975

Notes and Comments

appreciation of themselves, the qualities which he depicts himself as showing—and I believe truly—in his personal relations with them: honesty, fidelity, sincerity, and even generosity and respectfulness. And there is real delicacy of perception in such phrases as this in this Essay: "It costs her more to give this little than it costs another to give every thing."

I think this Essay may have come about in this way. Reading Virgil, in what seemed to him his old age, and these verses recalling to him the rapturous heats of youth, he dwelt on them with pleasure,—"even any small occasions of pleasure that I meet with, I seize upon them,"—dwelt on them with a delightful literary, as well as physical, pleasure; and then he began to question: "Why shouldn't I write of this pleasure, as well as feel it?" and from that there was but one step—sure to be taken—to "I will write of it." And he wrote with "the glowing of such fire as on the ashes of his youth did lie."

Very near the beginning he says: "Wisdom has her excesses, and has no less need than folly of moderation"; and we are reminded that one of the inscriptions in his library was: *Ne plus sapias quam necesse est, ne obstupiscas.*

In an earlier Essay, Montaigne criticises as regards its *sound*—its "numbers"—a sentence of Cicero in the *De Senectute: Ego vero me minus diu senem esse mallem, quam esse senem antequam essem*. That he sympathised with the thought is proved by his here translating the sentence and accepting it as his own—since he gives no hint that it is quoted: *J'aime mieux estre moins long temps vieil que d'estre vieil avant de l'estre.*

When Montaigne exclaims, on this same page, "Would

On Certain Verses of Virgil

I could take pleasure in playing with nuts or with a top! *Non ponebat enim rumores ante salutem,*" he drolly diminishes the sense, the weight, that this line has in the original. Cicero (*De Officiis*, I, 24) quotes it (from Ennius) when contrasting the conduct of Quintus Maximus (Fabius) with that of Cleombrotus, who, fearing odium, rashly gave battle to Epaminondas, whereby the power of the Lacedæmonians perished: *Quanto Q. Fabius Maximus melius! de quo Ennius:*

> Unus homo nobis cunctando restituit rem:
> Non ponebat enim rumores ante salutem.
> Ergo postque magisque viri nunc gloria claret.

(How preferable was the conduct of Quintus Maximus, of whom Ennius says: "One man, by temporising, set right our affairs; he indeed did not consider public sayings as much as the safety of the country, and therefore the glory of that man shines now and hereafter, and ever more brightly.")

Montaigne's humorously familiar use of this quotation suggests that it was a phrase that had sunk into his mind from the force of its serious meaning. It may be remembered that he says in another place:

"My citations do not always serve simply as comment. I do not regard them solely in the light of the use that I make of them; they often have in them, beyond what I say, the seed of a richer and bolder meaning; and often indirectly a more subtle suggestion, both for me who do not wish to express myself more fully and for those readers who enter into my thought."

One of the most animated expressions of Montaigne's

Notes and Comments

eager love of society—of *companionship*—occurs here: "If there be any one, any pleasant party, in country, in city, in France, or elsewhere, resident or travelling, to whom my temperament may be agreeable and whose temperaments may be agreeable to me, they have but to whistle and I will go to them and supply them with essays in flesh and bone." With this passage may be connected another in a later Essay, where, after repeating what he says here, that if he came to the knowledge of any man of worth who liked his writings he would readily go to him even if he were far off, "for the delightfulness of an agreeable companion can not be too highly bought, to my thinking," he adds that no long familiarity would be necessary for friendship, since *ce registre* completely reveals him.

What he says of the virtue of chastity concerning itself only with the will is a text which might be considered with advantage today. And the way in which in these pages, and the following ones on jealousy, he sets forth the conditions of social life may suggest the most serious considerations regarding the undesirableness of holding theories that are at variance with facts.

The eloquent page on *le bien dire*, and the following ones, are a vigorous enlargement of the same thought in the Essay "Of the Education of Children."

The passage immediately following, on his conditions in writing and on what "I have said to myself," can not be too carefully read and pondered as shewing not only his philosophy of his own authorship, but his singularly careful and discerning judgement of his own writings; and I think special stress should be laid on the "You often trifle deceptively," all the more that it is a posthumous addition. It seems to

On Certain Verses of Virgil

me to indicate that he had perceived himself to be often misunderstood in this respect.

When he says, "Some of my earliest Essays have a borrowed flavour," we must wonder whether he meant that they were derived from the ancients or his contemporaries.

What he says of the impromptu character of the activity of his mind, of his deepest and his gayest thoughts coming to him unexpectedly, usually in conversation, and when he could not put them on paper, is extremely interesting. What a loss to the world that he had no Boswell!

The "leaving books aside" connects itself logically with the "Let us leave Bembo and Equicola" of a previous page; the intermediate personal passage is quite a thing apart.

Skipping four or five pages, we come to the passage beginning: "What a monstrous animal" (is the man who shuns health and cheerfulness), which conveys in its very effective phrasing a warning of striking character to all the Pascal class of minds. It connects itself in feeling with a later page in this same Essay, where Montaigne declares that it is only reasonable for us to accept pleasure as readily as we do pain.

And in one of the last pages he dwells on the double power of the soul, both to cherish bodily pleasure and to infuse into the body enjoyment of pleasure of her own.

B. THE NOTES BY MR. IVES

1. *Mens intenta suis ne siet usque malis.*
 —Ovid, *Tristia*, IV, 1.4.
2. *Animus quod perdidit optat,*
Atque in præterita se totus imagine versat.
 —Petronius, *Satyricon*, 128.

1979

Notes and Comments

3.   *Hoc est*
Vivere bis, vita posse priore frui.
—Martial, X, 23.7.

4. See Plato, *Laws*, book II.
5. *Que je me chatouille.*
6. See Cicero, *De Senectute*, X. Montaigne quoted this passage in Book II, chap. 10, p. 552.
7. *A natura discedimus; populo nos damus, nullius rei bono auctori.*—Seneca, *Epistle* 99.
8.   *Non ponebat enim rumores ante salutem.*
—Ennius, in Cicero, *De Off.*, I, 24.
9. *Sibi arma, sibi equos, sibi hastas, sibi clavam, sibi pilam, sibi natationes et cursus habeant; nobis senibus, ex lusionibus multis, talos relinquant et tesseras.*—Cicero, *De Senectute*, XVI.
10. See *Ibid.*, XI.
11. *Auront prou.*
12.   *Misce stultitiam consiliis brevem.*
—Horace, *Odes*, IV, 12.27.
13. *In fragili corpore odiosa omnis offensio est.*—Cicero, *De Senectute*, XVIII.
14.   *Mensque pati durum sustinet ægra nihil.*
—Ovid, *De Ponto*, I, 5.18.
15.   *Et minimæ vires frangere quassa valent.*
—Idem, *Tristia*, III, 11.22.
16. Throughout this paragraph the personal pronoun refers to the mind.
17. *Par venues.*
18. *Esperdus.*
19.   *Ad nullum consurgit opus, cum corpore languet.*
—Maximianus (Pseudo-Gallus), I, 125.

1980

On Certain Verses of Virgil

20. *Dum licet, obducta solvatur fronte senectus.*
—Horace, *Epodes*, XIII, 5.

21. *Tetrica sunt jocularibus.*
—Sidonius Apollinaris, *Epistles*, I, 9.

22. *Tristemque vultus tetrici arrogantiam.*
—George Buchanan, *John the Baptist*, Prologue, 31.

23. *Et habet tristis quoque turba cynædos.*
—Martial, VII, 58.9.

24. See the *Laws*, book VII, near the beginning; also the *Timæus*, near the end.

25. See Cicero, *Tusc. Disp.*, III, 15.

26. See Pliny, *Nat. Hist.*, VII, 19.

27. *C'est une humeur bien ordonée de pinser les escris de Platon.*

28. See Diogenes Laertius, *Life of Plato*.

29. *Non pudeat dicere quod non pudet sentire.*—Source unknown.

30. See Plutarch, *Of the tranquillity of the mind*.

31. *Quare vitia sua nemo confitetur? Quia etiam nunc in illis est; somnium narrare vigilantis est.*—Seneca, *Epistle* 53.

32. See *Ibid*.

33. See Plutarch, *Of curiosity*.

34. *Nos mœurs.*

35. *Espousent les loix de la ceremonie et attachent là leur devoir.* The thought in this puzzling sentence seems to be that even criminals connect their deeds with external propriety; but it is not for those who sin against the law to find fault with those who (in their eyes) sin against society.

36. *Incrustations.*

37. *Et ne me chaut à combien.*

Notes and Comments

38. At this point Montaigne wrote, then erased, on the margin of the Bordeaux copy: *Plesante fantasie! Plusieurs choses que je voudrois dire à persone je le dis au peuple. Et sur mes plus secretes sciences et pensees renvoie à mon livre me plus privez amis.*

39. See Plutarch, *Apothegms of Kings*, etc.

40. See Diogenes Laertius, *Life of Socrates.*

41. *Ceux qui par trop fuyant Venus estrivent,*
Faillent autant que ceux qui trop la suivent.
—Verses of Amyot, from Plutarch, *That a philosopher should hold converse with princes.*

42. *Tu, Dea, tu rerum naturam sola gubernas,*
Nec sine te quicquam dias in luminis oras
Exoritur, neque fit lætum nec amabile
    quicquam. —Lucretius, I, 21.

43. *Agnosco veteris vestigia flammæ.*
—Virgil, *Æneid*, IV, 23.

44. *Nec mihi deficiat calor hic, hiemantibus annis.*
—Jean Second, *Elegies*, I, 3.29.

45. *Qual l'alto Ægeo, per che Aquilone o Noto*
Cessi, che tutto prima il vuolse et scosse,
Non s'accheta ei pero: ma'l sono e'l moto,
  Ritien de l'onde anco agitate è grosse.
—Tasso *Gierusalemma Liberata*, XII, 63.

46. *Et versus digitos habet.* —Juvenal, VI, 196.

47. *Dixerat, et niveis hinc atque hinc diva lacertis*
Cunctantem amplexu molli fovet. Ille repente
Accepit solitam flammam, notusque medullas
Intravit calor, et labefacta per ossa cucurrit.
Non secus atque olim tonitru cum rupta
  corusco

1982

On Certain Verses of Virgil

Ignea rima micans percurrit lumine nimbos.
              . . . Ea verba loquutus,
Optatos dedit amplexus, placidumque petivit
Conjugis infusus gremio per membra soporem.
           —Virgil, *Æneid*, VIII, 387-392, 404.

48.   *Quo rapiat sitiens venerem interiusque recondat.*
           —Virgil, *Georgics*, III, 137.

49. This passage must be interpreted by recognising the signification to Montaigne of the words *noblesse* and *vertu*. *Noblesse* indicated to him the position of men of rank—not only of high rank, but all those above "the people" and outside the clergy, physicians, scholars, and the like. *Vertu* to him did not so much imply goodness, as the quality of a gentleman, especially the quality of manliness.—G. N.

50. That is, if in its habitual qualities it resembles virtue.

51. *Vivante.*

52. *Genealogique et commune; de suite et de similitude; tirée par consequence, et consequence bien foible.*

53. He was the son of a well-born centurion, but was idle and a coward. See Plutarch, *Of false Shame*.

54. See Herodotus, VI, 60.

55. *Les ignobles.*

56. The nobles.

57. See Goulard, *Histoire du Portugal*, II, 3.

58.   *Optato quam junxit lumine tæda.*
           —Catullus, LXIV, 79.

59. That is, the answers to these questions.

60. *A le bien façonner et à le bien prendre.*

61. See Diogenes Laertius, *Life of Socrates*.

62. Man is to man either a god or a wolf. In the edition of 1530 of the *Adages* of Erasmus, *Homo homini lupus* is

1983

Notes and Comments

found on p. 78, and *Homo homini deus* on p. 271. The first sentence occurs also in Plautus, *Asinaria*, II, 4.88, and the other in Symmachus, *Epistle* 10.104.

63. *Et mihi dulce magis resoluto vivere collo.*
     —Maximianus (Pseudo-Gallus), I, 61.

64. *Fatum est in partibus illis*
     Quas sinus abscondit: nam, si tibi sidera cessent,
     Nil faciet longi mensura incognita nervi.
     —Juvenal, IX, 32.

65. *Venus huic erat utraque nota.*
     —Ovid, *Metam.*, III, 323.

The priest was Tiresias.

66. *Adhuc ardens rigidæ tentigine vulvæ,*
     Et lassata viris, nondum satiata, recessit.
     —Juvenal, VI, 128.

67. *Sit tandem pudor, aut eamus in jus:*
     Multis mentula millibus redempta,
     Non est hæc tua, Basse; vendidisti.
     —Martial, XII, 99.10, 7, 11.

68. *Motus doceri gaudet Ionicos*
     Matura virgo, et frangitur artubus
     Jam nunc, et incestos amores
     De tenero meditatur ungui.
     —Horace, *Odes*, III, 6.21.

69. *Et mentem Venus ipsa dedit.*
     —Virgil, *Georgics*, III, 267.

70. *Nec tantum niveo gavisa est ulla columbo*
     Compar, vel si quid dicitur improbius,
     Oscula mordenti semper decerpere rostro,
     Quantum præcipue multivola est mulier.
     —Catullus, LXVI, 125.

On Certain Verses of Virgil

71. *Nec non libelli Stoici inter sericos*
 Jacere pulvillos amant.
—Horace, *Epodes*, VIII, 15.

72. *Nimirum propter continentiam incontinentia necessaria est; incendium ignibus extinguitur.*—Unknown.

73. *Flagitii principium est nudare inter cives*
 corpora.
—Ennius, in Cicero, *Tusc. Disp.*, IV, 33.

74. *Omne adeo genus in terris hominumque*
 ferarumque,
 Et genus æquoreum, pecudes, pictæque volucres,
 In furias ignemque ruunt.
—Virgil, *Georgics*, III, 242.

75. *Nam tu, quæ tenuit dives Achæmenes,*
 Aut pinguis Phrygiæ Mygdonias opes,
 Permutare velis crine Licimniæ,
 Plenas aut Arabum domos,
 Dum fragrantia detorquet ad oscula
 Cervicem, aut facili sævitia negat,
 Quæ poscente magis gaudeat eripi,
 Interdum rapere occupet?
—Horace, *Odes*, II, 12.21.

76. *Quis vetat apposito lumen de lumine sumi?*
—Ovid, *De Arte Amandi*, III, 93.

77. *Dent licet assidue, nil tamen inde perit.*
—*Priapea*, III, 2.

78. *Ense maritali nemo confossus adulter*
 Purpureo Stygias sanguine tinxit aquas.
—Jean Second, *Elegies*, I, 7.71.

79. *Ah! tum te miserum malique fati,*
 Quem attractis pedibus, patente porta,

1985

Notes and Comments

      Percurrent raphanique mugilesque.
                                 —Catullus, XV, 17.
80.   *Atque aliquis de diis non tristibus optat*
      Sic fiere turpis.   —Ovid, *Metam.*, IV, 187.
81.   *Quid causas petis ex alto? fiducia cessit*
      Quo tibi, diva, mei?
                            —Virgil, *Æneid*, VIII, 395.
82.   *Arma rogo genitrix nato.*   —*Ibid.*, 383.
83.   *Arma acri facienda viro.*   —*Ibid.*, 441.
84.   *Nec divis domines componier æquum est.*
                            —Catullus, LXVIII, 141.
85.   *Sæpe etiam Iuno, maxima cœlicolum,*
      Conjugis in culpa flagravit quotidiana.
                                   —*Ibid.*, 138.
86.   *Nullæ sunt inimicitiæ, nisi amoris, acerbæ.*
                                —Propertius, II, 8.3.
87.   *Notumque furens quid fœmina possit.*
                                —Virgil, *Æneid*, V, 6.
88.   *Languidior tenera cui pendens sicula beta*
      Nunquam se mediam sustulit ad tunicam.
                                —Catullus, LXVII, 21.
89.   *Illud sæpe facit quod sine teste facit.*
                                —Martial, VII, 62.6.
90.   *Offendor mœcha simpliciore minus.*
                                     —Idem, VI, 7.6.

91. *Obstetrix, virginis cujusdam integritatem manu velut explorans, sive malevolentia, sive inscitia, sive casu, dum inspicit, perdidit.*—St. Augustine, *De Civ. Dei*, I, 18.

   92.   *Pone seram, cohibe; sed quis custodiet ipsos*
      Custodes? Cauta est, et ab illis incipit uxor.
                                   —Juvenal, VI, 347.

On Certain Verses of Virgil

93.   *Tot qui legionibus imperitavit,*
Et melior quam tu multis fuit, improbe, rebus.
                    —Lucretius, III, 1028, 1026.

94. *Fors etiam nostris invidit questibus aures.*
                    —Catullus, LXIV, 170.

95. *Materiam culpæ prosequiturque suæ.*
                    —Ovid, Tristia, IV, 1.34.

96. *Ubi velis, nolunt; ubi nolis, volunt ultro.*
                    —Terence, *Eunuchus*, IV, 8.43.

97. *Concessa pudet ire via.*   —Lucan, II, 446.

98. *Irarumque omnes effundit habenas.*
                    —Virgil, *Æneid*, XII, 499.

99.   *Belli fera mœnera Mavors*
Armipotens regit, in gremium qui sæpe tuum se
Rejicit, æterno devinctus vulnere amoris. . . .
Pascit amore avidos inhians in te, Dea, visus,
Eque tuo pendet resupini spiritus ore;
Hunc tu, diva, tuo recubantem corpore sancto
Circumfusa super, suaveis ex ore loquelas
Funde.   —Lucretius, I, 32-34, 36-40.

100. Of these words, those which do not appear in the passage of Lucretius are found in the verses of Virgil (*Dixerat*, etc.) quoted on p. 1151.

101. *Ces menues pointes et allusions verballes.*

102. *Contextus totus virilis est, non sunt circa flosculos occupati.*—Seneca, *Epistle* 33. Seneca's text reads: *Non fuerent circa flosculos occupati; totus contextus illorum virilis est.*

103. *Pectus est quod disertum facit.*—Quintilian, X.

104. *Nos gens appellent jugement langage, et beaux mots les pleines conceptions.*

Notes and Comments

105. In the sixteenth century, six elegies by Maximianus (fifth century) were published and were attributed to Cornelius Gallus. Montaigne quotes them ten times.

106. "Now in my latter time," he says, "I began to take my Latin books in my hand. And thereby a strange thing to tell you, but yet true: I learned not, nor understood matters so much by the words, as I came to understand the words by common experience and knowledge I had in things."—Plutarch, *Life of Demosthenes* (North's English version of Amyot's French translation).

107. *Si vous allez tendu.*

108. *Qui ont bon nez.*

109. *Les sciences.*

110. Leon Hebreo published in 1535 *Dialoghi de Amore*, which was almost as well known in Italy as Castiglione's *Cortegiano*. Montaigne owned a copy of it. Marsiglio Ficino is famous for his Latin translation of Plato, published in Florence at the end of the fifteenth century, which was the one used by Montaigne. He was the author of several other translations and of a considerable number of unimportant original works. Montaigne probably had in mind an early one, *De Voluptate*.

111. That is, those who have disguised them. *Dieu leur doint bien faire!*

112. Two Italian contemporaries of Montaigne, both authors of many works. Among those of the Cardinal Pietro Bembo (1470-1547) are *Gli Asolani*, dialogues on love, so called because they were supposed to take place at Asola. Mario Equicola (1460-1539) wrote at the age of sixty-five *Della Natura d'Amore*, spoken of "as a learned and serious work on a trivial subject."

On Certain Verses of Virgil

113. See Plutarch, *How to distinguish a flatterer from a friend*.

114. The proper form of the name is Antigenidas. See Plutarch, *Life of Demetrius*.

115. *Il est si universel.*

116. *A feinte.*

117. *Par similitude que par complexion.*

118. See Diodorus Siculus, XVII, 20.

119. See Diogenes Laertius, *Life of Zeno: Per Capparim . . . jurabat.*

120. See Idem, *Life of Pythagoras: Non per aërem quem spiro; non per aquam quam bibo.*

121. *Aux despens d'autruy.*

122. *Plus profondes resveries, plus folles.*

123. *Quænam ista jocandi Sævitia!* —Claudian, *In Eutropium*, I, 24.

124. *Ridentem dicere verum Quid vetat?* —Horace, *Satires*, I, 1.24.

125. *Nostri nosmet poenitet.*—Terence, *Phormio*, I.

126. See Leo Africanus, *Historical Description of Africa*.

127. In 1588: *en toute sorte de grandeur.*

128. *Ne se presente pas volontiers en public avec appetit.*

129. See G. Postel, *Des histoires orientales, etc.*

130. *Qui se prisent de leur mespris.*

131. *Exilioque domos et dulcia limina mutant.*
—Virgil, *Georgics*, II, 511.

132. See Herodotus, IV, 184; Pliny, *Nat. Hist.*, V, 8.

133. *O miseri! quorum gaudia crimen habent.*
—Maximianus (Pseudo-Gallus), I, 180.

Notes and Comments

134. *Et nudam pressi corpus adusque meum.*
—Ovid, *Amores*, I, 5.24.

135. *Postquam cupidæ mentis satiata libido est,
Verba nihil metuere, nihil perjuria curant.*
—Catullus, LXIV, 147.

136. *Cuius livida naribus caninis
Dependet glacies rigetque barba,
Centum occurrere malo culilingis.*
—Martial, VII, 95.10.

137. *Tanquam thura merumque parent:
Absentem marmoreamve putes.*
—Martial, X, 103.12, and XI, 59.8.

138. *Tibi si datur uni,
Quo lapide illa diem, candidiore notet.*
—Catullus, LXVIII, 147.

139. *Te tenet, absentes alios suspirat amores.*
—Tibullus, 1, 6.35.

140. Cf. what he says about them in connection with the ancient Greek and Roman "Academies," Book III, chap. 8, p. 1255.

141. *Brutalité.*

142. Cf. Book II, chap. 17, "Of Presumption": "Valour . . . has become a common quality."

143. *Toutes les approches se rendent necessairement substantieles.*

144. *Luxuria ipsis vinculis, sicut fera bestia irritata, deinde emissa.*—Livy, XXXIV, 4.

145. *Vidi ego nuper equum, contra sua frena
tenacem,
Ore reluctanti fulminis ire modo.*
—Ovid, *Amores*, III, 4.13.

On Certain Verses of Virgil

146. The following sentence of 1588 was omitted in the posthumous editions: *Ayant tant de pieces à mettre en communication, on les achemine à y employer tousjours la derniere, puisque c'est tout d'un pris.*
147. That is, to refuse him a child to bring up.
148. *Pati natæ.*—Seneca, *Epistle* 95.
149. *Experta latus, madidoque simillima loro*
　　　Inguina, nec lassa stare coacta manu,
　Deserit imbelles thalamos.—Martial, VII, 58.3.
150. *Et quærendum aliunde foret nervosius illud,*
　　　Quod posset zonam solvere virgineam.
　　　　　　　　　—Catullus, LXVII, 27.
151. *Si blando nequeat superesse labori.*
　　　　　　　　—Virgil, *Georgics*, III, 127.
152. 　　　　　　　*Ad unum*
　Mollis opus.　　—Horace, *Epodes*, XII, 15.
153. 　　　　　　*Fuge suspicari,*
　Cujus undenum trepidavit ætas
　　　Claudere lustrum.
　　　　　　　　　—Idem, *Odes*, II, 4.22.
154. *Indum sanguineo veluti violaverit ostro*
　Si quis ebur, vel mista rubent ubi lilia multa
　Alba rosa.　　—Virgil, *Æneid*, XII, 67.
155. *Et taciti fecere tamen convitia vultus.*
　　　　　　　　　—Ovid, *Amores*, I, 7.21.
156. *Si non longa satis, si non bene mentula crassa.*
　　　　　　　　　—*Priapæa*, LXXX, 1.
157. *Nimirum sapiunt, videntque parvam*
　Matronæ quoque mentulam illibenter.
　　　　　　　　　—*Ibid.*, VIII, 4.
158. *Esse unum hominem accommodatum ad tantam*

Notes and Comments

morum ac sermonum et volontatum varietatem.—Q. Cicero, *De Petitione Consulatus*, XIV.

159.   *Rimula, dispeream, ni monogramma tua est.*
                             —Th. de Bèze, *Juvenilia.*

160.   *Un vit d'ami la contente et bien traicte.*
                                    —Saint-Gelais.

161.   *Si furtiva dedit nigra munuscula nocte.*
                             —Catullus, LXVIII, 145.

162.   *Me tabula sacer*
       Votiva paries indicat uvida
             Suspendisse potenti
       Vestimenta maris deo. —Horace, *Odes*, I, 5.13.

163.   *Hæc si tu postules*
       Ratione certa facere, nihilo plus agas,
       Quam si des operam, ut cum ratione insanias.
                             —Terence, *Eunuchus*, I, 1.16.

164.   *Nullum intra se vitium est.*—Seneca, *Epistle* 95.

165.   *Dum nova canities, dum prima et recta senectus,*
       Dum superest Lachesi quod torqueat, et pedibus me
       Porto meis, nullo dextram subeunte bacillo.
                             —Juvenal, III, 26.

166.   See Xenophon, *Memorabilia*, I, 3.

167.   That is, philosophy.

168.   *Cujus in indomito constantior inguine nervus,*
       Quam nova collibus arbor inhæret.
                             —Horace, *Epodes*, XII, 19.

169.   *Possint ut juvenes visere fervidi,*
            Multo non sine risu,
            Dilapsam in cineres facem?
                             —Horace, *Odes*, IV, 13.26.

1992

On Certain Verses of Virgil

170. Charity, for the good of your soul.
171. *Nolo*
Barbam vellere mortuo leoni.
—Martial, X, 90.10.
172. *O ego di' faciant talem te cernere possim,*
Charaque mutatis oscula ferre comis,
Amplectique meis corpus non pingue lacertis!
—Ovid, *De Ponto*, I, 4.49.
173. *Quem si puellarum insereres choro,*
Mille sagaces falleret hospites
Discrimen obscurum, solutis
Crinibus ambiguoque vultu.
—Horace, *Odes*, II, 5.21.
174. *Importunus enim transvolat aridas*
Quercus. —Horace, *Odes*, IV, 13.9.
175. *Amor ordinem nescit.*—St. Jerôme, *Epistle to Chromatius.*
176. *Nam si quando ad prœlia ventum est,*
Ut quondam in stipulis magnus sine viribus ignis
Incassum furit. —Virgil, *Georgics*, III, 98.
177. *Ut missum sponsi furtivo munere malum*
Procurrit casto virginis e gremio,
Quod miseræ oblitæ molli sub veste locatum,
Dum adventu matris prosilit, excutitur,
Atque illud prono præceps agitur decursu;
Huic manat tristi conscius ore rubor.
—Catullus, LXV, 19.

CHAPTER VI

Of Coaches

A. THE COMMENT BY MISS NORTON

THE Essay opens with an introductory paragraph on the difficulty of ascertaining "the master cause" of any effect, and passes on to controvert Plutarch's belief that the cause of seasickness is fear. This, Montaigne says, he knows by experience is not the case, as he is very subject to seasickness and he is never afraid on the water—or elsewhere. He says, delightfully, that he has not courage enough to be afraid: if he were once overcome, he could never recover himself. In an earlier Essay he declares: "The thing I am most afraid of is fear."

He goes on to say that he hates travelling by coach, litter, or boat, or in any other way than on horseback. And speaking of coaches, he dwells for a moment on their ancient use in war, and then mentions the strange *attelages*—lions, tigers, stags, dogs, naked women, ostriches—that the Roman emperors made use of.

The strangeness of these inventions suggests the question of excessive expenses on the part of monarchs, which is admirably discussed for several pages, then passes into a striking sketch of the magnificence and luxury of the old Roman spectacles; and that leads to "the reflection which every one makes, but which can never be worn out, as to the indefinitely small proportion which our knowledge of past

Of Coaches

times bears to our ignorance of them."

Then he remarks how little we know of the present world, "the world that is slipping on while we are in it." Thence he diverges, as Sir Fitzjames Stephen has said (in his *Horæ Sabbaticæ*), "into a really beautiful set of reflections on the discovery of America, full of a delicate humour." He goes on to show how great were the natural gifts of the Mexicans and other natives of America, and how little they had gained except injury from the superior knowledge of their conquerors. This portion of the Essay has a peculiar interest, as M. Chinard has ably pointed out (*L"Exotisme américaine dans la littérature française au xvie siècle*, 1911), when studied in connection with the Essay "Of Cannibals" (Book I, chapter 31), written some eight years earlier.

There is an essential difference of character between them. As M. Chinard remarks: "In the first, Montaigne gave expression only to his curiosity, his liking for examining small and picturesque facts; in the later Essay, his conscience has been awakened, he regards the conditions under a more searching light, and he distinctly takes sides in the name of justice and humanity for the ancient possessors of the 'Terres Nouvelles' against their barbarous conquerors."

In 1580 Montaigne's thoughts were not less of the defects and prejudices of his compatriots than of the merits of savages; in 1588 he wears no longer his sarcastic smile; and his indignation gives him words that do him the honour because he is but little subject to such bursts of passion. He knew more than before of the facts and conditions of the conquest and of their horribleness; and his freedom of thought made him capable—more than any other of the defenders of the Indians in those days—of this noble appeal to

Notes and Comments

justice. After several pages about Cortez, Pizarro, and the kings of Mexico and Peru, he finishes the digression by returning "to the subject"—of coaches!

B. THE NOTES BY MR. IVES

1. *Namque unam dicere causam Non satis est, verum pluris, unde una tamen sit.*
—Lucretius, VI, 703.
2. See Aristotle, *Problemata*, sect. 33, question 9.
3. *Le jugement à la science.*
4. See Plutarch, *Natural Causes.*
5. *Pejus vexabar quam ut periculum mihi succurreret.* —Seneca, *Epistle* 53.
6. "Courage to let the courage sink."—Arthur Hugh Clough.
7. *Saines.*
8. See Plato, *Banquet*, near the end. Montaigne's quotation is not a translation, but a summary.
9. *Quo timoris minus est, eo minus ferme periculi est.* —Livy, XXII, 5.
10. Cf. Book I, chap. 18, p. 97: "The thing I am most afraid of is fear."
11. *En mon haut appareil.*
12. *Je n'en fais poinct à deux.*
13. See Diogenes Laertius, *Life of Epicurus.*
14. *Passions.*
15. Cf. Book I, chap. 26, p. 234: "My intellect was slow . . . my comprehension was tardy"; Book II, chap. 17, p. 883: "My mind is lazy and not keen. . . . My apprehension is slow and confused."
16. *Un rondelier.* See Chalcondylas, VII, 7.

Of Coaches

17. *Une pavesade.*
18. *Aiant une querelle.*
19. The Merovingians. See du Haillant, *Histoire des Rois de France.*
20. The phrase, "as if . . . tokens," is not found in the *Édition Municipale,* but was added in 1595.
21. Crinitus *(De Honesta Disciplina,* XVI, 10) may have been Montaigne's source for all three of these examples. For Antonius, see also Pliny, *Nat. Hist.,* VIII, 16, and Plutarch, *Life of Antony;* for Heliogabalus, the *Life* by Ælius Lampridius; for Firmus, the *Life* by Flavius Vopiscus. Firmus was not emperor, but one of the *minusculi tyranni,* although he is called *imperator* by Crinitus; Vopiscus speaks of his *sitting* on enormous ostriches.
22. See Isocrates, *Oratio ad Nicoclem,* VI, 19.
23. *Sur qui les belles robes pleurent.*
24. See the *Third Olynthiae.*
25. See Cicero, *De Off.,* II, 16.
26. See *Ibid.,* 15. This passage of Cicero has given rise to much discussion. No such "reproach" can be found in Aristotle, and in many editions of Cicero the name has been changed to "Aristo Ceus"; but in all extant MSS and early editions it is "Aristoteles."
27. See *Ibid.,* 17.
28. See Plutarch, *Life of Galba.*
29. *Toute magistrature.*
30. *Nulla ars in se versatur.*—Cicero, *De Fin.,* V, 6.
31. That is, liberality.
32. See Plutarch, *Apothegms of Kings,* etc.
33. Montaigne probably took this from J. Lipsius, *De Amphitheatro.*

Notes and Comments

34. *Quo in plures usus sis, minus in multos uti possis. Quid autem est stultius quam quod libenter facias, curare ut id diutius facere non possis?*—Cicero, *De Off.*, II, 15.

35. This parenthetical clause of 1588 was stricken out on the Bordeaux copy, but restored in 1595.

36. *Ils se taillent.*

37. See Seneca, *Epistle* 73.

38. Cyrus.

39. *Par declaration.*

40. See Xenophon, *Cyropædeia*, VIII, 2.

41. *Pecuniarum translatio a justis dominis ad alienos non debet liberalis videri.*—Cicero, *De Off.*, I, 14.

42. See *Ibid.*, II, 15.

43. See Crinitus, *De Honesta Disciplina*, XII, 7.

44.   *Baltheus en gemmis, en illita porticus auro,*
    —Calpurnius, *Eclogues*, VII, 47.
Taken by Montaigne from J. Lipsius, *De Amphitheatro*, from which this whole passage is derived, down to the last quotation taken from Calpurnius (p. 1233).

45.   *Exeat, inquit,*
    Si pudor est, et de pulvino surgat equestri,
    Cujus res legi non sufficit. —Juvenal, III, 153.

46.   *Quoties nos descendentis arenæ*
    Vidimus in partes, ruptaque voragine terræ
    Emersisse feras, et iisdem sæpe latebris
    Aurea cum croceo creverunt arbuta libro!
    Nec solum nobis silvestria cernere monstra
    Contigit, æquoreos ego cum certantibus ursis
    Spectavi vitulos, et equorum nomine dignum,
    Sed deforme pecus.
    —Calpurnius, *Eclogues*, VII, 64.

Of Coaches

47. *Quamvis non modico caleant spectacula sole,*
Vela reducuntur, cum venit Hermogenes.
—Martial, XII, 29.15.
48. *Auro quoque torta refulgent*
Retia. —Calpurnius, *Eclogues*, VII, 53.
49. *Vixere fortes ante Agamemnona*
Multi, sed omnes illachrimabiles
Urgentur ignotique longa
Nocte. —Horace, *Odes*, IV, 9.25.
50. *Et supera bellum Trojanum et funera Trojæ,*
Multi alias alii quoque res cecinere poetæ.
—Lucretius, V, 326.
51. See Plato, *Timæus*.
52. *Si interminatam in omnes partes magnitudinem regionum videremus et temporum, in quam se injiciens animus et intendens, ita late longeque peregrinatur ut nullam oram ultimi videat in qua possit insistere; in hac immensitate infinita vis innumerabilium appareret formarum.*—Cicero, *De Nat. Deor.*, I, 20.
53. *Exemplaires.*
54. *Jamque adeo affecta est ætas, affectaque tellus.*
—Lucretius, II, 1150.
55. *Cettuy-la;* that is, Lucretius.
56. *Verum, ut opinor, habet novitatem summa, recensque*
Natura est mundi, neque pridem exordia cœpit;
Quare etiam quædam nunc artes expoliuntur,
Nunc etiam augescunt, nunc addita navigiis sunt
Multa. —Lucretius, V, 330.
57. Cf. Book I, chap. 31, p. 271.
58. *Plein et membru que lui.*

Notes and Comments

59. Lucretius.
60. See Gomara, *Histoire Générale des Indes*, V, 13.
61. All this that follows was inspired by Gomara, *passim*.
62. *Faire son profit.*
63. *Mechaniques victoires.*
64. The Spaniards. This, too, is taken from Gomara.
65. The Pope.
66. The Spaniards.
67. The natives.
68. *Les honnestetez.*
69. Referring to the Essay, "Of Cannibals," Book I, chap. 31.
70. The Spaniards.
71. This account of the King of Peru (Attabalipa) has not been traced directly to any one source. The facts were in the air. The passage following, about the King of Mexico, is derived chiefly, with intentional divergences, from an Italian translation of Gomara's *Life of Cortes*.
72. Guatemotzin.
73. The Spaniards.
74. *Par armes.*
75. See Gomara, *Histoire Générale des Indes*.
76. Gomara was a Spaniard.
77. Of the Spaniards.
78. *Sur les lieux;* that is, in a foreign land.
79. Philip II.
80. *Un meuble reservé.*
81. See Gomara, *Histoire Générale des Indes*.
82. See *Ibid.*
83. See *Ibid.*

CHAPTER VII

Of the Disadvantage of Greatness

A. THE COMMENT BY MISS NORTON

THIS Essay might be entitled an Apology for Kings and Princes—for the unfortunate great. Montaigne's wide sympathies included poor peasants and poor princes in his compassion, and he saw the definitions of one and the other plane of human existence.

So it seemed to him that it was not a great sign of magnanimity to despise grandeur, no great wonder to refuse it; and he shrewdly suggests that the very glory of the refusal is a reward of ambition.

As for himself, he "cares too much for himself" to wish for a lofty position. He would like an increase in mental and physical qualities and in wealth, but not in power: he would rather be in the third place than the first, if they were both in Paris; he measures good luck, not by its might, but by its ease. He may admire Regulus more than Balbus, but he would rather be Balbus.

And, to come back to earthly greatness, the most difficult part in the world to play well is that of king. So unbounded a power it is difficult to keep in bounds; yet there is a peculiar incitement to virtue in being in a situation where every good act affects so many men, and where (like preachers) you are chiefly judged by the unexacting, easily

Notes and Comments

deceived, easily pleased common people. But this whole subject is one of those on which our interests make it difficult to pass sincere judgement; so let inflexible and impassible reason tell us what are the disadvantages of greatness.

First, that, out of respect, princes are treated disrespectfully: no man will fight against them; it is only their horses, not their fellows, that afford them an opportunity to shew their abilities in mastering opposition. They are never allowed the honour and pleasure of hazardous deeds; every thing gives way before them, as if by enchantment; they are kept aloof from their kind; their existence is not of life, but of sleep. The power and wealth of man lie in want.

Princes are deprived of all true praise; for the quality of kingship stifles the expression of all virtues that are not directly concerned with this office. A king can be nothing but a king, and his personality is wholly obscured by the light of his crown. His vices are fostered, not merely by approbation, but by imitation. And, in fine, to be not on a level with other men is to be at a disadvantage as regards success.

B. THE NOTES BY MR. IVES

1. Cf. Seneca, *De Tranquillitate Animi*, X.
2. *Fuite.*
3. *Que doivent faire ceux*, etc.
4. Cf. Book I, chap. 42, p. 351: *Quant au commander, qui semble estre si doux, considerant l'imbecillité du jugement humain et la difficulté du chois ès choses nouvelles et doubteuses, je suis fort de cet advis, qu'il est bien plus aisé et plus plaisant de suivre que de guider, et que c'est un grand sejour d'esprit de n'avoir à tenir qu'une voie tracée et à respondre que de soy.*

Of the Disadvantage of Greatness

5. Cæsar. See Plutarch, *Life of Cæsar*.
6. This sentiment is inscribed on a monument erected to Montaigne at Périgueux.
7. *Constitution.*
8. *Conduisant une vie tranquille et toute sienne.*
9. In *De Fin.*, II, 20, where he compares the two men greatly to the advantage of Regulus.
10. *Mais s'il me les falloit coucher sur la mienne.*
11. See Herodotus, III, 83.
12. *Il faut qu'elles s'entrepillent perpetuellement.*
13. G. Buchanan, *De jure regni apud Scotos* (1579), and A. Blackwood's reply: *Pro Regibus Apologia* (1581).
14. Buchanan's.
15. That is, to princes.
16. See Plutarch, *Of the tranquillity of the mind.*
17. See Idem, *How to distinguish a flatterer from a friend.*
18. *Elle vous plante trop à l'escart.*
19. Those of princes.
20. To the subject.
21. The royal position.
22. Princes.
23. *Qu'il n'est que par là.*
24. *Nostre veue s'y rompt et s'y dissipe, estant remplie et arrestée.*
25. Cf. Tacitus, Annals, II, 84. If this is Montaigne's source, his memory was very inexact.
26. See Plutarch, *How to distinguish a flatterer from a friend.*
27. See *Ibid.* But Plutarch said simply that he had seen *one man* do it.

Notes and Comments

28. See Plutarch, *How to distinguish a flatterer from a friend*.

29. Montaigne took this story from Spartianus (*Life of Hadrian*, XV) through Crinitus, *De Honesta Disciplina*, XII; and that of Pollio from Macrobius (*Saturnalia*, II, 4) also through the same passage of Crinitus.

30. See Plutarch, *Of the tranquillity of the mind*. But see Diogenes Laertius, *Life of Plato*, and Diodorus Siculus, XV, 6 and 7, for a different explanation of Dionysius's treatment of Plato.

CHAPTER VIII

Of the Art of Conversation

A. THE COMMENT BY MISS NORTON

THIS Essay does not teach the art of conversation, but rather the art of conversing with our fellow men, of holding converse with them, whether by oral speech or visible speech. As the conclusion of the Essay, we have a criticism of the writings of Tacitus, which might better, perhaps, have had a title to itself.

The opening pages have nothing to do with *conference* of any kind, save that Montaigne declares that he *confers* the knowledge of himself on the world through his Essays so that worthy men—*des honnestes hommes*—may profit

Of the Art of Conversation

by avoiding his imperfections.

When he begins his remarks on *la conference*, he does of course mean actual *speaking*, face-to-face talking,—more exactly, discussing,—and the delightful impression he gives of himself as a talker is scarcely impaired by his honest confession, on a later page, of his disagreeablenesses.

He indulges in a rather perilous paradox when he declares: "One does not do wrong to the subject when one forsakes it to find the best manner of treating it"; but we may believe that he meant only that good sense in the mode of discussing a subject is not less important than good sense in forming one's private opinion. And what he says regarding the learned follies in the manner of conducting public discussions in his day shows how widespread was the evil he condemned.

As he goes on to point out the true ends and objects of discussion, he naturally passes from that "questing" of truth which we make in company with our antagonist, to the solitary pursuit of it which is recorded on the printed page: and his turn of thought finds expression in the sentence which sounds more like the to-morrow of to-day than the long-ago yesterday of the sixteenth century. "I constantly take pleasure in reading authors without concerning myself about their knowledge, having regard to their manner, not their subject."

Montaigne did not believe that any man ever had captured, ever would, ever could capture the truth: but to *chase* it—ah! there is the pleasure! but it must be done intelligently, however eagerly.

There is something extremely interesting in Montaigne's annoyance at the lack of intelligence, the *sottise*, that he

Notes and Comments

came in contact with, and in his self-reproaches for this *fadaise* of his. And these self-reproaches lead him to wise thoughts regarding the relation there should be in our minds between our own weaknesses and those of others. "The sum of it is," he says, "that we must live with the living."

Then there comes a break in the Essay—not in the thought, but in the current of the expression: so little of a break in the thought that it merely gives me the impression that Montaigne perhaps here laid down his pen, or that his secretary, to whom he was dictating, went out of the room, and that he, walking back and forth in his library, thinking of what he was about to say, got the last part of the idea too completely in his mind, and when he began, started off at once with "The senses are our fit and primal judges," when he ought to have begun with "In intercourse, gravity of manner and a professional robe often have weight."

He did not better the arrangement by inserting in 1595 the long preceding passage. He illustrated here, as elsewhere, in a droll enough manner, his own remark: "Every man can speak with truth, but to speak with order, with prudence, with ability, few men have the power!"

Well, after we have got past the senses, and the gowns, and the gravity, and all the superficial appearances and ceremonies, the thought of the tyranny that these exercise keeps Montaigne's mind still dwelling on the frequent incongruity between the position a man occupies and what the man himself is; and from that he passes to the consideration of luck and ill-luck, returning to the contemplation of "a man promoted in dignity." He expresses his own divergence from popular judgements in a passage of admirable acute-

Of the Art of Conversation

ness and pointedness; the conclusion of which, bringing us fully, perfectly, back to methods of discussion, shews how completely that undercurrent runs through previous pages.

And now we really do find sane "admonitions"—what might be called maxims—about social intercourse, of which we, like Montaigne himself, may make *grand usage*. First, about fine-sounding phrases, and vague phrases—do not let them pass current too easily; on the other hand, when what is meant is foolish, do not try to "set right ignorance or stupidity." He speaks then of personal jests, of friends "rallying," "making fun" of one another; and these, which he enjoys, remind him of *jeux de main* (practical jokes?), which he hates.

And now he pauses again, and begins to consider by what, besides his demeanour *en conference*, he judges a man. "I ask him (in my own mind)," he says, "how contented with himself he is"; and this thought makes him want to tell us what he himself thinks of his Essay, and he declares that he does not know what to think; but, anyway, he is sure that the most famous books do not always do much honour to their authors; so, *fame* is not the only thing to consider. And some of the best things that authors say are not always, he has observed, original with them. ("Other writers," he seems to say between the lines, "borrow a good deal, as well as myself.") But this makes conversation about books, the discussion of books, awkward for persons who are not very well read, for they can not be sure whose *belle invention* they are praising. So I, Michel de Montaigne, am always on my guard about that!

He continues: "I have been reading Tacitus lately, because I had been talking about him with a friend of mine;

Notes and Comments

and do not you, my reader, agree with me that," etc. The sentences which break this criticism—"I dare speak not only of myself," to the end of the paragraph—were added in 1595.

The sentences on the last page are just a flourish—his *signature*.

B. THE NOTES BY MR. IVES

1. *De l'art de conferer.*
2. See the *Laws*, book XI.
3. *Nonne vides Albi ut male vivat filius, utque Barrus inops? Magnum documentum ne patriam rem Perdere quis velit.* —Horace, *Satires*, I, 4.109.
4. That is, to fear similar ones in himself.
5. *Par fuite que par suite.*
6. See Plutarch, *Life of Cato Censor.*—"Where did you learn your good manners?" "Of the bad-mannered."—Saadi.
7. *Son caquet.*
8. *Qui ne doit guere à la sottise en importunité.*
9. *Rejance = regence.*
10. *Cette tendreur du son ceremonieux des parolles.*
11. *Neque enim disputari sine reprehensione potest.*—Cicero, *De Fin.*, I, 8.
12. *Mon imagination.*
13. *Mais je romps paille.*
14. See Plutarch, *Of False Shame.*
15. *Qui se donnent sans forme.*
16. *Enfans de boutique.*
17. In Book VII, near the end.

Of the Art of Conversation

18. *Quester ce qui est.* In 1588: *quester la verité.*
19. *Foible de reins.*
20. *Se mutine à se faire tout plat.*
21. *Une querelle d'Alemaigne.*
22. *Sur la closture dialectique de ses clauses.*
23. *Nihil sanantibus litteris.*—Seneca, *Epistle* 59.
24. *Nec ad melius vivendum nec ad commodius disserendum.*—Cicero, *De Fin.*, I, 19.
25. *Voit-on plus de barbouillage au caquet des harengeres.*
26. *Sub aliena umbra latentes*—Seneca, *Epistle* 33.
27. *Desliées.*
28. Cf. Book I, chap. 26, p. 199: "Learning is a noble adornment, madame, and a marvellously useful tool. . . . In fact, it is of no true use in mean and low hands."
29. In the dialogues bearing the names of those two philosophers.
30. See Lactantius, *Institutiones Divinæ*, III, 28.
31. *Ce n'est pas à qui mettra dedans.*
32. *A nous en prendre à la gorge.*
33. Heraclitus. Cf. Book I, chap. 50, p. 403.
34. See Diogenes Laertius, *Life of Miso.*
35. *Volontiers.*
36. See Plutarch, *Of Hearing.*
37. *Stercus cuique suum bene olet.*
  —Erasmus, *Adages*, III, 4.2: *Suus cuique crepitus bene olet.*
38. *Age! si hæc non insanit satis sua sponte, instiga.*
  —Terence, *Andria*, IV, 2.9.
39. See Plato, *Gorgias.*
40. *Et la parliere et l'effectuelle.*

Notes and Comments

41. *Rarus enim ferme sensus communis in illa Fortuna.* —Juvenal, VIII, 73.

42. *Quand elle est mal estuyée.* See Plato, *Republic*, book VI.

43. *Humani qualis simulator simius oris,*
Quem puer arridens pretioso stamine serum
Velavit, nudasque nates ac terga reliquit,
Ludibrium mensis.
—Claudian, *In Eutropium*, I, 303.

44. See Plutarch, *How to distinguish a flatterer from a friend*, and *Of the tranquillity of the mind*.

45. *Principis est virtus maxima nosse suos.*
—Martial, VIII, 15.8.
Taken by Montaigne from the *Politics* of J. Lipsius, IV, 5.

46. Cf. Ovid, *Heroïdes*, II, 85.

47. See Livy, XXXVIII, 48.

48. See Plutarch, *Apothegms of Kings*, etc.

49. *Fata viam inveniunt.*
—Virgil, *Æneid*, III, 395.

50. *Les plus basses et laches, et les plus battues, se couchent mieux aux affaires.*

51. *Les personnes profanes.*

52. *Permitte divis cætera.* —Horace, *Odes*, I, 9.9.

53. Cf. Book I, chap. 47, pp. 381, 382: "So we are wont often to say, with good reason, that events and results depend for the most part, notably in war, upon fortune."

54. *Vertuntur species animorum, et pectora motus*
Nunc alios, alios dum nubila ventus agebat,
Concipiunt. —Virgil, *Georgics*, I, 420.

55. *Rencontrer = Reussir.*

56. See Thucydides, III, 37.

Of the Art of Conversation

57. *Ut quisque fortuna utitur,*
Ita præcellet, atque exinde sapere illum omnes
dicimus. —Plautus, *Pseudolus*, II, 3.15.
Taken from the *Politics* of J. Lipsius, IV, 9.
58. *A la mode des getons (jetons).*
59. See Plutarch, *Of Hearing.*
60. See Diogenes Laertius, *Life of Antisthenes.*
61. See Gomara, *Histoire Générale des Indes*, II, 77.
62. *Que nous nous enferrons, et aidons au coup outre sa portée.*
63. *Je ne les donnois qu'en nombre, on les recevoit en pois.* The sentence seems not wholly appropriate here.
64. *Qu'ils rencontrent.*
65. Cf. Plutarch, *Of the dæmon of Socrates.*
66. *Par espaulettes*—a phrase of Montaigne's coining.
67. *Videndum est non modo quid quisque loquatur, sed etiam quid quisque sentiat, atque etiam qua de causa quisque sentiat.*—Cicero, *De Off.*, I, 41.
68. That is, those who give judgement in general terms.
69. *Soufflez!*
70. See Diogenes Laertius, *Life of Aristippus.*
71. *Reparation.*
72. See Xenophon, *Cyropædeia*, III, 3.49.
73. *Auquel je veux grand mal.*
74. *Principians*—a word of Montaigne's coining.
75. *Au titre de la conference et communication.*
76. See Plutarch, *Life of Lycurgus.*
77. *Baissant joyeusement les oreilles.*
78. *Jeux de main.*
79. A figurative expression.
80. Probably the duc d'Enghien, killed in sport

Notes and Comments

(1546), and Henri II, killed in jousting by the comte de Montgommery (1559).

81. *Se battre en s'esbattant.*

82. *Ablatum mediis opus est incudibus istud.*
—Ovid, *Tristia*, I, 7.29.

83. See Commines, III, 12. Commines attributes the saying to his master, Louis XI.

84. *Beneficia eo usque læta sunt dum videntur exolvi posse; ubi multum antevenere, pro gratia odium redditur.* —Tacitus, *Annals*, IV, 18.

85. *Nam qui putat esse turpe non reddere non vult esse cui reddat.*—Seneca, *Epistle* 81.

86. *Qui se non putat satisfacere amicus esse nullo modo potest.*—Q. Cicero, *De Petitione Consulatus*, IX.

87. Cf. Book II, chap. 10, p. 549: "If I spend an hour in reading him [Cicero], which is a long time for me."

88. This sentence was omitted in 1595.

89. See Tacitus, Annals XVI, 16; Jean Bodin, *Methodus ad facilem historiarum cognitionem.*

90. Deaths commanded by the emperor.

91. This, after the semicolon, was omitted in 1595.

92. *A s'enfler.*

93. *Il me semble plus charnu, Seneque plus aigu.*

94. See Tacitus, History, II, 38.

95. As with Marius and Sylla.

96. *Patres conscripti* in the Latin.

97. See Tacitus, *Annals*, VI, 6. Cf. Suetonius, *Life of Tiberius.*

98. See Tacitus, *Annals*, XI, 11.

99. *Bas de poil.*

100. Those of Tacitus.

Of Vanity

101. *Genereuse.*
102. See Tacitus, *Annals*, XIII, 35.
103. It was a man. See Idem, *History*, IV, 81. "It is well to remember," says M. Villey, "that in *Le Contre-un* La Boëtie contested the authority of Tacitus, precisely because of the miracles he ascribed to Vespasian."
104. *Equidem plura transcribo quam credo; nam nec affirmare sustineo de quibus dubito, nec subducere quae accepi.*—Quintus Curtius, IX, 1.
105. *Haec neque affirmare, neque refellere operæ pretium est . . . famæ rerum standum est.*—Livy, I, Præfatio, and VIII, 6.
106. See Idem, XLIII, 13-15.
107. *Moi qui suis roy de la matiere que je traicte.*
108. *De quoi je secoue les oreilles.*
109. *Application.*

CHAPTER IX

Of Vanity

A. THE COMMENT BY MISS NORTON

SOME curious questions are suggested by this Essay. It has a marked irregularity of form, and, as familiarity with it increases, it seems almost as if two outlines, two forms, may be distinguished in it. Two different dates are found in it, each as being the date of its writing.

Montaigne refers twice to the death of his father, which took place in 1568, as having occurred eighteen years before the time when he was writing, which would make that time 1586; and on another page he speaks of the death of Pibrac (1584) as recent.

But he says: *Je suis envielli de huit ans depuis mes premières publications.* This would make the year 1588, as the first edition of the Essays was of 1580.

It may be said that perhaps this Essay was on the stocks for two years. The character of the opening pages is such that, written in the year of the publication of the edition of the Essays in which for the first time this Third Book appeared, they might serve almost as a preface to all the Essays.

These opening pages express Montaigne's recognition of the endlessness of his subject and of its (apparent) triviality, and uselessness (to the State), leading on to the remark that *escrivaillerie* is one sign of a nation's decadence.

But even worse than the folly of idle writing is his weakness, he says, in throwing every thing to the dogs when matters go badly; a despairing despondency that he expresses in one of those sentences of melancholy which, as the Saône with the Rhone, mingle with the large flow of his philosophy: *Ce m'est faveur que la desolation de cet Estat se rencontre à la desolation de mon aage.* He later fears that the *trahison* of his memory may be perceptible in these *revasseries*.

But, however imperfect his *revasseries* may be, *laisse, lecteur, courir encore ce coup d'essay et ce troisiesme alon-*

Of Vanity

geail du reste des pieces de ma peinture. He gives his reasons why he does not correct his writings (in essentials), but only adds to them, and he thanks *les honnestes hommes* who have accepted his efforts with good-will.

Later he says: *Je sens ce proffit inesperé de la publication de mes meurs, qu'elle me sert aucunement* [that is, *un peu*] *de regle*, and he adds, with some tone of disappointment, that, besides this profit, he had hoped, in making himself known to the world, for another gain, the happiness of finding a friend.

And still later: *J'escris mon livre à peu d'hommes et à peu d'années;* and this passage closes with a saddened sentence, to the effect that there will be no one by whom his memory will be cherished because of such affectionate and intimate knowledge of him as he had of his friend La Boëtie.

Interposed in these passages are others of a wholly different nature: page after page of cheerful garrulousness and conversational philosophy about his pleasure in travelling, merging into consideration of the wretched conditions of France; and his thought deepens, his voice strengthens, and the most serious questions of public importance are discussed with admirable vigour of intellect. He continues by describing his own personal position in the midst of the national troubles, and this leads him to the deeply interesting, much criticised, reflections on death. He then passes back to his travelling inclinations, and takes up the complaints brought against him for leaving his family, and for running the risk of dying away from home. He philosophises seriously on these points, so seriously that it carries him into reflections on the inconsistency between the moral laws that men lay down and their general conduct, the dis-

Notes and Comments

cussion of which forms an immense parenthesis of eight or ten pages, from *Je voy souvent qu'on nous propose des images de vie* to *J'avois à dire que je veus mal à cette raison trouble feste*, where he comes back to the subject of the captious difficulties raised by his friends.

It is very noticeable in these pages that in no Essay does Montaigne lay such stress on the necessity of careful and subtle attention on the part of his reader. In one passage he speaks of the mistakes that have occurred in the printing of the Essays:

Ne te prens point à moy, lecteur, de [fautes] qui se coulent icy par la fantasie ou inadvertance d'autruy; chaque main, chaque ouvrier, y apporte les siennes. . . . Où ils rompent du tout [that is, *tout-à-fait*] *le sens, je m'en donne peu de peine, car aumoins, ils me deschargent; mais où ils en substituent un faux, comme ils font si souvent, et me destournent à leur conception, ils me perdent. Toutesfois, quand la sentence n'est forte à ma mesure, un honneste homme la doit refuser pour mienne.*

B. THE NOTES BY MR. IVES

1. It is to be observed that "vanity" has not here its ordinary significance, but is used rather in the sense of the "Vanity of vanities, all is vanity," of the Preacher.

2. Montaigne evidently took this from Bodin, *Methodus*, etc., who confused a certain Diomedes, who lived about the sixth century A.D., with "Didymus grammaticus," of whom Seneca speaks (*Epistle 88*) as having written 4000 volumes.

3. Pythagoras imposed on his disciples a silence of five years.

Of Vanity

4. The original source of the last clause is Suetonius (*Life of Galba*), who gives the saying to the Emperor Galba. Montaigne evidently took it at second hand from some book where the first clause had been added and the personage not clearly indicated.

5. *L'affinement des esprits, ce n'en est pas l'assagissement en une police.*

6. *Vanité.*

7. See Plutarch, *Of Hearing.*

8. See Herodotus, VII, 209.

9. *Cappe:* a short cloak with a hood.

10. Cf. Book III, chap. 2, pp. 1100ff.

11. The precept that Montaigne refers to does not belong to Xenophon himself, but he quotes it in the *Cyropædeia* (I, 6.3) as having been said by Cyrus to Cambyses. Plutarch *(Of the tranquillity of the mind)* somewhat enlarges and explains it.

12. *Et faicts plus volontiers les doux yeux au ciel.*

13. See Seneca, *Epistle* 94.

14.   *Ipsa dies ideo nos grato perluit haustu*
      Quod permutatis Hora recurrit equis.
                    —Petronius, *Fragment* 678.

15.   *Aut verberatæ grandine vineæ,*
     Fundusque mendax, arbore nun aquas
       Culpante, nunc torrentia agros
    Sidera, nunc hyemes iniquas.
                    —Horace, *Odes*, III, 1.29.

16.   *Aut nimiis torret fervoribus ætherius sol,*
   Aut subiti perimunt imbres, gelidæque pruinæ,
   Flabraque ventorum violento turbine vexant.
                    —Lucretius, V, 215.

Notes and Comments

17. Plutarch *(Life of Paulus Æmilius)* tells of a man who, when his friends wondered at his divorcing his wife, shewed them his fine new shoe, saying: "There's not one of you who knows where it hurts my foot."

18. *Puisque je ne cerche qu'à passer.*

19. Poverty.

20. *Non æstimatione census, verum victu atque cultu, terminatur pecuniæ modus.*—Cicero, *Paradoxa*, VI, 3.

21. *Preste grande espaule.*

22. *Despiteusement.*

23. *L'escume.*

24. See C. Nepos, *Phocion*, I; Plutarch, *Life of Phocion*.

25. See Diogenes Laertius, *Life of Crates*.

26. See Plutarch, *How to restrain anger*.

27. The following sentences, down to "weigh upon me," were substituted in 1595 for this passage of 1588: *Or nous monstre assez Homere combien la surprise donne d'avantage, qui faict Ulysse pleurant de la mort de son chien et ne pleurant point des pleurs de sa mere; le premier accident, tout legier qu'il estoit, l'emporta, d'autant qu'il en fut inopinéement assailly; il soustint le second, plus impetueux parce qu'il y estoit preparé.* [See Plutarch, *Of the tranquillity of the mind*.] *Ce sont legieres occasions qui pourtant troublent la vie.* Montaigne made a curious blunder here, which was probably the reason the passage was omitted in 1595. When Ulysses meets his mother in Hades, nothing is said of *her* tears: "Anon came up the soul of my mother, dead... At the sight of her I wept." (*Odyssey*, XI.)

28. *Nemo enim resistit sibi, cum cœperit impelli.*—Seneca, *Epistle* 13.

29. *Stillicidi casus lapidem cavat.*—Lucretius, I, 313.

Of Vanity

30. *Ces ordinaires gouttieres m'enfoncent et m'ulcerent.*
31. *Tum vero in curas animum diducimus omnes.*
—Virgil, *Æneid*, V, 720.
32. See Diogenes Laertius, *Life of Diogenes*.
33. *Quin tu aliquid saltem potius, quorum indiget usus,*
Viminibus mollique paras detexere junco?
—Virgil, *Eclogues*, II, 71.
34. *Laissons en arriere nostre faict.*
35. *Sit meæ sedes utinam senectæ!*
Sit modus lasso maris, et viarum,
Militiæque! —Horace, *Odes*, II, 6.6.
36. *La philosophie politique.*
37. *Fructus enim ingenii et virtutis omnisque præstantiæ tum maximus accipitur, quum in proximum quemque confertur.*—Cicero, *De Amicitia*, XIX.
38. See Diogenes Laertius, *Life of Plato*.
39. *Multi fallere docuerunt, dum timent falli et aliis jus peccandi suspicando fecerunt.*—Seneca, *Epistle 3*.
40. *S'il nous en reste en gros de quoy faire nostre effect.*
41. This "eighteen years" dates this part, at least, of the Essay in 1586.
42. *Servitus obedientia est fracti animi et abjecti, arbitrio carentis suo.*—Cicero, *Paradoxa;* V, 1.
43. *Sensus! O superi, sensus!* —Source unknown.
44. *De l'ordre de sa police.*
45. *Et cantharus et lanx*
Ostendunt mihi me.—Horace, *Epistles*, I, 5.23.
The true text is: *Ostendat tibi te.*
46. See Plato, *Letter 9* (to Archytas).
47. *Qui que ce soit, ou art ou nature.*

2019

Notes and Comments

48. That is, wisdom.
49.   *Pejoraque sæcula ferri*
Temporibus, quorum sceleri non invenit ipsa
Nomen, et a nullo posuit natura metallo.
—Juvenal, XIII, 28.
50. *Nous sommes tantost . . . envieillis.*
51.   *Quippe ubi fas versum atque nefas.*
—Virgil, *Georgics*, I, 505.
52.   *Armati terram exercent, semperque recentes*
Convectare juvat prædas et vivere rapto.
—Idem, *Æneid*, VII, 748.
53. Poneropolis—city of criminals; later, Philipopolis. See Plutarch, *Of Curiosity;* Pliny, *Nat. Hist.*, IV, 11.
54. *És arts.*
55. *Telle peinture de police.*
56. See Plutarch, *Life of Solon.*
57. See St. Augustine, *De Civ. Dei*, VI, 4.
58.   *Ayme l'Estat tel que tu le vois estre;*
S'il est royal, ayme la royauté;
S'il est de peu, ou bien communauté,
Ayme l'aussi, car Dieu t'y a faict naistre.
—Gui du Faur, seigneur de Pibrac.
He was of Toulouse, and died in 1584, aged 55.
59. Paul de Foix (1528-1584), to whom Montaigne dedicated La Boëtie's poems, which he published in 1570.
60. *Non tam commutandarum quam evertendarum rerum cupidi.*—Cicero, *De Off.*, II, 1.
61. This is carelessly phrased in the original. Montaigne means that Pacuvius followed the right course.
62. That is, the government house.
63. See Livy, XXIII, 3.

Of Vanity

64. *Eheu! cicatricum et sceleris pudet*
Fratrumque; quid nos dura refugimus
  Ætas! Quid intactum nefasti
  Liquimus? unde manum juventus
Metu Deorum continuit? quibus
  Pepercit aris? —Horace, *Odes*, I, 35.33.
65.   *Ipsa si velit Salus,*
Servare prorsus non potest hanc familiam.
          —Terence, *Adelphi*, IV, 7.43.
66. See Plato, *Republic*, book VIII.
67. *Si malotru.*
68. See Seneca, *Epistle* 73.
69. See Plutarch, *Consolation to Apollonius*. Plutarch attributes the saying to Socrates, and so did Montaigne in 1588; but on the Bordeaux copy he substituted Solon, "perhaps," says M. Villey, "on the authority of Valerius Maximus (VII, 2, *ext.* 2)."
70.   *Enimvero dii nos homines quasi pilas habent.*
        —Plautus, *Captivi, Prologue*, 22.
71. This refers to a passage in a letter from Isocrates the philosopher to Nicocles, King of the Cyprians. Montaigne, not reading Greek, must have taken it from some other source than the original. Translated, the passage reads: "Envy not those who have the widest rule, but those who use to the best purpose the power they possess."
72.   *Nec gentibus ullis*
Commodat in populum, terræ pelagique
  potentem,
Invidiam fortuna suam. —Lucan, I, 82.
73.   *Nec jam validis radicibus hærens,*
Pondere tuta suo est. —*Ibid.*, 138.

Notes and Comments

74. *Et sua sunt illis incommoda, parque per omnes Tempestas.*
—Adapted from Virgil, *Æneid*, XI, 422: *Sunt illis sua funera, parque per omnes tempestas.*

75. *Deus hæc fortasse benigna Reducet in sedem vice.*
—Horace, *Epodes*, XIII, 7.

76. *De ceux que le ciel nous envoye et proprement siens.*

77. *Pocula Lethæos ut si ducentia somnos Arente fauce traxerim.*
—Horace, *Epodes*, XIV, 3.

78. See Quintus Curtius, VII, 1.94.

79. That is, the military profession.

80. *En saye.*

81. *Nihil est his qui placere volunt tam adversarium quam expectatio.*—Cicero, *Academica*, II, 4.

82. See Idem, *Brutus*, LX.

83. *Simpliciora militares decent.*—Quintilian, *Inst. Orat.*, XI, 1.

84. *En lieu de respect.*

85. *Mon invention presente.*

86. *Ce coup d'essay.*

87. He means that he does not alter the expression of his thoughts. Cf. a similar statement at the beginning of Book II, chap. 37, p. 1025.

88. *Petite subtilité ambitieuse.*

89. See Cicero, *Academica*, II, 22.

90. The printers.

91. He refers to the passage on p. 1301, where he quotes Juvenal: *An age worse than the age of iron . . .*

92. *Lucro cessante, emergente damno.*

Of Vanity

93. In 1588: *à laquelle je me mesle plus volontiers.*
94. *De longue main.*
95. See Plutarch, *Lives of the ten orators* (Lycurgus).
96. *Je crois bien.*
97. *J'aymeroy bien plus cher.*
98. *De la jalousie de ma regle.*
99. *Hoc ipsum ita justum est quod recte fit, si est voluntarium.*—Cicero, *De Off.*, I, 9.
100. *Quod me jus cogit, vix voluntate impetrent.*
—Terence, *Adelphi*, III, 5.44.
101. *Quia quicquid imperio cogitur exigenti magis quam præstanti acceptum refertur.*—Valerius Maximus, II.
102. The last clause was omitted in 1595.
103. *Est prudentis sustinere, ut cursum, sic impetum benevolentiæ.*—Cicero, *De Amicitia*, XVII.
104. He refers to what he calls the acquittal of his debt.
105. Grun states that Montaigne wrote on the Bordeaux copy of 1588, and then erased: *Jamais roy ne me dona un double en paiement ni en don.*
106. *Nec sunt mihi nota potentum Munera.* —Virgil, *Æneid*, XII, 519.
107. *Un essentiel grammercy.*
108. *In me omnis spes est mihi.*—A paraphrase of Terence, *Adelphi*, III, 5.9: *In te spes omnis, Hegio, nobis sita est.*
109. *Nous mesmes, qui est la plus juste adresse et la plus seure, ne nous sommes pas assez asseurez.* Some such paraphrase as suggested seems necessary; the meaning is very obscure.
110. See Plato, *Hippias Minor;* Cicero, *De Oratore*, III, 32.

Notes and Comments

111. *Biens estrangers.*
112. See Chalcondylas, II, 12.
113. See Goulard, *Histoire du Portugal*, XIX, 6.
114. See the *Nicomachæan Ethics*, IV, 3, referring to the *Iliad*, I, 503.
115. *D'estre tenu ny à autre ny par autre que moy.*
116. This sentence of 1588 was omitted in 1595.
117. See the *Nicomachæan Ethics*, IX, 7.
118. Xenophon; see the *Cyropædeia*, VIII, 4.4.
119. See Livy, XXXVII, 6 and 25, and XXXVIII, 27.
120. That is, of both life and fortune.
121. *Impius hæc tam culta novalia miles habebit?*
—Virgil, *Eclogues*, I, 71.
122. This is one of the references to his ancestors which have brought criticism on Montaigne, but which are open to various explanations. Only his father was born at Montaigne, where his grandfather and great-grandfather had lived; and they did not give their name to the place, but took their name from it.
123. *Quam miserum porta vitam muroque tueri,*
Vixque suæ tutum viribus esse domus!
—Ovid, *Tristia*, IV, 1.69.
124. *Tum quoque, cum pax est, trepidant formidine belli.* —*Ibid.*, III, 10.67.
125. *Quoties pacem fortuna lacessit,*
Hac iter est bellis. Melius, fortuna, dedisses
Orbe sub Eoo sedem gelidaque sub Arcto,
Errantesque domos.
—Lucan, I, 256, 257, 251, 252.
126. *Plein d'insipidité et indolence.*
127. *Je ne m'estrange pas tant de l'estre mort comme*

Of Vanity

j'entre en confidence avec le mourir.

128. See Plutarch, *How one may derive profit from one's foes.*

129.   *Tam multæ scelerum facies!*
                              —Virgil, *Georgics*, I, 506.

130. When Montaigne's father was mayor of Bordeaux he was sent as deputy to the Court, in 1554 or 1555. Michel, then a young man of twenty-one or twenty-two, may have accompanied him.

131. See Plutarch, *Of Banishment.* Cf. Book I, chap. 26 (Vol. I, p. 210).

132. *Je ne suis guere feru de la douceur d'un air naturel.*

133. See Plutarch, *Of Banishment.* Pliny (*Nat. Hist.*, XXXI, 3) says: "Kings of the *Parthians.*"

134. See Plato, *Apology.*

135. *Bien tendre.*

136. See Idem, *Crito.*

137. *Quoy? qu'il plaignoit l'argent de ses amis à desengager sa vie.* See Idem., *Apology.*

138. See Idem, *Crito.*

139. That is, of those which I accept from respect rather than from sympathy.

140. Cf. Book I, chap. 26, p. 204: "For this reason intercourse with men is wonderful for it [education], and travel in foreign countries . . . chiefly to bring back the characteristics of those nations and their manner of living, and to rub and file our wits against those of others"; also the first sentence of chap. 17 of the same book, p. 90.

141. That is, the stone.

142.   *Vires ultra sortemque senectæ.*
                              —Virgil, *Æneid*, VI, 114.

2025

Notes and Comments

143. Cf. Xenophon, *Cyropædia*, VIII, 8. All that Xenophon says is: "In summer the shade of trees and rocks does not satisfy them; but under those, men stand near them with artificial shades contrived on purpose."

144. *Je l'en mets au propre.*

145. He is speaking of his wife.

146. *Il n'adviendra, que je puisse, à personne d'avoir l'usage de ses biens, plus liquide que moy, plus quiete et plus quitte.*

147. The wives.

148. *A se desprendre et reprendre à secousses.*

149. That is, "conjugal friendship."

150. See Plutarch, *Common conceptions against the Stoics.*

151. *Ante oculos errat domus, errat forma locorum.*
—Ovid, *Tristia*, III, 4.57.

152. *Excludat jurgia finis....*
Utor permisso caudæque pilos ut equinæ
Paulatim vello, et demo unum, demo etiam unum,
Dum cadat elusus ratione ruentis acervi.
—Horace, *Epistles*, II, 1.38, 45-47.

153. That is, philosophy.

154. *Rerum natura nullam nobis dedit cogitationem finium.*—Cicero, *Academica*, II, 29.

155. A town on the island of Rugen. See Saxo Grammaticus, *History of Denmark*, book XIV.

156. *Uxor, si cesses, aut te amare cogitat,*
Aut tete amari, aut potare, aut animo obsequi,
Et tibi bene esse soli, cum sibi sit male.
—Terence, *Adelphi*, I, 1.7.

Of Vanity

157. La Boëtie.

158. See Plato, *Laws*, book XII.

159. *Ceux qui courent un benefice ou un lievre ne courent pas; ceux-là courent qui courent aux barres et pour exercer leur course.* The amplification of the text seems necessary to bring out the sense.

160. *La secte plus renfroignée.* See Plutarch, *Contradictions of the Stoic philosophers*, and *Of Banishment*.

161. *Pour le gratter justement ou il luy cuit, ou qu'on ne le gratte point du tout.*

162. *Sage femme,* the French term for midwife.

163. See Crinitus, *De Honesta Disciplina*, XVIII, 12.

164. *Cette partie n'est pas du rolle de la societé.*

165. *Prendre la chevre.*

166. *Composées* here would seem to have somewhat the sense of *solemn.*

167. *Mes mœurs.*

168. *Ma peinture.*

169. *Sans s'escarmoucher au vent.*

170. See Diogenes Laertius, *Life of Bion.*

171.   *Excutienda damus præcordia.*—Persius, V, 22.

172. See Plutarch, *How to distinguish a flatterer from a friend;* Cicero, *De Amicitia*, VI.

173. See Herodotus, III, 99, 100.

174. *Les offices communes.*

175. That is, with those nearest us.

176. *Tout un aage.*

177. It has been suggested that he refers to Louis XI.

178. Probably an allusion to King David. See *I Kings*, I, 2, 3.

179. This sentence of 1588 was omitted in 1595.

Notes and Comments

180. *Tant qu'il fuira.*

181. *Verum animo satis hæc vestigia parva sagaci
   Sunt, per quæ possis cognoscere cætera tute.*
   —Lucretius, I, 402.

182. The allusion is to the publication of La Boëtie's *Le Contr'un.* Cf. Book I, chap. 28, pp. 259, 260.

183. The last six lines were omitted in 1595—by Mlle de Gournay?

184. The bands of those who wished to die together. See Plutarch, *Life of Antony.*

185. See Tacitus, *Annals,* XVI, 19, and *History,* I, 72. They were condemned by the Emperor Nero to put themselves to death.

186. *Vitam regit fortuna, non sapientia?*
   —Cicero, *Tusc. Disp.,* V, 9.

187. *A la facilité du marché de ma vie.*

188. *De trousser mes bribes.*

189. *Non ampliter sed munditer convivium; plus salis quam sumptus.*—The first phrase is quoted by Nonius, XI, 19, but was probably taken by Montaigne from Justus Lipsius, *Saturnalium sermonum libri,* I, 6; the last is from C. Nepos, *Atticus,* XIII.

190. *Couverts et resserrez.*

191. The last clause was omitted in 1595.

192. *Si cum hac exceptione detur sapientia, ut illam inclusam teneam nec enuntiem, rejiciam.*—Seneca, *Epistle* 6.

193. *Si contigerit ea vita sapienti ut, omnium rerum affluentibus copiis, quamvis omnia, quæ cognitione digna sunt, summo otio secum ipse consideret et contempletur, tamen si solitudo tanta sit ut hominem videre non possit, excedat e vita.*—Cicero, *De Off.,* I, 43.

Of Vanity

194. See Idem, *De Amicitia*, XXIII.
195. See Xenophon, *Memorabilia*, II, 1.
196. *Me si fata meis paterentur ducere vitam*
  Auspiciis. —Virgil, *Æneid*, IV, 340.
197. *Visere gestiens,*
Qua parte debacchentur ignes,
Qua nebulæ pluviique rores.
—Horace, *Odes*, III, 3.54.
198. The quotation marks indicate imaginary speech.
199. King Henri IV supped and slept at Montaigne, December 19, 1584. On October 23, 1587, he was there again and remained some days.
200. *Quæ te nunc coquat et vexet sub pectore fixa?*
—Ennius, in Cicero, *De Senectute*, I. Taken by Montaigne from J. Lipsius, *De Constantia*, I, 8; but he has changed the text, which is: *Quæ nunc te coquit et versat sub pectore fixa.*
201. *Nunquam simpliciter fortuna indulget.*—Quintus Curtius, IV, 14.
202. *Nulla placida quies est, nisi quam ratio composuit.* —Seneca, *Epistle* 56.
203. *A le prendre à la lettre.*
204. *Cela mesme me nourrit.*
205. *Et que j'ay ou m'en divertir commodéement.*
206. *Alter remus aquas, alter mihi radat arenas.*
—Propertius, III, 3.23.
207. *Dominus novit cogitationes sapientium, quoniam vanæ sunt.*—Psalm XCIV, 55.
208. *Quisque suos patimur manes.*
—Virgil, *Æneid*, VI, 743.
209. *Sic est faciendum ut contra naturam universam*

2029

Notes and Comments

nihil contendamus; ea tamen conservata propriam sequamur.—Cicero, *De Off.*, I, 31.

210. The daughter of Cato of Utica, who killed herself when she learned of the death of Brutus, her husband, after the battle of Philippi. See Plutarch, *Life of Brutus*.

211. Perhaps Antoine Muret, or Théodore de Bèze.

212. See Plutarch, *Of Hearing*.

213. See *Ibid*.

214. Diogenes Laertius in his *Life of Xenophon* speaks of Xenophon's love for Clinias.

215. *Curentur dubii medicis majoribus ægri.*
 —Juvenal, XIII, 124.

216. See Diogenes Laertius, *Life of Antisthenes*.

217. See Idem, *Life of Diogenes the Cynic*.

218. See Antoine de Guevara, *Golden Letters*.

219. *Nemo satis credit tantum delinquere quantum
 Permittas.* —Juvenal, XIV, 233.

220. *Olle, quid ad te
De cute quid faciat ille, vel illa sua?*
 —Martial, VII, 9.1.

221. *Let loix qui nous condamnent à ne pouvoir pas nous condamnent de ce que nous ne pouvons.*

222. *Mes mœurs mesme, qui ne disconviennent de celles qui courent à peine de la largeur d'un poulce.*

223. *Exeat aula
Qui vult esse pius.* —Lucan, VIII, 493.

224. See the *Republic*, book VI.

225. See *Ibid*.

226. *At tu, Catulle, obstinatus obdura.*
 —Catullus, VIII, 19.

227. See Plato, *Gorgias*.

Of Vanity

228. See Trebellius Pollio, *Triginta Tyranni.*

229. *L'innocence civile. Innocence* = freedom from wrong-doing.

230. *J'aymerois bien à voir en Xenophon.* This phrase has the same ironic sense as in English: "I should like to see him do it," and means: "I should be surprised to find in Xenophon." Montaigne had in mind the passage of Charles V through France in 1540, and he contrasts the tone of Xenophon's day with that of his own, and with that of other periods. But see Xenophon, *Agesilaus,* III and IV.

231. *Ces babouyns capettes.*

232. *Egregium sanctumque virum si cerno, bimembri*
Hoc monstrum puero, et miranti jam sub aratro
Piscibus inventis, et fœtæ comparo mulæ.
—Juvenal, XIII, 64.

233. Antony, Octavius, and Lepidus.

234. *Quo diversus abis?* —Virgil, *Æneid,* V, 166.

235. *Cette farcissure*—about the inconsistency between precepts and practice.

236. The *Phædrus.*

237. The ancient writers.

238. Two plays of Terence.

239. Sylla's name is said to have been given him because of his colour. Says Amyot, in a note to his translation of Plutarch's *Life of Sylla:* "*Syl* in Latin signifies ochre, which turns red when it is put into the fire."

In his *Life of Cicero,* Plutarch says: "I think that the first who bore the name of Cicero was some personage of note, and that, from love of him, his descendants did not drop that name but were very glad to retain it; although many made fun of it, because *cicer* means a dried pea, and

Notes and Comments

the great Cicero had a wart or something of the sort on the end of his nose, which resembled a dried pea, and they said that he was called Cicero because of that."

Torquatus (surname of Manlius) comes from the Latin *Torquis*, a necklace. The name was given to him because of a necklace that he took from a Gaul in single combat. See Livy, VII, 10; Aulus Gellius, IX, 13.

240. *Un art leger, volage, demoniacle.* See Plato, *Ion.*

241. *Je vais au change.*

242. *Il luy faut certes quitter la maistrise et preeminence en la parlerie.*

243. See Plato, *Laws*, book IV.

244. *Nihil est tam utile quod in transitu prosit.*—Seneca, *Epistle* 2.

245. See Aulus Gellius, XX, 5.5; Plutarch, *Life of Alexander.*

246. Rome.

247. *Retrogradation et reflexion.*

248. See Diogenes Laertius, *Life of Arcesilaus.* Montaigne first called the friend Appelles, which is the name given by Plutarch in telling the story in *How to distinguish a flatterer from a friend.* On the Bordeaux copy of 1588, after reading Laertius, he changed the name to Ctesibius.

249. See Cicero, *De Fin.*, V, 1.

250. *Tanta vis admonitionis inest in locis! Et id quidem in hac urbe infinitum; quacumque enim ingredimur in aliquam historiam vestigium ponimus.*—*Ibid.*, 1 and 2.

251. *Ego illos veneror et tantis nominibus semper assurgo.*—Seneca, *Epistle* 64.

252. *Laudandis preciosior ruinis.*
—Sidonius Apollinaris, *Carmina*, XXIII, 62.

Of Vanity

253. *Ut palam sit uno in loco gaudentis opus esse naturæ.*—Pliny, *Nat. Hist.*, III, 5.

254. *Nos humeurs.*

255.   *Quanto quisque sibi plura negaverit,*
A dis plura feret. Nil cupientium
Nudus castra peto.
... Multa petentibus
Desunt multa.
—Horace, *Odes*, III, 16.21, 22, 42, 43.

256.   *Nihil supra Deos lacesso.*—*Ibid.*, II, 18.11.

257. *Mais, gare le heurt!* Formerly a cry of drivers of cattle, or of persons meeting at cross-roads.

258.   *Fortunæ cætera mando.*
—Ovid, *Metam.*, 11, 140.

259. *Bona jam nec nasci licet, ita corrupta sunt semina.*—Tertullian, *Apologetica.*

260. *Quod Horatius Maximus, Martius Cecius, Alexander Mutus, almæ urbis conservatores de Illustrissimo viro Michaele Montano, equite sancti Michaelis, et a Cubiculo Regis Christianissimi, Romana civitate donando, ad Senatum retulerunt, S.P.Q.R. de ea re ita fieri censuit.*

CUM veteri more et instituto cupide illi semper studioseque suscepti sint, qui virtute ac nobilitate præstantes, magno Reip. nostræ usui atque ornamento fuissent, vel esse aliquando possent: Nos majorum nostrorum exemplo atque auctoritate permoti, præclaram hanc Consuetudinem nobis imitandam ac servandam fore censemus. Quamobrem cum Illustrissimus Michael Montanus Eques sancti Michaelis, et a cubiculo Regis Christianissimi, Romani nominis studiosissimus, et familiæ laude atque splendore et propriis virtutum meritis dignissimus sit, qui summo Senatus Popu-

Notes and Comments

lique Romani judicio ac studio in Romanam Civitatem adsciscatur, placere Senatui P.Q.R. Illustrissimum Michaelem Montanum rebus omnibus ornatissimum, atque huic inclyto Populo charissimum, ipsum posterosque, in Romanam civitatem adscribi, ornarique omnibus et præmiis et honoribus, quibus illi fruuntur, qui Cives Patritiique Romani nati aut jure optimo facti sunt. In quo censere Senatum P.Q.R. se non tam illi Jus Civitatis largiri quam debitum tribuere, neque magis beneficium dare quam ab ipso accipere, qui hoc Civitatis munere accipiendo, singulari Civitatem ipsam ornamento atque honore affecerit. Quam quidem S.C. auctoritatem iidem Conservatores per Senatus P.Q.R. scribas in acta referri atque in Capitolii curia servari, privilegiumque hujusmodi fieri, solitoque urbis sigillo communiri, curarunt. Anno ab urbe condito CXƆCCCXXXI. post Christum natum M.D.LXXXI.III. Idus Martii.

Horatius Fuscus sacri S.P.Q.R. scriba.
Vincent. Martholus sacri S.P.Q.R. scriba.

261. That is, ourselves.

CHAPTER X

Of the Management of One's Will

A. THE COMMENT BY MISS NORTON

SAINTE-BEUVE has said of this Essay that it was inspired by Montaigne's remembrances of his mayoralty. This is to a high degree true, but the Essay is greater than this alone would indicate. It is an admirable plea for the point of view which considers the *man* as, in every sense, of more importance than the *office;* which estimates what a man can *do* as of little consequence in comparison with what he can *be*, and can be *for himself alone*. Since (in theory) all the work of public life is, at bottom, for the purpose of obtaining happiness for men as individuals, Montaigne aims at once at the result (he does not say so), and urges, only by the expression of his own opinion, every man to make *himself* "happy." It need scarcely be indicated that the weakness in this revolutionising and "impressive" reasoning is the fact that it is not entirely a matter of will, of personal effort, but of spiritual good-fortune, if happiness is attained in unhappy circumstances, if a scourged slave can be content; and it is not easy, and it is questionable if it be right, for a free man—using "freedom" and "slavery" in their widest application—to be happy in the presence of misery, without doing his utmost to relieve it. And to do one's "utmost" in this direction is the kind of life of which

Notes and Comments

Montaigne says: "This fashion of life that I praise in another I do not like to follow myself: and I am not without excuse."

His "excuse" is set forth in this Essay, as elsewhere, wonderfully well, but not convincingly. But perhaps no Essay is of more valuable weight than this in balancing the mind justly, in opposition to the influences of to-day, concerning the claims of the active and the inactive life. And nowhere has Montaigne's voice more personal authority than here, being the voice of one whose ability in *work*, in active work, is as unquestionable to those who carefully study his life as in *meditation*.

But his all-justifying "excuse" is something he never himself thought of in that light: the production of the Essays. It is impossible not to believe that he has served and aided more fellow men by this means than he could have done by any devotion to public interests during his lifetime. And the conclusion that must always be reached is that each man must—and *should*—act according to his nature.

I think this Essay might well begin on the last page of the preceding one, with the sentence: "This common fashion and custom of looking elsewhere than at ourselves," etc. Montaigne goes on to assert (ironically) that mankind does well not to "consider" itself, to look always elsewhere than inwards, and then, quoting the Delphian oracle, he cries out with scorn to think that man, the poorest of all animals, should be the only one who foolishly embraces the universe.

This is a fit introduction to the opening of this Essay, where he says that he himself does not attempt to embrace the universe, that both from nature and by effort he "es-

Of the Management of One's Will

pouses very few things." And he states admirably *why* he will "not go far from himself"; he describes excellently those whose minds "find rest in motion; who busy themselves about the quarrels of one neighbour, and the pulse of another, and the will of a third."

Then he turns to his own public employment as mayor, to explain his acceptance of it and to describe his mode of executing it. The thought of his father's mode of executing it leads him back to the same reflection as before, that the greater number of the rules and precepts current in the world assume it to be a fine effect to turn us away from ourselves.

He dwells still on the character of the friendship we owe to ourselves, setting forth that it implies public duties, and he utters the noble truth: "He who does not live somewhat for others scarcely lives for himself." Returning later to the claims of public affairs, there is a sentence that has been too much overlooked in depicting Montaigne as an easy-going egotist: "I would not that he should refuse his attention, his steps, his words, his sweat, and his blood if there be need."

In the letter, dated May 22, 1585, addressed by Montaigne (mayor) to M. de Matignon, then lieutenant for the king at Bordeaux,—a letter of which Sainte-Beuve says: "It shews us Montaigne in the full exercise of his office, and in all the activity and vigilance in his power. The *soi-disant* idler had, at need, many more of these active qualities than he promised,"—he assured the marshal: "We shall spare nothing, neither our care, nor, if need be, our lives, to retain every thing under subjection to the king." Sainte-Beuve remarks: "Montaigne was not prodigal of protestations and phrases, and what with others would be a mere form is here a real and verified engagement."

Notes and Comments

To return to the Essay itself: Montaigne, speaking of public affairs in general, passes from depicting the manner in which many men *assume* them—incorporate themselves in them—to speak of his own personal separation from them, and of his relation to the public parties of his day, and then of the relation of the people to the public parties, declaring: "It is a mistake to throw ourselves so headlong in pursuit of our inclinations and our interests." As who do? "The feverish parties," I think, of the preceding page; "the minds which stupidly see things only by halves."

These several pages in the spirit of the prayer, "Lead us not into temptation," are interesting and characteristic, and so peculiarly *undulating* and living that no dead résumé can be made of them.

B. THE NOTES BY MR. IVES

1. Sainte-Beuve's article on "Montaigne maire de Bordeaux" (*Nouveaux Lundis*, VI) should be read, without fail, in connection with this chapter. A letter from Montaigne to the maréchal de Matignon, which is to be found in several editions of the Essays, should also be read; and there is another letter of similar character, which was discovered only in 1863, and has not often been printed.

2. *Le sens.*

3. These last clauses are very obscure.

4. See Plato, *Laws*, book VII.

5.   *Fugax rerum, securaque in otia natus.*
                                —Ovid, *Tristia*, III, 2.9.

6. *Si je mordois à mesme.*

7. *De les prendre en main, non pas au poulmon et au foye.*

Of the Management of One's Will

8. *Que j'ay dans mes entrailles et dans mes veines.*
9. *Cette humeur commune.*
10. Seneca, *Epistle* 22. Montaigne translates the words after quoting them.
11. See Idem, *Epistle* 94.
12. See Idem, *De Brevitate Vitæ*, III, 1.
13.   *Incedis per ignes*
    Suppositos cineri doloso.
              —Horace, *Odes*, II, 1.7.
14. *Messieurs.*
15.   *Uterque bonus pacis bellique minister.*
         —Virgil, *Æneid*, XI, 658.
16. Pierre Eyquem, Montaigne's father, was chosen mayor of Bordeaux for two years, August 1, 1554.
17. *Imperiti enim judicant, et qui frequenter in hoc ipsum fallendi sunt ne errent.*—Quintilian, *Inst. Orat.*, II, 17.28.
18. See Plutarch, *How to distinguish a flatterer from a friend.*
19. *Il est vrayment du cabinet des Muses.*
20. *Qui sibi amicus est, scito hunc amicum omnibus esse.*—Seneca, *Epistle* 6. The text of Seneca is changed.
21.   *Non ipse pro charis amicis*
    Aut patria timidus perire.
             —Horace, *Odes*, IV, 9.51.
22. See Plutarch, *Of Banishment.*
23. *L'un va bien sans l'autre.*
24. See Seneca, *Epistle* 62.
25. See Idem, *De Ira*, I, 12.
26.   *Male cuncta ministrat*
  Impetus.   —Statius, *Thebaïd*, X, 704.

Notes and Comments

27. See Seneca, *De Ira*, I, 15 and 16.
28. *Festinatio tarda est.*—Quintus Curtius, IX, 9.12.
29. *La hastivité se donne elle mesme la jambe.*
30. *Ipsa se velocitas implicat.*—Seneca, *Epistle* 44.
31. The King of Navarre, afterward Henri IV.
32. *Il est toujours chez soi.*
33. See Seneca, *Epistle* 16, 7 and 9.
34. *Nam si, quod satis est homini, id satis esse potesset,*
    Hoc sat erat; nunc, quum hoc non est, qui credimus porro
    Divitias ullas animum mi explere potesse?
    —Lucilius, book V, quoted by Nonius Marcellus, *De Differentia*, etc., V, 98.
35. See Cicero, *Tusc. Disp.*, V, 32.
36. See Seneca, *Epistle* 18.
37. See Plutarch, *That vice alone suffices to make man unhappy.*
38. *Sufficit ad id natura quad poscit.*—Seneca, *Epis.* 90.
39. See Diogenes Laertius, *Life of Cleanthes*. It was Zeno who said this of Cleanthes.
40. *Quo mihi fortuna, si non conceditur uti?*
    —Horace, *Epistles*, I, 5.12.
41. In this passage of 1595, from the quotation from Horace above, the text of 1588 is considerably expanded and modified.
42. In 1582, Pope Gregory XIII reformed the calendar by dropping ten days.
43. *En despit de mes dents.*
44. *Cette forme m'est passée en substance, et fortune en nature.*

2040

Of the Management of One's Will

45. See Seneca, *De Tranquillitate Animi*, X.
46. *S'entend voisine reflexion et essentielle.*
47. *De pointe.*
48. *Mundus universus exercet histrioniam.*—A fragment of Petronius, taken by Montaigne from J. Lipsius, *De Constantia*, I, 8.
49. *Se prelatent.*
50. *Les bonnetades.*
51. *Tantum se fortunæ permittunt etiam ut naturam dediscant.*—Quintus Curtius, III, 2.18.
52. *Neque extra necessitates belli præcipuum odium gero.*—Source unknown.
53. *D'autant que je voy communement faillir au contraire.*
54. *Non tam omnia universi quam ea quæ ad quemque pertinerent singuli carpebant.*—Livy, XXXIV, 36.
55. Montaigne tells in the *Journal de Voyage* (Rome) of the criticisms of his book made by the censor, and that among them objection was taken to what he said of heretical poets (Théodore de Bèze) in the Essay "Of Presumption" (Book II, chap. 17).
56. See Livy, VI, 18.
57. *De ceux que les singeries d'Apollonius et de Mahumed embufflerent.*
58. *Une grande moderation.*
59. *Je me penche à l'opposite de son inclination, comme je la voy se plonger et s'enyvrer de son vin.*
60. See Plutarch, *Apothegms of the Lacedæmonians*.
61. See Idem, *Apothegms of Kings*, etc.
62. *Melius non incipient quam desinent.*—Seneca, *Epistle* 72.

Notes and Comments

63. *Faisant luicter les maux par la vigueur de la patience.*
64.   *Velut rupes vastum quæ prodit in æquor,*
 Obvia ventorum furiis expostaque ponto,
 Vim cunctam atque minas perfert cœlique
  marisque,
 Ipsa immota manens.
       —Virgil, *Æneid*, X, 693.
65. That is, such men.
66. That is to say, we must provide against the feelings that may arise, not against meeting the storm.
67. See Diogenes Laertius, *Life of Zeno*.
68. See Xenophon, *Memorabilia*, I, 3.13.
69. This sentence was omitted in 1595.
70. Xenophon. See the *Cyropædeia*, V, 1.2-8.
71. *Là vous les prendrez sans vert.*
72.   *In tam diversa, magister,*
 Ventus et unda trahunt. —Source unknown. Montaigne translates the lines before quoting them.
73. *Propension tyrannique. Propension* was introduced into the language by Montaigne.
74. See Seneca, *Epistle* 85.
75. See *Epistle* 116.
76. See *Epistle* 85.
77. *Etenim ipsæ se impellunt, ubi semel a ratione discessum est; ipsaque sibi imbecillitas indulget, in altumque provehitur imprudens nec reperit locum consistendi.*—Cicero, *Tusc. Disp.*, IV, 18.
78.   *Ceu flamina prima,*
 Cum deprensa fremunt sylvis, et cæca volutant
 Murmura, venturos nautis prodentia ventos.
       —Virgil, *Æneid*, X, 97.

Of the Management of One's Will

79. *Convenit a litibus, quantum licet, et nescio an paulo plus etiam quam licet abhorrentem esse; est enim non modo liberale paululum nonnunquam de suo jure decedere, sed interdum etiam fructuosum.*—Cicero, De Off., II, 18.

80. *Sans avoir ouy pis que mon nom.*

81. The reference here is to the war in 1476 between Charles the Bold and the Swiss. Commines (V, 1) says: *Et pour quelle querelle commença cette guerre? Ce fut pour une chariot de peaux de mouton que monseigneur de Romont prit à un Suisse en passant par sa terre.*

82. The civil war between Marius and Sylla. Plutarch (*Life of Marius*) narrates that, when Marius was on the point of obtaining possession of the person of Jugurtha, the latter fell by treachery into the hands of Sylla, who afterward always used a seal commemorating this, *pour faire despit à Marius.*

83. See Plutarch, *How to learn whether one improves and benefits by the practice of virtue.*

84. See Plutarch, *Of False Shame.*

85. See Diogenes Laertius, *Life of Bias.*

86. *Vous vous soubmettez.*

87. *Abscinduntur facilius animo quam temperantur.*—Source unknown.

88. The Stoics.

89. Cf. Book I, chap. 54, p. 417: "The simple peasants," etc.

90. *Felix qui potuit rerum cognoscere causas*
Atque metus omnes et inexorabile fatum
Subjecit pedibus strepitumque Acherontis avari!
Fortunatus et ille deos qui novit agrestes,
Panaque, Sylvanumque senem, Nymphasque

Notes and Comments

91. *sorores!* —Virgil, *Georgics*, II, 490.
*Jure perhorrui
Late conspicuum tollere verticem.*
—Horace, *Odes*, III, 16.18.

92. As mayor of Bordeaux.

93. *Cum semper natura, tum etiam ætate jam quietus.* —Quintus Cicero, *De Petitione Consulatus*, II.

94. *Si elles se desbauchent par fois.*

95. *J'ay un agir trepignant.*

96. *Neque submissam et abjectam, neque se efferentem.*—Cicero, *De Off.*, I, 34.

97. *Ny les choses qui nous oignent, au prix de celles qui nous poignent.* "Montaigne," says M. Villey, "doubtless recalled, in connection with the play upon the words *oignent* and *poignent*, the popular couplet:

Oignez vilain, il vous poindra;
Poignez vilain, il vous oindra."

98. See Plutarch, *How to distinguish a flatterer from a friend.*

99. See Idem, *Life of Alexander.*

100. See Plato, *First Alcibiades.*

101. See Plutarch, *How to learn whether one improves and benefits by the practice of virtue.*

102. *Non nobis, Domine, non nobis, sed nomini tuo da gloriam.*—Psalm CXV, 1.

103. See Plutarch, *Common conceptions against the Stoics.*

104. See Cicero, *De Off.*, II, 22.

105. *Quæ est ista laus quæ possit e macello peti?*—Idem, *De Fin.*, II, 15.

106. *Mihi quidem laudabiliora videntur omnia quæ*

Of Cripples

sine venditatione et sine populo teste fiunt.—Cicero, *Tusc. Disp.*, II, 26.

107. *Je n'avois qu'à conserver et durer.*

108.   *Mene huic confidere monstro!*
Mene salis placidi vultum fluctusque quietos
   Ignorare.   —Virgil, *Æneid*, V, 849, 848.

Montaigne has inverted the order of the lines, and omitted *jubes* after *ignorare*.

CHAPTER XI

Of Cripples

A. THE COMMENT BY MISS NORTON

IN the preceding Essay, Montaigne has said how much the reform in the calendar (which, in France, went into effect in 1582, when they passed at once from the 9th to the 20th of December) bothered him. Here he recurs to it, to contemplate it from his familiar point of view, the uncertainty of human "reason."

The thought on the next page, that men, with regard to the facts set before them, occupy themselves more readily in seeking the reason than the truth of them, is the opening of the most definite argument for doubt that occurs in the Essays. Elsewhere we have seen Montaigne apparently curiously credulous; here the scales decidedly dip on the other

2045

side; and, as Voltaire said: "The man who would learn to doubt should read this essay." He will learn here how to doubt wisely, intelligently, calmly, contentedly, with no touch of the spirit of the scoffer. He will learn the reasonable sources of doubt—its rightful causes—as derived from the conditions of human nature.

M. Villey has well stated Montaigne's own attitude. "When he comes forth from doubt, and he comes forth very resolutely, it is alone the authority of the fact that obliges his reason to accept it. Whenever he can clearly mark the meaning of facts, he comes to a decision; and he remains in doubt in all cases where the facts do not seem to him to dictate an answer. The Essay 'Of Cripples' has much significance from this point of view."

The passage beginning "I myself" is a convincing proof of the slight dependence to be put on human testimony, on the expressions of opinion. It is questionable whether Montaigne is not lacking in sound judgement in what he says on the next page: "For my part what I should not believe when asserted by one man, I should not believe if asserted by a hundred." Cumulative testimony is surely different, not merely in *degree* but in *kind*, from a solitary testimony. Like a composite photograph, it proves the facts that the independent assertions testify to.

This Essay indicates, as can be constantly observed in Montaigne's pages, how much interested he was by "miracles," by the inexplicable; he tells countless stories of "such matters," for the truth of which he vouches as little as he seeks for the cause. His verdict was: "The Court understands nothing of this"; but it is evident that the pleadings entertained him. And it may have been, it seems to me, be-

Of Cripples

cause he in some measure foresaw, as Bacon foresaw, that some of these wonders would be explained, not denied, by the clear-sightedness of coming science.

A propos, ou hors de propos, of this question of beliefs, of opinions,—of their grounds,—he comes to beliefs about cripples, and from this paragraph the Essay received its irrelevant name.

B. THE NOTES BY MR. IVES

1. The extra day in leap year.
2. *Jusques à ce qu'on fust arrivé à satisfaire exactement ce debte.*
3. *Que nous n'avons encore achevé d'arrester.*
4. That is, astronomy. See Plutarch, *Roman Questions.*
5. *Subjection et apprentissage.*
6. *Sur le vuide que sur le plain.*
7.   *Dare corpus idonea fumo.*   —Persius, V, 20.
8. *Il n'en est rien.*
9. *Ita finitima sunt falsa veris ut in præcipitem locum non debeat se sapiens committere.*—Cicero, *Academica,* II, 21.
10. That is, with miracles.
11. *Insita hominibus libidine alendi de industria rumores.*—Livy, XXVIII, 24.
12. See Seneca, *Epistle* 81.29.
13. Cf. Book I, chap. 9, p. 41: "In truth, lying is an accursed vice"; and Book II, chap. 17, p. 877: "My soul, by its nature, shuns falsehood, and hates even to think a falsehood."
14. *Quasi vero quidquam sit tam valde quam nil sapere vulgare.*—Cicero, *De Divin.*, II, 39.

Notes and Comments

15. *Sanitatis patrocinium est insanientium turba.*—St. Augustine, *De Civ. Dei*, VI, 10.

16. *Apprehension.*

17. *En l'architecte de tels ouvrages.*

18. *Qui les reconnoistroit en leur giste.*

19. *Miramur ex intervallo fallentia.*—Seneca, *Epistle* 118.

20. *Nunquam ad liquidum fama perducitur.*—Quintus Curtius, IX, 2.

21. See Cicero, *Academica*, II, 47.

22. See Plato, *Theætetus.* Iris, as the messenger of the gods, represents the highest knowledge, that is, philosophy. Thaumas (not Thaumantis) is wonder.

23. The report was printed in 1560.

24. Montaigne refers to the *cause célèbre* of the false Martin Guerre, which the elder Dumas introduced in his story of *The Two Dianas*.

25. See Valerius Maximus, VIII, 1, *ext.* 2.

26. *Cettuy-cy en est.*

27. *Soit qu'il l'employe au faict d'autruy, soit qu'il l'employe contre soy-mesme.*

28. *Majorem fidem homines adhibent iis quæ non intelligunt.*—Source unknown.

29. *Cupidine humani ingenii libentius obscura creduntur.*—Tacitus, *History*, I, 22.

30. *Je vois bien qu'on se courrouce.*

31. *Videantur sane, non affirmentur modo.*—Cicero, *Academica*, II, 27.

32. See *De Civ. Dei*, XIX, 18.

33. *Captisque res magis mentibus quam consceleratis similis visa.*—Livy, VIII, 18.

Of Cripples

34. See St. Augustine, *De Civ. Dei*, XVIII, 18.
35. *Que nostre volonté en fust tenue à la justice.*
36. *C'est par maniere de devis que je parle de tout, et de rien par maniere d'advis.*
37. *Nec me pudet ut istos fateri nescire quod nesciam.* —Cicero, *Tusc. Disp.*, I, 25.
38. *Des complexions.*
39. See Tasso, *Paragon dell'Italia alla Francia.*
40. See Suetonius, *Life of Caligula.*
41. See Plutarch, *Political Precepts;* Erasmus, *Adages* (*cothurno versatilior*).
42. See Plutarch, *Of False Shame;* Seneca, *De Beneficiis,* II, 17.
43. *Seu plures calor ille vias et cæca relaxat*
     Spiramenta, novas veniat qua succus in herbas;
     Seu durat magis, et venas astringit hiantes,
     Ne tenues pluviæ, rapidive potentia solis
     Acrior, aut Boreæ penetrabile frigus adurat.
     —Virgil, *Georgics,* I, 89.
44. *Ogni medaglia ha il suo riverso.*—Italian proverb.
45. See Cicero, *Academica,* II, 34.
46. *Monts et merveilles.*

CHAPTER XII

Of Physiognomy

A. THE COMMENT BY MISS NORTON

IN this Essay, as in some others, the reason for the title does not appear till toward the end: the word "physiognomy" does not occur for some thirty pages. It always interests me to trace out the possible origin of this seeming unfitness of the title, and in this case I find the following explanation.

It is evident that Montaigne's thoughts were at this moment much occupied by Socrates, and, lover of beauty that he was, in thinking of him he had felt over and over again how much he regretted that Socrates had "a figure and face so ill favoured and so unfitting the beauty of his soul"; and thus being led to consider what and how much the physiognomy means, he thought it a good subject for an Essay. But, the title being written, it was of the soul of Socrates that he began to think more than of his body, and for some pages he discourses admirably on him and his philosophy. The character of this philosophy leads Montaigne to comment on what he has been observing lately in the peasants—*les pauvres gens*—around him; and from this the transition is natural to a long account of *nos troubles*—the civil war and the plague—and his own share of them.

Sainte-Beuve, in writing of this Essay (*Causeries de*

Of Physiognomy

Lundi, IV, 93), says: "The consolation that Montaigne here offers to himself and to others is as lofty and as beautiful as human consolation, without prayer, can be." On another page he remarks: "All this chapter is fine, touching, fitting, giving evidence both of a noble stoical elevation and of the easy and kindly nature that Montaigne by good right said had been given him by birth and education."

A valuable and forever timely part of the Essay is the praise that follows of *simplicity*, of keeping close to nature, to simple and natural conditions of feeling, of which Socrates's address to his judges, "of unimaginable loftiness, true, frank, and just," is a perfect example. These pages deserve immortality. They are chiefly concerned with our feelings about death, but they are of large outlook and inclusion.

From these high moral thoughts, Montaigne slips easily into remarks on the simplicity of the *style* of Socrates, and from these to half-jesting about the ornamentation of his own style from a superabundance of quotations, in which matter he had "yielded to public opinion." The sentence with which he closes this passage about his own writings— "I have chosen the time when my life all lay open to my sight"—is delightfully like him.

(Sainte-Beuve has somewhere happily said—he can not be quoted too often—that when Montaigne speaks of himself and judges himself, he should always be listened to with smiling intelligence—with something of his own smile.)

Then he enters abruptly on what he was thinking of when he sat down to the Essay—the appearance of Socrates; from that he passes to "physiognomy" in general; from that to his own looks (illustrated by two stories), and so to his own

Notes and Comments

goodness of heart, which makes him merciful even to the wicked; and thus he closes this most interesting meditation, for which still another title might be "A Eulogy of Socrates."

B. THE NOTES BY MR. IVES

1. Cf. Book II, chap. 12, p. 722: "For the opinions of men are received in continuance of ancient beliefs, by authority and on credit."
2. See Plato, *Banquet*.
3. Socrates.
4.   *Servare modum, finemque tenere, Naturamque sequi.*   —Lucan, II, 381.
5. Cf. Cicero, *De Off.*, I, 26.
6. *Mais ravala plustost et ramena à son point originel et naturel, et lui submit la vigueur,* etc.
7. Socrates.
8. *Les plus beaux effects.*
9. That is, toward the primitive nature of man.
10. *Ut omnium rerum, sic litterarum quoque, intemperantia laboramus.*—Seneca, *Epistle* 106. Taken by Montaigne from J. Lipsius, *Politics*, I, 10.
11. See Tacitus, *Agricola*, IV.
12. *Paucis opus est litteris ad mentem bonam.*—Seneca, *Epistle* 106.
13. *Quand je me trouve au propre.*
14. *Quæ magis gustata quam potata delectant.*—Cicero, *Tusc. Disp.*, V, 5.
15. *Tout ce qui plaist, ne paist pas.*
16. *Ubi non ingenii, sed animi negotium agitur.*—Seneca, *Epistle* 75.

Of Physiognomy

17. *A le voir suer d'ahan pour se roidir, et pour s'asseurer, et se desbattre si long temps en cette perche.*

18. *Magnus animus remissius loquitur et securius.*—Seneca, *Epistle* 115.2.

19. *Non est alius ingenio alius animo color.*—Idem, *Epistle* 114.3.

20. The text of 1588 has *nous esveille*, which was omitted in 1595.

21. *Simplex illa et aperta virtus in obscuram et solertem scientiam versa est.*—Seneca, *Epistle* 95.

22. The civil wars.

23. *Non armis sed vitiis certatur.*—Source unknown.

24.   *Hostis adest dextra lævaque a parte timendus,*
        Vicinoque malo terret utrumque latus.
                —Ovid, *De Ponto*, I, 3.57.

25.   *Nostre mal s'empoisonne*
    Du secours qu'on luy donne.
—Source unknown; the lines are found in Bouchet's *Les Serées*, but M. Villey thinks that he took them from Montaigne.

26.   *Exuperat magis ægrescitque medendo.*
               —Virgil, *Æneid*, XII, 46.

27.   *Omnia fanda, nefanda, malo permista furore,*
    Justificam nobis mentem avertere deorum.
—Catullus, *Epithalamium of Thetis and Pelius*, 406.

28. That is, according to individual judgement.

29. That is, in managing troops than in leading them.

30.   *Hunc saltem everso juvenem succurrere seclo*
    Ne prohibite!   —Virgil, *Georgics*, I, 500.

31. See Valerius Maximus, II, 7, ext. 2.

32. See Frontenius, *Stratagematica*, IV, 3.13.

Notes and Comments

33. This must refer to the commander of the military order known as the Knights of Rhodes, or Knights of Malta, who had possession of the island of Rhodes until 1522, when that island was seized by the Turks, and the Knights were given the island of Malta.

34. See G. Postel, *History of the Turks*.

35. See Paul Jovius, *History of his own time*.

36. As civil war.

37. *L'usurpation de la possession tyrannique.* See Plutarch, *Life of Brutus*.

38. See Plato, *Epistle* 7 (To the kinsmen of Dion).

39. That is, as not being a Christian.

40. *A qui on aye en bon escient persuadé.*

41. *Nihil in speciem fallacius quam prava religio, ubi deorum numen prætenditur sceleribus.*—Livy, XXXIX, 16.

42. See Plato, *Republic*, book II.

43. When he was writing this. See p. 1419 *supra*.

44.   *Undique totis*
  Usque adeo turbatus agris.
     —Virgil, *Eclogues*, I, 11.

45. *Quæ nequeunt secum ferre aut abducere*
   perdunt,
  Et cremat insontes turba scelesta casas.
     —Ovid, *Tristia*, III, 10.65.

46. *Muris nulla fides, squallent populatibus agri.*
    —Claudian, *In Eutropium*, I, 244.

47. *M'en eust deu de reste.*

48. *Perspicuitas enim argumentatione elevatur.*—Cicero, *De Nat. Deor.*, III, 4.

49. *Sit mihi quod nunc est, etiam minus; et mihi*
  vivam

Of Physiognomy

Quod superest ævi, si quid superesse volent di.
—Horace, *Epistles*, I, 18.107.

50. *Je les eusse plus gaillardement souffert à la foule.*
51. *Les subornemens qu'on me faict pour me tirer en place marchande.*
52. *La condition de mes mœurs.*
53. *Potentissimus est qui se habet in potestate.*—Seneca, *Epistle* 90.
54. *Rien ne chatouille qui ne pince.*
55. *Tantum ex publicis malis sentimus quantum ad privatas res pertinet.*—Livy, XXX, 44.
56. *En lieu de sureté.*
57. The health of France.
58. From the civil convulsions of the time.
59. *De porter la main au devant de la playe.*
60. *Quelque tenue contre la fortune.*
61. *Mista senum et juvenum densantur funera; nullum*
    Sæva caput Proserpina fugit.
    —Horace, *Odes*, I, 28.19.
62. *Et c'est le bon que.*
63. *L'apprehension.*
64. *Videas desertaque regna.*
    Pastorum, et longe saltus lateque vacantes.
    —Virgil, *Georgics*, III, 476.
    Montaigne substitutes *videas* for *vident*.
65. *Chauma pour long temps.*
66. See Diodorus Siculus, XVII, 105.
67. See Livy, XXII, 51.
68. See Plutarch, *Of the love of parents for their children.*

2055

Notes and Comments

69. *Exilia, tormenta, bella, morbos, naufragia meditare.*
—Seneca, *Epistle* 91.

70. *Ut nullo sis malo tyro.*—Idem, *Epistle* 107.

71. *Parem passis tristitiam facit pati posse.*—Idem, *Epistle* 74.

72. See *Ibid.: Ita nos non ad ictum tantum exagitamur, sed ad crepitum.*

73. That is, in midsummer.

74. *Jettez vous en l'experience.*

75. See Seneca, *Epistle* 13.

76. See Idem, *Epistle* 24.

77.   *Curis acuens mortalia corda.*
—Virgil, *Georgics*, I, 123.

78. *Minus afficit sensus fatigato quam cogitatio.*—Quintilian, *Inst. Orat.*, I, 12.

79. See Seneca, *Epistle* 30.

80.   *Incertam frustra, mortales, funeris horam*
    Quæritis, et qua sit mors aditura via.
—Propertius, II, 27.1.

81.   *Pœna minor certam subito perferre ruinam,*
    Quod timeas gravius sustinuisse diu.
—Maximianus (Pseudo-Gallus), I, 277.

82. *Et difformer la fin de son total.*

83. *Tota philosophorum vita commentatio mortis est.*
—Cicero, *Tusc. Disp.*, I, 30. A reminiscence of a passage in Plato *(Phædo)*. Cf. Book I, chap. 20, p. 103.

84. *Le bout, non pourtant le but.*

85.   *Quo me cumque rapit tempestas, deferor*
    hospes. —Horace, *Epistles*, I, 1.15.

86. See Suetonius, *Life of Cæsar*. Cf. Book II, chap. 13, p. 821.

Of Physiognomy

87. *Plus dolet quam necesse est qui ante dolet quam necesse est.*—Seneca, *Epistle* 98.

88. *Voulans devancer et regenter les prescriptions naturelles.*

89. *Environ en ce sens.* This may be called a reminiscence—it is hardly even a paraphrase, not at all a translation—of scattered passages in Plato's *Apology*. There is much more of Montaigne in it than of Plato.

90. See the *Odyssey*, XIX, 163.

91. *D'ainsi vous maintenir.*

92. See Diogenes Laertius, *Life of Socrates;* Cicero, *De Oratore*, I, 54.

93. See Seneca, *Epistle* 31: *tenor vitæ per omnia consonans.*

94. See Plutarch, *Of Envy and Hatred.*

95. *Un discours, en rang et en naïfveté bien plus arriere et plus bas.*

96. *Inartificielle.* Purely a Montaigne word, used only in this place, and found in no dictionary but Littré's.

97. *Republique.*

98.   *Sic rerum summa novatur.*—Lucretius, II, 75.

99.   *Mille animas una necata dedit.*
                              —Ovid, *Fasti*, I, 380.

100. In this passage of 1595 the text of 1588 is only slightly expanded.

101. *J'eusse parlé tout fin seul.*

102. That is, with these "borrowed embellishments."

103. *Ravadeurs.*

104. In this reference Montaigne had vaguely in mind the general tone of the dialogue of Plato called *Euthydemus*, or, possibly more directly, a confused remembrance of

Notes and Comments

what Socrates there says—not about compilations of commonplaces, but about the composers of speeches to be used by others.

105. A president of some "parliament."

106. In 1588: *Je desrobe mes larrecins et les desguise* (omitted in 1595).

107. That is, those devoted to what is natural and true.

108. This sentence of 1588 was omitted in 1595.

109. Apparently he began to write about 1572, when he was thirty-nine.

110. This evidently alludes to the friendship of Mlle. de Gournay.

111. *Qui ne sentent au.*

112. *Et ne traicte à point nomme de rien que du rien, ny d'aucune science que de celle de l'inscience.*

113. *Qu'il eust rencontré un corps si disgratié.*

114. *Ipsi animi magni refert quali in corpore locati sint: multa enim e corpore existunt quæ acuant mentem, multa quæ obtundant.*—Cicero, *Tusc. Disp.*, I, 33.

115. *Qui est toutesfois la plus imperieuse.*

116. This sentence of 1588 was omitted in 1595.

117. See Cicero, *Tusc. Disp.*, IV, 37.

118. Socrates. See Diogenes Laertius, *Life of Aristotle*.

119. See *Ibid*.

120. See Quintilian, *Inst. Orat.*, II, 15. Athenæus (XIII) gives credit for the scheme to the advocate, Hyperides, himself.

121. Καλὸς καγαθός.

122. See the *Gorgias*. Plato says nothing about their being trivial.

123. See Aristotle, *Politics*, I, 3.

Of Physiognomy

124. See Diogenes Laertius, *Life of Aristotle*.
125. *Cruement.*
126. *Preud'hommie scholastique.*
127. *Sans les mœurs.*
128. *J'ay un visage favorable et en forme et en interpretation.*
129. *Quid dixi habere me? Imo habui, Chreme!*
—Terence, *Heautontimoroumenos*, I, 1.42.
130. *Heu! tantum attriti corporis ossa vides!*
—Maximianus (Pseudo-Gallus), I, 238.
131. *Avoit merveilleusement chaussé les esperons.*
132. The last two clauses (1588) were omitted in 1595.
133. *Je ne fus pas si tost esventé.*
134. The words in brackets were omitted in 1595.
135. *Tunc animis opus, Ænea, tunc pectore firmo.*
—Virgil, *Æneid*, VI, 261.
136. *Jam prece Pollucis, jam Castoris implorata.*
—Catullus, LXVI, 65.
137. The parenthetical clause was omitted in 1595.
138. That is, his bearing.
139. *Ut magis peccari nolim quam satis animi ad vindicanda peccata habeam.*—Livy, XXIX, 21.
140. See Diogenes Laertius, *Life of Aristotle*.
141. *Qui ne suis qu'escuyer de trefles.*
142. See Plutarch, *Of Envy and Hatred*.
143. See Idem, *Life of Lycurgus*.

CHAPTER XIII

Of Experience

A. THE COMMENT BY MISS NORTON

IT is to be regretted that this last of all the Essays, written in 1587, is not one of the most interesting. Some of the pages are undesirably garrulous about his physical conditions, and there are many extravagant paradoxes arising from ignorance and also from thoughtlessness and (despite the title) from inexperience.

But in other respects it is expressive of Montaigne's temper of mind in what seemed to him his old age. It, in every sense, records his "experience" of life. It is so peculiarly personal in tone that it is only those who have long associated with Montaigne who can read it rightly; it is not till the erroneous traditional views of Montaigne's character have disappeared that the general reader will understand this Essay at all truly. It has little solidity, but it is like a lusty vine beautifying the dead wall of life; and none of its grapes is sour. The sweetness, the serenity, the sadness of our dear, gay, and vehement and irritable friend, touch these pages with softer lights than gleam almost anywhere else. The course of life—experience—made Montaigne more sensitive physically and mentally than in youth, but more wise; and his wisdom resolved itself into a love of life "such as it has pleased God to grant us."

Of Experience

His "experience" leads to no complaints about the order of things in heaven or on earth, and as little to raptures of memory or of hope. He is simply and calmly *content*.

Had Montaigne known the Thoughts of Marcus Aurelius, he might have quoted in this Essay the words: "Pass then through this little space of time conformably to nature, and end thy journey in content, just as an olive falls off when it is ripe, blessing the earth which produced it, and thanking the tree on which it grew."

We desire to *know*, the Essay begins by saying; but experience is as uncertain a guide as reason, because of its infinite diversity; in jurisprudence no countless number of laws can equal or control the instances of its variety. Therefore the fewer laws we make, the better, all the more since nature's laws are better than man's. Lawyers are as poor members of society as physicians, and even our language becomes obscure in legal matters.

Almost it would seem as if in all things explanations but added difficulties; to interpret the interpretations is harder than to interpret the original matter. Feeble minds are entangled in the perplexities of learning: generous minds in the search for knowledge find no end to their investigations.

So there are countless books about books. He himself has been led to comment on his own writings. There are more doubts about the opinions of Luther than Luther himself suggested about the Holy Scriptures; and such dissensions resolve themselves into the meaning of words. He returns to the thought on an earlier page of the diversity of human actions and the effect of this upon the laws, and he says: "Neither do events entirely differ from one another; every thing has some likeness to every thing else. But all instances

Notes and Comments

are imperfect, and consequently imperfect also all results of experience. And the laws can bring things into connection only by hook and by crook. The private laws of ethics are difficult enough to lay down, but public laws of general guidance are yet more so, and our justice is a perfect witness to human incompetence." And he gives illustrations and comments. Then, after a moment's personal rejoicing that he himself has never fallen into the hands of the law, he passes into the weighty and interesting passage about the foundations of the law. And then follows the interesting page (added in 1595) about the rules of nature and the *doulx chevet*—the soft pillow for a sound head secured by indifference, by incuriosity.

The previous pages might be entitled "Of the Laws of France, and Law in general," the following ones "Of the Knowledge of Oneself." On this subject he dwells for four pages; and then passes to the knowledge of others induced by knowledge of oneself: a knowledge which he confesses is in his case attained as gropingly, and to be uttered in as desultory points—*articles descousus*—as all other knowledge.

He returns to his self-knowledge with an interesting little bit of self-portraiture: and from his own dealings with princes passes to the consideration of the man who *should* be their adviser, and of the need kings have of such men.

Then, at last, begins the Essay "Of Experience": it so clearly begins here, with "In fine, all this medley" (p. 1473), that I am almost inclined to believe that he affixed the preceding pages merely because he did not see what else to do with them, and because he saw the word "experience" on the first page. Montaigne's "reading over" of his own

Of Experience

writings was certainly very irregular, and at times very reluctant; and there is reason to believe, there are many indications, that sixteenth-century authors did not read their own proof-sheets. I think Montaigne never considered one of his Essays in the light of a *whole*. I think he calls them truly pieces of *marqueterie;* they are mosaics, made up of separate stones set in irregular patterns; I am audacious enough to believe that an editor might be trusted, and might trust himself occasionally, to rearrange them slightly.

The pages that follow are a record of his bodily life, of his own physical experiences, his bodily habits and conditions, and those of others, with special study of his experience of the stone. There is a paragraph—interesting but quite misplaced—on the life of a soldier. Equally misplaced is the delightful passage about his father and his father's wish to connect him with *le peuple*. And, apropos of his teeth, there is a fine stoical passage about old age.

Then he passes to the consideration of the proper manner of enjoying physical pleasure, and the charming passage, "When I dance, I dance . . . " introduces the naturalness, the honourableness of enjoying such pleasures—of studiously delighting in prosperity. All these pages are eminently characteristic, most admirable in their serene and self-possessed wisdom: and any abstract of them would be idle: they are to be read and re-read.

The last page is the most characteristic possible: there could not be a more fitting conclusion to the Essays: it seems to sum them all up. His humour is in the sentence beginning "Much good does it do us to mount on stilts"; his wisdom in the next; his sensitiveness and tenderness in the next; and the words with which he introduces the beautiful conclud-

Notes and Comments

ing citation from Horace are the words with which the reader may phrase his thought of Montaigne himself: "the protector of health and wisdom, but cheerful and companionable."

B. THE NOTES BY MR. IVES

1. *Per varios usus artem experientia fecit,*
Exemplo monstrante viam.
—Manilius, *Astronomica,* I, 59.

2. Cicero (*Academica,* II, 18) says that there were several men at *Delos* (not Delphi) who had this faculty.

3. See Plutarch, *Of Envy and Hatred.*

4. See Seneca, *Epistle 113: Exegit* [*natura*] *a se ut quæ alia erant et dissimilia essent et imparia.*

5. *En leur taillant leurs morceaux.*

6. *Ut olim flagitiis, sic nunc legibus laboramus.*—Tacitus, *Annals,* III, 25.

7. See G. Bouchet, *sérée* IX.

8. *Escholiers de la jurisprudence.*

9. See *Ibid.*

10. See Plato, *Republic,* book III.

11. *Confusum est quidquid usque in pulverem sectum est.*—Seneca, *Epistle* 89.3.

12. *Difficultatem facit doctrina.*—Quintilian, *Inst. Orat.,* X, 3.16.

13. Cf. Book II, chap. 12, p. 785.

14. *Mus in pice.*—Latin proverb; see Erasmus *Adages,* II, 3.68.

15. See Plutarch, *Common conceptions against the Stoics.* These dogs are not mentioned in any fable of Æsop, and Montaigne undoubtedly took the anecdote from Plu-

Of Experience

tarch, through Amyot. But Amyot says that the dogs were after certain *cuyrs* (hides) that they saw on the water, and that they died rather than touch them. Amyot's word *cuyrs* is an accurate translation of Plutarch's δερμάτων.

16. See Diogenes Laertius, *Life of Heraclitus*. In the *Life of Socrates*, Laertius attributes to him a similar remark.

17. *Tournevire*—a word introduced by Montaigne.

18. Through his oracle.

19. See Aristotle, *Nicomachæan Ethics*, IV, 13.

20. The significance of this term has never been satisfactorily explained.

21. See Plutarch, *Of the plurality of friends*. Cf. Plato, *Meno*.

22. See St. Augustine, *De Civ. Dei*, XXI, 8.

23. *Justice*, here used in the sense of administration of the law.

24. It was Philip of Macedon. See Plutarch, *Apothegms of Kings*, etc.

25. *La raison de la cause . . . la raison des formes judiciares.*

26. See Plutarch, *Political Precepts*.

27. See Idem, *Of the delays of divine justice*.

28. *Juste de soy.* See Diogenes Laertius, *Life of Aristippus*.

29. See *Ibid*.

30. See Plutarch, *Life of Alcibiades*. Alcibiades was in hiding, and some one who recognised him said to him: "How is this? have you no faith in your country's justice?" —"Yes, indeed," he replied, "when it is a question of any thing else; but when my life is at stake, I would not trust my own mother, for fear lest, by mistake, she should put in

Notes and Comments

a black bean when she meant to put in a white one." (One was the sentence of condemnation, the other of acquittal.)

31. See G. de Mendoza, *History of China*.

32. See Plato, *Gorgias*.

33. *Metaphysics*, the study of supernatural things; *physic*, the study of natural things.

34. *Qua Deus hanc mundi temperet arte domum;*
Qua venit exoriens, qua deficit, unde coactis
Cornibus in plenum menstrua luna redit;
Unde salo superant venti, quid flamine captet
Eurus, et in nubes unde perennis aqua,
Sit ventura dies mundi quæ subruat arces,
Quærite, quos agitat mundi labor.

—The first six lines are from Propertius, III, 5, 26; the last from Lucan, I, 417.

35. *Université*, in the Latin sense.

36. *Avec grand raison;* the phrase is ironical.

37. *Trop sophistiqué*.

38. In 1595: *Cicero*.

39. *Et emperiere et populaire*.

40. The words in brackets were omitted in 1595.

41. *Fluctus uti primo cœpit cum albescere vento,*
Paulatim sese tollit mare, et altius undas
Erigit, inde imo consurgit ad æthera fundo.
—Virgil, *Æneid*, VII, 528.

42. Apollo. See Plutarch, *On the meaning of the word Ei*.

43. See Plato, *Charmides*.

44. See Xenophon, *Memorabilia*, IV, 2.24.

45. See Plato, *Meno*.

46. See Xenophon, *Memorabilia*, IV, 2.24 and 29.

Of Experience

47. *Une constante froideur et moderation d'opinions.*

48. *Nihil est turpius quam cognitioni et perceptioni assertionem approbationemque præcurrere.*—Cicero, *Academica*, I, 13. The true reading is: *Neque hoc quidquam esse turpius,* etc.

49. See Plutarch, *Of Brotherly Love.*

50. Antæus.

51. *Cui, cum tetigere parentem,*
Jam defecta vigent renovato robore membra.
—Lucan, IV, 599.

52. The phrase replaces this of 1588: "the wisest man who ever lived, by the testimony of gods and men."

53. See Diogenes Laertius, *Life of Antisthenes.*

54. *Sed neque quam multæ species, et nomina quæ sint,*
Est numerus. —Virgil, *Georgics*, II, 103.

55. *Sola sapientia in se tota conversa est.*—Cicero, *De Fin.*, III, 7.

56. See Livy, XLI, 20.

57. See the *Gorgias.*

58. *Dum melior vires sanguis dabat, æmula necdum*
Temporibus geminis canebat sparsa senectus.
—Virgil, *Æneid*, V, 415.

59. *Quod sit esse velit, nihilque malit.*
—Martial, X, 47.12.

60. See Tacitus, *History*, I, 15.

61. *Exemplaire assez à prendre l'instruction à contrepoil.*

62. *Opination.*

63. Montaigne seems to have misunderstood the passage in Tacitus (*Annals,* VI, 46), which says that Tiberius

Notes and Comments

ridiculed those who after *thirty* years had need of advice about health.

64. See Xenophon, *Memorabilia*, IV, 7.9.
65. See Plato, *Republic*, book III.
66.   *Tandem efficaci do manus scientiæ!*
              —Horace, *Epodes*, XVIII, 1.
67. The words in brackets were omitted in 1595.
68. *Eschanson:* the official whose duty it was to taste the food offered to a king or other great personage.
69. Augsburg: Augusta Vindelicorum.
70. See *Epistle* 90.
71. See Plutarch, *Platonic Questions*.
72. *Si nous sçavions trouver leur jour.*
73. See Diogenes Laertius, *Life of Pyrrho*.
74. *Un tabut de ses valets plain de licence.*
75. See *Epistle* 56.
76. See Diogenes Laertius, *Life of Socrates*.
77. That is, that had died of disease. See Seneca, *Epistle* 108.
78. See Seneca, *Epistle* 108.
79. See Plutarch, *Of Banishment*.
80.   *Ad primum lapidem vectari cum placet, hora*
    Sumitur ex libro; si prurit frictus ocelli
    Angulus, inspecta genesi collyria quærit.
              —Juvenal, VI, 576.
81. See Plutarch, *Life of Philopœmen*. It was not he who said it, but some men whom he was questioning.
82. See Idem, *How to restrain anger*.
83. This sentence was omitted in 1595.
84. *Se sont mis en chartre.*
85. See Plutarch, *Life of Cæsar*.

Of Experience

86. *Homo mundum et elegans animal est!*—Seneca, *Epistle* 92.
87. *Allez croire.*
88.   *An vivere tanti est?* ...
    Cogimur a suetis animum suspendere rebus,
       Atque ut vivamus vivere desinimus.
    Hos superesse reor quibus et spirabilis aer,
       Et lux qua regimur redditur ipsa gravis?
             —Maximianus, (Pseudo-Gallus), I, 155, 247.
89. *Quem circumcursans huc atque huc sæpe Cupido,*
    Fulgebat crocina splendidus in tunica.
                     —Catullus, LXVI, 133.
90. *Et militavi non sine gloria.*
                   —Horace, *Odes*, III, 26.2.
91. *Sex mi vix memini sustinuisse vices.*
                   —Ovid, *Amores*, III, 7.26.
92. *Inde tragus, celeresque pili, mirandaque matri Barba meæ.*   —Martial, XI, 22.7
93. *Defienda me, Dias, de my.*
94. Physician to Henri II of France.
95. That is, J. C. Scaliger, of Padua.
96. This is the only suggestion that Montaigne was ever wounded, but it seems to come in naturally enough here, where he speaks of himself as *soldat et Gascon*.
97. See Plutarch, *Of Garrulity*; Diogenes Laertius, *Life of Carneades*.
98. *Est quædam vox ad auditum accommodata non magnitudine, sed proprietate.*—Quintilian, *Inst. Orat.*, XI.
99. See Plutarch, *Of Hearing*.
100. See Plato, *Timæus*.

Notes and Comments

101. See Cicero, *Tusc. Disp.*, III, 6.
102. *Universel et à tout sens.*
103. *Defluxions.*
104. *Indignare si quid in te inique proprie constitutum est.*—Seneca, *Epistle* 91.
105. *Stulte, quid hæc frustra votis puerilibus optas?*
—Ovid, *Tristia*, III, 8.11.
106. See Plato, *Republic*, book III.
107. *Non secus instantem cupiens fulcire ruinam,*
Diversis contra nititur objicibus,
Donec certa dies, omni compage soluta,
Ipsum cum rebus subruat auxilium.
—Maximianus (Pseudo-Gallus), I, 171.
108. See Plutarch, *Of the tranquillity of the mind.*
109. See Plutarch, *How to restrain anger.*
110. *Il est temps qu'ils commencent à se lascher et desmentir.*
111. *Saxifrage.*
112. Cf. Book II, chap. 37, pp. 1025, 1026.
113. *Quæ venit indigne pœna dolenda venit.*
—Ovid, *Heroïdes*, V, 8.
114. *Raillant à pauses avec les dames* (1588); changed in 1595 to: *bouffonant à pauses avec tes gens.*
115. See Seneca, *Epistle* 78.
116. *En quoy j'en doibs estre quitte.*
117. *Prompte et soudaine.*
118. This is the reading of 1588; in 1595, forty years was changed to *un aage*, and fourteen years to *un autre [aage].*
119. See Plutarch, *Common conceptions against the Stoics.*

Of Experience

120. See Plato, *Phædo*.
121. See Cicero, *De Senectute*.
122. That is, when the body is sound.
123. See Diogenes Laertius, *Life of Plato;* Plato, *Laws,* book VII.
124. See Plutarch, *Political Precepts,* and *That a prince should be a scholar.*
125. *Les corvées.*
126. *Sur le pavé.*
127. *A faute d'apparence.*
128. See the *Republic*, book V.
129. *Pulchrumque mori succurrit in armis.*
—Virgil, *Æneid*, II, 317.
130. *Vivere, mi Lucili, militare est.*—Seneca, *Epistle* 96.
131. That is, youth.
132. *Non hoc amplius est liminis, aut aquæ*
  Cœlestis, patiens latus.
—Horace, *Odes*, III, 10.19.
133. *De chausser ainsin un teinct et un port trouble et de mauvais prognostique.*
134. *Nec vitiant artus ægræ contagia mentis.*
—Ovid, *Tristia*, III, 8.25.
135. *Quis tumidum guttur miratur in Alpibus?*
—Juvenal, XIII, 162.
136. *Res quæ in vita usurpant homines, cogitant,*
  curant, vident,
 Quæque agunt vigilantes, agitantque, ea sicut in
  somno accidunt,
 Minus mirandum est.
—Cicero, *De Divin.*, I, 22; verses taken from a play of Attius (*Brutus*).

Notes and Comments

137. See the *Timæus*, book II.
138. See Cicero, *De Divin.*, I, 25.
139. The inhabitants of the Atlas mountain range.
140. See Herodotus, IV, 184.
141. See Cicero, *De Divin.*, II, 58.
142. See Diogenes Laertius, *Life of Pyrrho*.
143. See Aulus Gellius, XV, 8.2. Montaigne is mistaken here. The opinion of Favorinus (an orator of the second century B.C.) was, according to Aulus Gellius, the same as Montaigne's.
144. *Où qu'il s'applique.*
145. *Ils ont bon temps.*
146. *Per quæ luxuria divitiarum tædio ludit.*—Seneca, Epistle 18.
147. *Si modica cœnare times olus omne patella.*
—Horace, *Epistles*, I, 5.2.
148. *Magna pars libertatis est bene moratus venter.*—Seneca, Epistle 123.
149. That is, the children's.
150. See Plutarch, *Lives of Agis and Cleomenes*.
151. See Plutarch, *Life of Flaminius*.
152. See Idem, *Life of Pyrrhus*.
153. See Suetonius, *Life of Augustus*.
154. *Une reglée collation.*
155. *Comme si elle estoit entiere.*
156. See Herodotus, I, 32.
157. ἄριστον μέτρον —See Diogenes Laertius: "that excellent mediocrity, so highly commended of old, and especially by Cleobulus, one of the seven sages of Greece."
158. *Omnia quæ secundum naturam fiunt sunt habenda in bonis.*—Cicero, *De Senectute*, XIX.

Of Experience

159. See Plato, *Timæus*.
160. *Vitam adolescentibus vis aufert, senibus maturitas.* —Cicero, *De Senectute*, XIX.
161. *Fais mes jours gras des maigres.*
162. See Seneca, *Epistle* 18.
163. See Idem, *Epistle* 19.
164. See Plutarch, *Banquet of the seven wise men*.
165. *J'estois monté d'une coife à un couvrechef, et d'un bonnet à un chapeau double.*
166. See Suetonius, *Life of Augustus*.
167. See Erasmus, *Adages*, II, 3.1. According to Pliny (*Nat: Hist.*, XXVIII, 17) it was *Demetrius* (a physician) who laid down this rule in a book about the number four.
168. According to Athenæus (II, 2) it was not Cranaus, but Amphictyon, his successor.
169. The phrase in brackets was omitted in 1595.
170. *J'ay arresté plus malaiséement en mesme point.*
171. *Encore que j'y sois assis, j'y suis peu rassis.*
172. The words in brackets were omitted in 1595.
173. See Diogenes Laertius, *Life of Chrysippus*.
174. See Plutarch, *That virtue may be taught*.
175. See Seneca, *Epistle* 15.
176. See Plato, *Protagoras*.
177. See Aulus Gellius, XIII, 11.
178. *Ce n'est pas une feste peu artificielle et peu voluptueuse qu'un bon traittement de table.*
179. It may be remembered that it was *"en une grande fête et compagnie de ville"* that Montaigne met La Boëtie.
180. *Qui ne manie que terre à terre.*
181. See Cicero, *Tusc. Disp.*, V, 7.
182. *Tantost avant, tantost arriere.*

Notes and Comments

183.   *Sincerum est nisi vas, quodcunque infundis
             acescit.*   —Horace, *Epistles*, I, 2.54.

184. See Cicero, *Tusc. Disp.*, V, 17. The assertion of Critolaus was somewhat different; it was to the effect that the good qualities of the soul outweighed all other advantages.

185. That is, the object presented by the imagination.

186. *Intellectuellement sensibles, sensiblement intellectuels.*

187. See Diogenes Laertius, *Life of Aristippus*.

188. See *Nicomachæan Ethics*, II, 7, and III, 11.

189. In 1588: "There are some of our youths who ambitiously declare that they tread them under foot."

190. The words in brackets were omitted in 1595.

191. This sentence was omitted in 1595.

192. See Cicero, *Academica*, II, 45.

193. See St. Augustine, *De Civ. Dei*, VIII, 4.

194. *Appendicules et adminicules.*

195. See Plutarch, *Life of Brutus*.

196.   *O fortes pejoraque passi
     Mecum sæpe viri! nunc vino pellite curas;
         Cras ingens iterabimus æquor.*
                                    —Horace, *Odes,* I, 7.30.

197. *Cui cor sapiat, ei et sapiat palatus.*—Cicero, *De Fin.*, 11, 8.

198. See Cornelius Nepos, *Life of Epaminondas*.

199. In 1595 this was changed to "Scipio the elder, a person worthy to have a celestial origin attributed to him." (Livy, XXVI, 19; Valerius Maximus, I, 3.5.) The earlier text corresponds with the facts.

200. A game of competition between two persons in

Of Experience

soonest picking up some object. See Cicero, *De Oratore*, II, 6. This reference again is to the younger Scipio.

201. Montaigne supposed Scipio to have had a share in writing some of the comedies of Terence. See Suetonius, *Life of Terence*. Cf. Book I, chap. 40, p. 334.

202. See Livy XIX, 19. The elder Scipio is referred to.

203. This sentence was omitted in 1595. But cf. Book II, chap. 36, p. 1024.

204. See Xenophon, *Banquet*, II, 15. Socrates was but sixty-nine when he died.

205. See Plato, *Banquet*.

206. See *Ibid*.

207. See Diogenes Laertius, *Life of Socrates*.

208. Montaigne was misled here by a mistake made by Diodorus Siculus. It was not Socrates, but Isocrates, who went to the rescue of Theramenes.

209. See Plato, *Banquet*.

210. See *Ibid*.

211. See Plato, *Banquet*.

212. *Le peuple se trompe.*

213. See Seneca, *Epistle* 39.

214. See Diogenes Laertius, *Life of Eudoxus*.

215. *Eodem enim vitio est effusio animi in lætitia quo in dolore contractio.*—Cicero, *Tusc. Disp.*, IV, 31.

216. *D'en esteindre l'une que d'estendre l'autre.*

217. 1See Plato, *Phædo*; cf. Book II, chap. 20, p. 910.

218. See Idem, *Laws*, book I.

219. See *Ibid.*, book I.

220. See *Ibid.*, book II.

221. *Stulti vita ingrata est, trepida est, tota in futurum fertur.*—Seneca, *Epistle* 15.

Notes and Comments

222. *Je consulte d'un contentement avec moy.*

223. *Morte obita quales fama est volitare figuras, Aut quæ sopitos deludunt somnia sensus.*
—Virgil, *Æneid*, X, 641.

224. See Arrian, V, 26.220.

225. *Nil actum credens, cum quid superesset agendum.* —Lucan, II, 657.
The reference in Lucan is not to Alexander, but to Cæsar.

226. *Sapiens divitiarum naturalium quæsitor acerrimus.* —Seneca, *Epistle* 119.

227. See Diogenes Laertius, *Life of Epimenides;* Plutarch, *Banquet of the seven wise men.*

228. *Omnia quæ secundum naturam sunt æstimatione digna sunt.*—Cicero, *De Fin.*, III, 6. The quotation is taken, with some modification, from two sentences.

229. *Les plus humaines et nostres.*

230. *Quand elle se met sur ses ergots.*

231. *Intrandum est in rerum naturam et penitus quid ea postulet pervidendum.*—Cicero, *De Fin.*, V, 16.

232. See Plato, *Laws*, book VII.

233. *Qui velut summum bonum laudat animæ naturam, et tanquam malum naturam carnis accusat, profecto et animam carnaliter appetit, et carnem carnaliter fugit; quoniam id vanitate sentit humana, non veritate divina.*—St. Augustine, *De Civ. Dei*, XIV, 5.

234. *Stultitiæ proprium quis non dixerit ignave et contumaciter facere quæ facienda sunt; et alio corpus impellere, alio animum; distrahique inter diversissimos motus?* —Seneca, *Epistle* 74.

235. The meditation of the "venerable souls."

236. This sentence was omitted in 1595.

Of Experience

237. *Nous faudra-il chier en courant?* See Planudes, *Life of Æsop.*

238. See Quintus Curtius, IV, 7.29 and 30; VIII, 5.13.

239. See Idem, VI, 9.

240. *Dis te minorem quod geris, imperas.*
—Horace, *Odes*, III, 6.5.

241. *D'autant es tu dieu comme*
Tu te recognois homme.

—See Plutarch, *Life of Pompeius:* "As he left the city of Athens, he read two couplets which had been written in praise of him; one within the gate, which ran:

'D'autant es tu dieu comme
Tu te recognois homme';

and the other outside the same gate:

'Nous t'attendions, nous te voions,
Nous t'adorons, et convoyons.'"

242. *Frui paratis et valido mihi,*
Latoë, dones, et, precor, integra
Cum mente; nec turpem senectam
Degere, nec cythara carentem.
—Horace, *Odes*, I, 31.17.